Drug-Impaired Professionals

DRUG-IMPAIRED PROFESSIONALS

Robert Holman Coombs

HARVARD UNIVERSITY PRESS
Cambridge, Massachusetts, and London, England   1997

Library of Congress Cataloging-in-Publication Data

Coombs, Robert H.
   Drug-impaired professionals / Robert Holman Coombs.
      p.   cm.
   Includes bibliographical references and index.
   ISBN 0-674-21673-3 (alk. paper)
   1. Professional employees—Substance abuse.
2. Professional employees—Rehabilitation.
3. Substance abuse—Treatment.
I. Title.
RC564.5.P76C66   1997
362.29'086'22—dc21   96-37926

Designed by Gwen Nefsky Frankfeldt

For all in the human family who have suffered from the desolating sickness of chemical dependence

Contents

Preface

Drug abuse is at least as prevalent among highly regarded professionals as among the general public. This book describes the nature of the problem, the self-destructive dynamics involved, and the range of recovery tools and programs available.

For years I conducted two seminars at UCLA to which I invited chemically dependent physicians to share their experiences and answer students' questions. The extraordinary revelations that emerged during those sessions prompted further investigation, in the form of in-depth interviews.

From 1992 through 1995 my assistants and I spoke with 91 addicted professionals (66 men and 25 women)—21 physicians and medical students, 11 dentists, 13 pharmacists, 12 nurses, 21 attorneys, and 13 pilots; 19 experts (12 men and 7 women) who assist them in recovery; and 5 other people who felt that others might benefit from their experiences: a nurse who worked in the office of an addicted doctor, an oral surgeon whose chief resident was addicted, a pharmacy assistant who worked in a large university hospital, the spouse of an addicted pilot, and the father of a physician who died from an overdose. We found these people by networking with known former addicts and professional organizations. Once assured of our motives and trustworthiness, they spread the word, and others contacted us and expressed willingness to be interviewed. In all, we interviewed people in 21 states, the District of Columbia, and two Canadian provinces. Each interview, averaging one to one-and-a-half hours, was tape recorded, transcribed, and edited as necessary to preserve confidentiality.

The life experiences included in the following pages will, I hope, make clear both that no one is immune to addiction and that recovery is worth the physical, emotional, and spiritual struggle involved.

Drug-Impaired Professionals

I

CHEMICAL DEPENDENCY: AN OCCUPATIONAL HAZARD

ONE

The Secret Sickness

"This is a disease that tells you that you don't have it. It's the only disease I know that argues with you and says, 'Look, despite all the evidence, you don't have a problem.' "

(JD, age 64)

"I didn't think it could happen to me because I'm too smart and I have all this knowledge. I'm unique, a doctor, a cut or two above the average citizen. When I found out I was addicted, I was devastated. It sneaked up on me and had me by the throat before I even had an inkling that I had a problem."

(MD, age 50)

"When I was asked what could have been done to help me with my addiction, I told them, 'Bring it out into the open by letting people know it's an occupational hazard. Get the secret out of the closet.' "

(MD, age 34)

A recent headline in the *Los Angeles Times* proclaimed: "Doctor Convicted of 2nd-Degree Murder in Two Traffic Deaths." The accompanying story told how a 32-year-old physician, known for his humanitarian care of impoverished AIDS patients, had killed two people and critically injured three others while driving under the influence of alcohol and other drugs (Cekola and Owen 1994). When a jury found him guilty on two counts of murder—the verdict mandates a prison term of 18 years to life—family and friends in the courtroom sobbed. "He was given a gift to save lives, and look what he's done with it," one of the survivors remarked. "He took two lives."

Such stories are especially shocking when they involve "pedestal professionals"—physicians and other health care professionals, airline pilots, and attorneys—because society regards these people as role models. Carefully selected and arduously trained in the acquisition of specialized skills, licensed and monitored by regulatory boards or agencies, they are the people on whom we rely to protect our health, our safety, our liberty, our lives.

"Pedestal professionals" occupy a world far removed from winos on skid row or crack addicts in jail—our stereotypical view of addicts (see Woodruff 1992). Yet these widely respected and admired professionals are no less vulnerable than other people to emotional impairment or addictive illness. In fact addiction may come with the territory (Vaillant, Brighton, and McArthur 1970). According to Douglas Talbott, founder of the Talbott-Marsh Recovery Center in Atlanta, Georgia, "Drug addiction is an occupational hazard of practitioners of the healing arts just as black lung is for miners" (quoted in Redmond 1979, p. 51). Indeed, the prevalence of substance abuse is probably higher among professionals than among those they serve.

Addiction, called "a secret sickness" by the Texas Young Lawyers Association (1990), affects people at every level of society, and they become expert at hiding it. "By definition," a former cocaine addict explained, "the addict is a person who is living secretly. The treatment is to help them come out of that secret life to a place where they can deal with their shame and guilt and anger and suffering and remorse and be open with other people" (ibid.). "We are only as sick as our secret," a physician confirmed. "Addicts hide their secrets from others because of shame. The public view is that addicts are scum, and you are ashamed. This means that you will not ask for help, so there's no way out except dying or being caught" (KCET Video Lifeguides 1991). The most important aspect of treatment is breaking the secret. "When I came back from treatment," another physician reported, "I told people the truth, that I had a drug problem. It was hard to do, but it liberated me, and now I can joke about it" (MD, age 34).

Many addicted professionals graduate in the top third of their classes. They tend to be efficient, hard-working, and admired by their colleagues. Addicted nurses, for example, typically earn degrees beyond basic training, and their colleagues regard them as very capable (Clark 1988; Green 1989). "I've always been an overachiever," said a pharmacist who began using drugs after pharmacy school. "No matter what I did, I always wanted to be the best at it. In high school I excelled in sports and grades, and in college I was president of my class and fraternity and was one of the top five graduates academically. I was Mr. Wonderful, Big-Man-on-Campus, the whole bit, a very ego-pleasing existence. My wife married this fantastic human being, this superachiever, and then ten years later realized that she was married to a drug addict" (PharmD, age 41).

Many professionals, like the ones cited in this book, are high-functioning and respected in their communities. However, their drive to achieve may be part of an underlying "addiction to perfection" and a need to define themselves in terms of what they can produce and possess. In that sense they epitomize our culture's emphasis on outer-directed goals and values: money, power, and prestige. They try harder, do more, and go higher. When fear and exhaustion close in, when there are not enough hours in the day and the nights are too long, drugs and alcohol make going that extra mile or getting a good night's rest possible.

The chemicals produce their desired effects for a while, but slowly, insidiously, they change from a help to a hindrance. Recovering alcoholics in Alcoholics Anonymous have a saying: "First the man takes a drink; then the drink takes a drink; then the drink takes the man." The addict loses control and becomes enmeshed in behaviors that, if unchecked, lead inexorably to professional and financial ruin, destruction of personal and professional relationships, homelessness, and mental and ultimately fatal physical illness. Professionals caught in this devastating chokehold, like any other addicts, are unable to self-correct. As their conduct spirals downward, they are overwhelmed by profound feelings of guilt and shame and put their clients and associates at risk. Recovering addicts say that this "pitiful and incomprehensible demoralization" leads to the "gates of insanity and death" (MD, age 34).

Consider the downward path of a high-achieving dentist who was training to be an oral-maxillofacial surgeon. After finishing at the top of his dental-school class, he won a highly coveted place in the dental surgery program. "The year I applied," a classmate recalled, "there were 260 who applied for three spots" (DDS, age 35). Five years later while under the influence of drugs he was killed while trying to push his stalled car from the center lane across a busy metropolitan freeway. "He had access to a lot of IV [intravenous] medications," the same associate recalled. "He'd bring them home to medicate his wife so she could sleep after her father's death. As an oral surgeon, he could order large quantities of Demerol and Valium and Brevital to put patients to sleep while doing molar extractions. He would give some to the patients and keep some for himself."

A grieving father of an anesthesiologist-in-training who had died from a drug overdose described his son as "very, very bright, always near the head of his medical school class. He made the dean's list year after year and for three years of residency showed superb work habits, helpfulness, technical proficiency, and an unfailingly cheerful disposition. He had a fine scholastic mind, read *very* fast, and retained it all." He was found dead by his wife after injecting himself with Sufenta, a substance 100 times stronger than heroin and more addicting than crack cocaine. His father remarked sadly, "It is simply beyond understanding how this could have happened . . . he was extraordinarily intelligent and certainly knew about all the dangers."

Guardians of the Secret

Perhaps more than anyone else, professionals are motivated to keep their addictions secret: their careers depend upon their professional reputation, and their sense of self depends upon their careers. Asking for help involves admitting to a problem that could destroy their reputation, so many professionals face their addictions alone. One by one, they give up the things they value. The last thing to go is the career—unless they die first. "Since I'm a pharmacist and a professional, I didn't tell anybody about how much I used," a former addict confessed. "I didn't talk about it. It was a secret. I was the only person who knew" (PharmD, age 43). Some professionals will go to great lengths to maintain the secret. "It took the worst kind of suffering to open my eyes," said a dentist, "but I now know we have an infinite capacity to fool ourselves."

> If anyone had said I was a drug addict, I would have told him he was a liar and just full of it. It did not occur to me that I had a problem until I overdosed . . . Sitting around in my apartment one night, I injected myself with a much larger dose of cocaine than I thought. I

started convulsing, and barely made it to the phone to call an emergency service.

He continued:

My staff knew about the problem and one staff member quit, but the rest stayed . . . They thought they were helping me and in that way they enabled me to keep using. I missed days of work when I'd call in; I wanted to go out and use that day, and they'd have to cancel all my patients and reschedule them. I graduated to shooting cocaine and heroin. By then the quantities were incredible. I started out snorting a couple of lines a night and ended up injecting and snorting about three grams a day. My wife threw me out. I moved to one of the worst urban areas in the state, and lived in a residential hotel. I loved every minute of it because the drugs were at my front door-step. My practice was my practice, and my social life was out on the street, so to speak, and that's where I made all my purchases.

One night I ended up getting stabbed by a guy who I thought was my friend . . . We fought and he stabbed me with a 3-inch blade, puncturing my abdomen. Fearing for my license, I avoided hospitals and went to my office. I did a primary internal suture and a secondary suture and placed myself on high dosages of antibiotics. I had so much cocaine and heroin in me that I didn't feel anything. I healed nicely and moved out of the downtown area. I didn't have to go to the hospital and I wasn't reported. If someone said to me that I had to stop, my position was that I had a lot of willpower and could do anything I wanted to, and if I wanted to stop tomorrow I could. I believed that up to the last day. I have yet to see a person that can set it aside, clean themselves up and walk into recovery. For me it took the ultimate consequence, a near-death episode to begin to acknowledge that I might have a problem.   ("A Foolish Capacity" 1990)

Associates often help conceal the secret by ignoring, making excuses for, or otherwise covering up a colleague's addiction. "We don't want to admit there are lawyers out there who are drunks and addicts," an attorney commented. "That would reflect poorly on the profession. So we don't talk about it" (JD, age 41). Enabling strategies that shield the addict from the legal, social, and work-related consequences of continued use worsen the behavior and deepen the pathology. A dentist recalled, "Once I used cocaine for two to three days straight; I had stayed up all weekend. When I walked into the office, the ladies put me in bed and canceled all my patients" (DDS, age 47). No healing can occur until the secret is broken.

The addicted professional fears the loss of a practice and, even more devastating, the loss of a license to practice; the office staff fears reprisal and termination of employment; the family fears discovery by the community; the spouse fears loss of income and disintegration of the family; peers face loss of respect for the profession; professional licensing boards fear that harm will come to the public and embarrassment to the professional society; close friends fear that friendships will be terminated. So everyone tiptoes around the problem, maintaining a conspiracy of silence (see Oberg 1989).

A state or federal license gives the addict an advantage in maintaining the secret. Not only does it provide an income and a professional identity; it also guarantees easy drug access and coverup. Motivated to protect their licenses at all costs, addicted professionals become expert in defending themselves and their actions. However, it becomes progressively more difficult to avoid embarrassing scenes, and the circle of silence shatters when the humiliating secret is painfully revealed. The user may be the last to realize that it is no longer a secret. "Alcoholics always *think* they are secret drinkers," an attorney explained. "There was a lot of excessive drinking in the firm and perhaps they did not notice, but I do not remember anyone else spending hung-over days hiding in their office fearing encounters with clients or partners expecting clear thinking. The continued crisis of my personal life I tried to keep secret, too, but I am sure that tale could be read on my face" ("A Woman's Story" 1989, p. 296).

Since their professional activities are the last aspects of their lives to fail, addicted professionals may continue working for years before their problems become obvious. When their addiction surfaces at work, personal and social lives are often wastelands. Using just enough chemicals to keep a slight "buzz" at work, they usually maintain a level of professionalism barely adequate to the task.

There is often a reluctance to step in and say anything about drug problems to a professional colleague—a hesitancy to face negative facts or to make the other angry. Colleagues may cover up for the addicted nurse, for example, by allowing a lighter work schedule, poorly supervised night duty, accepting lies as reasons for errors or absences, or otherwise deferring confrontation about the addicted behavior. "In dentistry, as well as the other professions," Cassell (1979, p. 54) remarked, "they try to protect their co-professionals because they have a special relationship . . . the worst thing you can do is not to do anything." Even flagrant violations of professional decorum may be played down by supervisors and colleagues, as this pharmacist pointed out. "One of the drug companies threw an open house at a pharm conference with an open bar, and I proceeded to get beyond drunk. I threw up all over the place with my boss, preceptor, and everybody else around. When I got back home I was called into the director's office and asked if the stress was maybe getting to me. Nothing was said about the possibility of my having an alcohol problem" (PharmD, age 44).

The confidentiality expected of professionals can hide a professional's addiction. Although an oral surgery resident overdosed and had two cardiac arrests in the ambulance en route to the emergency room, he was not reported.

> The ER doc, the friend of our chief, made a confidential phone call to him saying that one of his residents had overdosed—the bloods that were drawn while he was unconscious verified that. But because it was of a confidential nature, this information was not released. The resident denied the problem and refused urine and blood tests. He denied everything and wouldn't admit he had been in the hospital or the ambulance. He said, "It never happened, and you can't prove it." And the records were confidential. When he was later dismissed from the program for erratic behavior, he hired a well-known law firm and filed a lawsuit against the university.

To disguise the signs of his IV injections, this same trainee wore long-sleeved anesthesia gowns and would scrub in when no one else was around. A colleague recalled,

> One day I got there late and saw the tracking lines up his arm very clearly. When I asked him about it he said that his cat had scratched him. It was frustrating because all nine of us residents knew about his problem. Our chief would sit in conferences with us and discuss with us what we could say. He explicitly told us we couldn't say anything to anybody outside the training program because it would be a breach of confidentiality and violate his due process. (DDS, age 35)

Airline pilots are often enabled by their fellow pilots. "The guys in the cockpit know who the drinkers are, and they protect each other by looking the other way," a pilot (age 45) reported. "The denial of these guys seems much more evident than it is with other professional groups" (airline treatment expert).

Law firms avoid unfavorable exposure by adopting the attitude: "We don't have that problem here." All too often, Hickey (1990, p. 38) explains, drinking and other addiction problems are ignored, covered up, or ended by firing the impaired attorney. When an attorney is forced to appear before a disciplinary board as a result of client complaints, unless the offense is egregious board members typically sweep it under the table. "If he's been a good lawyer but then starts dropping the ball, they say, 'Hell, we know Joe. He's a good lawyer; there couldn't be anything wrong with him' " (JD, age 64).

Identifying addicted colleagues is rarely a simple matter, and professionals are trained to wait for clients to come to them, not vice versa. The rationale is that a person cannot be helped unless he asks for help. Moreover, with an increase in lawsuits, professionals are reluctant to assume additional risks by intervening in their associates' personal lives. Even when they are willing to intervene, colleagues rarely know how to proceed. To whom does one report an addicted associate? If a report is made, what will be done about it? Will the addicted colleague be hurt professionally, and will there be repercussions for the informer? In a society that conditions children to avoid "tattletales" and "snitching," is it unrealistic to expect professionals to report impaired colleagues and to do so with little experience or understanding about who might be hurt?

Despite the understandable pressure on the addict's associates to maintain the circle of secrecy, society cannot afford to tolerate his continued use. "When a treating person is actually or potentially dangerous to clients," Bissell and Jones (1981, p. 101) noted, "we must take whatever action is necessary to protect those clients. Any one of us would wish to be stopped by our peers rather than allowed to do harm."

This is how the chair of an anesthesiology department addressed the problem.

> When I was a first-year resident, I heard that one of the previous year's graduating residents had died of a drug overdose. They said he was an excellent anesthesiologist and was well liked—a natural-born leader. One morning, about a month before he was to finish the program, he didn't show up to do his cases, so someone from the de-

partment called his home. His roommate answered, and when he went to see if the resident had overslept, he found him on the floor, dead.

Later on in my first year, the department chairman called a special meeting. Everyone had to come. He stood there at the podium and said he had been told about a couple of residents' use of drugs at parties. He said, "You might think that what you do socially has nothing to do with what you do here. Well, let me tell you something. I confronted a resident in the not-so-distant past with information I had regarding his use of recreational drugs and he told me, 'What I do on my own time is my business.' He was one of my best residents. He's dead now, and I'm here to tell you that if you are using drugs 'on your own time' *it isn't only your business!* I learned the hard way that it is *my* business, and any of you who are using recreational drugs must stop. If you need help, get it. If you don't know where to get help, ask me and I will tell you. I promise you that if you come to me for help, I will not throw you out of the program. I also promise you that if you continue to use drugs, I will throw you out. It's your choice. You know who you are. I don't want any more dead residents."   (MD, age 44)

Professional "Immunity" to Addiction

Elitist attitudes, common among professionals, facilitate addiction. Feeling too smart and well educated to become addicted, professionals can develop a false sense of security. Asked if he ever felt immune to addiction, a dentist replied, "Absolutely. Big-time. In fact, it could have killed me. Nearly did" (DDS, age 46). "Physicians learn to disassociate themselves from danger to be able to cope with it," Vaillant, Brighton, and McArthur pointed out (1970, p. 369). "For effective patient care, every physician must engender in himself the belief that 'It can't happen to me.' "

Most people think that addicts and professionals have nothing in common; they are mutually exclusive. "When someone told my wife I was an addict, she said, 'He couldn't be. He's a pharmacist' " (PharmD, age 47). A physician said, "I was under the delusion that because I was an MD I had some kind of entitlement or uniqueness that would allow me to float through things without any difficulty. I learned the hard way that this is not true; it's absolutely erroneous. It was very tough for me to get real and realize that I'm a human being" (MD, age 50).

Training in the health sciences contributes to a feeling of invincibility. "I knew too much about drugs to become addicted," a pharmacist reasoned. "I was at low risk because I was intelligent and knew about drugs. I was armed with information" (PharmD, age 48).

Because they can recite the product information for pharmaceuticals, health professionals mistakenly assume that they will automatically recognize and control the adverse effects of drugs on themselves. But they have just enough drug education to get into trouble. "I definitely felt immune," an addicted nurse said, "because I was an expert with drugs" (RN, age 40). A dentist commented, "It was my arrogance about my knowledge of pharmacology, pathology, and the pathophysiology of inflammatory disease in general that fed the flames of my denial. I was my own patient and had a fool for a doctor" (Oyler 1986, p. 5).

McAuliffe's (1984) in-depth interviews with addicted health practitioners found them highly knowledgeable about the possible adverse effects of drugs; some had even treated patients for addiction. But they discounted personal risks, reasoning that they understood drugs, had used them successfully in their clinical practice, and were too smart to let their use get out of hand; if they used the drug only occasionally, nothing bad would happen.

Professionals receive little or no education about the progressive stages of addiction and how to remedy its problems. Health professionals may know that alcoholism is associated with sclerosis of the liver or depression, but they are rarely aware that addiction progresses through predictable stages, each with its particular signs and symptoms. "I had all this knowledge but no training whatsoever in addiction. So, I thought, 'I'm a nurse. I should be able to handle this' " (RN, age 70).

Because society places them on a pedestal, some professionals feel they are, or should be, invulnerable to the problems that afflict "ordinary" people. According to an addictionologist who has treated hundreds of them, they are "an elite group of egotistical professionals who are constantly under an enormous amount of stress, work horrendously long hours, make lots of money and are *always* surrounded by drugs and have a unique capacity to rationalize their addictive behavior" (Jules Trop quoted in Rosenblatt 1989, pp. 9–10).

Addicted physicians have what Talbott calls an "M. Deity syndrome" (quoted in Wright 1990, p. 1023): (1) a strong and deeply felt need to help, (2) professional grandiosity and omnipotent feelings such as "only I am able to help this patient," (3) an orientation to immediate solutions such as symptomatic relief that disregard long-term consequences, and (4) an inability to handle their own feelings if treatment that could provide immediate relief is withheld.

A recovering physician who had reached the point in his addiction to cocaine where he was either constantly high on coke or crashing said, "I *never* considered that I was an addict. I was a doctor! . . . I saw it as my right to relax and release stress because I was under such an incredible amount of pressure" (Rosenblatt 1989, p. 11). When finally investigated he was defiant and viewed the whole thing as legal harassment. "I would scream, 'I'm a doctor! How dare you!' " Similarly, a young surgeon, challenged about his cocaine use, responded with a condescending smile, "This is my right. I use cocaine recreationally. I understand the drug and what it does. I am a physician" (ibid., p. 9).

Physicians are not the only professionals with inflated images of self. A common theme among addicted dentists, according to one observer, is the attitude, "I'm a professional, a dentist. I'm above such commonperson problems." But, he notes, "It becomes all too apparent that dentists are just as human as anyone else" ("I'm a Chemically Dependent Dentist" 1990, p. 17). A dentist recovering from addiction recalled, "they put handcuffs on me and hauled me off to jail. They'd hold me overnight, but the next morning I'd walk out of jail saying to myself, 'I'm a dentist, I'm above all this stuff' " ("A Near Fatal Combination" 1990).

Because they manage the health care of others, nurses, too, may feel superior. "I always kept myself apart because I thought I was special," one said. "I thought I was different, smarter than others. I could treat myself. When I had pain I'd think, 'I need IV morphine, I need Demerol—I have it!' " (RN, age 42; see also Barde and Pick 1993).

Hickey (1990, p. 37) contends that many attorneys have difficulty admitting to themselves that they cannot manage their drinking. It doesn't fit with their self-image. "It's awfully hard for people in controlling positions to acknowledge that they are controlled by alcohol." "Yes, yes, it's true that I felt I was immune," an attorney acknowledged. "I felt that all the time. I dealt with clients who were in all kinds of trouble because of their booze. But I was rich and professional and it happened to the other person, not me" (JD, age 61).

Airline pilots also "tend to see themselves as invincible. They see themselves as different from the average citizen because they are in a super-responsible position" an airline employee assistance program (EAP) representative remarked. "I'm a cracker-jack pilot," reasoned a pilot (age 45). "It can't happen to me; I'm not a skid-row character." A treatment expert described the addicted pilot's attitude like this: "How can I be an alcoholic when I'm the captain of a 747 aircraft? Everyone admires me. I'm controlling my drinking, and it hasn't quite affected my job performance." Although every other aspect of his life may be affected, "once he puts on his uniform and performs his duties in a professional manner, he becomes immune."

Professional pride gets in the way of accepting help. Self-confident and independent professionals are accustomed to handling personal problems on their own. An addicted physician, for example, can pull rank on anyone who confronts him about his drug use. "I used to tell people, 'Don't give me any crap about this! I majored in psychopharmacology as an undergraduate, and I know what the side effects are. When you know as much as I do, then you can talk to me' " (MD, age 38). When a telephone caller recommended treatment, a physician was incensed. "I replied, 'Well, screw you. You're probably *Mister* Smith, not *Doctor* Smith. How could you give *me* instructions?' And I hung up" (MD, age 57).

Drug-abusing professionals may go undetected longer than other groups because their relative affluence and prestige isolate them for a time from the full impact of their addiction. Furthermore, because clients put them on a pedestal, professionals are likely to ignore their own fallibility, to dissociate from the dangers of drugs, and to adopt the grandiose attitude "It can't happen to me" (Vaillant, Brighton, and McArthur 1970, p. 369). Those who work with addicted physicians say that "MD stands for 'Massive Denial.' "

Addiction: An Equal Opportunity Destroyer

The impact of substance abuse on professionals and their associates can be devastating. Obsession with alcohol and other drugs undermines physical and mental health; it also diminishes and destroys personal and professional lives. "Addiction kills people," said a pharmacist. "It just flat out kills them; it slowly kills you physically, morally—if you ever had any morals—and in the end spiritually. You are dead, dead, dead!" (PharmD, age 46). An interview study of 86 pharmacists recovering from chemical dependency found that 44 had been arrested, and 24 had spent at least one night in jail. Forty-five had experienced unemployment because of drinking or other drug use, 16 had lost their licenses, and 18 had attempted suicide, 13 by drug overdose. Ironically, use of chemicals had interfered with their lives long before they were consciously worried about it (Bissell, Haberman, and Williams 1989).

The addict's family suffers profoundly. A study of 67 physicians and 133 nurses living with a chemically dependent person found their confidence and self-esteem damaged (Williams, Bissell, and Sullivan 1991). At work they had difficulty concentrating, and their absenteeism, errors, poor judgment, and patient neglect increased. Many reported anxieties and health problems that they attributed to living with an addict. More than one-third were depressed, one-third had also become chemically dependent—half of these after living with the addict—and 12 percent had attempted suicide.

Professionals entrusted with their clients' welfare can do great damage, even causing death. Addicted health care professionals have difficulty upholding the ethical imperative dating from the time of Hippocrates: "Do no harm." Nonmalfeasance, accepted as the guiding principle of attorneys' professional conduct, aims to protect clients not only from disability and death but also from physical and fiscal harm, pain, damage, and loss of liberty and property. However, as addiction progresses, deteriorating work performance increasingly places clients at risk.

The economic cost of addiction is staggering to the individual, the employer, and society. For example, in 1989 the total estimated cost of an addicted nurse to an employer would have paid the annual salaries of two staff nurses or financed the education of a nursing student from high school through graduate training (LaGodna and Hendrix 1989).

ATTENDANCE DEFICITS AND EXCESSES

Work absenteeism is manifested in failure to appear on Monday mornings, leaving early, taking lengthy lunches, excessive use of days off and sick leave, and absences without notification. Addicted professionals often call in to request compensatory time at the beginning of a work shift, disappear from the work site, have long unexplained absences, make improbable excuses, and take long trips to the bathroom or to stockrooms where drugs are kept. "My job performance was okay," a nurse recalled, "but my attendance was bad. I would not show up or even call in. Then the next day I would say, 'Oh, I thought I had the day off. You're kidding me? Oh, no!' The majority of the people on that floor were chemically dependent, and we were all very good actors. Finally it became so bad that the head nurse, a very codependent person, confronted us" (RN, age 40).

Unreliability in keeping appointments and deadlines, another early sign of addiction, is common among addicted professionals. A physician complained of a colleague, "He didn't show up when he was supposed to, and he let other people do his work for him. He slept a lot and just wasn't available" (MD, age 50). An attorney recalled, "I missed court appearances because I couldn't wake up in the morning. I was withdrawn and couldn't function without my drugs" (JD, age 48). A physician commented, "I was nicknamed 'old sleepy-head'—I was always late scrubbing up and late for rounds because I didn't want to show up with alcohol on my breath" (Cruse 1981, p. 299).

Health professionals addicted to narcotics spend excessive amounts of time in the hospital near their drug supply. They volunteer for overtime and are at the hospital when off duty. "I find it funny," an anesthesiologist remarked, "when people talk about the signs of addiction as being poor attendance at work and not showing up. That's alcoholism, just the opposite of what happened to me. With Fentanylism it is *showing up* and working 24-hour days and relieving somebody for their cases. It is being Super Doc. *That's Fentanylism!*" Another anesthesiologist commented, "I was a nice guy in the OR [operating room] and would relieve you of any of your cases, especially if it was a heart patient and a lot of Fentanyl was used. I would go in and offer to relieve you, let you get a cup of coffee. Then I'd sample from the large amount of Fentanyl we had in the case" (American Society of Anesthesiologists and Janssen Pharmaceutica 1994).

Addicted professionals gradually shift their work to settings in which they can more readily indulge their habits and avoid detection. They eat lunch alone, avoid informal staff get-togethers, and lose interest in outside activities. "It's easy for an impaired nurse to 'hide,' " a nurse acknowledged. "I prefer to work the night shift, when staffing is minimal and there are no supervisors or visitors around" (Alexander and O'Quinn-Larson 1990, p. 57). "As my relationship with drugs intensified," another nurse recounted, "I preferred being alone rather than socializing at lunchtime. This was the time I could go home and sneak a few drinks" (Kendall 1987, p. 87).

In the surgical suite, addicted doctors and nurses typically request frequent bathroom relief (where they use drugs) and are difficult to find between cases because they are taking short naps. Working alone, they refuse lunch and coffee breaks in order to divert drugs. They often assist in administering opiates in the post-anesthesia recovery room, and their patients complain of pain out of proportion to the amount of narcotics charted on the anesthesia records. Their record keeping becomes sloppy and unreadable, and they sign out ever-increasing quantities of narcotics and chart inappropriately high dosages. Their long-sleeved gowns hide needle marks and help them cope with frequent chills.

Meetings, schedules, and deadlines, the essence of the attorney's work, are crucial for professional success. Addicted attorneys may neglect routine tasks. A chemically dependent attorney said, "Telephone calls went unreturned. Depositions were missed and rescheduled. Hearings were set and reset. Trial continuances were routinely filed because I was not prepared. Promises of status reports to clients went unfulfilled . . . My drinking was out of control and I was, in fact, not doing my job" ("A Hard Charging . . . Trial Lawyer" 1989, p. 294).

Professionals feel profound shame when they fail to meet minimum professional standards. "When I finally realized that I was an alcoholic lawyer, I was devastated," one said. "I had known some alcoholic lawyers who had become the joke of the courthouse. Everyone had to work around them. They missed filing dates and had mistrials when they didn't show up on the second day of the trial. I just didn't want to be an alcoholic lawyer, but I was!" (Texas Young Lawyers Association 1990). "I missed a statute of limitations, which is unforgivable for a trial lawyer like me," another lamented. "I was supposed to file the client's lawsuit within two years of the accident date. When I missed the date, the client had a lot of heartache and filed a legal malpractice claim against me. I caused a lot of people a lot of trouble by not taking care of their business in a timely way. And when I didn't file lawsuits on time, they sued me" (JD, age 64).

UNPROFESSIONAL APPEARANCE AND PERFORMANCE

Personal appearance and hygiene typically deteriorate as the addictive illness progresses. According to one dentist, he was the only one unaware of "the unmistakable stench of stale alcohol on his breath. Even if I *saw* a patient (and I didn't knock them out of the chair with my breath), I didn't *do* anything" (Wamsley 1978, p. 30). His patients soon found themselves another dentist.

An embarrassed attorney's hands trembled noticeably in a legal meeting. "We all had to sign some papers, and my hands were shaking so hard the others looked startled. I finally got it signed" (JD, age 64).

Eventually many addicts begin to vacillate between fatigue and hyperactivity. They sway or stagger, slur their speech, and use profane and obscene language.

Addicted professionals may be confused and have difficulty concentrating or recalling details and instructions. Ordinary tasks require greater effort and consume more time. "There were times at work when I was totally stoned," said a pharmacist. "I couldn't type, I couldn't count, and if I hadn't had an experienced technician helping me, they would have had to lock the doors and send people to other pharmacies. The boss was a mile and a half away from the pharmacy and never asked me what was wrong, even though he probably had people asking about me. But of course I never made mistakes—it was always somebody else" (PharmD, age 46).

The addict's work style spasmodically alternates between periods of high and low productivity, but performance is generally lowered by missed deadlines, mistakes due to inattention, poor judgment, and bad decisions. "I was making a lot of money for my law firm, but I reached the point where I was incapacitated when the chemicals didn't kick in anymore," an attorney recalled. "I became paralyzed by fear and guilt and worried about getting caught for stealing. I would sit in the office for an hour or two at a time and stare at the phone—terrified that it wasn't going to ring because I knew it needed to if I was going to make money, and terrified that it would ring because I was afraid that somebody would find out what I was doing. I was literally paralyzed" (JD, age 64).

Intoxicated clinicians may respond inappropriately to emergency calls and decline in efficiency, thoroughness, and quality of patient care. "Did I ever drill drunk? Drilling under the influence?" a dentist asked rhetorically. "No, but I was severely impaired by fatigue, withdrawal and lack of concentration too many times" (Reid and Dr. L 1990).

As memory suffers and output declines, inefficient and careless work patterns worsen. "My daily habits were horrible, and my desk was a mess," an attorney confessed. "There would be times when my law partners wouldn't know where I was or what I was doing, and that troubled them. I would drink all night and then try to smooth myself out with Valium so I could work during the day" (JD, age 64). Recalling how his life became a nightmare, another attorney said, "My professional life suffered beyond belief. I began to appear in court, as well as in the office, intoxicated on a regular basis. On two occasions, I actually fell asleep during a trial . . . I had become an embarrassment to my family and the profession. I had also become very dangerous to myself as well as others" ("A Progressive Disease" 1992, p. 251).

STRAINED RELATIONS AT WORK

Interpersonal relations with colleagues, staff, and clients suffer. A study of 300 addicted nurses found that many experienced mood swings, irritability, memory losses/blackouts, poor attitudes, anxiety, intenseness, and inappropriate secretive behaviors (Sullivan, Bissell, and Leffler 1990). "My moods had little correlation with what was occurring in my life," a nurse recalled. "One hour I was personable and calm, the next hostile and irritable. When I was high, I often had telephonitis" (Kendall 1987, p. 87).

During drug withdrawal professionals are preoccupied, nervous, irritable, impatient, and demanding of others. Rarely admitting errors or accepting blame, they give implausible excuses for absences and oversights. Interpersonal friction develops when addicts overreact to real or imagined criticism and hold unreasonable resentments. "After a while," a physician recalled, "nice old doc became that grumpy SOB, slamming phones, chewing out staff, projecting [personal faults] onto others" (Cruse 1981, p. 299).

Compassionate relations with clients become increasingly difficult for a professional crippled by addiction. "I wasn't emotionally available to really care about my patients," a psychiatrist explained. "I was full of emptiness and had no idea how to follow through with patients, so I had to go through the pretense of caring; and this gave me much guilt" (MD, age 57).

Colleagues and staff who initially try to protect the professional eventually become resentful when the addicted colleague does not pull his own weight and the continuity of care, client safety, and teamwork diminish. Relationships can be strained beyond repair when behavior becomes intolerable.

SERIOUS ERRORS THAT ENDANGER CLIENTS

Everyone makes mistakes, of course, but addicted professionals exceed acceptable limits. According to the Federation of State Medical Boards, more than 10,000 physicians are sanctioned each year by state medical boards for misconduct ranging from drunkenness to patient abuse. In *10,289 Questionable Doctors* (Public Citizen Health Research Group 1994b), a 2,100-page nationwide summary of doctors unfit to practice medicine, a state-by-state listing indicates doctors who misused drugs, were convicted of criminal charges, provided substandard care, or were negligent. Yet state boards discipline less than half of one percent of the practitioners responsible for the estimated 150,000 to 300,000 deaths or injuries to Americans each year as a result of medical negligence.

Intoxication, blackouts, hangovers, and withdrawal may harm patients. "I was a good nurse," one said. "But I worked a lot with hangovers and made lots of mistakes when coming down off acid" (RN, age 35). One dental patient was startled when the practitioner, while preparing the patient's teeth, began to jerk uncontrollably as a result of his addiction to meperidine (Aston 1984).

Life-endangering situations occur when a surgeon or anesthesiologist is intoxicated. Bending over his patient, an anesthesiologist cautiously lifted the face mask while pretending to adjust it and inhaled deeply to share the patient's Penthrane. After repeated deep inhalations, he nearly lost consciousness in the operating room. Later, "The patient was waking up and I was out cold," he reported (Sullivan, Bissell, and Williams 1988, p. 13).

A physician heard his surgeon father-in-law say that he didn't think he could operate sober (MD, age 35). Similarly, a medical intern in the emergency room told how alcohol "helped" him deal with a small child requiring a tracheotomy.

> The nurse asked me to take over. I remember moving into the room, but because I was in a total blackout, I have no memory of doing the tracheotomy. Fortunately, the child's life was saved, the "trach" was completed, and I found myself thinking that because the procedure had turned out so well, maybe being in a blackout was a good way to do surgery and I should experiment with the effects of alcohol on surgical performance.   (MD, age 57)

Work errors due to chemical effects are not uncommon in medical settings. "I booked a couple of operations for the wrong day," a nurse confessed. "And on another night I was involved in an emergency that I don't remember. Then there was the time I found a bottle in the doctor's locker and took the booze myself in the middle of the afternoon and passed out on the OR floor" (RN, age 70).

What do other operating room personnel do when the surgeon is intoxicated? "I remember seeing a physician come to surgery who was probably drunk, but I didn't say anything because I was afraid he'd say something about me. I was terrified that he had my number. A lot of surgeons can operate better drunk than sober" (MD, age 50). When an intoxicated surgeon nearly killed his wife, he rushed her to the emergency room. "I gave her the wrong thing for her seizure. The ER doc knew something was screwed up, but to protect me, he reported it was due to seizure and not to drug overdose. This really pissed off the paramedic guy who had taken her to the ER. She went home that night, and I promised to never use again, but of course I did" (MD, age 40).

A first-year resident in oral surgery recalled how his intoxicated senior resident put patients at risk.

> His bad judgment was shown when operating on a young diabetic who should never have had surgery; minimally he should have been monitored very closely before surgery. When the patient came in at 0630 for an 0800 surgery, the admitting resident hadn't been told about his condition because the senior resident was afraid it might prevent the surgery and hinder his own progress. To graduate he was required

to do a certain number of surgeries of different types. While being prepared for surgery, the patient fell unconscious and went into a coma.   (DDS, age 35)

On another occasion this same surgeon almost fell asleep in the operating room with an activated power instrument in his hand, a reciprocating saw whose blade goes back and forth to cut through facial bones. "It's very sharp, and he fell forward as if he was going right into the patient's eye! The way it's supposed to work is you first retract all the oral soft tissue near the bone, then place the blade in the mouth, start to irrigate, then step onto the pedal that activates the saw blade. But he started the saw before it was in the patient's mouth! His whole body was leaning into the patient when we stopped him. When we asked if he was okay, he said, 'I've been up all night for a 36-hour shift' " (DDS, age 35).

Another physician reported an error that nearly caused a patient's death.

When my addiction reached its height I needed to shoot up every two hours. So, if an open-heart case took four or five hours, I'd have to leave in the middle of the operation, go to the men's room in the OR suite, get my fix, and then go back to the operating room and continue surgery. I was so quick, I could inject myself faster than most people actually go to the bathroom.

During one 20-hour neurosurgical operation, my relief came every two hours or so and I went off for my Fentanyl fix. But later that night, my relief didn't show up for hours. I became edgy and distracted because I was experiencing withdrawal.

I was so distracted, I injected a blood product into the wrong port of a catheter. It caused a blood clot that went to the patient's lung, and the patient arrested. We gave him every drug imaginable—adrenalin, calcium, bicarbonate—and we shocked him with the defibrillator pads a half-dozen times before his normal heart rhythm was restored. Luckily, he suffered no ill effects from the arrest. People arrest during surgery for no apparent reason sometimes, so no one realized that my mistake had caused the arrest.   (Pekkanen 1988, pp. 221–222)

The addicted pilot can jeopardize the well-being of an entire cargo of passengers. When a DC-8 crashed in 1977, killing all on board, the pilot was found to have three times the blood alcohol level permitted for driving a car, according to the National Transportation

Safety Board findings (Flynn et al. 1993). In 1988 an airline accident took the lives of both pilots and seven passengers leaving Denver's Stapleton International Airport. The NTSB investigation concluded that the captain's performance had been impaired by his preflight use of cocaine. "We really can't say if he suffered from withdrawal," the investigator reported. "The most likely effect on the pilot was fatigue from cocaine-induced insomnia" (Fotos 1989).

A 1984 report by the NTSB cited alcohol use as a common factor involved in fatal commercial-aviation accidents. During the period 1975–1981 the board found that 10.5 percent of fatal general-aviation crashes resulting in 742 fatalities involved pilots whose autopsies showed positive blood tests for alcohol. An additional 6.4 percent of commuter-airline crashes and 7.4 percent of air-taxi crashes involved pilots with positive toxicological evidence of alcohol use. Fortunately, fatal crashes of major U.S. air carriers are rare, but the number of nonfatal aircraft accidents and near misses caused by alcohol may be higher (National Transportation Safety Board 1984; Yesavage and Leirer 1986).

In 1990 three Northwest Airline pilots were convicted of flying on too much alcohol and too little sleep. Although they had had many drinks the previous night, they climbed into the cockpit, thus displaying their impaired judgment. They were taken into custody by police after a citizen's arrest by an FAA inspector who had received an anonymous tip about their drinking. One pilot's defense was that he could tolerate more booze than the average man ("The High and the Mighty" 1990).

Rationalizations abound. "I have never had a blackout in an airplane, but I have flown with great hangovers," one pilot (age 54) boasted. "I've had blackouts and been in jail cells on layovers, but I've never had a blackout while flying. I suppose this is pride in the job." Another pilot (age 50) who had never flown inebriated but had done so with a hangover said, "Although this made it more difficult for me to keep up a level of performance, I didn't fall down to the level of other [sober] pilots. That may sound self-inflating, but my skill level was so high it would have taken a great deal to bring it way down to the point where it was unsafe."

A strong correlation exists between chemical dependence and malpractice. For example, the State Bar of California found that as many as 50 percent of the disciplinary problems that came before it—2,500 in 1989—involved chemical dependency (Haldane 1990). Similar results have been found in other states (Spilis 1992).

The lying and cheating that go hand in hand with addiction put clients at great risk. A now sober physician described an addicted colleague as "unreliable, a liar, a thief, and a cheat—one of us" (MD, age 49). A nurse confessed, "I used to steal my patients' drugs at work. I would say, 'Mr. So-and-So has chest pain and needs MS IV.' Then I'd give him Valium, which was not locked up. He'd get something, go to sleep, and I'd get his morphine. I was injecting up to 10 milligrams of IV morphine, and at the same time I was always drinking and using street speed wherever I could get it. I was a garbage can" (RN, age 42).

Patients whose medications are stolen not only suffer unnecessary pain but also are billed for the medication. "I literally stole drugs from patients and cost them money," a physician recalled. "I'd wait six hours after their last dose, then write another dose on the chart and take it myself. I'd justify it by saying, 'She doesn't need that quite yet' " (MD, age 36). It's easy to steal from patients, as a nurse pointed out.

> People were coming back from surgery, and I had access to their pain meds. When someone has had surgery, or is an older patient or confused, they don't know what meds they have or don't have, so it's easy to give them half a dose. I'd give the patient half a dose and take the syringe into a bathroom and take the other half. You don't want to be too obvious by going into the staff bathroom too many times, so I'd use the patient's bathroom.   (RN, age 40; see also Alexander and O'Quinn-Larson 1990, p. 56)

This is how an emergency room physician stole cocaine from patients.

> We kept liquid coke in the ER to treat patients with nosebleeds, so I used to pray for nosebleeds to come in. I would have the nurse put the coke into a syringe, then when I sent her out of the room to get some obscure piece of equipment, I filled up another syringe with water and switched the syringes. I packed the patient's nose with water until the bleeding stopped and then I would go into the bathroom to do 100 percent pure coke. Sometimes I saved up the coke and put it in a nasal spray bottle and gave it to all my friends. We would walk around snorting the coke. Then I made friends with a hospital phar-

macist who liked to do coke, and she would steal pure coke crystals out of the coke bottle and we would go up on the roof in the middle of the night and do crazy stuff while using. I was always high when I was at work. Thank God I never killed anyone because I easily could have; my judgment was really messed up.   (MD, age 38)

It is not uncommon for addicted lawyers to steal clients' money. The Georgia Bar, for example, reports that more than 80 percent of disciplinary cases involving offenses related to client security funds have been linked to substance abuse (Spilis 1992).

Addicted attorneys get into trouble when they accept retainers but show no progress toward delivering the promised legal services. Not only do they fall behind in accounting to the client; they also sometimes commingle funds with their office or personal expenses instead of holding them in trust. "The problem with lawyers is that we steal," a recovering addict explains. "We call it 'borrowing' when we use other people's money. But whatever you call it, it comes down to stealing. For most state bar associations, if you commingle your client's funds with your own, you are history—you're no longer a lawyer" (JD, age 60).

ILLICIT DRUG TRAFFICKING

A few health practitioners augment their incomes by writing prescriptions for an extra supply of narcotics or diverting office-stashed drug supplies. Prescription drugs are easier to obtain, less expensive, and usually of better quality than street drugs. And the potential profits are enormous. For example, Dilaudid, a powerful narcotic substitute for heroin, reportedly retails for $2 per tablet, whereas on the streets it may sell for $50–100 (Weikel 1996; see also Jalon 1986). Goldman (1981) estimates that prescription drug trafficking in the United States is a $25-billion-a-year business (see also Haislip 1993).

According to Aston (1984), an estimated 1 or 2 percent of physicians, dentists, and pharmacists—sometimes working together—generate almost all prescription drugs sold for illegal use in the United States. For example, a 1985 sting operation in Los Angeles resulted in civil and criminal actions against 34 people and conviction of 7 physicians, 5 clinic owners, 3 independent drug dealers, and a pharmacy owner (Jalon 1986).[1]

Prevalence of Drug Use

How many health professionals, attorneys, and commercial pilots are chemically impaired? Like scattered pieces of a jigsaw puzzle, the data provide a fragmentary picture. Relatively few rigorous studies have been conducted. Virtually no research data exist for dentists, and only a few studies have been reported for other professions. Because the American Medical Association was the first to acknowledge the secret sickness in its ranks, more research data exist about medical students and physicians than about the other professions combined Moreover, surveys based on self-reports are likely to underestimate the prevalence of chemical impairment among those surveyed. Addicts, often in denial, tend to hide this stigmatizing problem—even from themselves—and are less likely than others to complete accurately or to return questionnaires seeking information about their use of substances (Bissell 1989).

THE GENERAL PUBLIC

We live in an addiction-prone, drug-consuming society focused on individual achievement and self-fulfillment through acquisition of wealth, status, and power. Chemical dependency, one aspect of the broad spectrum of addictive behaviors, is in the spotlight because of the public's increasing awareness of its costs to the individual, the family, and society.

Millions of Americans suffer and die from alcohol and drug abuse that often goes undiagnosed and untreated. About 43 percent of U.S. adults (76 million people) have been exposed to alcoholism in their families. They either grew up with, married, or had a blood relative who was an alcoholic or a problem drinker (Schoenborn 1991).

The extent of the problem is reflected by the Hallmark Card Company's greeting cards, T-shirts, coffee mugs, and other items for recovering alcoholics/addicts and their friends, relations, and associates. The company's marketing research found that at least 15 million Americans were currently attending support groups for alcohol and drug addictions and 100 million more—nearly half the population—supported their efforts to stay clean. With so many in the recovering community, Hallmark tapped into this "inspirational gold mine" with uplifting messages like "You expected a miracle and you got one" and "Your recovery is something I had hoped and prayed for" (Yates 1992).

A national probability sample of U.S. households (*Preliminary Estimates from the 1995 National Household Survey on Drug Abuse* 1996) found that 52 percent of Americans age 12 and older had used alcohol during the month preceding the survey. Asked about the use of any illicit substance, 6.1 percent of the same population responded that they had used during the past month.

Researchers in a collaborative project of the National Institute of Mental Health and research teams at Duke, Johns Hopkins, UCLA, Washington University at St. Louis, and Yale interviewed 20,291 people age 18 and older from five U.S. cities in 1980–1984. They learned that one in six Americans (16.7 percent) had been plagued with a substance abuse disorder at some point during their lifetime; 13.5 percent revealed abuse or dependence from alcohol and/or 6.1 percent from another drug (Regier et al. 1990).[2]

PHYSICIANS

Are physicians more or less likely than the general public to abuse drugs or become chemically dependent? Those who believe doctors are no more likely to abuse drugs than the general population cite Brewster (1986), who concluded that physicians are similar to the general public when alcohol and other drug dependence are considered together. Her conclusion came after she reviewed the literature and mailed a questionnaire to 510 male and 490 female physicians in Ontario, Canada, asking: "Have you ever been treated for problems with alcohol or other drugs?" Responses showed that 1.2 percent of the physicians and 1.3 percent of the general population in that region had received treatment.

Other researchers, however, report that physicians are more likely than nonphysicians to abuse alcohol and other drugs. One of the first studies, a 20-year follow-up of 268 college men, revealed that the 46 who became physicians used significantly more drugs than the other respondents (Vaillant, Brighton, and McArthur 1970). By the time they were 50, drug use—regular use of tranquilizers or intermittent use of sleeping pills, amphetamines, and minor tranquilizers—among the physicians was twice as great as among the other graduates. Dependence on alcohol or drugs that damaged them occupationally and socially was even more prevalent among the physicians—9 percent of the doctors versus 1 percent of the controls (Vaillant 1982).

A national survey of 9,600 randomly selected U.S. physicians (Hughes et al. 1992), compared with results from the *National Household Survey on Drug Abuse* (1991), found physicians significantly more likely to use alcohol and prescription medications—especially minor opiates (for example, codeine and Darvon) and benzodiazepine tranquilizers (for example, Valium and Xanax)—and less likely to use cigarettes and illicit substances (for example, heroin, cocaine, and marijuana).

Significant differences have also been found among medical trainees. Myers and Weiss (1987) report that residents are five and a half times more likely to use sleeping pills than those under age 30 in the general population. A national survey of resident physicians (Hughes et al. 1991), compared with young adults similar in age, found residents to have higher rates of alcohol use (5 percent had drunk alcoholic beverages daily during the past month) and benzodiazepines , but lower use rates of other drugs, such as marijuana, cigarettes, cocaine, barbiturates, and heroin. Drug use for recreation—to have a good time, to feel good, or to experiment—was the predominant reason given for using two legal and four illicit substances. Self-treatment for medical purposes, to relieve tension, or to relax was the primary reason for use of three prescription substances. Amphetamines were used primarily to improve work performance and alertness.

A large random study of fourth-year students from 23 representative U.S. medical schools (Baldwin et al. 1991) found medical students more likely than two similar-age national comparison groups to use alcohol, tranquilizers, and psychedelic drugs other than LSD, but less likely to have used eight other substances in the past 30 days or past year (see also Clark and Daugherty 1990). Clark (1988) found that alcohol-abusing medical students—about 18 percent of the class—had better first-year grades and better overall scores on the National Board of Medical Examiners test (Part I) than their classmates.

How many practicing physicians become chemically dependent? A look at California's physicians, representing about 10 percent of the nation's doctors, suggests that the number is substantial. Between 1980 and 1995 about 1,300 licensed California physicians—of a total of about 76,000—contacted the state diversion program, which diverts chemically dependent doctors from the criminal justice system into treatment and carefully monitors their recovery (Medical Board of California 1995). In addition, an informal 1990 study led the program's director to conclude that there were at least 1,300 other physicians who had sought recovery outside the diversion program. In short, from 1980 through 1995 at least 2,600 California physicians had received treatment (Gladden 1994). Many others, still in denial, avoid treatment altogether. The Medical Board of California (1995) estimates that 13,600 California physicians (18 percent) abuse alcohol or other drugs during their lifetime and 2 percent should be in treatment at any one particular time.

Hughes and colleagues' (1992) study of 9,600 randomly selected U.S. physicians found that 8 percent of the responding physicians admitted having abused or been dependent upon alcohol or other drugs during their lives. Other studies, suggesting rates of alcohol abuse for physicians ranging between 13 and 14 percent, are consistent with the 13.5 percent rate of alcohol disorders in the adult population recently reported by the National Institute of Mental Health. Differing methods and criteria for defining alcohol abuse undoubtedly contribute to these differing results.

Of all physicians, anesthesiologists seem at highest risk (Gualtieri, Cosentino, and Becker 1983; Gallegos et al. 1988; Lutsky et al. 1991). They have ready access to drugs, and the practice of anesthesiology is usually extremely demanding, often involving life-and-death decisions, isolation, long hours, competition with colleagues, and confrontation with demanding surgeons. William Farley, an anesthesiologist, noted,

> I've been able to uncover, without too much work, 25 [overdose] deaths among anesthesiologists that have occurred in the last two years, and 19 of these have been residents. I've talked with many of the departments where these tragedies occurred and in virtually every case was told, "This resident was the best and the brightest." "This was absolutely the last person we suspected might have a problem with drugs." "This resident was ticketed down stream to become our chief resident." (American Society of Anesthesiologists 1994)

In 1993 the chairman of an anesthesia department at a prestigious university told me that about 30 percent of his staff were addicted and two had recently died from overdoses. This situation caused him so much stress that, at the recommendation of his dean, he had taken a sabbatical year off.

PHARMACISTS

Pharmacists and pharmacology students have drug-use patterns similar to those of physicians and medical students, but at a slightly lower prevalence. A 1984 questionnaire sent to 510 randomly selected pharmacists in a New England state and to 470 students from the state's pharmacology schools (McAuliffe et al. 1987b) found that 46 percent of the pharmacists and 62 percent of the students had used a controlled substance without a prescription in the past year. The study also found that 18 percent of the pharmacists and 35 percent of the students who had ever used drugs either became drug dependent or were at risk for drug abuse.

How do pharmacology students compare with the general population? A 1987 survey of 272 pharmacy students at two midwestern pharmacy schools (Tucker, Gurnee, and Sylvestri 1988) found their use of alcohol (89 percent) similar to that of other college populations but significantly higher than that of young adults in the general population (68 percent). Problem behaviors related to alcohol use were unexpectedly high; 34 percent reported blackouts or periods of amnesia, and 10 percent had had four or more episodes of binge drinking—defined as five or more drinks per occasion—in the month preceding the survey.

How many practicing pharmacists use drugs to such an extent that their work is impaired? A 1984 survey mailed to all licensed pharmacists in North Carolina revealed that 43 percent of the 1,370 respondents knew at least one pharmacist who had personal problems severe enough to interfere with performance of everyday activities. Nearly one-third had worked with someone with an alcohol-abuse or addiction problem (Normark et al. 1985).

NURSES

There are few research data to assess the extent of drug use among nurses. Schwartz-Barcott and Schwartz (1990) analyzed the responses of 256 nurses to questions about drug use in a large national telephone survey of 20,000 U.S. citizens by the University of Chicago's National Opinion Research Center. Asked if they drank liquor, wine, or beer, significantly more nurses (83 percent) than the larger sample (66 percent) said they did (see also Smith et al. 1989; Trinkoff and Storr 1994).

Another survey, mailed to 5,000 U.S. nurses by the editors of two popular magazines, with more than 2,000 responding, found that only 3 percent reported illicit drug use on a regular basis—at least once a month (Naegle 1988). Five percent of the nurses had felt a persistent need for alcohol at some time in their lives; and 3 percent said that alcohol use had adversely affected their performance in terms of missing work, having trouble getting along with others, practicing below standards, seriously considering suicide, or causing an accident. "Many nurses" (number unspecified) penned comments like these on their questionnaires: "A lot of nurses drink and occasionally come to work with hangovers"; "I see alcohol abuse as a more overwhelming problem than drug use; a lot of nurses drink excessively."

A study of 143 currently working registered nurses, ages 18–65, identified in a 1980–1984 NIMH-sponsored probability sample of households in five major U.S. metropolitan areas, found no greater use of alcohol or illicit drugs than a matched comparison group of 1,410 nonnurses (Trinkoff, Eaton, and Anthony 1991). But the use patterns of both groups were substantial. One-third (32.9 percent) of the nurses and 35.1 percent of the comparisons had at some time in their lives used illicit drugs without a prescription (or exceeding prescription) to get high.

To what extent are nurses impaired by chemicals? Eight percent of the nurses surveyed by Trinkoff and Storr (1994) admitted that they had abused drugs, and 2 percent confessed to an alcohol problem. Trinkoff, Eaton, and Anthony's study found that 1 in 20 (4.9 percent) nurses, compared with 8.8 percent of nonnurses, had experienced pathological use of alcohol; that is, they had a history of at least one of these symptoms: need for daily use, inability to cut down, bingeing to intoxication lasting 48 hours, blackouts, or continued drinking despite physical problems caused by the drinking.

How does pathological use affect their work? According to a 1984 report by the American Nurses' Association (Solari-Twadell 1988), 68 percent of all state board actions against nurses stem from substance abuse (see also Green 1989). In 1994 the number of disciplinary actions increased to 2,100, with 47 state boards reporting

(Sheets 1995). "Addiction is a tremendous problem in our profession," said the secretary-treasurer of International Nurses Anonymous, an unofficial network of nurses who are in a 12-step recovery program (1995).

DENTISTS

Few empirical studies address the prevalence of substance abuse among dentists, but anecdotal data suggest the number may be substantial. For example, a dentist quoted by Rankin and Harris (1990, p. 7) said that within a five-year period in his suburban area—a three-mile radius—a 47-year-old dentist had died from acute alcoholism and five others had lost their clinical licenses; two were addicted to cocaine, one to Demerol, and two others to nitrous oxide. A statewide survey of 370 Michigan dentists found that 48 percent of the respondents knew a colleague with an obvious substance abuse problem. Another 39 percent were aware through hearsay (Peterson and Avery 1988).

About 55 percent of all cases filed from 1977 through 1984 before the Texas Board of Dental Examiners were related to drug offenses (Sandoval, Hendrickson, and Dale 1988). During the same period action was taken against 109 Oregon dentists (22 percent of the cases) for various drug-related offenses: overprescribing, prescribing outside the scope of dentistry, and self-administration. The most common drugs consumed were meperidine (Demerol; 25 percent), alcohol (17.9 percent), diazepam (Valium; 10.7 percent), nitrous oxide (7.1 percent), oxycodone (Percodan; 7.1 percent), and secobarbital hydrochloride (Seconal; 7.1 percent) (Clark, Chiodo, and Cowan 1988).

ATTORNEYS

A study of North Carolina attorneys found that 16.6 percent consumed three to five alcoholic drinks a day (North Carolina Bar Association 1991). This finding came from a questionnaire mailed to 11,810 licensed attorneys asking them about the quality of their lives. The report discusses no other substance.

A 10 percent random sample of Washington State attorneys revealed that one-third had suffered from depression, problem drinking, or cocaine abuse (Benjamin, Darling, and Sales 1990). Eighteen percent were problem drinkers, and 5 percent had suffered from both alcoholism and depression. Although less than 1 percent reported currently abusing cocaine, about 26 percent had used cocaine previously. Those who had practiced longer were more susceptible to drinking problems; 18 percent of the lawyers who had practiced from 2 to 20 years had developed problem drinking, compared with 25 percent who had practiced 20 or more years. Years in legal practice, however, did not affect the percentage of attorneys who suffered from depression or cocaine abuse. A comparison of Washington and Arizona attorneys by the same investigators found that both states had similar occurrences of depression, problem drinking, and cocaine abuse (Benjamin, Sales, and Darling 1992).

State records show that a high percentage of attorneys in trouble with licensing boards suffer from chemical abuse. The president of the California State Bar indicates that at least one in seven California lawyers has a serious substance abuse problem. Half of the 5,000 legal misconduct cases investigated each year by the California Bar are linked to substance abuse (Haldane 1990).

A status report from the American Bar Association asserts that 13 of every 100 students who graduate from an accredited law school show signs of drug/alcohol dependency (Robbins and Branaman 1992). A disproportionately large number of individuals in the legal profession are at risk for chemical dependency.

A national study of 3,388 law students at 121 accredited U.S. law schools found that 14 percent had drunk alcoholic beverages 10 or more times during the previous month, and 3.8 percent admitted to daily use. When compared with college and high school graduates of similar age (23–33), law students show significantly higher usage rates for alcohol and psychedelic drugs other than LSD for lifetime, past-year, and past-month use. Law students also report significantly higher usage rates than other college graduates for past-year marijuana use, past-year and past-month tranquilizer use, lifetime and past-year LSD use, past-year use of opiates other than heroin, and past-month barbiturate use. The survey also documented increased use and frequency of usage of some substances as students progressed through law school, and among older law students. The pattern is most dramatic for alcohol—compared with first- and second-year students, third-year students use significantly more alcohol, both daily and monthly (Association of American Law Schools 1993).

Extrapolating from the data in the law student survey, the Association of American Law Schools concluded that substantial percentages of current law students are very frequent users (and at least occasional abusers) of alcohol and that somewhat lower but still significant percentages of law students are recent users of illicit drugs. "There may be as many as 4,900 (3.8%) law students nationally who are already using alcohol on essentially a daily basis, and over 15,000 (11.7%) may have abused alcohol at some point since entering law school. Over 10,600 (8.2%) may have used marijuana within the past 30 days, and almost 1,700 (1.3%) may have used cocaine during the same period" (Association of American Law Schools 1993, p. 12).

PILOTS

Little is known about how many commercial pilots use marijuana and other illicit drugs, but a serious alcohol problem clearly exists. In two questionnaire surveys of 2,000 private and professional pilots, Ross and Ross (1988) found that 16 percent of the respondents admitted to heavy drinking (an average of more than five drinks per occasion, two or more times monthly, or an average of more than two drinks daily), with no difference between private and professional pilots.

To what extent do pilots suffer from problem drinking or chemical dependence? Barton Pakull, chief psychiatrist of the Federal Aviation Administration's Aviation Medical Program, reports that more than 2,000 pilots have returned to flying after completing the FAA's Chemical Dependency Program (Pakull 1996; see also Markham 1981; Harper 1983).

In July 1991 the *Washington Post* reported that the FAA had systematically compared the records of 170,000 licensed pilots with their auto driving records in the National Driver Register and found that 4,000 had drunk-driving records. Eighty-four cases were sent to the FAA chief counsel for possible action. The FAA was working through checks on the remainder of the country's 680,000 licensed pilots, 146,000 of them commercial pilots (Phillips 1991; see also Martinez 1987; Nather 1989).

According to the FAA (Gordon 1991), nearly 400 of the 47,000 pilots employed by U.S. passenger airlines have been convicted of an alcohol-related motor vehicle offense. "Although the FAA's driving record checks are only about one-third complete, officials said they cover virtually all pilots of passenger planes because they must undergo medical reviews at least once a year. Of the 205,000 U.S. pilots checked thus far against computer records, 5,568 were found to have alcohol- or drug-related traffic convictions in the last three years" (p. 3A).

In Perspective

We think of professionals entrusted with the public welfare as role models, not drug abusers or addicts. But addiction is no respecter of persons; professionals fall prey as often as other people—if not more so.

All addicts become skilled at concealing their drug habits and subsequent problems, but chemically dependent professionals, clever and imaginative, develop ingenious schemes and rationalizations to cover up their drug habits. Their associates, having a big stake in the professional's goodwill and success, often enable the addiction and thus delay recovery. Most at risk are the addicted professionals' patients and clients.

The drug problem in America is much more pervasive than is commonly recognized. As a nation we usually target the most visible addicts—those in our inner cities who use illicit drugs. Fanned by uninformed political rhetoric, we prosecute and imprison them. Rarely do we notice or publicize professionals and other white-collar drug abusers who have much easier access to controlled substances. Our national understanding about the nature of chemical dependency and those who succumb to it is faulty.

TWO

Addiction's Defining Nature

"The first time I used Demerol it was like dying and going to heaven. I thought I had found Nirvana. But I could never get the virgin experience back again, and within a week I was hopelessly addicted."

　(MD, age 50)

"I figured I had a problem with alcohol and had better do something about it. So I stopped. Then I got myself half a jug of wine as a reward for stopping drinking."

　(JD, age 48)

"To this day, after seven years clean and sober, I still think about drinking and using."

　(RN, age 40)

Ignorance and naiveté contribute unnecessarily to the addiction of many professionals. This chapter reviews a few of the things all professionals should know: types of drugs and drug users, addiction's defining characteristics, and its underlying biological, psychosocial, and spiritual dynamics.

Psychoactive Drugs: Status and Effects

Socially acceptable psychoactive drugs[1]—alcohol, found in beer, wine, and "spirits" or "hard" liquor; nicotine, found in tobacco;[2] and caffeine, found in coffee, tea, chocolate, and cola[3]—are readily available and used despite awareness of their widely publicized adverse effects. Other drugs—central nervous system (CNS) depressants,[4] narcotics,[5] and stimulants[6]—are controlled through doctors' prescriptions but can be used inappropriately. Illegal street drugs such as marijuana, heroin, cocaine, LSD (lysergic acid diethylamide), and PCP (phencyclidine) are covertly marketed and used.[7] "Designer drugs," illegally developed and sold by amateur chemist profiteers, approximate the effects of controlled substances.[8]

Legal, accessible, and socially acceptable, alcohol is seldom regarded as a drug and does not carry the same stigma. "I didn't do drugs," said a nurse. "I always knew that drugs were illegal, but it was okay to drink because I could buy it" (RN, age 37). A physician recalled, "I was chairman of our hospital committee for impaired physicians. Back in those days the hospital furnished dinner and wine. So when the addicts came in before us, we would sit there drinking our wine while chewing them out for their drug use. Alcohol was okay; the only rule was that you just didn't come to work with alcohol on your breath or with the shakes" (MD, age 75).

Drugs vary in legal and social status and in the degree to which they are regulated by the Drug Enforcement Agency (DEA). The DEA classifies drugs by schedules from I to V according to their potential for abuse. Schedule I drugs are classified as the least useful and most dangerous.[9]

A license to practice medicine does not automatically grant doctors the privilege of prescribing "controlled substances." They must apply directly to the DEA for authorization to prescribe medications in Schedules II, III, and IV. Schedule II drugs cannot be prescribed by telephone, and there are no refills; they require special prescription forms issued by the DEA to doctors approved after an additional application process. Schedule III drugs require a new prescription after six months or five refills. Schedule IV drugs also require a new prescription after six months or five refills but have less severe penalties for illegal possession than Schedule III drugs. Authorization is not required for Schedule V drugs (for example, Lomotil) and is not granted at all for Schedule I drugs (for example, heroin) except for scientific research.

Individual drugs have several different names: a technical name based on its structure, one or more proprietary or brand names, and several slang names. For example, methaqualone is the chemical name for Quaaludes, called "ludes" on the street. A street drug is usually procured from a drug dealer in certain areas of a city and is usually manufactured in unregulated and illegal laboratories. Its potency and purity are usually unpredictable. A pharmaceutical drug is manufactured and marketed by a pharmaceutical company; its purity and potency are strictly regulated and standardized and are clearly stated on the label.

Alcohol, at one end of the psychoactive drug spectrum, is legally available to adults in unlimited quantities. It is glamorized and widely accepted as an integral part of many social and business functions. Heroin, at the other end, is a highly restricted, Schedule I drug; illegal use is punishable by imprisonment. Each year about 7,000 people die from heroin abuse and 100,000 from alcohol abuse (Massing 1992, p. 38).

Addiction treatment specialists typically use the words "addict" and "alcoholic" interchangeably because a person who is addicted to one substance is susceptible to addiction to all other psychoactive drugs. Miller and Gold (1988b; 1990) report that over 80 percent of cocaine addicts are also addicted to alcohol, and 53 percent of these are addicted to hashish or marijuana.

Alcoholics who avoid other drugs sometimes regard themselves as superior to those addicted to illegal drugs. "I didn't think of alcohol as a drug," a nurse remarked (RN, age 70). An alcoholic attorney confessed, "I was terrified of drugs, absolutely terrified. I distinguished myself from drug addicts—you know, the man with the golden arm going through crazy withdrawals. I looked down on them, represented them in court, and lectured them about the importance of controlling their drug habits. I didn't consider alcohol a drug. Now that I'm sober, I'm embarrassed to think about it" (JD, age 56).

A narcotic-dependent nurse had to fight to stay in Alcoholics Anonymous because alcoholics disdained her. "I had a bad experience in AA back in 1981 when there were no Narcotics Anonymous programs," she recalled:

> I came up against the old-timers' mentality. They didn't want me in the program, and a lot of them resented me for being there. At an AA retreat for women, a group of them drew up a petition to get me out. But the retreat leader told them that if anybody was going to leave, it would be them. I stood up at a meeting and said, "Look, I know about your petition; I know I make a lot of people uncomfortable, but if I leave, I die." There was dead silence. I really believed that if I left, I would die.   (RN, age 56)

The atmosphere is more tolerant now. Widespread experimentation with recreational drugs in the 1960s reduced the social stigma associated with drug use and made it more commonplace, even a sign of status—such as cocaine use among the affluent. Many AA members, recovering from addictions to drugs *and* alcohol, now identify themselves as "alcoholic-addicts," and AA's 12-step model has been diversified to include such groups as Narcotics Anonymous and Cocaine Anonymous.

Drug-User Continuum

Drug users vary in their level of involvement and intensity of dependence. The most straightforward way to explain variations is to use a five-point continuum. At one end are abstainers who never use drugs (Type 1), and at the other are those who are so physically and psychologically dependent that drug use dominates their lives. In between are social users (Type 2), drug abusers not yet chemically dependent (Type 3), and addicts who are physically but not psychologically dependent (Type 4). Of course, in reality individuals seldom fit neatly into a particular category. A person categorized as an abstainer, for example, may, on rare occasions, drink. Moreover, psychological dependence, not precisely defined, varies by degree, and individuals may shift during their lifetime from one category to another. For example, an attorney remarked, "I started out as a social drinker, using alcohol as a social lubricant. Then I started escalating and eventually crossed that invisible line that every alcoholic does. I gradually changed from a social drinker to a mean, ugly, angry person" (JD, age 61). Later he became a total abstainer.

Most drug abusers and addicts (Types 3, 4, and 5) regard themselves as social drinkers/users (Type 2). "I was a maintenance drinker," acknowledged an attorney. "I went through all the stages but thought I was a social drinker. Oh, I can't be an alcoholic, I reasoned, because I never drink alone. I always made sure that I was someplace where I could ask people to drink with me" (JD, age 41). Another attorney recounted how he came to recognize his alcoholism:

> Throughout my adult life I was a daily drinker; I thought that was what normal people were supposed to do, and I couldn't imagine life without alcohol. Then I represented a young man charged with driv-

ing while intoxicated. When questioning jurors about their drinking habits so I could get people that drank like my client, I asked one woman if she considered herself a social drinker, and she assured me that she was. I inquired, "Mrs. V., what do you consider social drinking?" She explained that she and her sister had a glass of wine at Thanksgiving and a highball around the holidays. I hadn't heard the term "highball" since 1940, so I questioned her a little further. "What about the person who comes home after a hard day and just has a couple of drinks to round off the sharp edges to relax?" She looked at me very quizzically and asked, "Why would anyone drink every day?" I really couldn't answer that, and I excused her. Then I proceeded to lose the case. I had come across a different definition of social drinking. My definition was that I was a social drinker if I was standing up.   (JD, age 60)

ABSTAINERS (TYPE 1) AND SOCIAL DRINKERS/USERS (TYPE 2)

Abstainers (Type 1), who make up about one-third of the population (Institute of Medicine 1989), do not use alcohol or other drugs. Social drinkers/users (Type 2), who constitute the majority of the population, occasionally use alcohol and other drugs in social settings and have no trouble restraining or discontinuing their consumption. They typically limit their use to parties or religious occasions when drinking/drugging is expected, and they rarely experience significant personal problems from use of these substances either at home or at work.

Users in the next three categories frequently jeopardize their own and others' health and well-being.

DRUG ABUSERS (TYPE 3)

The nickname "party animals" aptly describes Type 3 users. These individuals, considerably more numerous than alcoholics and addicts, use substances excessively.[10] Like Type 2 users, their use typically occurs in social settings. However, Type 3 users consume more heavily, and intoxication is usually the purpose of their get-togethers. Unlike addicts, however, their use is sporadic (usually on weekends), and they are not physically dependent, although their use of intoxicants may eventually escalate. Partying—"getting blasted," "plastered," or "smashed" with the peer group—is a valued activity, a way to enjoy social acceptance.

Many college students exemplify this type (Commission on Substance Abuse at Colleges and Universities 1994). A study sponsored by Columbia University's Center on Addiction and Substance Abuse has found a startling increase in binge drinking during the past 15 years, especially among women. Defined as the consumption of more than five cans of beer or five glasses of wine at a single sitting, binge drinking is now practiced by almost half of all college students. "Once thought of as a male rite of passage," an investigator asserts, "alcohol abuse has now become a woman's rite of passage" (Eaton 1994, p. A21).

The Stanford University marching band was reprimanded for "arriving at a football game drunk" and "urinating on the field" in full view of television cameras, the press, and several thousand people attending the game (Bishop 1990). An auto accident in Bowling Green, Kentucky, seriously injured two college students who had been drinking at a bar that advertised a "bladder buster" special—half-price drinks until the first person in your party uses the restroom ("Bladder Buster" 1992).

"Chug-a-lugging," the rapid ingestion of alcohol—usually beer—is a popular practice among some youths and sometimes leads to death. But drug abuse is not limited to students. Following the third quarter of a Citrus Bowl football game, the public address system was turned over to a group called the Zonies, a club of 3,000 fans who regularly buy end-zone tickets. After paying homage to a beer keg deposited on a pedestal at one of the goal lines, they chanted, "Zonies don't care who's in the game; the teams on the field all look the same. Zonies don't care who is here, as long as we have ice-cold beer." The newspaper columnist remarked, "Yes, these were adults" ("Questionable Call" 1992).

PHYSICALLY BUT NOT PSYCHOLOGICALLY DEPENDENT ADDICTS (TYPE 4)

With frequent use of alcohol or drugs, the body's internal chemistry adapts to the ingested substance, inducing physical dependence. When the substance is withheld, the adapted body chemistry is thrown off balance, and withdrawal signs and symptoms occur. Abrupt and total cessation of the ingested substance, called "cold turkey," produces a rapid and intense detoxification of the adapted body chemistry.[11] After enduring the discomforts of withdrawal, Type 4 users, who are not psychologically dependent, can "walk away" from chemical dependence and "never look back" (Waldorf,

Reinarman, and Murphy 1991). Although they experience cravings and withdrawal symptoms and may enjoy a psychological boost from drugs, they do not rely on these substances to cope with daily life.

Patients inadvertently addicted to drugs prescribed by their physicians can become Type 4 users. When an automobile accident caused brain trauma to a university professor, a physician encouraged him to try a new drug—a benzodiazepine (Xanax)—to alleviate the anxiety and depression caused by his sudden loss of mental acuity. When the professor declined, saying he didn't want to be addicted, the doctor mistakenly assured him that the drug was not addicting. "When I realized that I was hooked on this miserable stuff, I hated it and wanted to get off. I tried cold-turkeying it, but had a severe panic attack in which I thought I was dying. It took months to get this poison out of my system" (PhD, age 49). A person physically addicted by such means would be incensed to be labeled an addict. Though highly motivated to be free from "chemical slavery," such inadvertent addicts must endure the withdrawal process until their nervous systems resume normal functioning.

Situational addicts, including some Vietnam veterans, provide another example of Type 4 users. Narcotic use and addiction were very common among military personnel in Vietnam. In 1970–71 almost half (45 percent) of enlisted men tried narcotics, and 20 percent reported feeling "strung out" or addicted. Having used heroin and other narcotics heavily for a considerable time, they suffered the classic symptoms of withdrawal for at least several days. Almost 11 percent tested positive for drugs in urine samples taken at departure; yet a year after returning to the United States, only 5 percent were still addicted (Robins 1993, p. 1044). This outcome contrasts markedly with those for nonveterans treated at the federal narcotics hospital in Lexington, Kentucky, during the same period: six months after treatment, two-thirds were re-addicted. Moreover, further follow-up revealed that "only 12% of those addicted in Vietnam had been addicted at any time in the three years since returning and . . . the addiction had usually been very brief" (ibid., p. 1045). According to Robins, "It was not treatment that explained this remarkable rate of recovery. Only one third of the men addicted in Vietnam received even simple detoxification while in the service and only a tiny percentage of Vietnam enlisted men went into drug abuse treatment after returning—less than 2% of those who used narcotics in Vietnam" (ibid.).

Surprisingly, Robins also found that, for this group, recovery did not require abstinence. Although nearly half of the Vietnam addicts tried narcotics again after return, only 6 percent became re-addicted. Even regular heroin users became re-addicted in only half the cases. "This surprising rate of recovery, even when re-exposed to narcotic drugs," she points out, "ran counter to the conventional wisdom that heroin is a drug which causes addicts to suffer intolerable craving that rapidly leads to re-addiction if re-exposed to the drug" (Robins 1993, p. 1046).

How do we explain this? The drug itself does not "cause" addiction. Other factors, such as context, are more important. Clearly, some Vietnam veterans were only situationally addicted. During the horrors of an unpopular war, they used easily available, high-quality, socially approved drugs. When they returned to civilian life, psychoactive substances offered little psychological advantage. After detoxifying, most walked away from the drugs or used them only intermittently for recreation. They recovered sufficiently to establish or renew meaningful connections with schools, families, churches, and other social support structures that provided the psychological nourishment drugs only simulated. Those who were unable to recover from the horrors of war or to reconnect with an ambivalent populace were most vulnerable to substance abuse and addiction precisely because their emotionally supportive connections with others had been shattered.

Waldorf, Reinarman, and Murphy's (1991) life-history interviews with 122 current and 106 former cocaine users in northern California also illustrate the differences between Type 4 and 5 users. A chain-referral technique—"snowball sampling," in which one respondent recommends another—provided information from a hidden and hard-to-reach population about who does and does not quit drugs without formal assistance. The subjects exemplifying Type 5 addicts experienced severe crises and profound despair—including contemplation of suicide. After several unsuccessful attempts to stop using cocaine, they usually sought formal treatment of some kind and adopted AA's view that they were "powerless over drugs." Most of the sample, however, appear to have been Type 4 addicts: they were able to stop using drugs without formal help because they "did not have severe, underlying psychological problems or other addictions. Stopping cocaine abuse was a surprisingly straightforward and relatively trouble-free process for them," Waldorf, Reinarman, and Murphy report (1991, p. 228). Although most in this group had a difficult time abstaining even temporarily if the drug was readily available, "with varying degrees of effort and anguish, they 'just walked away' from cocaine and 'never looked back' " (pp. 271–272).

Although these Type 4 users had used cocaine heavily for a number of years, they maintained a stake in conventional life. "What keeps users from going over the edge with cocaine [going from Type 4 to Type 5] or allows many of them to climb back, is the investment in their everyday lives" (Waldorf, Reinarman, and Murphy 1991, p. 219). Most of them "worked regularly, maintained homes, and were responsible citizens . . . and did not see themselves as being particularly deviant . . . or distinct from other people they knew" (ibid., p. 220). In other words, most of these heavy users did not need to make major changes in their lives to stop using cocaine. They used drugs for pleasure and discontinued them when the disadvantages outweighed the advantages. As the ratio of positive to negative consequences tips toward the negative—from "fun" to "painful"—Type 4 addicts stop using.

PHYSICALLY AND PSYCHOLOGICALLY DEPENDENT ADDICTS (TYPE 5)

Many Type 5 addicts, like the professionals we studied, also have a big stake in their careers and families, but they do not simply walk away from drugs when the reward-pain ratio shifts. They depend on the drug's psychoactive effects to cope with life. When unpleasant and disruptive events accelerate, rather than discontinuing the drug as Type 4 addicts do, they increase the dosage, switch to other drugs, or try to titrate various substances. Instead of blaming drugs for their spiraling decline, they regard them as the solution.

Although physically addicted Type 4 users experience cravings when discontinuing, they can manage them. By contrast, Type 5 users continue to medicate their feelings even as their lives deteriorate. In short, they are psychologically "hooked." This saying among AA participants captures the difference between Type 5 addicts and other drug users: "When your drinking interferes with your work, you're in trouble. When your work interferes with your drinking, you're an alcoholic."

Although Type 5 users may try to stop and may even succeed, they cannot *sustain their abstinence* without others' help. Once begun, they cannot restrain themselves. The expression "one drink, one drunk" conveys this reality. Chemicals are their "best friend"—their elixir—and viable connections to other life structures wither and die.

This dentist's experience illustrates the obsessive preoccupation and irrationally compulsive behavior of such an addict.

> For 20 years I was a maintenance drinker. I'd drink every night, and overindulge at every social occasion. I got into several auto accidents, but other than that it had really no effect on my life or career. Only my wife could tell I had a problem. My curiosity led me to other drugs—most notably nitrous oxide in the comfort of my own office. I'd had the equipment in my office for years. One day, for some reason it caught my attention. I decided to try it. I put the mask on at 80% for a couple of minutes. Immediately I was hooked. Five-minute sessions turned into hours, until it got to the point I wouldn't go home for dinner. My wife would come down to the office at 11 P.M. and scream at me. "It's time to come home." I'd say, "F—— you, I'm going to keep doing it." I'd stay there all night, just barely getting myself together in the morning in time to work on patients.   ("A Near Fatal Combination" 1990, p. 25)

Unlike Type 2, 3, and 4 users, Type 5 addicts have a permanent, chronic chemical dependence—both physical and psychological. Untreated, it eventually becomes debilitating and often fatal; it gets worse, never better. The Type 5 addict who quits can never be a "social user" again. As the saying goes, he has become a pickle and cannot return to being a cucumber. Relapse, the *sine qua non* of addictive behavior, occurs when the recovering addict or alcoholic slips back into "old habits"—thoughts, feelings, and behaviors that then lead, gradually or precipitously, to resumption of the addictive pattern. The substance abuse during relapse is often worse than the abuse before sobriety, as if the addiction had progressed invisibly in the interim. A period of sobriety, no matter how long, confers no protection from the ravages of addiction during a relapse. Conditions supporting sobriety must be consciously maintained, and warning signs of relapse must be heeded. The recovering addict is motivated to avoid that first drink or drug by the memory of the miseries of chemical dependence and by appreciation of the rewards of sobriety.

A nurse described how difficult life is for someone psychologically dependent on drugs as well as how satisfying recovery can be.

> In recovery I've found peace, the peace that I had been looking for all the time. I've also had less fear and more freedom. Before I had to stay high enough so that I could talk to somebody on the phone or even go to the grocery store to get some bread. If I didn't stay high, I'd be so paranoid I'd just walk off. When I first went into treatment, I was so paranoid I refused to sleep in pajamas; I slept in my clothes and shoes so I would be ready to run. I never knew when—maybe in the middle of the night—I would have to hide. There was always somebody after me or something that might happen. When I first caught sobriety, it represented normality, freedom from constant fear, and taste of peace.   (RN, age 40)

The remainder of this book is mostly about Type 5 addicts, those who are both physically and psychologically dependent.

Addiction's Defining Characteristics

Definitions of addiction are slippery. Type 5 addicts—those who are both physically and psychologically dependent—typically exhibit these overlapping characteristics: tolerance and withdrawal symptoms, compulsive use, loss of control, continued use despite adverse consequences, preoccupation with drugs, progressive neglect of role obligations, and denial and other forms of distorted thinking. The patterns of addiction interact with the addict's life experience, character, and temperament. No two addicts are identical. Some vary significantly in one or more characteristics.

TOLERANCE AND WITHDRAWAL

As the body adjusts to—tolerates—the drug's pharmacologic effects through repeated intake, an increasing dosage is needed to obtain the intensity and duration of the original experience. The continual user must take more drugs to avoid the psychological distress and physical discomfort that accompany withdrawal, ranging from flulike symptoms to seizures or even death. A treatment expert illustrated this process with the case of a social drinker who became physically and psychologically dependent.

> A woman came to me who, though she had been a social drinker throughout her adult life, became chemically dependent. She and her husband had a nightcap after dinner and drank at parties. No problem. Once in a while they'd get drunk on New Year's Eve—normal social drinkers all their lives. Three years ago her husband died of a heart attack, and she, in her grief, had trouble sleeping. When she complained her friend said, "Why don't you have a glass of wine when you go to bed?" She took this advice and fell asleep with no problems. After about two months she had to have two glasses of wine, and then three. Because she's taking so much fluid when she goes to bed, she wakes up to urinate at 3:00 A.M., and then she can't get back to sleep. So she graduates to brandy, a stronger form of the same drug. One glass of brandy, then two, and then she's waking up in the morning with trembling hands, so she has to have one in the morning to go to work.

Then he explained:

> Here's a woman who has no personal or family history of alcoholism and yet, with an abrupt psychological event of enormous magnitude, begins using alcohol, not as a social lubricant, not as a nice little ritual with her hubby, but for the drug effect. Then she begins to notice tolerance: to get the effect, she has to drink more and more. A psychological factor altered her body's resistance to developing alcoholism. She has now stopped and has become abstinent. Can she go back to social drinking? No; she tried, but her inability to do that brought her to my office.

Chronic use of most psychoactive drugs gradually induces physical dependence. During the prolonged administration of morphine, for example, the body compensates for the continued presence of this pain-relieving drug, which is an analgesic and central nervous system depressant, by increasing the number and sensitivity of target receptors to offset the morphine-induced suppression of the CNS. The result is mitigation of the drug's impact, which necessitates an increase in dosage to restore the original desired effect. "When we bathe our brain cells in chemicals over time, the brain cells become adjusted to those chemicals," explained an addictionologist. "Then if you discontinue the chemical use, the discomforting physiological reaction is called withdrawal. It is a common problem with alcohol, barbiturates and tranquilizing drugs. A hypersensitivity is developed to the drug that will never change. Once a person is withdrawn from a chemical, he will remain hypersensitive to it; his chemical addiction can be triggered at any time if he is re-exposed to the chemical" (Elliot n.d.).

Some professionals gradually develop an enormous tolerance. "I was taking 20 cc of Fentanyl at a time, two to five times the lethal dose," an anesthesiologist confessed. "If you gave a healthy person 4 cc straight, there's a good chance he would die of respiratory arrest; clearly, 10 cc will kill you. I would go into the bathroom, take twice this amount, go to the OR [operating room], and do surgery, not even feeling high" (MD, age 34).

Certain addicts, like this pharmacist, become extremely toxic after ingesting massive amounts of chemicals: "At the worst period of my addiction, I was taking 150 Percodan tablets just to get through the day—25 at a time without water. After a while there was no high involved. I used them just to get rid of the withdrawal symptoms. I had built up my tolerance to such a level with these narcotics that I could take 25 at a time and still function" (PharmD, age 41). Asked about what this did to his health, he replied: "It ate a big hole in my stomach. When I went to rehab I had a huge ulcer that they treated as life-threatening. But I didn't care about killing myself; I needed those drugs. I had pain, but I was more worried about getting rid of the withdrawal symptoms than I was about the pain in my stomach. Just give me the drugs to get through the day and leave me alone. If I die, I die."

The gradual process of increased tolerance for nitrous oxide is described by a dentist interviewed by Redmond (1979, p. 50):

> It started so simply—so easily. After a long day at the chair, I thought a little nitrous oxide to relax me wouldn't hurt. But over a period of time my tolerance increased to the point that I was taking it straight, without any oxygen. It seemed almost logical, at times. It worked quicker than alcohol and there was no tell-tale breath. I began to live for 5 o'clock when I could turn it on.

Withdrawal experiences vary widely from person to person and from episode to episode. The nature and severity of withdrawal symptoms are determined by the type of the drugs used, the amount and duration of use, and the user's physiological and psychological responses.

Withdrawal symptoms from alcohol, for example, often begin four to six hours after decreasing or discontinuing intake: morning tremors, nausea, sweating, insomnia, depression, irritability, restlessness, apprehension, and mild difficulties with concentration. As these symptoms become more severe, the alcoholic drinks and uses other substances earlier in the day and may even awaken in the middle of the night to ingest them. Full-scale withdrawal, called delirium tremens, or "the DTs," may include seizures, disorientation, and hallucinations (*Alcohol and Health* 1990).

Withdrawal from sedatives and hypnotic drugs, including the "minor tranquilizers," can also result in DTs, although the severity and time sequence of withdrawal events will differ for each drug (Sullivan, Bissell, and Williams 1988, p. 57). Exceptionally high doses of marijuana can produce withdrawal symptoms, including irritability, insomnia, tremor, sweating, and gastrointestinal complaints (Schuckit 1995a).

Not long ago cocaine was misrepresented as a "safe" drug because, unlike heroin and other addictive drugs, cocaine's withdrawal symptoms are not always obvious to an observer and, in some cases, the user. However, cocaine and amphetamines are highly addictive. Although some withdrawal signs may seem relatively mild, others are more serious, such as severe depression, anhedonia (inability to experience happiness), subjective discomfort, and drug hunger (Sullivan, Bissell, and Williams 1988, p. 56). More extreme reactions to abrupt cessation of heavy cocaine use, especially when freebased or smoked as crack, are characterized by agitation and intense cravings, called "Jonesing," and may include paranoid delusions, explosive violence, and hallucinations. Withdrawal from heavy methamphetamine use is similar.

Those in advanced stages of addiction sometimes experience severe withdrawal, as this pharmacist testified. "I wanted to quit and figured, 'I'll get through this on my own. Then I'll feel better and stay stopped.' But the withdrawal symptoms were too severe, and I went into DTs and had auditory and visual hallucinations. My mom called, and I was acting bizarre and telling her about all kinds of fearful hallucinations. She and my dad put me in a psychiatric hospital" (PharmD, age 45). Even under hospital supervision, he went into a three-day coma. "They were pounding me full of phenothiazine," he said, "but I got worse and worse and worse." Before the hospitalization he had been in a 10-day blackout. The only thing that he could remember was "It was the lowest time of my life, and I felt awful. I had run out of the stuff that used to make me feel better and couldn't get anything or do anything to make me feel better."

Withdrawal pain is emotional as well as physical. "I was stressed and anxious," a surgeon explained. "The psychological withdrawal—knowing that there were only one or two shots [of Demerol] left—was more of a problem to me than the actual physical withdrawal" (MD, age 40). Another physician agreed: "In the movies about drug addicts you see narcotic withdrawal as being physically painful. For me there was some of that, but mostly it was emotional. I was nervous, uptight, and climbing the wall with anxiety. I was panicky and starving for air; I felt that I was deep underwater and was swimming furiously to get to the top. I needed relief so badly! I knew all I needed was a shot of drugs and within seconds it was 'Ahhhhh!' " (MD, age 34).

COMPULSIVE USE

Addicts continue to seek drugs even when they experience no pleasure or withdrawal symptoms. Berridge and Robinson (1995) explain that changes eventually take place in the brain so that the addict craves the drug of choice and compulsively seeks it even without anticipation of pleasure or dreading the discomfort from withdrawal.

Addiction involves an illogical, irrational, irresponsible, continued, repeated use of a substance as it destroys an individual's life (Smith, Talbott, and Morrison 1985). Characterized by an irresistible impulse to use drugs, it is described by one addict as a "vise-like grip" (Starr 1989) and by another as like having "two hands grabbing [you] by the back of the neck and pushing [you] into the gutter" (Holloway 1991).

Compulsive disorders are characterized by repetitive, ritualized acts and intrusive, ego-alien ("ego-dystonic") thoughts. Many alcoholics and addicts, from skid row to the boardroom, report voices intruding into their minds—"a whispering in the ear"—telling them to use drugs or to rebuke those who try to persuade them not to use. Whenever someone told him that he was drinking too much, an inner voice told one attorney, "Screw 'em, he can't talk to you that way" (JD, age 56). Another attorney recalled, "These voices whispered in my ear, saying 'Look, you don't have a problem' " (JD, age 41). "Worn down by insidious voices" in his head that "never shut up," a physician injected himself with Demerol. This narcotic "launched me to another universe," he said. "No wonder people become addicted to this stuff" (Wall 1991).

In AA these voices are jokingly called "The Committee." "I've heard a lot of other alcoholics describe their minds as sort of a committee," an attorney explained. "The voices never shut up. One guy I know says his mind is like a Greyhound bus with about 50 passengers and no driver. One at a time these personalities get up and drive the bus and the other 49 bitch about where they're going. And they never get anywhere. The only way to quiet all those voices— stop all the yapping—is to drink and do drugs" (JD, age 41). "As you recover, the voices get quieter," another attorney reported. "Now most of my hours are very peaceful no matter what's going on" (JD, age 56).

A dentist whose addiction to nitrous oxide escalated from 30 minutes twice weekly to 36 hours straight without a bathroom or water break recounted the addictive inner dialogue like this: "My most frightening moment came one morning when I arrived at the office. My assistant seated a man for an emergency endo opening [root canal]. I numbed the patient and then left the room to use just a bit. I couldn't return!" The assistant had to make an excuse to the patient and refer him to a nearby dentist. "You can imagine how frightened my assistant had become," the dentist recalled. "Canceling patients and making excuses was bad enough, but when she heard me having conversations with myself and answering in a voice other than my own, it was too much for her" (Williams 1992, pp. 39–40).

We can only speculate about the origin of these "voices." The "observing ego's" awareness of different aspects of the self, and even "talking" to oneself, are within the range of the normal person's experience. When some aspect of the self escapes the control of the observing ego, it can take on its own "voice" and become intrusive, leading, in extreme instances, to the subjective experience of "possession" by one or several disembodied entities. The range of interpretations varies from manifestations of pathological brain chemistry to spiritual darkness.

Some psychotherapists focus their therapeutic approaches on addressing the conflicts expressed by "subpersonalities" that emerge in conflicting "voices" and "energies," some of which appear to the client to take on a life of their own and may even seem "demonic" (Stone and Winkelman 1989). For many Type 5 users, this phenomenon is one aspect of their compulsion to use and of their experience that they are powerless to stop.

The power of an addiction can be gauged by what the addict will forfeit for the drug. Psychologically dependent addicts value drugs above everything else. Their drug of choice—alcohol, cocaine, narcotics, or other substances—comes before family, personal health, personal finances, and sometimes even food, shelter, and freedom from imprisonment (Sullivan, Bissell, and Williams 1988). They will do whatever it takes to obtain them, as this nurse's account illustrates.

> I started taking narcotics from the hospital. I simply signed the drug out to a patient who had a standing order for pain medication, and for the next year and a half, I stole drugs every day. Patients missed their pain medications because of me. I would give them the anti-nausea shot that is prescribed along with narcotics, and I would take their pain shot home. I even stole pain medication from my own son when he broke his arm.   (Hodge 1988, p. 88)

Despite guilt, shame, and self-loathing, such addicts are unable to break this downward cycle. "I hated what I was doing," this nurse recalled. "Every morning I would say to myself, 'Please, God, don't let me take drugs today.'" Even then, she confessed, "I never thought of myself as an addict" (ibid.).

A similar story was told by a dentist. "When the oral surgeon would come to our office, I would steal his Demerol and put water back in the bottles. The obsession was terrible. I'd come into the office pledging, 'I'm not going to do it!' But suddenly I was. I'd feel guilty as hell watching his patients get that watered-down Demerol. 'How could I ever do that? I'm a good dentist, a good person.' Despite my shame and guilt, the same thing happened all over again" (DDS, age 46). "Every day I went to work," recounted an addicted nurse who was dealing drugs to physicians and other nurses, "I promised myself that I'd stop taking and selling drugs. But every day I continued" (Carol 1986, p. 42).

Although Type 4 addicts use willpower successfully to discontinue drugs, Type 5 addicts cannot. A physician who had been in treatment three times for Demerol addiction reported: "Within a week I was using again. Somebody as badly addicted as I was cannot be relieved miraculously of the obsession and compulsion in 30 days; the obsession is still there; I still think of using. I know I'm an alcoholic addict and the disease is always waiting around the corner to get me. It is a terrible revelation, but I have absolutely no control over it. If I rely on my own willpower I'll wind up using again" (MD, age 50).

LOSS OF CONTROL

Impaired control is the inability to limit the quantity of drugs consumed, the duration of the drug-using episode, and the problematic behavioral consequences. "One day I was drinking and could actually stop when I wanted to; the next day it was impossible" (JD, age 64). The Type 5 addict's loss of control is permanent and progressive. It cannot be "cured," only arrested. "You never recover from drug and alcohol addiction," said an addicted dentist (DDS, age 45).

Although Type 4 addicts can quit without outside help, few, if any, psychologically dependent addicts can remain permanently abstinent on their own, and they rarely seek help until they are desperate. Usually, someone else must confront them and encourage them to get help. According to Anglin, Brecht, and Maddahian (1989), sincere, self-initiated treatment admissions constitute as little as 5 percent of the total addict population. Professionals are no more likely to reach out for help. Douglas Talbott (1996) reported that of the approximately 6,000 health professionals treated there—3,500 of whom were physicians—about 5 percent were self-referrals.

Despite tremendous inner struggles, the addict's willpower succumbs to the drug's addictive power. "I couldn't stop," an attorney acknowledged (JD, age 42). "I tried stopping on my own, but something would always happen to trigger me." Another attorney recalled:

> I was hired on a big case in a neighboring state. I stayed sober and successfully handled the case. As alcoholics are prone to do, I decided to celebrate my good fortune by having one drink. I did not understand that one drink triggers a drunk. After my one drink I ended up spending five days lost in that state having bizarre experiences with some weird people. I learned I was powerless over alcohol. (Texas Young Lawyers Association 1990)

An addict may defy all rules of common sense and yield to the craving at the worst possible times. Sooner or later he winds up intoxicated when he wanted to stay sober and had every rational incentive to do so. "Alcohol created more stress than it eliminated," an attorney noted. "I had this constant struggle: 'Will I drink today or won't I? I won't today, but what about tomorrow?' Every day I went through the mental turmoil of wanting to drink but not wanting to. 'Boy, what happens if I do?' The night before a trial you know that you need to be alert and get a good night's sleep; but I would wind up drinking at the worst possible time. It was bizarre!" (JD, age 57; see also "From Joker to Justice" 1992).

Stung by memories of embarrassing drug-related behaviors—sometimes rationalized as "party silliness"—the Type 5 addict frequently attempts to establish rigid "rules" regarding the use of his drug: "I will never drink before 5:30 P.M."; "I will never use at school or at the office"; "I will have only two drinks." Inevitably these "rules" prove ineffective as the addict develops ingenious ways to procure, conceal, and use substances. The addict's lifestyle pivots upon covert activities such as sneaking drinks, snorting cocaine, or whiffing nitrous oxide.

Brief periods of abstinence are typically followed by intolerable withdrawal symptoms and deepening emotional pain. Each addict goes through stages of dark despair, believing that there is something wrong with him mentally and hating himself for wasting his talents and troubling, and even harming, his family and others. As coping mechanisms normally used to deal with daily stresses disintegrate, the user perceives that drugs are his only source of relief. As he descends to deeper levels of psychological dependence, the addict's grasp of reality becomes tenuous and his denial profound.

Some academics (for example, Peele 1992) challenge the idea that an addict's loss of control is progressive and permanent and that addiction can be only arrested, never "cured." To buttress their case, they cite cases of addicts who have discontinued without others' aid (see, for example, Granfield and Cloud 1994). In all likelihood these cases are Type 4 addicts who, though physically hooked, are not psychologically dependent.

CONTINUED USE DESPITE ADVERSE CONSEQUENCES

Harmful consequences motivate reasonable people to stop using, but this is not the case for psychologically dependent addicts. An addicted aviator recounted the compelling hold of addictive substances: "There was a point in my time with the airlines that if I had been confronted with the choice, 'You're going to have to quit drinking or die,' my selection would have been to die" (pilot, age 58).

Addicts use chemicals because they create powerful feelings and mask negative ones. "I used drugs because I loved them," a physician explained. "I *loved* them! They were wonderful! I loved to get high" (Pekkanen 1988, p. 228). Hoping to reexperience the "high" or to escape painful feelings generated by internal conflicts and/or external stress, addicts ignore the drug's miserable and destructive aftereffects.

Adverse drug-related consequences may be physical (for example, withdrawal syndromes, liver disease, gastritis, anemia, and neurologic disorders) or mental and psychological (for example, impaired cognition and changes in mood and behavior). They may also be interpersonal (for example, marital problems, child abuse, and other troubled relationships), occupational (for example, client abuse and strained relationships with employer, colleagues, and staff), legal, financial, and spiritual (Morse and Flavin 1992).

Hangovers, the least of an addict's health worries, are repeatedly ignored by addicts when the next drug-using opportunity presents itself.

I suffered a tremendous hangover and vowed not to put myself through such misery again. Broken vows of abstinence characterized my twenty years of drinking. I would frequently waken at night with what I described as "cotton-mouth" and a splitting headache and I would go through the house and pour all the alcohol down the sink. The next day I would find myself writing "wine" on the shopping list. (Kathleen 1992)

A physician described his drug-related discomfort, anxiety, and embarrassment: "Being preoccupied with drugs is like being at a party and having the gastric flu with diarrhea and terrible stomach cramps. I may be talking to my boss, and all I can think about is my stomach cramp. Then as I feel it going further and further down . . . I think, 'What am I going to do?' . . . I have to keep up an appearance of being competent and hide the fact that I'm distressed with this embarrassment." Such preoccupation, he explained, "is a regular occurrence for many alcoholics and addicts who are having a conversation or trying to do a job at work . . . you can think of nothing but when the next drink or shot or fix will come" (KCET Video Lifeguides 1991).

An addict's life is filled with embarrassing and humiliating experiences. An intoxicated dentist left his office when he became too sick and shaky to treat his first patient. His hygienist watched him throw up in the parking lot. One day he ripped his hand on the lathe in the lab, being too drunk to realize the motor was on when he was changing the cutting wheel. He fired his valuable dental assistant in a rage early one morning, but couldn't recall why. He was humiliated when a patient, a small boy, asked him why he shook so much and the boy's mother asked him to transfer the records to another dentist (Kloeffler 1986).

A physician addicted to Demerol who had been in and out of treatment several times said, "I shot up a lot. Once I passed out and fell into the cabinet; another time I shot up and fell into the toilet. I had lost everything—my license, my wife, my family. I had nothing left and had nowhere else to turn. It was either get straight or die. That was my choice" (MD, age 50).

Blackouts, a dangerous early symptom seen commonly among alcoholics, involve memory loss lasting minutes, hours, or days during which, to an outside observer, the individual continues to function normally (Kabb 1984). Physicians have confessed to conducting surgery while in blackouts, and nurses have worked all or part of a shift with "absolutely no memory of the events that occurred." For example, an "unhappy and lonely" nurse said, "I liked the high feeling, the busy feeling, the rush; I really liked that. It would come on quickly, and I liked the build-up and the rush. But then I would black out and wouldn't remember." (RN, age 37). "Over the years," an attorney explained, "I suffered other smaller blackouts. However, instead of acknowledging these as blackouts, I would chalk them up to 'daydreaming.' To this day, I do not know how many times I left a location and arrived at another location unable to remember at all my journey between those two points. It is truly a miracle that I am still alive, considering the number of times that I drove a car in a state of mobile unconsciousness" ("Me? An Addict?" 1992, p. 255).

Addicts recall with a great deal of guilt and shame risking others' lives. "I never wanted to be like my father, who was emotionally abusive," a nurse recalled. "But I did all the same things, every one of them. Night after night after night I drove my kids while intoxicated. I paid $130 for each car seat so my kids would be safe in the car with a drunk behind the wheel. I risked their lives by driving in a blackout! Thank God I didn't run over one of them" (RN, age 37).

Death and near-death experiences caused by overdosing also occur. Some are actually suicide attempts. "I remember taking massive doses of Valium and cardiac pills the second time I tried to commit suicide," a pharmacist recalled. "They should have killed me, since I took enough to make a horse bleed. I woke up with my AA sponsor slapping me in the face. For some reason I saved all the empty containers—that saved my ass. I had 32 different drugs in my system, and for 24 hours they didn't know if I would make it or not" (PharmD, age 49).

While intoxicated, otherwise rational professionals can become assaultive. For example, in 1985 the Delaware Bar was shaken with the news that a Delaware attorney on the eve of his thirty-seventh birthday had killed his wife and two young sons with a shotgun and then turned the weapon on himself. His blood-alcohol content was over three times the amount legally defined as intoxicating. He had been cross-addicted to painkilling prescription drugs and was facing imminent bankruptcy (Moore 1991).

How can reasonable people become involved in such destructive situations? The answer is that, once addicted, these individuals are no longer reasonable. The psychological strength of the addict's habit distorts his formerly rational responses to life situations. He may loathe himself for his outrageous behaviors. But the bizarre logic of an addictive mind rules out rational decisions, as evidenced by this comment: "Junkies look for Fentanyl because some people die from it, so it must be good stuff" (Gallagher, 1986, p. 31).

PREOCCUPATION WITH DRUGS AND NEGLECT OF ROLE OBLIGATIONS

Addicts focus obsessively on obtaining drugs and their anticipated effects. "At first alcohol was my hobby," an attorney recalled, "but as time went by, it became my sole recreation" (JD, age 57). Addiction involves an intimate relationship—with a substance. A pharmacist compared the feelings drugs give with falling in love.

> Consider the rush of infatuation and the enjoyment of being with that special person. Much of the day is spent thinking of that person, and lifestyle changes are made to maximize interaction with him or her. My love affair with drugs gave me those same feelings. I enjoyed the feeling of intoxication and I felt confident, secure, and accepted. Before I went to a social function, I was more interested in whether or not drugs and alcohol would be there rather than who would be there.   (Kendall 1987, p. 85)

A physician who became addicted in medical school recalls the high he received just by anticipating use of drugs. "I remember walking into a pharmacy soon after I received my medical degree and experiencing almost orgasmic excitement knowing that I could have any of the drugs that were on the shelves" (Rogers 1995).

"My every waking thought was about supporting my drug addiction," a pharmacist confessed:

> The thought of living without drugs was enough to drive me crazy. My addiction was not only a physical thing; there was a heavy psychological addiction, too. My mental condition focused constantly on getting through the day. "Okay, I know I need 150 Percodans to get through the day today, but I have only 140." I would plan how to steal them. And God help me if I had to go out of town; I would need 1,000 pills for a five-day trip. I had to find them and take them with me. I had stashes all over the house, the car, the garage. There are still hundreds of pills out there. God only knows where they are.   (PharmD, age 41)

Like this pharmacist, other addicts clandestinely stash their drugs to ensure a ready supply. An alcoholic pilot whose father-in-law was also alcoholic remarked that "he had bottles stashed everywhere.

When I braked his car, 9 or 10 pint bottles—some empty, some half full—would come sliding out from under the seat" (pilot, age 57).

Anticipating the next drug experience occupies much of the addict's time. "Part of the excitement was just getting ready," an attorney acknowledged (JD, age 48). But preoccupation diverts time and energy from important life concerns. "Every part of my life centered upon drugs," a pharmacist said. "I didn't care about my family or my job. I cared about my job because that was the way I got my drugs" (PharmD, age 41).

Professional performance deteriorates as addiction progresses. "I never saw a patient *except* through the befuddled haze of a monumental hangover," an alcoholic dentist recalled.

> While I should have been thinking about a proper diagnosis or a logical treatment plan, my mind was filled with thoughts of how many hours it would be until I could crack the bottle and have a little sip to relax. My shaky hands and my numbed mind weren't capable of undertaking *anything* that required precision or dexterity. So my office rapidly became a "referral bureau." The only things I actually *did* were the things that could have been handled by a moderately competent sophomore dental student.   (Wamsley 1978, p. 28)

DENIAL AND OTHER DISTORTED THINKING

A chemically dependent person usually loses the ability to perceive and acknowledge his addiction. This denial is a product of (1) the drug's pharmacologic effect on memory and the power and influence of euphoric recall, (2) psychological ego-defense mechanisms such as suppression and repression, and (3) associates' unwitting enabling behaviors (Morse and Flavin 1992, p. 1013). The following note, written by an addicted attorney, illustrates the mental confusion that underlies denial. It was sent by a solo practitioner to the state bar to be given to their disciplinary agency. Sadly, the sender had not been found at the time of this writing.

> To whom it may concern: I can't take things anymore. Please find enclosed the keys to my office. This letter is intended to be received as a resignation from the Bar. Please have someone let my clients know. If there are expenses, I have numerous cases for which I have not as yet billed amounting to probably over $20,000. I truly regret any hardships my leaving may cause, but as I said, I just can't take it anymore. I am cracking up. My secretary is familiar with my practice, if you need help sorting things out, she can do better than I. Her

number is . . . With this letter I give you the authority to make whatever contacts you need to in order to straighten up my affairs. I no
longer have the ability to do that. I don't know what is happening to
me, but I can't think anymore . . .   (Muccigrosso and Spilis 1992a, p. 1)

Addicts ignore clear evidence of declining health. "Physically, my
body was just deteriorating," a nurse recalled. "I went down to 89
pounds because of my heavy use of cocaine and the crack. I had a
lot of health problems . . . that I denied. And I remember one of my
last binges, being in a hotel room, using crack, and actually dou-
bling over on the bed, getting chest pain, and pain down my left
arm—I know what all these signs are—but not cluing in on the fact
that this is really getting out of hand." After she finally got her
breath back, she picked up the pipe again. "I put another rock on,
knowing that this might be my last one. And yet the compulsion to
use that drug was there and I couldn't stop" (Barde and Pick 1993).

Addicts typically view drugs as the solution to their problems
rather than the source, and they develop plausible explanations for
their drug use (see Jim 1992). This dentist's rationalization illustrates
his bizarre thinking: "I've always been a real sensitive person," he
said. "When people are going through discomfort, they don't like
being at the dentist, and that really puts pressure on me. I almost
felt my patients' pain sometimes, so I took medication for them. I'd
think, 'God, this is gonna really hurt, so I better take some'" ("A
Near Fatal Combination" 1990).

A nurse rationalized intravenous injections of narcotics for a simple headache. "At one point when I was using IV morphine, I won-
dered if this was an addiction. But I thought, 'It couldn't be; not me.
I'm taking it because I have a headache.' IV morphine for a headache? Doesn't everybody?" (RN, age 42).

Bizarre thinking sometimes puts others at risk, as this dentist's
story illustrates.

Eventually, my staff and partners walked out on me. Colleagues were
threatening to report me to the board, and they did. But the risk of
losing the right to practice my profession had no effect on me. In the
end, it was the risk of losing my family that shook me up. I got to the
point where I knew there was nothing in me that could keep me from
doing the stuff over and over again. I decided it would be best if I
killed my wife and kids so they wouldn't suffer the same addiction.

That's how an addicted mind works. Twice I was turned down in my attempts to buy a gun to kill my wife. I was also trying to get drugs to poison my children so they wouldn't have to suffer. Fortunately, my wife took the kids and left me before I had the chance to end it my way.   ("A Near Fatal Combination" 1990)

Sometimes denial develops early in the parental homes. "At 19 I was diagnosed by two different physicians as being alcoholic. But my family said, 'Not our little Billy. He will outgrow this!' The whole family was into booze and denial. When I got into drugs, my brother, a heavy boozer, thought it was amusing" (PharmD, age 47). Professional training also reinforces denial through its demands for superhuman performance. "All doctors must learn to employ denial, or self-deception, in order to practice medicine," Gallagher (1986, p. 31) observes. "They learn to tell themselves they are not tired when they haven't slept enough; they harden themselves against the cries of patients undergoing painful procedures; they put aside personal problems when they walk into the hospital. The same technique, often used unconsciously, allows them to deny their own painful addiction."

Addicted professionals become expert at concealing their addiction. They make every effort to appear normal at work. Addicted nurses, for example, may take particular pains that their uniforms are immaculate and their nails on their shaking hands are trim and clean. They expend great effort in job performance to make up for lapses (Sullivan, Bissell, and Williams 1988, pp. 23–29).

To avoid detection, an airline executive in New York explained, "Pilots keep two sets of medical records: one from their real doctor who treats them, and the other for the one they visit for recertification. They keep these medical records separate and unknown to others." "Guys who become pilots are extremely physically fit but usually psychologically unsophisticated," a treatment expert in California noted. "They work hard to keep themselves fit, and it is hard for them to admit to any kind of problem that may affect their career. Because they have a real love affair with flying, they deny any medical problem and never go to a doctor for *any* reason."

Addicted professionals, however, cannot maintain a proper cover indefinitely. The truth eventually becomes obvious to others. Until recently it was widely believed that addicts could not be helped until they "hit bottom" and recognized the need for help. This myth assumed that they would understand the problem and know where to find help when the pain became too great (Crosby and Bissell 1989). Generally speaking, however, the delusional system that develops with drug abuse usually requires external help. Assistance must come from caring associates who intervene to help users grasp the reality of their self-destructive situation.

A broken back and his wife's departure shook this physician's denial:

> I was living in an empty examining room in a medical office building because I had no place else to go. I wasn't practicing medicine at all to speak of during these years because it had become so painful. I was admitted to the hospital after having an alcohol convulsion of such severity that I broke my back in four places and tore the humeral heads off of both shoulders. I woke up strapped to a gurney with my arms over my chest and my wife leaning over me telling me that she was leaving! I laughed! I thought that was hilarious. That was part of the insanity . . . I had been hooked on pills and alcohol and had faked out others and myself for ten years and didn't realize until then that I was physically ill.   (KCET Video Lifeguides 1991)

The Roots of Addiction

Is addiction a self-inflicted condition among moral weaklings who lack character and willpower, hopelessly inept people who should be punished? No. Research and clinical experience contradict this common assumption. Those best informed regard addiction as a disorder involving biological, psychosocial, and spiritual factors. Although a few ideologues argue that the "tree" of addiction has only one root—usually either biological or psychosocial—most addictionologists see its bases as more complex (Peck 1991), an illness of the whole person involving an interplay of body, mind, and spirit (Clarno 1986).

BIOLOGICAL ROOTS

The biological root of addiction—brain function—draws on decades of research with alcoholics and their offspring.[12] The importance of heredity as a dominant risk factor in alcohol addiction, well established by more than 100 studies conducted before 1970 and hundreds more since then, confirms that predisposition to alcoholism is genetically transmitted (U.S. Department of Health and Human Services 1985). Until recently, however, very little research has been done on the physiology of those who use other drugs.

The disease concept of addiction, promulgated in 1935 when Alcoholics Anonymous came into existence, gained support 20 years later when the American Medical Association accepted the view that alcoholism is a disease. Much later, in 1990, the National Council on Alcoholism and Drug Dependence and the American Society of Addiction Medicine also went on record as saying that alcoholism is a primary, chronic disease influenced by genetic, psychosocial, and environmental factors (Lewis 1991).

This medical model of addiction asserts that chemical dependence is, first, *describable:* its symptoms can be identified, and it is a *primary* disease, not necessarily a symptom of a more "serious" problem. Second, it is *progressive:* its course can be predicted. Over time, drug consumption gradually and insidiously affects the central nervous system, causing a multitude of secondary problems. Symptoms may temporarily plateau, but they continue to worsen with repeated drug use. Third, it is *chronic:* susceptibility to compulsive drug use continues throughout the addict's lifetime. It is not reversible, since there is no known cure; without intervention, it tends to get worse, never better. When an addict starts using again, even after a long period of abstinence, his condition usually deteriorates until it becomes as bad as or worse than when he quit. Fourth, chemical dependence is potentially *fatal.* Organ damage increases, and physical deterioration accelerates. The possibility of accidents, overdosing, or suicide while users are under the influence increases inexorably. Addicts generally die considerably sooner than nonaddicts.

Because addiction is not caused by virulent microorganisms or by wildly proliferating malignant cells, proponents of the medical model sometimes have a difficult time convincing others that addiction is a disease. Diabetes, another progressive, chronic illness of unknown etiology, is cited as an analogue. Like addiction, diabetes has no cure, but its progress can be slowed. "Diabetics do not become diabetic from eating too much sugar," explains Wharton (1989). "They eat too much sugar because they are diabetic." Similarly, "Alcoholics and drug addicts do not become addicts because they drink too much alcohol or take drugs. They drink too much alcohol or take drugs because they are addicts. The genetic pattern of inheritance of diabetes and addiction is the same."

Neuroscientists now regard addiction as a "chemical deficiency" disease similar to Parkinsonism (caused by insufficient dopamine in a part of the brain) and diabetes (caused by a lack of proper insulin release in the pancreas) (Erickson 1995). Biologic researchers believe that the compulsion to drink or to use other drugs is driven by a neurochemical abnormality in the brain that influences CNS regulation of feeling (LeDoux 1994). "There is one part of the brain that most drugs of abuse seem to affect," explains a National Institute on Drug Abuse (NIDA) executive (National Institute on Drug Abuse 1993). "Called the 'brain reward system,' it controls our feeling states and emotions. Drugs of abuse, unfortunately, have the unique capacity to directly affect the brain reward system, bypassing the normal channels of information processing," according to Marvin Snyder, NIDA's acting director (ibid.). "When you take a drug and use it repeatedly, there are fundamental changes that happen in your brain, and over time, those changes basically change the way you view the world."

A healthy brain sends and receives messages through a network of billions of nerve cells called neurons. Messages travel from one neuron to the next across spaces called synapses. Chemical molecules (neurotransmitters) carry the messages across these synapses. Each nerve cell has receptors to receive messages from the other neurons. Psychoactive drugs interrupt this process, affecting emotions, perceptions, and bodily functions.

The brain is a malleable organ that changes structure and function according to what it experiences. "The brain is constantly 'wiring,' 're-wiring' and possibly 'unwiring' itself, forming and re-forming synapses between neurons," Kotzsch (1993, p. 160) explains. Psychoactive drugs alter normal brain functioning. Cocaine, for example, interrupts normal functioning in the brain's reward system, where mood and energy are controlled. Cocaine prevents dopamine, the chemical transmitted with the "feel-good" message, from being reabsorbed into the cells that sent it. Instead, it remains in the synapse between neurons and keeps firing pleasure messages. Because so many of these messages come all at once, the cocaine user feels extremely good—euphoric! But as the cocaine wears off, the user feels worse, and more cocaine is needed to regain the euphoric feeling—eventually even to feel normal.

Some researchers think dopamine is destroyed while trapped in the synapses, so that less is available for subsequent "feel-good" signals. Others suspect that the brain stops making dopamine receptors in the nerve cells, reducing the number of pleasure messages the neurons can receive. As the brain loses its capacity to send and/ or receive messages, the user loses the ability to feel good without the drug.

Animal studies indicate how powerful drugs can affect the reward center of the brain. "Once conditioned, animals willingly participate in physically damaging activities to get more drugs. They will swim through acid baths, stand on hot plates while the temperature is increased, ignore personal grooming, not eat or drink, lose interest in sex and even sometimes die of self-neglect to get more drugs" (Jacobsen 1991). In their biopsychological theory of addiction, Berridge and Robinson (1995) maintain that repeated intermittent ingestion of addictive drugs combined with stimuli associated with drug taking sensitizes certain neural systems so that the drug has a more powerful effect on those systems. This neural sensitivity is so persistent that the user seeks to use the drug even if it brings no pleasure. This intense longing for the drug may even be on an unconscious level; addicts who can't understand why, want drugs more even though they may like them less. Only a reversal of this sensitization could "transform the brain and mind of an addict back to the brain and mind of a nonaddict" (Berridge and Robinson 1995, p. 76).

The irreversible nature of addiction may reflect the brain's revised function in response to chronic drug ingestion. "Once addicted, always addicted," observed a once-addicted physician who now specializes in addiction medicine. "Our brain is wired like the telephone company's circuitry; the circuits still work after a long period of nonuse. The 'lines' in our brain that were established by drugs are still there waiting for us after a long abstinence" (MD, age 40).

According to most treatment experts, people addicted to one mood-altering chemical cannot safely use any other. Although the precise mechanism for this cross-dependency is not fully understood, the pleasure center of the addict's brain apparently cannot discern which chemical is providing a euphoric payoff. Consequently, the potential for addiction may generalize over all categories of psychoactive drugs.

Some specialists surmise that addicts have a special, genetically determined sensitivity to the euphoric effects of psychoactive chemicals. Drawing on research evidence that the biological offspring of alcoholics have a higher risk for alcohol problems than those from nonalcoholic families, Blum and colleagues (1996, p. 132) argue: "An inborn chemical imbalance that alters the intercellular signaling in the brain's reward process could supplant an individual's feeling of well being with anxiety, anger or a craving for a substance that can alleviate the negative emotions." This imbalance, dubbed the "reward deficiency syndrome" by one of the researchers, "manifests itself as one or more behavioral disorders."

Studies of twins show that chemically dependent people often have a preferred drug. These findings indicate that some addicts may be treating themselves for undiagnosed deficiencies in neuro-biochemical functioning—that drug selection, rather than being a random choice, results from an interaction between the drug's psychopharmacologic action and the dominant painful feelings with which the person struggles (Peters 1990a).

Adoption studies in Scandinavian countries, where family records are most complete, show that young twins adopted from alcoholic families into nonalcoholic homes have the same risk for becoming alcoholic that they would if they stayed in the alcoholic family. Conversely, children adopted into alcoholic families from nonalcoholic families have no greater risk of alcoholism than if they were raised by their biological nonalcoholic parents (Miller 1991; see also Goodwin 1985).

Some addicted professionals are fatalistic about the genetic roots of their addiction, and this attitude precludes preventive action. "I'm an addicted person," a nurse explained. "My son is also an addictive person because he's got alcoholism on both sides of his family. He has a 60 percent chance; those are the stats now. Yeah, he's just waiting to happen" (RN, age 42). Similarly, a physician said, "I knew at an early age that whatever I grew up to be, I would also be an alcoholic. It was part of my life and part of the life of everybody else around me" (MD, age 57).

Some addictionologists dispute that there is a specific genetic link to alcoholism. Gelernter, Goldman, and Risch (1993) reviewed studies on genetics and alcoholism and concluded that the available data do not support previous studies indicating a genetic link; rather, the results of these studies can best be explained by sampling error and ethnic variation.

Although genetic factors may put a person at risk to become an addict, as they do other health problems, they do not predestine him. Noble and colleagues, who discovered a common gene pattern among severe alcoholics (1994) and cocaine addicts (1993), caution that having the gene pattern does not doom a person to abuse, but it increases their risk. My view is that addiction is the end result of an interactive process involving social, psychological, and spiritual factors among biologically vulnerable persons.

PSYCHOSOCIAL ROOTS

Although there is no evidence that addicts have a common personality profile, an abundance of research shows that addictive behaviors are shaped by behavioral reinforcement. Addicts, like all humans, learn to repeat behaviors that make them feel good or relieve unpleasant feelings. They become psychologically dependent on drugs as a result of consistent positive reinforcement during the early stages of drug use.

The social-learning perspective asserts that people use drugs to get pleasurable feelings or to block negative ones. Immediate reinforcement conditions users to seek and use more drugs. Once addicted, an individual is further reinforced in his desire to use when the drug relieves the discomfort of withdrawal. In this regard, Davies (1992, p. 160) defines addiction as "learned helplessness," a condition that hinders an individual's attempts to take an active and constructive role in his or her health-related behavior.

Research has shown that even expectations about an impending drug intake can affect a user's mood. Addicts report they feel better just *thinking* about the drug. Some addicts experience druglike effects when they assume they have consumed drugs but actually have been given only a placebo (*Alcohol and Health* 1990, p. 53).

After repeated reinforcement, the addict learns "cues" that stimulate his central nervous system. He is primed and reacts with craving and change in autonomic (involuntary) response when presented with conditioned cues (cue reactivity). Some drugs, such as those taken intravenously (for example, Fentanyl) or smoked with high potency (for example, crack cocaine), have very high cue reactivity because they provide the most immediate reinforcement. "I've had many cases of professionals who have told me about their reactivity to a Fentanyl cue," a New York addictionologist commented. "For one doctor just seeing that vial made him drool; his profound autonomic response to the vial overwhelmed him."

Cues may include people, places, and things associated with drinking or using drugs, such as needles, syringes, drugs, or the drug closet. "It's totally unrealistic," the same treatment expert noted, "to put addicts in treatment away from all their cues and triggers and then, without deconditioning, put them back into an environment where they will be flooded with cues that trigger their autonomic response, and expect them not to respond to them again. Before going back to work they must be exposed to the cues—the drugs, the situations, the meds. It's important that we help them extinguish their reactive responses in a safe and controlled environment."

Long before they first use it, some children acquire expectations about the euphoric benefit of alcohol and the convivial settings in which it is consumed. These early expectations strongly predict drug-using behavior. Compared with nonusers, drug users typically expect more positive effects from drugs and spend more time with drug-using friends. They often think drugs increase physical and social pleasure and social capability (*Alcohol and Health* 1990, p. 53). Although drugs usually have the opposite effect, users often believe that drugs make them more attractive, relaxed, alert, and sexually responsive.

Children and adolescents learn to value and use drugs through role modeling; that is, they imitate their drug-using peers and associates. In some cultures and groups, they also learn at an early age that drinking and using other drugs are not only tolerated but expected, and that these activities confer social recognition from those who also indulge in these behaviors. Pleasure comes not only from the pharmacologic effects of the drugs but also from the psychological reward of being liked and accepted. During adolescence, the latter is an even more powerful reinforcer than the former.

Not only do adolescents respond to what parents and other significant associates define as appropriate; most also expect to drink as adults. In our society, addictive substances are widely available, openly advertised and sold. They are also stocked in many homes, and youngsters are significantly more likely to use drugs if their parents do (Fawzy, Coombs, and Gerber 1983). Kandel and associates (1978) found that 82 percent of drinking families raise youths who also drink, while 72 percent of abstaining families produce abstainers. Home is mentioned by adolescents as a drinking site second only to peer parties. Youths tend to use a greater variety of substances than their parents. They emulate parental drug behaviors, but generalize this imitative pattern to illicit as well as licit drugs (Fawzy, Coombs, and Gerber 1983).

Social learning may account for differences among cultural groups. For example, Italians and Jews, who usually use alcohol in highly controlled circumstances, have traditionally low rates of alcoholism. By contrast, Irish Catholics, Mexicans, and Poles have very high rates. These differences may reflect the way each culture defines alcohol. Teenagers conform to adult patterns in the home, which reflect the religious and ethnic communities to which the family belongs (Kaufman and Borders 1988).

Family pathology, as well as genetics, can explain the generational continuity of addiction in families. Children raised in homes where substances are abused experience more emotional impairment and, like their parents, cope by turning to alcohol and other drugs to mask the psychic pain caused by emotionally distressing family circumstances. The typical family profile of drug-abusing adolescents is one in which the youth feels unloved and rejected by uninvolved and emotionally distant parents. Relationships are particularly tense with a drinking father who abuses other family members.

Children of alcoholics experience more headaches, anxiety, and sleep deprivation and exhibit more aggressive behavior. Alcoholic sons of alcoholic fathers have high rates of passive dependency. In contrast, healthy families who share positive affect are significantly less likely to produce drug-abusing offspring (Fawzy, Coombs, and Gerber 1983).

SPIRITUAL ROOTS

Addiction is regarded by many recovering addicts and those who assist them as a manifestation of spiritual poverty. Psychoactive drugs temporarily mask isolation and emptiness and simulate peace of mind. As one attorney put it, "The bottom line in addiction is lack of spirituality" (JD, age 55).

Hiatt (1986) points out that the spiritual dimension, a powerful resource for healing and communication, is fundamentally experiential and intuitive rather than conceptual, comprised of direct experiences and manifest in concrete behaviors. Most important, "the spiritual dimension has an integrative function for the individual. It brings the seemingly disparate parts of the personality and fragmented nature of experience together into a single whole. It also provides direction and may be experienced as a striving to better oneself or to achieve harmony with the world" (p. 8). Hiatt also notes that "like physical and psychologic development, spiritual development is lifelong and follows an uneven, step-wise course. Spiritual crises and encounters are nodal points in spiritual development" (p. 9).

Vaillant's (1983) longitudinal studies found that participants in Alcoholic Anonymous, a program based on spirituality and altruistic service, are more likely to achieve long-term sobriety than those in either medical or psychological treatment. AA participants believe that acceptance of a "Higher Power" is crucial to recovery. AA's "Big Book" (*Alcoholics Anonymous* 1976), which uses the term "spiritual awakening" many times, indicates that these "awakenings" are not necessarily sudden or spectacular, but often are gradual transformations.

> With few exceptions, our members find that they have tapped an unsuspected inner resource which they presently identify with their own conception of a Power greater than themselves . . . Most of us think that this awareness of a Power greater than ourselves is the essence of spiritual experience . . . we wish to say that any alcoholic capable of honestly facing his problems in the light of our experience can recover, providing he does not close his mind to all spiritual concepts. (*Alcoholics Anonymous* 1976, pp. 569–570)

Some discount spirituality because it cannot be measured by scientific methods. But scientific method, limited to empirical phenomena, can neither confirm nor deny the reality of extrasensory experiences. Those who embrace scientism—the doctrine that empirically unmeasurable phenomena are either nonexistent or un-important—usually fail to realize that their own position rests on metaphysical assumptions that cannot be measured by the episte-mological method they espouse. "The mind denies that which it can't understand and we are a mentally identified culture," a phy-sician explains. "In valuing the mind as much as we do, we have a cultural tendency to deny mystery, to deny the spiritual" (Remen 1991, p. 62). But, she adds, "Denying the spiritual is bad for your health" (p. 64).

Until recently, western medicine has virtually ignored spiritual health. Of all the aspects of personal health—biological, psycholog-ical, environmental, and spiritual—the last has received the least attention (Sandor 1994). Remen (1991) explains, "Much illness may have its roots in unrecognized spiritual distress—issues of isolation, of anger, the feelings people have that they don't matter or that nobody matters to them . . . there is a general lack of meaning and purpose and significance that seems to underlie illness. What we call stress might really be spiritual isolation" (p. 64).

"What is spiritual isolation?" Remen asks. "Basically to me it seems that it is living with a closed heart . . . It is very interesting how often the process of physical healing runs concurrent with the healing of the heart. A greater altruism, a greater compassion, seems to occur in different people as you work with them through severe illness" (1991, pp. 64–65).

A mechanistic, biomedical model of health emerged at the turn of the century, supported by a rapid enhancement of scientific knowledge and medical technology. A reductionist view of the hu-man organism (Kuhn 1988), it defines man as the component parts of his biological machinery (McKee and Chappell 1992). Patients are often alienated from their highly specialized, mechanistically ori-ented clinicians who, rather than treating the whole person, focus on body parts.

Challenged by research showing the impact of social support and other psychosocial factors on health and illness, health care practi-tioners eventually adopted a biopsychosocial model. More recently, some have proposed that this model also include spiritual aspects. "All four parameters are interrelated and interdependent to the ex-tent that failure to address illness in one may significantly limit the therapeutic efficacy of prescriptions focused on the others," Kuhn (1988, p. 98) argues. "The organism heals only as competently as the 'weakest' or 'sickest' element. To be healthy is to be whole, involving the optimal function of body, mind, and spirit in whatever the social context."

According to this view, the person who is spiritually healthy is sensitive and vitally connected to the unseen energies that vibrate between living things, not unlike the vibrations that pass between tuning forks or radio signals between transmitters and receivers. Toxic chemicals, like corrosion in a radio, inhibit and impair spiritual health. Numerous addicts who have made an effort to grow spiritually, have found inner peace and even joy—euphoric feelings that psychoactive drugs only simulate.

Although spiritual phenomena are not measurable by empirical methods, their consequences are. Byrd (1988), for example, studied the efficacy of prayers with 393 hospitalized patients in a coronary care unit. Patients were randomly divided into two groups. Neither they nor their therapists were aware of each patient's assignment. For patients in one of the groups, someone outside the hospital, unknown to them, prayed for their rapid recovery, for prevention of complications and death, and for other healing benefits until the patient was discharged from the hospital. Results show that the patients in the prayer group had statistically significantly better overall outcomes: they needed fewer antibiotics, diuretics, and intubation/ventilation and had less congestive heart failure, fewer episodes of pneumonia, and fewer cardiac arrests.

"Who has not, during a time of illness or pain, cried out to a higher being for help and healing?" asks Byrd (1988). "Prayer is the most powerful form of energy that one can generate," notes Alexis Carrell, medical scientist and Nobel laureate. "It is a force as real as terrestrial gravity" (quoted in Davis 1992, p. 19). Davis, a psychotherapist, agrees. He credits prayer with benefiting him much more than nine years of psychoanalytic therapy. An agnostic who first experimented with prayer at age 61, he reports, "I don't believe this change can be explained on the basis of a mere psychologic process like suggestion, for it did not result from any hope, expectation, or fantasy. Whatever this experience was, it caused by far the most profound and lasting change in my personality and in my life. It was an answer to prayer, not only my own prayer, but—as I learned later—the prayers of others for me" (ibid., p. 20).

In Perspective

Like other chronic illnesses, addiction has many components— some physiological, others psychosocial, and still others spiritual. Western medicine has until quite recently ignored the psychosocial and spiritual aspects of addiction and other illnesses. In-depth interviews with recovering addicts make the interplay between these factors clear.

Much confusion exists about drugs and the nature of chemical dependence. Consider the turbulent history of cocaine. Once an ingredient in Coca-Cola and immensely popular, it was considered a safe drug; but as the evidence of cocaine's damaging effects accumulated, nonmedicinal use was outlawed and the drug removed from cola drinks. On the other hand, until very recently heroin never enjoyed widespread middle-class acceptance. Consistently viewed as evil, severe sanctions have been levied against those who use it. By contrast, alcohol causes many more problems than all illicit substances combined, but it has been glamorized, advertised, and made widely available. Few consider alcohol a drug; even alcoholics sometimes look down on other addicts with disgust.

The definition of chemical dependence has also shifted. For many years the definition focused mostly on tolerance, withdrawal, denial, and preoccupation. Then, because the physiological effects of cocaine did not seem to fit this description, the definition changed to the three c's—compulsive use, loss of control, and continued use despite adverse consequences.

Other definitional conflicts exist. Although some regard addiction as a genetically determined disease, others argue that it is a learned behavior. The confusion about addiction is most apparent in the controversy about whether addicts can quit using without specialized treatment. Many argue that addicts cannot, but others disagree, citing studies of addicts who quit by themselves once their circumstances changed. It seems most likely that addiction results from an interactive process involving social, psychological, and spiritual factors among the biologically vulnerable.

Making a distinction between levels of addiction—particularly between Type 4 and Type 5 addicts—eliminates some of the confusion. However, our knowledge about addiction is still at an elementary level. Because very few experts who study or treat addicts have received comprehensive training, it is not surprising that their views of addiction, its treatment, and prevention are so divergent and territorial.

THREE

Emotional Health versus Impairment

"Our profession really sets you up to become an addict and a workaholic, which I've found in my life to be equally destructive."

  (MD, age 38)

"When I was on drugs I was somebody I really wasn't. They helped me play out what I thought I should be—a very loving and accepting type of doctor, the kind you see on television—the perfect doctor. I was able to handle anything all the time and never have to do any emotional processing. That's kind of the hallmark of my life—to avoid the feeling part."

  (MD, age 35)

"The best relationship I ever had, consistent and faithful, was with alcohol and drugs. It's the only relationship I knew how to do—the only relationship I was faithful to for 15 years."

  (RN, age 40)

Ironically, professional training can impede healthy emotional development. The recruiting system typically favors those who are willing to sacrifice a well-balanced and emotionally enriching lifestyle to attain the required academic grades and aptitude test scores, and the socialization system reinforces emotional isolation (Coombs 1986; Coombs and Paulson 1990; Coombs, Perell, and Ruckh 1990). "My best interests as an individual were pushed to the wayside in order to achieve the school's goals," an addicted dentist complained (DDS, age 43). "The neglect of emotional development is a gross problem in medical training," a physician agreed. "When I introduce myself at codependency meetings, I always say I'm recovering from the effects of medical training" (MD, age 38).

Vaillant and colleagues (1972) pointed out that the altruistic care of other people is a superb form of psychological adaptation to life, but only if the self is cared for. Speaking to a class at Harvard Medical School about doctors who fail to do this, Vaillant (1982, p. 21) advised, "You should make sure that when you give to others, you're also given to . . . [You should] pay attention to getting care for yourselves in order to care for others. Physician, cherish thyself."

Physicians and dentists in California have very high rates of suicide, more than twice those in the general population (Singleton 1989). Nationally, the suicide rate for the general population is about 15 per 100,000, but the rate among physicians is about 77 per 100,000. According to a study of Oregon physicians on probation with the state licensing board, the rate, if extrapolated to a large population, would approximate 20,000 per 100,000—one in five (Crawshaw et al. 1980).

For the depressed professional, suicide offers one option, psychoactive drugs another. "You don't have time when you're in training to take care of yourself," an attorney pointed out. "Alcohol provides a quick fix. It takes too much time to go canoeing or cross-country skiing, but alcohol is virtually instant" (JD, age 50). This physician chose the drug "solution" while a medical student.

> I did extremely well as an undergraduate and was a star athlete. On the first day of medical school they told us how wonderful we were to be there—and for the next four years they told us how stupid we were. In my first quarter, the girl I planned to marry told me she didn't feel the same way about me. I became depressed and had a hard time keeping up with the enormous amount of material. A psychiatrist put me on an antidepressant that made me feel tired and kept me from concentrating. Then, miraculously, I found a wonder drug. I could do a few lines of cocaine, and I was no longer depressed and could function quite well in my studies. I did two weeks of studying in a 48-hour period, staying up all night. It not only helped me function; it made me feel wonderful.   (MD, age 40)

However, this solution was short-lived. "When I got heavily into this drug, it disrupted my physiologic state. I had extreme chest pains and palpitations. I lay in bed saying, 'Dear God, if I survive this episode, I promise I will never do this again.' But as my heart rate lowered, I was at the pipe again. To help come down, I used alcohol, marijuana, benzodiazepines, and Quaaludes. I'd swear off and then experience anhedonia and be right back in the circle again."

Falling Short of the Professional Ideal

Fully competent professionals are emotionally mature and do not neglect their own emotional needs. Impaired professionals, such as Type 5 addicts, fall short in nurturing their inner lives and as a result are less capable of providing sensitive care to their clients.

There are two, interdependent areas of professional competence, both vital to professional effectiveness. The first is cognitive know-how, an understanding of the problems related to professional action (the head); the second is sensitivity to emotional needs, the ability to establish rapport and to deal compassionately with clients (the heart). Health professionals and pilots must also have competence in a third area: the manual dexterity necessary to carry out procedures essential to their clients' well-being (the hands). Whereas well-functioning professionals demonstrate a balanced competence in all three areas, impaired professionals are underdeveloped in one or more, usually the heart (Coombs 1986; Coombs, May, and Small 1986; Coombs and Paulson 1990; Coombs and Virshup 1994).

Institutions providing professional training generally ensure that their graduates are intellectually and technically competent (the head and hands), but most have a dismal record of encouraging fledgling professionals to develop emotionally. This omission puts trainees at high risk for burnout, depression, substance abuse, and emotionally unrewarding lifestyles.

All too often professionals resort to psychoactive drugs to compensate for emotional deficits. Compellingly appealing, they provide quick energy, exhilaration, relaxation, and peace of mind. These chemical substitutes, however, impede the development of healthy coping skills.

EMOTIONAL ISOLATION AND NEGLECT

Training centers that equate professionalism with the suppression of emotion foster emotional isolation, which is at the core of professional impairment. In teaching hospitals, for example, good clinicians are expected to control their emotions at all times. Privately feeling overwhelmed and anxious, many trainees develop a profound sense of personal inadequacy (Coombs 1978). So, like their mentors, they project a calm exterior, compounding their emotional isolation. "In medical school there is little interest in emotions," a physician recalled. "It is mostly academic. There isn't much feeling for the patient as an individual. He is just a number, and all we were interested in was having the same diagnosis as the professor and doing what he did" (MD, age 75).

Scientism typically dominates the curricula and milieu of professional training centers, reinforcing a narrow focus on technical knowledge. Trainees are expected to be analytical and emotionally aloof. To express personal feelings among associates is to risk appearing "soft" or "weak"—in short, "unprofessional." "Emotional development is completely neglected in medical training," a physician observed. "In fact, it is discouraged except in psychiatry residency. So if students can't deal with the stress of medical school, they are looked at as wimps" (MD, age 38).

The problem is even deeper than emotional neglect. "They not only don't address emotional development," a nurse remarked; "they sometimes make matters worse by abusing you emotionally" (RN, age 40). Recent studies show that emotional mistreatment of medical students is pervasive (Sheehan et al. 1990; Silver and Glicken 1990; Wolf 1994).

In male-dominated training centers a tough-guy attitude is highly valued. Medical students in anatomy and autopsy rooms, for example, are expected to dissect human bodies with apparent equanimity. Rarely given an opportunity to discuss their feelings about these emotionally unsettling experiences, they adapt by chronically suppressing or intellectualizing them. This emotional sterility sometimes carries over into their personal lives, resulting in restless sleep and fitful dreams (Finkelstein 1986).

The intellectualized attitude also pervades other professional training centers. "In law school it's all intellectual," an attorney noted. "There's no encouragement to express emotions. You pretend it's not there by maintaining a cool and calm facade. It's okay to be falling apart as long as you don't show it. The law school motto is like the television commercial: 'Don't ever let them see you sweat!' It's okay to be terrified; just don't ever show it." He added, "When your insides are in turmoil, your outside must look cool and col-lected. There's something wrong here" (JD, age 64). And lawyers carry this facade throughout their careers. The same attorney con-tinued: "I can't recall a time when a lawyer ever admitted to me that anything he ever did caused him any anxiety or fear or concern. When fear paralyzed me I dealt with it by becoming angry, and the anger kicked me into action. There are a lot of angry lawyers out there."

Curriculum reform is needed if trainees are to avoid addiction and other manifestations of emotional impairment. The same attor-ney urged: "Law school curricula need to address the lawyer's emo-tions. Tell students honestly that they and their clients will experi-ence fear, and that the jury won't like you when you or your witness become angry in the courtroom."

Emotional development is also neglected in airline pilots' train-ing. As a result, noted an EAP representative, "Pilots who become addicted have a very hard time in their recovery. They don't know how they feel. They're taught that men are not supposed to feel or be emotional." "Pilots deal with the world in a cognitive way and are not hip to identifying their feelings," an airline executive ex-plained. "It's a very macho profession. Training is very stressful, and there's nothing that addresses their emotions. No counselor is provided when they have a problem; it isn't a part of the pilot's culture."

OVERWORK

Imbalanced lifestyles, common among professionals from the in-ception of their training, also contribute to emotional impairment. The professional-school recruiting process typically favors those who single-mindedly pursue admission at the expense of the social experiences necessary for the development of a broad and emotion-ally expressive personality. Although admissions committees like to see a "well-rounded" individual—one who lists volunteer service activities, travel, and athletics—they typically require such a high level of scholastic achievement that most applicants can devote very little time and energy to other pursuits—just enough to make them appear well-rounded on the application forms. Recruits are usually competitive, narrowly specialized, self-sacrificing, grade conscious, bookish, and emotionally inexpressive. Trusting in technology and hard science, they value a mechanistic, quantifying approach, with little regard for feelings and other less measurable aspects of life (Coombs and Paulson 1990).

Professional training tends to impose an imbalanced lifestyle. During the first seven months of medical school, for example, profound lifestyle changes affect physical and psychological health. Among first-year medical students, Wolf and Kissling (1984) found a significant decrease in physical activity, sleep, nutrition, leisure, recreational activities, and general healthy feelings.

Professional students are expected to work excessively long hours, and sleep deprivation is common. In law school, for example, first-year students are generally overwhelmed by the workload, with little time left to sleep, relax, or enjoy friends and relatives (Benjamin et al. 1986). First-year grades control the distribution of honors, law review, job placement, and, because of the importance accorded these by the law faculty, a sense of self-worth. Third-year students, many of whom work part-time while trying to keep up with their demanding studies, complain about insufficient time for rest and sleep. And lawyers are not unique in this regard. "I had no idea what I was getting into," said a nurse. "None. I've worked 18-to-22-hour days and then gone back the next day with only two hours' sleep. I don't know how much more I can take" (RN, age 37).

Postgraduate residency training for physicians, sometimes requiring 100-to-140-hour work weeks, demands physical and emotional stamina. Many high-stress situations severely tax emotional resilience.

> Medical training implants a sense that no matter how hard you work and no matter how much you memorize, it's never enough. A sense of fear and guilt is instilled in you that if you don't study everything, if you didn't read that article or chapter, you may hurt or kill someone. So most doctors live completely slanted lives. They know a tremendous amount about medicine but can't talk about art, music, literature, or sports. It's just tragic how few outside interests most doctors have.   (MD, age 38)

Chronic overwork intensifies emotional problems. Gradually severing ties with family members and neglecting restorative activities that offer rest and diversion adversely affect the technical quality of work as well as relationships with clients and others. Unrewarding social encounters contribute to greater frustration, creating a vicious cycle. Work addiction is as destructive as drug addiction, a physician explained. "It may not cause a quick death, but its outcome is the same; it robs life of its quality just as drugs and alcohol do. People in training need to be made aware of the potential for getting swallowed up by medicine and be encouraged to maintain other interests and balance work with a healthy lifestyle" (MD, age 38).

An oral-surgery resident told how an authoritarian system damages trainee well-being:

> As first-year residents we took call on 24-hour shifts, and I could see 36 patients in one Saturday. We had lots of emergencies, especially on "Friday/Saturday night knife and gun call," where I might see 15 to 16 broken jaws in one evening; they don't come in with toothaches, but with jaws broken through windshields, etc. It took a great deal of energy and strength. If you offended your senior resident, he could retaliate by assigning you an extra day (Sunday), making 72 hours straight, and then you'd have to immediately resume your normal weekly Monday-to-Friday work schedule.

Imagine how this trainee felt when he realized that his senior resident was addicted:

> Whenever there was an emergency I was to call him, and he was supposed to come in as my backup. But when I phoned him, his attention span was literally just a few words; he couldn't hold a thought. Right in the middle of a sentence he'd start talking to his dog. It was very bizarre, given the gravity of the situation and his refusal to come in. Once I called him to say we had a patient who needed emergency surgery. Between talking to his dog he told me to give the patient a local anesthetic. I said that the patient would die while I was doing that and if he didn't get in here quickly, I would call one of the ENT [ear-nose-throat] docs. He said, "If you do, you'll be in *big* trouble." There was a turf war going on between us and ENT, but I called them anyway because I didn't want to kill anybody.   (DDS, age 35)

EMOTIONAL PATHOLOGY

Long and arduous training for a career can cause professionals to lose perspective. The emotionally healthy individual regards her career as only one component of her success and self-image. But many professionals invest so much in their careers that the career shapes their self-concepts. The realization that society places them on a pedestal only reinforces their sense that they *are* their careers. It is a rare physician, for example, who does not pen "M.D." after his signature, even in nonclinical contexts. "When I went home and took off my white coat, there was nothing there," a nurse lamented. "Without drugs, there was no person" (RN, age 39).

The pursuit of excellence, constantly trying to prove one's competence by impressing a critical audience—usually professional peers—in order to feel good about oneself, easily leads to an unbalanced and emotionally unrewarding lifestyle characterized by physical and emotional exhaustion, anxiety, irritability, and depression. In order to appear competent and strong, some professionals chronically suppress anxiety, doubt, and feelings of inadequacy—emotions that cry for expression. They are easily seduced by mood-altering drugs that provide relief.

Therapists are usually available to trainees who manifest serious emotional problems, but little is done to prevent these problems. And trainees may be reluctant to blow their emotional covers by seeking help even when it is available. "There was no emotional support for the student," a dentist recalled:

> I had a lot of psychological problems, but I was afraid if I told anyone I would be busted and not be allowed to finish school. It's very difficult to be honest, especially with an instructor, if you're afraid they will turn you in and keep you from accomplishing what you've worked all your life to achieve. Only occasionally does someone care, but the bottom line is to just keep quiet if you want to get through.   (DDS, age 37)

Mentors rarely encourage self-care activities. "They usually have an hour during orientation day when they tell you to take care of yourself, and then the rest of the time—about 80 hours a week or more—they tell you to work harder" (MD, age 36). An addicted pediatrician became psychologically dependent on Valium when a medical school psychiatrist prescribed it to help him cope with stress. "I learned in my preclinical years in medical school what everyone else learned—biochemistry, anatomy, physiology, histology, pathology, and pharmacology. But I wasn't taught any nonchemical coping skills for dealing with stress. None of my professors even said to me, 'Learn how to take care of yourself. If you're not healthy, you're of no use to anyone' " (Rogers 1995).

According to Bowermaster (1988), completing dental school requires students to become self-denying. Relegating their personal lives to secondary importance leads to an inability to recognize and deal with the emotional needs and conflicts that arise within themselves and their families.

Norton (1989) describes a profile of the typical chemically dependent pharmacist. Demanding of self, she has a tendency to deny or ignore tension, depression, boredom, and unhappiness, and expresses more guilt about drug use than do others in the general public. Her drug use is solitary. She is responsible and has self-control and conventional life attitudes.

Taught that the patient's needs come first, good nurses put others' needs before their own (Sikora 1988; Solari-Twadell 1988). To live by this creed, nurses develop strong denial mechanisms to suppress their own emotional pain, fears, and anxieties. Drugs provide a way to keep going, to excel and achieve. Diminished self-worth manifests itself in the "caretaker mentality," the need to care for others. But "the Florence Nightingale image" may cause them to push themselves beyond their own stamina. "Nurses are socialized into believing that they care for the world," said nursing consultant Evelyn Carroll (Barde and Pick 1993). They neglect their own needs "because they're so busy caring for everybody else. And you'll find nurses feeling that there's always more they ought to be doing; no matter how much they do, it's never quite enough."

The collective denial of emotional pathology existing in training institutions exacerbates these problems. An embittered anesthesiologist who nearly died from a drug overdose received less concern from his associates than is commonly given to patients.

> Whenever a patient dies in the OR, a grand rounds is held after a thorough research, with two or three docs presenting the details with slides, etc., to the entire department. It's a big deal when a patient dies. But when a doctor dies from addiction, as they regularly do here—about one a year in this teaching hospital—it's no big deal. They say, "Oh, that's too bad. Let's put a little article about addiction in everyone's mailbox." Why isn't it a big deal when one of us dies? It's a rotten shame!   (MD, age 34)

In a class of medical students assessed from the first day of school until several months before graduation, 12 percent showed considerable depressive symptoms during the first three years, and 25 percent (the largest proportion) were symptomatic after the end of the second year (Clark and Zeldow 1988).

The changes that occur during internship, the first year of physician postgraduate training, follow a predictable cycle: initial stages of excitement and anxiety followed by self-doubt and then, later in the year, periods of fatigue, defeat, and depression (Girard et al. 1980). Depression increases significantly over the course of the year, with many interns experiencing fits of crying and despair (Martin 1986).

During a five-year period (1979–1984), 56 percent of the internal-medicine training programs in the United States granted leaves of absence to medical residents because of emotional impairment. An average of one percent of internal medicine house staff require leaves of absence, with the rate twice as common for female residents (Smith, Denny, and Witzke 1986). Other studies report that women trainees experience more psychological distress than their male counterparts. Loneliness, depression, suicide, and marital conflict are reported at higher rates for women than for men. Because female residents are given less social support than their male counterparts, they are more vulnerable to the adverse affects of stress (Coombs and Hovanessian 1988; see also Hurwitz et al. 1987).

A resident interviewed by Hurwitz and colleagues (1987, p. 165) conveys the emotional exhaustion experienced by a physician-in-training:

> This residency engenders a fair amount of bitterness. We work a minimum of 80 hours a week, sometimes 120 . . . My social life is nonexistent with respect to men and sexual relationships. My last date was more than a year ago, my last superficial one-night stand six months ago . . . At this point I do not have the confidence to believe that I will ever achieve a caring relationship, let alone one that could be fun or frolicsome. I do have my supports in friends but my schedule allows me to see them a maximum of once or twice a month . . . No delayed gratification can replace these last years of being or feeling young with [age] 40 fast looming. I am not suicidal, but there are times it takes all my inner resources to put one foot in front of the other . . . I would not object vehemently to not waking up. Sleep is one of the great luxuries; I am chronically sleep-deprived.

Small wonder that many professionals use drugs or commit suicide, sometimes by drug overdosing. "There are lots of physicians who are trained to think they must never make a gross error, and if they do, they will be a total failure," a doctor noted. "Some of them commit suicide. It's better to switch careers midstream than to do that. Sell shoes or whatever, but be happy, be a real person and count for something" (MD, age 36).

Chemical Magic

Alchemists in the Middle Ages earnestly searched for elixirs, mythical substances to remedy all diseases and ills, restore youth, prolong life indefinitely, and convert base metals into gold. Drug users, modern-day alchemists, seek elixirs in the form of alcohol and other drugs. Like magic, psychoactive drugs convert boredom into excitement, self-doubt into confidence, fatigue into energy, anxiety into calmness, and psychic pain into peace of mind. "I started off with alcohol, and it fixed my feelings of fear, shyness, and anxiety," a nurse explained. "I found that with drugs I could change my mood and have more control. Alcohol as a depressant was one way, but with drugs I could go up, down, or sideways" (RN, age 40).

The most common theme in Type 5 addiction is a reliance on drugs to feel good. "When I first used codeine," a pharmacist remarked, "I thought, 'Eureka! I've found it!' It made all my problems, worries, and troubles go away" (PharmD, age 46). Type 5 addicts regard their drugs as "best friends" because they magically comfort their troubled souls. "It was the missing link I had been looking for all my life," said an attorney (Resnick 1990).

An addict's drug choice reflects the correlation between its psychopharmacologic effect and the feeling sought. A survey of drug use among fourth-year students at 23 medical schools (Baldwin et al. 1991) found they used alcohol, marijuana, cocaine, and psychedelics to relax, feel good, and have a good time; they used tranquilizers for relaxation and amphetamines to stay awake and improve performance. Khantzian (1985) notes that narcotic addicts use opiates because they soften powerful feelings of rage and aggression and that cocaine relieves depression and sluggishness.

Psychoactive drugs create personality transformations almost instantly. Called "cosmetic psychopharmacology" (Kramer 1993) and "a coat of Teflon for human beings" (Mehren 1993, p. E1), psychoactive drugs miraculously ease painful emotional problems—at least initially. "Alcohol was the magic potion I had been looking for all my life," remarked an attorney. "The first time I used amphetamines, the magic was there. I could pull all-nighters and feel really good" (JD, age 61).

A dentist describing his first experience with nitrous oxide said, "It was a legal, inexpensive attitude adjustment. Man, this is great .. I could achieve an 80–90% concentration .. All that had to be done was hang up the hose, wait a few minutes and drive home; no side effects, just what the doctor ordered" (Dr. Jon 1992). A pharmacist and nurse agreed: "I used the pills and alcohol to turn me into somebody that I wasn't" (PharmD, age 49). "I felt very powerful under the influence; I was an altogether different person, and other people said I *was* a different person" (RN, age 35).

SELF-CONFIDENCE AND SOCIAL SUCCESS

Psychoactive drugs enhance sociability by giving a psychological lift and relieving anguish and tension. "I used alcohol as a social lubricant," a pilot (age 54) reported. "It became a crutch, a thing to lean on when I was apprehensive or unsure."

Many addicts learn the magical power of drugs during adolescence when their self-esteem and confidence are shaky. "At age 13 I discovered that ingesting chemicals could help me feel better and cope with life," an attorney recounted. "My first chemical was alcohol, but I moved on to other chemicals along the way. I discovered that when under the influence of drugs or alcohol, I was cool, brilliantly witty, charming, and no longer the smallest guy in the crowd. I was no longer the young kid, but a real member of the group. I no longer feared failure of any kind" ("Me? An Addict?" 1992; see also "The Appearance of Propriety" 1989).

Some drugs, like heroin and alcohol, buffer awareness of stress (O'Doherty 1991). "For me alcohol was like a gift from Above," an attorney recalled. "It was a way to escape from my painful adolescent feelings of inferiority. From my very first drink to my very last drink, I drank for only one reason: to escape . . . I never felt comfortable in a social setting unless I was drinking. When confronted with a room full of people I experienced a painful feeling of anxiety, feeling like I was just not good enough and would never fit in. When I drank I became a talkative, bubbly person" ("Personal Stories of Recovery" 1991). "Somewhere in high school they must have taught a class in how to live life, and I missed it," a pharmacist said with a laugh, "but alcohol helped me to function. It took away my inhibitions and gave me the ability to be part of the group" (PharmD, age 46).

A longitudinal study of students, beginning in preschool and extending through age 18, found that drug-using adolescents are frequently maladjusted and show a distinct personality syndrome marked by interpersonal alienation, poor impulse control, and emotional distress. Psychological differences between frequent drug users and others can be traced to the quality of parenting received in earliest childhood. Problem drug use was found to be a symptom, not a cause, of personal and social maladjustment (Shedler and Block 1990).

Adolescent insecurities are often carried forward into adulthood. "Although I was 33," an attorney recalled, "the same insecurities that plagued me as a teenager plagued me in my law practice. Alcohol helped me have a sense of competence and fit in" (Texas Young Lawyers Association 1990). "Whenever I wanted to go to a cocktail party where there were important people," a pilot (age 53) confessed, "I felt I needed a few drinks to allay my anxieties. I knew I would be uptight."

Drugs also enhance sexual intimacy. "Alcohol helped me deal with women," the same pilot acknowledged. "When under the influence I could womanize and do a lot of things I couldn't do without alcohol." A dentist said that marijuana and Quaaludes removed lifelong feelings of inadequacy about his sexual capabilities. Another dentist used cocaine as "bait" to seduce women who he felt would probably reject him as a sexual partner (Rosecan, Spitz, and Gross 1987).

RELIEF FROM PSYCHIC PAIN

Drugs appeal to those in psychic pain—described by a physician as "emotional agony in need of relief" (MD, age 50). "It was a way to anesthetize my feelings," a dentist commented (DDS, age 45). "Psychache," a term coined by Shneidman (1993), refers to this pain. "We all recognize the words headache, earache, backache, toothache—and we intuitively know what those words mean," he explains (p. 145):

> In roughly the same sense, *psychache* refers to the hurt, anxious, soreness, aching psychological *pain* in the psyche, the mind. It is not psy-

chogenic pain of a body part; it is not phantom limb pain; it is an intrinsically psychological pain—the pain of excessively felt shame, guilt or humiliation, or loneliness, or fear, or angst, or dread of growing old or of dying badly—or whatever. When it occurs, its reality is introspectively undeniable. Suicide occurs when the psychache is deemed by that person to be unbearable.

This physician treated his psychache with drugs:

> I had to function in the OR, but when I went home I used drugs to fall asleep. I was so miserable that the only state of consciousness that was not painful was unconsciousness. I'm not being melodramatic. I would sit there shooting up a barbiturate or sedative, waking up and shooting up again, going through that night after night, shooting myself into unconsciousness until it was time to go to work the next day.   (MD, age 34)

A perfectionist pharmacist became addicted after receiving a doctoral degree in pharmacy with honors, being elected to the National Pharmacy Honor Society, and subsequently becoming director of pharmacy services at a major urban hospital. "I had all the symptoms of being successful. I had a lovely wife and a family and a fine job and was respected in my chosen profession. The only problem was that I didn't feel successful and I had an empty feeling down deep inside . . . I found myself using alcohol and pills to shut out those ungrounded feelings of insecurity and inadequacy" (Hirning 1991, p. 14).

The quest for perfection, an expectation cultivated in professional schools, reinforces the value of psychoactive drugs. Calling cocaine his "comforter," an attorney recalled: "I was always my own worst critic. No matter how good someone said I was, I wasn't good enough. No matter what I won, it wasn't satisfying. Eventually taking cocaine to the office became as normal as carrying a wallet" (McGlone 1991; see also "Two Sides to Every Story" 1992).

For the emotionally malnourished, drugs have great appeal. "Depression runs in my family," an attorney remarked. "Two of my uncles committed suicide. I was depressed from age nine. My fourth-grade teacher asked me why I was so sad and why I didn't play with other children. I always felt like an outsider. In the beginning alcohol gave me a lift, made me feel okay" (JD, age 41). "Considering the family I grew up with it's lucky I'm not insane," a dentist stated. "I used drugs as a survival mechanism" (DDS, age 46).

A wife, describing her pilot husband as "a person in pain," explained that his low self-esteem came from being sexually molested by an older sister and harassed by older neighborhood boys. "But alcohol erased that and got him going. Hey, for a moment, he wasn't in pain."

ENHANCED WORK PERFORMANCE

Stimulants and other drugs can temporarily enhance performance at school, work, and elsewhere. "At first I had an incredible record," a prosecutor reported. "I'd take these pills and could think quicker. I didn't lose many cases" (JD, age 47).

Stimulant drugs like "dexies" (Dexamyl and Dexedrine) meet the professional's need for energy. "Speed got me up in the morning and made me feel good," a nurse confided (RN, age 45). "These little wonders," as a dentist called the pills, condensed his study time and provided euphoria and a feeling of energy and omnipotence (Arthur 1982, p. 45).

Tranquilizers and narcotics can also enhance performance, as this pharmacist reported. "I was in the senior class play in pharmacy school and had a lot of butterflies in my stomach. A pharmacist colleague said, 'Here, take a couple of these before you go on, and you'll feel fine. I did, and my performance was phenomenal; I was a knockout, the star of the show; I brought the house down," he said with a laugh. "From then on I used them whenever I needed to perform as toastmaster, chair a meeting, or whatever" (PharmD, age 49). "I began to use Percodan for dental pain," another pharmacist said. "I found it gave me a feeling of well-being—it made me feel like Mr. Wonderful! I could do tons of work and handle situations better" (PharmD, age 41).

PLEASURE

One need not have an emotional disorder to be enticed by a chemical elixir. In the early stages, alcohol and other drugs are often used just to have fun, to celebrate, as this criminal defense attorney's experience illustrates:

> I considered myself upbeat and I drank to celebrate life's little victories. I am a respected and accomplished lawyer, so I had victories to

celebrate. For many years I avoided drinking over painful experiences, believing that this would prevent me from developing the disease of alcoholism. In the end I drank for good reasons, for bad reasons, mostly for no particular reason at all. I found myself drinking when I had no particular desire to do so.   (Kathleen 1992)

During a very stressful day in dental school, a dentist recalled, a classmate gave him a few 10 mg Valium tablets. "The feeling that came over me was far better than any I ever had while drinking. I had never felt that good. I also discovered that drinking a few beers later that day potentiated the wonderful feelings I had experienced earlier." He explained, "I justified my drug usage by rationalizing that if I worked hard I would indeed treat myself to some good feelings." Later, he recalled, "I would 'treat' myself to a Demerol cocktail at the end of my working day. Then after a few weeks I would not only 'treat' myself to one after work, but one just before bed time . . . By this time I had begun taking both Valium and Demerol during the day just to maintain a certain feeling of being normal" ("I'm a Dentist and a Drug Addict" 1990, p. 18). For such individuals, being under the influence eventually becomes the norm, and any deviation from the norm causes discomfort—even feelings considered normal by nonaddicted people.

The advertising industry bombards us daily with media messages equating alcohol and pharmaceutical products with health, sociability, and well-being. Who can resist the promise that by simply ingesting these substances we can think faster, reason more clearly, have more energy, feel less fatigued, be less anxious, and be happier? Why hold back when by taking a drink we can have more friends, more adventure, and be more popular, attractive, and sexy? Considering the propaganda, it is surprising that more people do not become drug-dependent.

Almost all the professionals interviewed for this book said that drugs at first improved their lives—lifted their feelings when they were low and enhanced positive moods. "The thought would come repeatedly to me in a variety of circumstances that a drink would make it better," an attorney recalled. "If it was good times, we'll have more fun if we have a few drinks. If it's bad times, a drink will lift us up and take away the tension" (Texas Young Lawyers Association 1990). "Alcohol did more for me than for other people," a pharmacist explained. "People would say, 'Why don't you just quit?' I would say, 'Honey, if it did for you what it does for me, you would have done it too' " (Reimenschneider 1990).

Chemical Servitude

Continued use of chemicals eventually pulls the user into pain and despair. "Before you know it, you cross over a line and are addicted," a nurse warned (RN, age 70). When this happens, a physiological and psychological adaptation takes place and drugs turn from friend to enemy. An attorney who crossed over the line tried to quit alcohol and cocaine because, he said, "I could no longer deal with the feelings of remorse and self-hate which followed every drinking and drugging episode. Suicide was an ever-present thought . . . I could not cope with my day-to-day responsibilities. My substance abuse had seriously eroded my ability to think clearly and to take care of the work that had to be done" ("Personal Stories of Recovery" 1991, pp. 163–164).

Despite this reality, Type 5 addicts continue using in ever-increasing amounts, hoping to relive the initial experience—or at least feel normal. The psychic pain inevitably gets worse. "Every day I woke up to a nightmare," a dentist recalled. "There was no self-respect, only self-loathing. I feared everything and everyone. I couldn't even begin to sort out the jumble of emotions inside me. The only way I knew to quiet those anxieties and fears was to anesthetize them with drugs and alcohol" ("The Seduction of a Substance Abuser" 1988, p. 177).

An attorney described how "speed" initially enhanced his performance but then made his life hell:

> A criminal client came into my office and when I bemoaned the fact that I was going to be working on a brief all night, she gave me about half an ounce of meth [methamphetamine]. She told me that a few lines would keep me going all night. Wow! A new lawyer tool! I could be super-lawyer! My opponents at the D.A.'s office would only work 8–5, but I, super-lawyer, could work around the clock! And so it began. But then the elixir stopped working. Line by line, day by day, I sank into a hell from which I barely escaped . . . Every waking moment was torture, frantic and insane. I was quickly becoming broke, paranoid and impotent. All I had dreamed of—money, a reputation, family, a home—was being converted to money, then to cocaine and then smoked or snorted away. The bar complaints came next. My wife

kicked me out of the house, forced me to live in my office. I became the target of law enforcement investigations. I became financially destitute. I needed help. I knew I had a problem. I had tried quitting cocaine before, but had failed miserably.   (Mark 1992)

As more and more drugs are ingested, the body's normal processes are adversely impacted. "I found this magical drug that helped me fall asleep," explained an addictionologist who had himself been addicted.

It was wonderful! I would just reach over and put one of those in my mouth, and I would be out. What happened over the course of many weeks and months, though, is that my body became adapted to the Quaaludes. My brain said, "Why should I create the neurochemical in this guy's head to help him fall asleep when he takes this magical pill that works so effectively on cue?" In other words, my brain quit producing the normal chemicals that helped me fall into a healthy sleep and I needed more and more of the drug for it to be effective. When I quit using Quaaludes, it took weeks for my body and mind to adjust so that I could fall asleep normally.

Kern (n.d., p. 57) explains: "Every time we take something, the part of our brain that produces sleep chemicals shuts down a bit, and then still more, until eventually our brain's chemical plant grinds to a slow halt."

Type 5 addicts become psychologically dependent only on substances that make them feel better; if a substance doesn't contribute to a good feeling, they don't repeat it. Cocaine users, for example, realize an immediate euphoric high, a jolt of elation followed by a fall, a depression. But with continued use, good sensations don't come as often, and the cocaine user rarely gets much of a high. Instead, she uses it just to feel normal. Similarly, heroin addicts and alcoholics frequently say that they don't drink or do drugs to make them feel good—they do it just to feel okay.

Myers (1992) explains "the opponent-process principle": "Even in the short run," he says, "emotions seem attached to elastic bands that snap us back from highs or lows. For many pleasures we pay a price, and for much suffering we receive a reward" (pp. 54–55). He cites as examples new mothers who experience relief or euphoria after the pain of childbirth, or parachutists who feel elated after a terrifying jump, or people who get the blues after a holiday.

Emotional "muscle," like physical muscle, develops by struggling with problems. As there can be no growth without overcoming resistance, struggle is a necessary prerequisite for personal development (Kern 1993). Using chemical elixirs to avoid unpleasant feelings interferes with and frustrates the normal processes of healthy emotional growth. When a chemical is used to address problems of loneliness, boredom, depression, and anxiety or simply to fulfill the desire to be happier, it bypasses the normal processes of growth—struggling—and impedes development of the healthy coping skills necessary for dealing with life's problems.

Meehan (1984, p. 53) explains: "A teenager on drugs *does not grow emotionally*. All that grows is the magnitude of his problems. That is why drugs are so devastating to young, unformed psyches. Exactly at the time when young people need to learn how to deal with adult problems, drugs give them a means of sidestepping those problems ... Drugs are not a means of finding oneself, as many people pretend. In fact, they keep one from doing so." A pilot (age 48) observed, "Alcohol had been a tranquilizer for my emotions and helped me deal with the problems I was afraid to handle. But it not only stopped fixing my emotional problems; it made them worse." "I used alcohol as a coping mechanism," said an attorney. "The longer I used it, the more I excluded other coping mechanisms. It insulated me from life, from all of life's little travails and the fear that I used to carry around" (JD, age 47).

Emotional atrophy occurs as the addict, turning to her elixir, forgets previously learned ways of dealing with frustration and psychic pain. Stashing drugs in a variety of ingenious places to provide an ever-available emotional crutch, the addict deprives herself of the opportunity to recognize and deal with uncomfortable feelings and challenging experiences. "Living is painful," Hutchinson (1987) notes, and healthy emotional development requires "pain work."

Once drugs are discontinued, the recovering addict must return to where he left off in his emotional development—to that emotional age when he started using drugs to cope—and begin there. Though his body age may be 45, his emotional age may be only 15. "Drinking retarded my emotional development and growth as a person," an insightful attorney reflected. "It retarded my growing up. In the last few years I've just begun to catch up" (JD, age 57). This reality explains the dread addicts experience at the prospect of living without their elixir. It also explains the high relapse rate among those who try to quit—for to discontinue drugs is to let go of the only thing that makes them feel good and in control. "You know, if you've been drinking a long time, you may not have the skills to live another way," a recovering nurse explained. "Being willing to try a new way of life is very scary and confusing. It takes a lot of courage to change when [your addiction] is the only thing you know" (Reed 1992, p. 58).

After years of quieting uncomfortable feelings with drugs, facing those feelings can be terrifying. A nurse in treatment who had been required to meditate said, "They wanted me to be still, but I had never been still. I feared being still because if I stopped and sat down long enough I would start to feel, and that frightened me" (RN, age 40). As one treatment expert explains, "I used to discharge people from the treatment center with the advice, 'The more uncomfortable you are with your feelings in the next 28 days, the better—because if you aren't uncomfortable, you aren't growing' " (Kern 1993).

Accelerated Emotional Growth

Accelerated emotional development occurs when addicts begin to face life's problems without their chemical crutches. This attorney's experience exemplifies the transition: "I used alcohol to feel comfortable, to avoid feeling scared; I wanted to feel that everything was okay. But toward the end that feeling got harder and harder to get because the drug was not working. Now when I'm emotionally distraught about something I go to more 12-step meetings. I've discovered that I can withstand a lot more than I ever thought I could" (JD, age 34).

Recovering addicts may startle others by saying they are glad to be alcoholics/addicts. "It's hard for people not in recovery to understand, but I'm really glad I'm a drug addict," a pharmacist said. "My addiction allowed me to find a fantastic way to live. I'm really happy" (PharmD, age 41). "It's a whole new life for me," a nurse agreed. "If I had never been a drunk, I would never have found AA and would never have experienced the growth and felt the freedom I have today. Without this whole new way of living, I would still be the insecure little girl that I was before, feeling that I wasn't as good as others and could never be perfect. I learned in AA that it's okay to make mistakes, and that gave me great freedom" (RN, age 70).

When forced to confront their feelings, addicts develop qualities of heart typically neglected by professionals. "There is no doubt that being an alcoholic is the best thing that ever happened to me," a pilot (age 56) reflected, "because once I got into recovery I began to work on me and to get healthy. Then some really good things happened." "In a sense my addiction has been a blessing," an attorney said. "I'm now a better lawyer. I wasn't bad before, but I'm better now. I was an abysmal failure as a husband, son, and father, but now I'm pretty good at all those, too" (JD, age 64).

Experts agree that recovering addicts become better people than they were before their addictions. "In a lifetime of medicine," Reimenschneider (1990, p. 8) observes, "I have found that alcoholism [addiction] is the only disease in which, when a patient gets well, he is more well than before he became ill." "Most will agree," notes the director of the Texas Pharmacists Recovery Network, "that pharmacists come out of recovery programs better pharmacists than they were before. They are better in the profession and they treasure their licenses because they know what it is like to have their license— and their lives—in jeopardy" (Richardson 1990, p. 16).

A physician's clinical effectiveness improved when he was forced to deal with emotional pain. He set up a new practice directly across the street from the partners who had thrown him out. It doubled in size during the first six years of his sobriety.

Self-esteem soars when the recovering addict likes the new person he is becoming. "I'm a much more honest person and much more aware of other people's pain," a nurse enthused. "Before, I was a very good liar. Now I am rigorously honest" (RN, age 42). A pilot (age 53) changed from a "smart-ass with all the answers to almost everything" to one who has left behind his masculinity hangups and resentments. "I've found inner peace," he said. "I now understand myself and others, and this has benefited me greatly."

A physician who used drugs and excessive work to numb the residual pain of his mother's suicide when he was only eight years old said, "I've learned that feelings don't kill me. Instead of running from my feelings, I now encourage them to come up so that I can process them and work through them. Even though some are painful, I celebrate that I have them and I can discuss them with my AA sponsor and with other friends or with a therapist when I need to. I don't allow them to fester and cause me to act out in a self-destructive way" (MD, age 38).

Spiritual growth, a common experience for those who recover from addiction, is savored as a "triumph of the soul." "My wife and I developed a wonderful, loving relationship; I made new friends, I became involved in recreational activities I had abandoned; my thinking ability made a quantum leap, my physical health returned; and for the first time in my life, I experienced spiritual growth" ("Out of the Abyss" 1991; see also Jim 1992).

Note the new perspective of this physician who described herself as "a food addict, a love addict, and a drug addict":

> It's hard to imagine that I've gotten from there to here in only eight years. I was absolutely miserable, a self-centered, unhappy woman filled with self-pity. I used to read about Maslow's self-actualizing person, and it would break my heart because I knew that it was not possible for me to be that kind of person. But now I think, "Who cares about Maslow?" I'm becoming the kind of person God wanted me to become and it's just a trip! I now have joy in my life. I've never had joy before. Horror, negative intensity, tension, and passion, yes, but never joy.   (MD, age 50)

Interpersonal relationships improve dramatically, as one attorney explained: "Today my relationships are better because I have so much less to hide; and the less I hide from others, the stronger those relationships are because I understand that today people know and accept the real me, and not the me I pretended to be for so many years" ("Me? An Addict?" 1992, p. 255).

Improved family life and emotional growth go hand in hand. "The quality of my marriage has improved 200-fold," a pilot (age 53) enthused. "We now have a very trusting, caring relationship between us." A dentist remarked:

> I'm now the spiritual leader of my house. I have a great deal of pride in raising three kids with a second wife, and we have a wonderful relationship. The other night my 12-year-old daughter went through a hormonal explosion that was comical. She raged at me, but I just listened and didn't respond defensively. I also shared with her my vulnerability and inadequacies. It took 20 to 30 minutes, and when she was through she gave me a hug and a kiss. When I walked into

my bedroom my wife said, "What a great dad." Ten minutes later my daughter knocked on the door and kissed both me and her "wicked" stepmother. (DDS, age 43)

Service enhances personal fulfillment. "I now spend a lot of time helping other people," an attorney remarked. "But I get more out of it than I give" (JD, age 64). A pilot (age 58) agreed: "Helping somebody who is still using helps me grow and be empathic. It's made me a more sensitive and understanding person."

After discontinuing his drug use and regaining his license, an attorney opened an office with $300 he had "scraped together." Out of practice for six years, he was delighted to schedule his first client. Then his AA sponsor called, saying, "Cancel the client. We have to go to Fresno tomorrow to take a lawyer to an AA meeting." He protested that at least 20 others could be called to go with the sponsor, but his complaints were unheeded.

> I was so upset. But to make a long story short, I went. When I tried to reschedule the client he got another attorney. When I came back from sitting with this guy all day long the horrible depression I had been in for six months—this deep dark depression—was gone! It finally dawned on me that what had happened was that I had got out of thinking about myself for an entire day. It taught me a tremendous lesson that I will never forget and helped put my priorities in the right order. (JD, age 61; see also Burke 1991)

Type 5 addicts can become happy and productive once they are chemically abstinent. The outcome, of course, depends upon how much effort they make in developing emotionally and spiritually. "The key is," Kern (1993) explains, "the 'life' they create must be more fulfilling than the life they had with the drug."

In Perspective

Psychoactive substances are most alluring to those who, like this dentist, lead emotionally and spiritually unfulfilling lives: "Something in my life was missing, and substances seemed to fill the gap" (DDS, age 43).

Professional training does little to nourish emotional health. Although trainees develop ample intellectual and hands-on skills, they become emotionally impaired when they neglect family, friends, and other outlets for nurturing. Most training centers have programs to assist those who "crash and burn"—become seriously depressed, suicidal, or chemically dependent—but relatively few offer preventive programs; emotional and spiritual well-being is not a priority. "In training we were taught to be good pharmacists, but we weren't taught to be good human beings," a graduate complained. "We weren't taught to feel, to be in touch with our emotions or be human" (PharmD, age 49).

Capitalizing on the popular quest for easy cures to life's dilemmas, giant industries advertise and market alcohol and other alluring substances with promises of well-being. "The message is: "If you feel bad, there's something wrong with you" ("It's O.K. to Feel Bad" 1994).

Once addicted, Type 5 users cannot simply toss drugs aside and walk away, because their coping skills have withered. It is terrifying for them to consider a day without drugs, and some regard death as a better alternative. Is it any wonder that so few addicts voluntarily quit, or that so many of those who do quit quickly relapse?

II

DEVELOPMENTAL DYNAMICS

FOUR

Vulnerabilities

"My first thought in the morning was 'Where's the medicine [codeine]'? Then I would whip down four ounces of this syrup. Once I remember thinking, 'God, you're an addict.' But my brain would come back with the message, 'No big deal, you're a doctor; you can get this stuff for the rest of your life. You're the smoothest, kindest, most loving family doctor in the world.'"

(MD, age 35)

"When I was in the Air Force we had happy hour every night, and you were expected to be there. Everyone was drinking and having a good time. Occasionally someone would get drunk, but it never seemed like there was anything wrong with drinking. It was just part of the scene."

(Airline EAP representative)

"As a child I was unloved or unlovable. I had a feeling of inferiority; I was less than other people and didn't fit in. But when I took a drink or drug, all those feelings left. I could interact with other people and feel as good on the inside as others looked on the outside."

(PharmD, age 41)

Professionals—especially health professionals—are particularly vulnerable to drug abuse. They attend colleges where recreational drug use—especially alcohol—is the norm and matriculate to professional schools that promote a view of drugs as a way to solve human problems. Open-ended careers, those with no established starting and quitting times, encourage overwork, unbalanced lifestyles, and self-neglect. Some professionals, coming from emotionally abusive families, select professional careers for the status and approval they never received at home. When their careers fail to meet emotional and spiritual needs, these high-achieving, perfectionist caretakers, like so many of their parents, turn to alcohol and other drugs. These risk factors—together with the tendency of professionals to feel immune to addiction—greatly increase their chances of drug involvement.

Emotionally Impaired Family

Growing up in an emotionally damaging family, as many professionals do, puts them at high risk for drug abuse.[1] Psychoactive drugs temporarily mask the emotional pain caused by parental neglect or abuse and seem the perfect solution for those raised in such homes. "If I had to say what is at the core of my addiction," a physician acknowledged, "I would say it was my dysfunctional upbringing" (MD, age 38). A dentist commented, "I was in a dysfunctional family my entire life. I think I was destined to be a drug addict no matter what" (DDS, age 45).

Studies substantiate that many professionals come from dysfunctional families. Bowermaster (1989) estimates from surveys at various dental schools that over 35 percent of all dental students, compared with 10 percent of the general population, are raised in families with a history of chemical dependency. A study of 361 students from all four dental classes at the University of Texas Health Sciences Center at San Antonio revealed that 15 percent had a family history of alcoholism and 17 percent a family history of illicit drug use (Sandoval et al. 1990). A survey of 140 students in two Kentucky dental schools found that 35–39 percent had an alcoholic parent or grandparent (Sammon et al. 1991).

The professionals interviewed for this book readily acknowledged the relationship between family pathology and addiction. "We all talk about our dysfunctional families at meetings of the International Doctors of Alcoholics Anonymous" (MD, age 50). "Of the addicted nurses that I know," a nurse observed, "I can't think of one who didn't come from a dysfunctional family. Although their parents were not necessarily alcoholics or addicts, their families didn't work together or function as healthy families" (RN, age 70).

Only 13 percent of the addicted professionals interviewed considered their parental families emotionally healthy. The remainder (87 percent) said at least one parent (usually the father) was emotionally restricted—cold and aloof. Depressive family interactions included rigid rules, workaholic or "rage-aholic" behaviors, lying, sexual abuse, and "double-talk." "My father was an extremely advanced alcoholic," a nurse recalled. "Even at my birth he was into long-term blackouts. Whenever he would come back—he had tuberculosis and went away for long periods—I hated it because of the violence that he brought. As a child I always said that I would never be like him and drink" (RN, age 56).

Violent experiences, indelibly imprinted in memories, create fear. "When my dad started drinking, it got absolutely insane," an attorney said. "I've seen him rip toilets out of floors. I'd sleep with one eye open afraid that he was going to come home drunk. I'd worry about what was going to happen or which one of us kids was going to go flying. It got all twisted" (JD, age 56). A physician recalled:

My mother and father were chronic alcoholics. My father drank a bottle of whiskey every day, but he managed it well. My mother, on the other hand, was a fall-down drunk. I remember coming home one afternoon when I was about nine and seeing my mother lying on the kitchen floor. She had passed out, but the maid said that she was resting her back and needed a hard surface. When my mother was drunk there was violence in our home, and she occasionally tried to molest me sexually or exhibit herself inappropriately. My father beat her up once when she tried to climb into bed with me. It was the first time I had heard human bones splintering. I ran and told the maid that my daddy was murdering mommy. The rest of the family listened to the radio and pretended that nothing was happening. Nothing was ever spoken about that incident except to say that my mother had bumped into a door and had fractured her maxilla. Everyone in the family was dedicated to each other's personal destruction. I was the only person to whom everyone could speak. (MD, age 57)

To make matters worse, violent episodes are usually unpredictable as the alcoholic parent alternates between being "wonderful" and "dreadful." "There was such a fine line, and he could change in half an hour depending on how much vodka he had in the glass," a nurse remarked (RN, age 40). A dentist said, "It was like having two fathers. When sober my father was this nice, intelligent, gentle person, but when drunk he turned into a raving, physically abusive maniac" (DDS, age 48).

Though less physically violent, other dysfunctional families are no less emotionally abusive.

> Thankfully my dad never hit us, but he would yell and scream. Many nights he'd make us sit in the truck for hours on end while he was in the bar. We lived five miles out of town on a ranch, and we would wait in the truck three to five hours at a time for him to come out of the bar. The three of us would take turns going in and getting the keys to the truck so we could turn on the light to do our homework. On a cold winter night it could be 20 below zero. My mom would call the bar, and he'd have the bartender tell her that he wasn't there. What was my mom to do? Walk to town in the freezing weather with two babies in her arms?   (RN, age 37)

Imagine the emotional pain caused by this drunken father's devastating verbal assaults on his teenage daughter:

> My dad was real, real weird—*really* weird—and very, very violent toward my Mom and me. He called me a "whore" and "trash." He insulted my friends and wouldn't come out to meet the people I dated. On my sixteenth birthday his present to me was an expression, "Sweet sixteen and never been missed." I was enraged at everything and wanted to run far, far away. I was an addiction waiting to happen.   (RN, age 42)

Low self-esteem is a predictable outcome of such childhood experiences. "I certainly had very low self-esteem," a nurse said. "My father was an alcoholic. He wasn't the type who pushed and yelled, but there was silence in the family—and mother and the rest of us constantly worried about how it looked to the neighbors. I got the feeling that I wasn't any good because the neighbors didn't think my father was any good. I wanted to be loved and liked, so I thought if I was perfect, people would have to like me" (RN, age 70).

Emotionally abused children, "stuffing" their feelings and suppressing brutal and emotionally devastating memories, eventually lose conscious awareness of feelings. "It took me a long time to realize that I had any feelings," an attorney commented. "I don't know where the feelings go when you don't feel anything" (JD, age 44).

Silence and denial are typical in emotionally impaired families. "Nobody admitted that my dad was an alcoholic," an attorney said. "My dad died of sclerosis of the liver, but nobody talks about it. My brother won't talk about my being an alcoholic. He told his daughter that I had an allergy. Our whole family was weird about it" (JD, age 40). A nurse recalled, "There was no healthy way to deal with the issues and problems, so we sought our answers and solutions elsewhere—in drugs and stuff" (RN, age 40).

The effects of such abuse may last a lifetime. A nurse, for example, found it hard to talk to a psychiatrist about her depression. "Growing up in a home where there is alcoholism and secrecy, and having kept everything secret for so many years, it's hard to open up; you don't like to talk" (RN, age 54).

Addicted professionals describe their childhood home environments not only as secretive but as rigidly oriented to rules and hard work, with little or no expression of positive sentiment. "My parents were stern, and there was no hugging or that sort of thing," a pharmacist recalled (PharmD, age 49). "I was supposed to go to school, come home, study, and then go to work," a dentist said. "There was no leisure time" (DDS, age 37). A physician explained, "The family message was 'Don't feel, don't laugh, don't tell others about our family' " (MD, age 60).

Overachievement and overwork characterize professionals raised in emotionally impaired families. A brilliant record of academic and other achievements can do wonders for one's self-esteem. "I felt that getting good marks in school would make my mother proud and possibly make my father love me," a lawyer said. "I overachieved my way all through law school. I looked forward to being called to the bar, as I thought I would finally feel worthwhile rather than empty and hollow. My mother, of course, attended the ceremony. My father was off getting drunk somewhere" (Lawyers Assistance Programme 1992, p. 623). "I always tried to overachieve to compensate for our family problems," a pharmacist confirmed. "I was captain of the baseball, basketball, and football teams in school. I became president of my grade school and in my high school, but that didn't fill the void. For the next 26 years I looked for ways to get high. I was an addict waiting to happen" (PharmD, age 47).

The helping professions appeal to individuals from emotionally damaging families for two reasons: the high status can compensate for their damaged self-esteem, and they are accustomed to the caregiver role. To keep things manageable in their families, they had to be perfect and to keep their parents happy. "I had a hard time raising you, Mom," a young man told his alcoholic mother (DeShields quoted in Hudson 1994, p. C1). "I never got to be a kid," a nurse said; "I was the oldest child and had to be responsible and take care of my brothers and sisters" (RN, age 45). An attorney recalled, "I was the hero, the caretaker, a superperfect kid. By the time I was three I had to take care of Mom and keep her happy. If I didn't, she would bitch to Dad, and he'd start hitting, and all hell would break loose. So I went from age 2 to 20 real fast" (JD, age 48).

For professional trainees with abusive backgrounds, emotional abuse from mentors comes as no surprise, and its incidence is high. In one study of medical students (Silver and Glicken 1990), 46 percent of 431 respondents reported being abused by insulting or humiliating comments, sexual harassment, intentional neglect, or unfair grading. A similar survey of third-year medical students found that 79 of 98 respondents (81 percent) had seriously considered withdrawing from school because of mistreatment (Sheehan et al. 1990). Two national surveys of fourth-year medical students in 1991 and 1992 found that about 40 percent had been publicly belittled or humiliated during their medical training (Association of American Medical Colleges 1991, 1992a). The problem has been so pervasive that in 1992 the American Association of Medical Colleges issued a statement encouraging all medical schools to develop and implement policies to reduce the incidence of mistreatment (1992b).

Men and women from dysfunctional families may create their own destructive units. People tend to seek the familiar in interpersonal relationships; so those with negative self-concepts typically select others who derogate them. Swann and colleagues (1992) found that those with positive self-esteem are more committed to spouses who think well of them than partners who regard them negatively. Conversely, persons with poor self-regard are more committed to spouses who think poorly of them. In other words, there is a tendency to select a partner who confirms one's self-concept— even if it is negative and fraught with detrimental consequences (Swann, Hixon, and de la Ronde 1992).

Of course, not all addicted professionals come from unhealthy families. "I was an only child who was raised by two loving parents," a dentist reported. "They weren't alcoholic nor abusive, just loving, caring parents. But I had trouble dealing with peer interaction, and when I drank alcohol it filled that void" (DDS, age 43).

Those who view addiction as a genetically induced disease sometimes dispute the role of dysfunctional families. For example, a judge recalled, "My parents were married 53 years, and I never heard a harsh word between them. Neither drank, and they were loving toward all of us ... I grew up in a happy household and achieved many honors." These circumstances led him to conclude that "most alcoholics, if not all, are born alcoholics" (Leahy 1991, p. 52). An attorney agreed. "It is a common misconception that one must come from a so-called 'dysfunctional family' to develop the disease of alcoholism. This is not true. People from good backgrounds who consider themselves generally satisfied with life can develop this disease. Because alcoholism results from a biological defect in the way an individual processes alcohol, it can develop in anyone with a certain genetic predisposition" (Kathleen 1992).

Other addicts acknowledge that although their families were dysfunctional, "all families are dysfunctional to some extent" (JD, age 64). "I think we *all* grow up in dysfunctional families," a physician asserted (MD, age 34). A pilot (age 61) agreed: "Each individual has to take responsibility and not blame his problems on his childhood."

Informal Encouragement to Use Recreational Drugs

The term "recreational drug use" refers to social tolerance and encouragement of alcohol use and, to a lesser extent, marijuana and cocaine use. In this country, drinking has generally come to be regarded as a hallmark of gracious living and the cocktail party circuit as a means to enhance career and social status. The ability to "drink well" is not only socially acceptable but highly valued in some professional circles—and almost required in others (Kahler 1989). An attorney reported that her employers "asked me to go out on the first night and have a drink. I said no. They called me in the next day and told me that drinking with the clients was sort of part of my job. I thought I had died and gone to heaven!" (JD, age 44).

Many professionals grew up in communities where drinking was regarded as a normal part of everyday life. "I came from an Irish-Catholic background that considered alcohol very important in our daily lives," an attorney said. "Everybody did it. Getting drunk wasn't considered a major problem; in fact it was kind of a rite of passage. So I drank, first as an altar boy. I was into serious drinking when I was 17" (JD, age 70).

In some families, wine and other alcoholic drinks are an integral part of meals and social occasions. "I always thought it was sort of glamorous and grown-up to drink. Having a good time meant drinking a little too much" (JD, age 57). Youngsters emulate drinking parents. "I always saw alcohol as something you do when you get home from work or at social functions," a pharmacist acknowledged. "To this day my father has a Manhattan when he comes home from work. It's a ritual" (PharmD, age 26). A pilot (age 58) added, "My father, his brothers, and my brothers are all oriented toward alcohol as entertainment, as a social outlet, an expression of good times. Drinking was reinforced all along because I liked the approval of these people."

In most cases, young men and women come to professional training centers straight from college campuses where the attitude toward drinking and, to a lesser extent, recreational use of other drugs is generally permissive and even encouraging. A Core Alcohol and Drug Survey of 78 U.S. college and university campuses from 1989 through 1991 reported that 66.8 percent of students prefer to have alcohol at campus social events. Eighty-six percent had used alcohol the previous year, and 42 percent had binged with five or more drinks at one time (*American Council on Alcoholism News* 1993). Former surgeon general Antonio Novella observed that "college students spend more money on alcohol than on textbooks" (Eigen 1995, p. 269).

The annual consumption of alcoholic beverages for the more than 12 million college students in the United States is well over 430 million gallons (National Clearinghouse for Alcohol and Drug Information, cited in Williams 1994). A national study found that college students do more heavy drinking than their noncollege peers: 40 percent of the college students compared to 34 percent of their age peers had drunk five or more drinks in a row in the previous two weeks. Although they may be less likely to drink on a daily basis, college students are more likely to participate in heavy weekend drinking (Johnston, O'Malley, and Bachman 1994, p. 151). A study of 720 freshmen at 13 "heavy-drinking colleges" (Wechsler 1994) found that half "get smashed" in their first week at college.

Many freshmen regard drunkenness as an integral part of college life.

A 1991 national survey of college and university administrators shows that alcohol abuse by students is a serious and increasing problem on campuses. College administrators believe that alcohol use contributes to 70 percent of the violent behavior that occurs on campus, to 40 percent of student academic failure, and to 44 percent of student emotional problems (Anderson and Gadaleto 1991). The presidents of 35 major universities and deans of 1,100 colleges of education concluded that college and universities need to provide better education about substance use and abuse, particularly for prospective teachers (Hackett, Henry, and Manke 1991).

At a time of life when social acceptance is extremely important, the pervasive view among college students is that drinking is expected and fun (Eigen 1992). And they drink despite adverse consequences. "When I was in college I drank a whole pint of vodka and passed out. My roommates told me that I had thrown up in bed, but it didn't faze me in the least. As a matter of fact, they considered it macho and heroic to have done that and survived. Everyone laughed and giggled and thought it was neat" (pilot, age 53).

Recreational use of alcohol continues in professional school. Incoming students are often welcomed by the preceding class with a party serving alcoholic drinks. "They open the door to medical school and say, 'Hi, how are you? What would you like to drink?' It's our way of life" (MD, age 50).

Recalling their days in college and professional school, physicians describe alcohol as the prevailing social lubricant. "All our functions were imbued with alcohol. It was romantic and fun and provided a lot of camaraderie. Drinking was part of being a medical student and was supported by everyone in the environment" (MD, age 50).

A physician who refrained from drinking in college couldn't resist in medical school. "Before starting college my dad said, 'They'll probably offer you alcohol, but I want you to know what it's like.' So he poured me several ounces of scotch, and I took great gulps that burned my throat. I coughed and sputtered and blew it out my nose and figured that if that is what alcohol is like, I'll drink Coke." In medical school, however, it was a different story:

> I think everyone in the fraternity house must have been alcoholic be-
> cause they were so methodical about the way they went about it. We
> had the longest bar on campus built behind a wall that looked like a
> furnace. We could cool four kegs of beer at a time and had rigged a
> device that could lift kegs of beer to the third floor and plug them into
> what had been the gaslights. Someone had replumbed the entire house
> so that through gravity we could feed cold beer into any room. Every
> Sunday morning the pledges were required to clean out the system.
> Drinking was the thing to do.   (MD, age 61)

Professional students trying to abstain from alcoholic drinks may
experience considerable peer pressure. "When I started medical
school in 1983," a physician recalled, "out of my class of 169, there
were no more than 5 other nondrinkers. As one of the nondrinking
students, I came under regular and frequent pressure from many
members of the freshmen class to drink alcohol when I attended
class events." This pressure, much greater than he had experienced
in high school or college, made him feel stressed and alienated.
When he approached the dean about having alcohol-free social
events, the latter laughed and predicted that social functions bereft
of alcohol would be poorly attended by the students and not supported by the alumni association (Bohlmann 1995).

Alcohol and drug users regard abstainers as "squares" and avoid
them. "I didn't hang around with classmates who weren't using,"
a nurse recalled (RN, age 40). "I had the choice to associate with
people who had healthier lifestyles," a physician admitted, "but I
avoided them and surrounded myself with 'cool' people" (MD, age
38).

Drinking expectations continue into postdoctoral training.
"When I was a resident," a physician remarked, "everyone in the
department was supposed to throw a party. They were always
pretty nice parties with lots of booze. When it came to one guy's
house, he had a nice dinner but only had wine. We were pissed off
because he didn't serve any good hootch" (MD, age 50).

A typology of origins to addiction, proposed by McAuliffe and
colleagues (1985), compares recreational, therapeutic, and instrumental users. *Recreational* addicts begin using drugs with friends on
social occasions to satisfy their curiosity and to be part of the group.
Therapeutic addicts begin drug use, usually at the direction of a physician or dentist, to relieve physical pain, but in some cases as self-

treatment, especially to cope with emotional pain. *Instrumental* drug use begins with the use of stimulants to relieve fatigue and improve performance. Among those in the health professions, McAuliffe (1984) notes, drugs are used for all three purposes, but recreational use of drugs other than alcohol is a recent phenomenon. A new type of physician addict has emerged, one addicted to such so-called recreational drugs as marijuana and cocaine.

Recreational drug use is also pervasive in other professional schools. "The group that I ran with drank all the time," an attorney said. "I thought those nuts that didn't drink were prudes; I looked at them with disdain" (JD, age 64). Drinking behavior in professional training often assumes a pattern. "My law school friends and I had a tradition," recalled another attorney. "On Friday nights we'd meet in this hotel and drink until the bar closed down" (JD, age 37). After heavy studying, another said, "we rewarded ourselves by drinking. It was our golden apple for working hard" (JD, age 54).

Happy hour becomes a daily habit for some student professionals. "The summer before I graduated I worked for a dentist who introduced me to scotch. We would work late, until 7 or 7:30 P.M.; then, when the last patient left, he'd haul down a bottle of Black & White. We would drink it warm with a tapwater chaser. I drank to excess that summer every day at happy hour" (DDS, age 67).

More than half of the schools that responded to a law school survey reported that alcohol is always or often served at faculty receptions. Eighty-three percent said it is sometimes served at joint student-faculty functions, but one-third reported that these practices had declined during the last ten years (Association of American Law Schools 1993).

Alcohol is virtually mandatory in some law practices. "To be accepted at the Firm, it seemed to me, one was required to drink and to drink heartily. One of the Firm's recruiting rituals back then was the 'whiskey test,' in which fresh-faced recruits were invited to drinks with the senior partners to see if they had the 'right stuff.' I passed with flying colors" ("A Hard Charging, Hard Drinking Trial Lawyer" 1989, p. 293).

Another attorney recalled, "When I was in law school, one of my heroes was a hard-living, hard-drinking attorney, and I wanted to be his protégé. I'd look at him and say, 'That's the way I want to be'" (JD, age 56). Another attorney asked rhetorically, "What is there about being an attorney that makes you more at risk for chemical dependency?"

> You can go to any city, large or small, and at the end of the day you will find the lawyers getting together at the bar, getting to know each other, exchanging views, talking about their cases. Drinking becomes part of their life. When attorneys get sober, one of the biggest things they miss is drinking martinis with the guys while talking shop about their work. We do that probably more than any other profession. You can go to some bars at 5:00 P.M. and find 90 percent of the people there are lawyers.   (JD, age 48)

Pilots who receive their training in the military routinely use alcohol for recreational purposes. "In my 12 years in the Marine Corps I drank—boy, did I drink! It was not only accepted; it was expected, almost required." "We always had happy hour every night. There was always a club somewhere that sold dime drinks, and you really couldn't afford not to drink," a pilot (age 58) explained. Another pilot (age 45) elaborated:

> Our squad skipper had a motto that "everything runs better on alcohol" and "we don't trust anybody who doesn't drink." If somebody in the squadron didn't drink, he was an outsider, a weirdo, an oddball, and a real troublemaker. We were encouraged, if not socially coerced, to abuse alcohol. It was a badge of courage to drink, and we thought it was funny when a guy would get hurt the next day or was a little bit slow getting off the target or something. "Look at his wings wobble," that kind of crap.

A Defense Department study concluded that the rate of heavy drinking in the military is nearly twice that of the civilian population. The military continues to sell cheap, untaxed liquor at base stores and to permit happy hours at clubs where drinks can be bought for as little as 25 cents (Wertsch 1992).

The entertainment media reinforce the perception that drinking and other recreational drug use is expected of successful professionals. The once-popular television show "M*A*S*H," for example, showed Hawkeye Pierce, the congenial, witty, compassionate, and skilled surgeon using humor and alcohol to cope with the strain of long hours in surgery amidst an endless stream of wounded and dying soldiers. He distilled spirits in his tent and served martinis in stemware near the battlefront. A heroic model of the hard-drinking physician, Hawkeye "deserved" to drink, and drinking never affected his technical competence. Who could criticize a hero for high-volume drinking when, with technical skill and compassion, he repeatedly saved the lives of young soldiers? Ironically, professional stature may be the biggest obstacle to recognizing that one has a drinking problem (Clark et al. 1987).

The infamous 1991 Tailhook convention—an annual three-day party where 4,000 Navy and Marine Corps aviation officers (including 25 admirals) consumed $33,500 worth of alcohol—illustrates the pathological outcome when drug abuse becomes institutionalized. After a seven-month investigation, 140 officers were disciplined for public lewdness, sexual assaults of at least 83 women, and other misconduct. According to a news account, many were so drunk by nine o'clock on the first night that "the hallway reeked of the smell of beer, urine, and vomit, but things were destined to get far uglier as the night wore on" (Kempster 1993, p. A1). Many of the younger officers who attended felt these excesses were condoned by the top brass since, despite significant misconduct at previous conventions, the Navy continued to support the Tailhook Association and its annual meeting.

Easy Access to Drugs

Alcoholic beverages and street drugs are readily accessible to most people, but professionals—especially health professionals—have much easier access to controlled substances.

HEALTH CARE PROFESSIONALS

A survey of 500 physicians and 504 medical students (McAuliffe et al. 1987) found that nearly all the physicians and 65 percent of the students have easy access to drugs. "I used to read the *Physicians' Desk Reference* like it was a novel," a physician reported. "I looked for new controlled drugs, and when I found one that sounded great, I would mail order 1,000 of them. I could order 1,000 barbiturates for 20 to 30 dollars. If I liked them I'd order 5,000. Access was no problem for me" (MD, age 38).

Some nurses consider easy access as part of their employee benefit package. Inventorying, stocking, and administering drugs and writing up their effects may seem to be permission to self-administer (Hallgren and Beach 1989). Inadequate monitoring of controlled substances facilitates stealing, and working in a critical care specialty surrounded with psychoactive drugs increases the likelihood of illicit drug use (Trinkoff and Storr 1994). An addicted operating-room nursing supervisor, responsible for monitoring medications, felt like a fox in the chicken coop. "My task was to check all the drugs. I worked very hard, but every chance I had I would sneak a little to make sure I had a supply for myself. I would fill all my little prescriptions and take a few pills for myself. It was very insidious, and I felt very guilty" (RN, age 70).

Easy access to drugs also contributes to chemical dependence among dentists. "It was a *big* influence, the one thing that I credit with sinking my boat," one remarked. "I might have been able to control my drug use if it hadn't been for such easy access to drugs. The cookie jar was there, and it was just too much temptation for me" (DDS, age 46). "I maintain to this day that if I hadn't had easy access to cocaine, I never would have become an addict," said another dentist (DDS, age 47).

Nitrous oxide, used to relax dental patients, appeals to the dentist for the same reason. "It is very tempting to use," a dentist remarked. "It leaves no odor and can be purchased in big enough quantities so that no one will notice 'just a little missing.' It's virtually impossible to detect in the bloodstream unless you catch someone in the act" (Donald A. Krzyzak quoted in Smith 1992, p. 8).

A clinical license greatly facilitates access. "When I got my dental license," a dentist confessed, "I was able to secure voluminous quantities of drugs, and I used them a lot" (DDS, age 49). "Demerol became my drug of choice, and there wasn't a day that I didn't use it," another remarked. "I just went over to the pharmacy and got it in bulk order" (DDS, age 46).

Drugs used for sedation and anesthesia are easily available to the dental surgeon. "I did surgery as a result of wanting to prescribe more drugs for myself and justify my use. The narcotics habit is no longer with me, thank God, but because of all my experience I now have the ability to do surgery" (DDS, age 49).

Most health care professionals do not have to exert themselves, since the drugs come to them in the form of free samples from pharmaceutical companies. "Drug reps are always coming around," a dentist reported, "so I could get whatever I wanted. I would never have gotten addicted to Demerol or Xanax or Halcion if they hadn't. I could easily have gotten addicted to cocaine—anybody can get cocaine—but I wouldn't have become addicted to these other drugs" (DDS, age 37).

"Eating the mail"—ingesting drug samples—is considered a career benefit by some addicts. "I never had to worry where my supply was coming from," a physician recalled. "I could always call up my pharmaceutical representative and get what I wanted; no questions asked" (American Pharmaceutical Association 1992, p. 14).

An older physician recalled his delight when, as a medical student, he attended a monthly meeting where pharmaceutical representatives touted their products. "In medical school we had a thing called 'Drug Day,' and we loved it! Once a month we would walk around the auditorium with a shopping bag, and the drug reps would give us samples. We would pick up some great stuff—Dexedrine, Ritalin—we loved that; it was wonderful! One of my addicted colleagues said, 'I owe everything I am or ever will be to Smith, Kline and French, who made Dexedrine' " (MD, age 50).

Nurses employed in physicians' offices also use the drugs provided by pharmaceutical representatives. "I worked for a doctor who had a back cabinet full of stuff provided by the reps who came around. You could just go in there and get whatever you wanted. I would tell the doctor, 'I can't get rid of this headache; I need something,' then I'd take whatever I wanted" (RN, age 42).

Stealing drug samples from colleagues also occurs. "When I was an intern, I used to steal people's free samples from their mail to get their amphetamines. The drug companies sent free samples of Dexedrine, and I ate them all. I'd never been away from home before. I was in a big city hospital, and I was pregnant. I didn't know what the hell was going on. Amphetamines saved my life" (MD, age 60).

"Pad power" is commonly used by clinicians to support their drug habits. "The availability of drugs is so easy, I could write myself a prescription for anything I wanted," a physician remarked. "An honest pharmacist would question it, but I would put somebody else's name on it. A pharmacist told me once not to put my family name on the prescription. 'You should always put somebody else's name on it,' he said" (MD, age 75).

It is much easier for nurses than for patients to obtain a doctor's prescription. Feigning illnesses such as urinary or kidney problems, headaches, or back pain, they simply ask physicians to write them prescriptions. "We are much freer than other people to medicate ourselves," said a nurse. "A doctor is much more free in giving medication to me than to someone she doesn't know. We just trust each other more" (RN, age 45). "We call them 'hall prescriptions,'" another nurse explained. "Just ask any M.D. in the hall, and he whips out his pad and, without asking any questions, writes a prescription" (RN, age 70).

A nurse may also steal the prescription pad and forge the physician's signature. "I forged more than 1,000 prescriptions and I was fired from six different hospitals before I was treated," one confessed. Another recovering nurse reported, "By the time I got treated, I was taking between 80 to 100 pills a day" (Jarvis 1984).

Stealing from patients takes many forms. "It's easier to cop a chemical in the ER than on the floor," a nurse noted, "because you can give a patient some Vicodin and keep half for yourself. It's so busy and loud and noisy in the ER; there isn't as much control as there is on the hospital floors" (RN, age 40). Other nurses dilute the drugs. "It is child's play to cut the pharmacy supply . . . and who is going to believe the patient who complains that his medication is not as strong as it used to be?" (Kendall 1987, p. 88; see also Beck and Buckley 1983).

This nurse finessed an ample drug supply by encouraging patients to request pain medication and then keeping half for herself.

> Some nurses would just walk in, flip the patient over, give the shot, and walk out. But I sat on the patient's bed and talked with them, showed interest in pictures of their family, asked if they wanted juice, gave them a back rub, and then said, "Would you like something for pain?" They would say, "Sure." Initially they got half and I would keep half, but then eventually I kept it all and gave them placebos. I helped them find relief by psychological suggestion, telling them that the drug was going to work in about 10 minutes, and it always did! I know it was crazy, but these people thought I was a fantastic nurse. One with a broken hip told me, "I want to tell you something, you are the only one that when I get a shot, it works. I think some of those other nurses are using my medication!"   (RN, age 56)

Clinicians who work in intensive care units, emergency rooms, and surgical suites are at particularly high risk to use narcotics such as Demerol and Fentanyl (Sullivan, Bissell, and Williams 1988; see also Pekkanen 1988). An anesthesiologist who worked in a surgery suite tied an IV tubing to his leg and attached it to an expandable bottle inside his sock. Working behind a surgical screen that separated him from the surgeons, "he would quickly and skillfully put a spritz of the drug into the catheter, and it would collect under his sock. If he worked on four surgery cases that morning, he would have enough to have a wonderful drug dinner plus a little extra," a colleague recalled.

The chair of a hospital committee that investigates impaired physicians told of an anesthesiologist who stole entire trays of 12 to 24 bottles. He would inject these drugs into a hidden container, and, when no one was looking, throw the empty bottles into an air-conditioning duct. He reasoned that a single vial would attract attention on an audit, but that if an entire tray was missing, they would assume an accounting error.

Hospitals have tightened their regulations, and stealing has become more difficult. But clever professionals still outwit these control procedures. "Now narcotics have to be signed out by two people. But if you look hard enough you can find another person who uses drugs, and they will cover up for you" (RN, age 37). An emergency room physician told how he and his cocaine-using associates kept themselves well supplied for several years by taking turns stealing vials of sheep's blood used in experiments from the hospital. Since the classic treatment for a nosebleed is to administer a 10 percent solution of cocaine to contract the capillaries, one would squirt the blood up his nose and walk into the emergency room with a "nosebleed." Then he took the cocaine solution to a deserted lab and evaporated the liquid, leaving pure crystallized cocaine. "There was a whole network of us, doctors at different hospitals," one said. "In fact, we worked it out so that one of us was always on emergency-room call during the weekends." When the cocaine was available, "the weekend festivities would begin. The party lasted for almost four years." Somebody finally caught on because the hospitals in the area were having to restock so much cocaine. "We were all amazed that it went on as long as it did" (Rosenblatt 1989, p. 10).

Since psychoactive drugs are stockpiled in pharmacies, employment there for an addict is like being a kid in a candy store. Circumventing auditing procedures is particularly easy when the pharmacist owns or manages the drugstore. "There wasn't anyone looking over my shoulder," one explained (PharmD, age 46). "I was completely on my own," another added. "As director of a hospital pharmacy in a major metropolitan area, I had the power of attorney to give narcotics. I just didn't sign them into stock when they came in. I used to order cocaine by the ounce. Two ounces at a time, one for me and one for the hospital. One time I used 20 grams in two days" (PharmD, age 45).

A pharmacist described how skillful he became in manipulating others:

> I stole thousands of Percodan tablets, a Schedule II drug that must be prescribed and accounted for each and every day. I was good with people. I made friends with the inspectors, and when they came around I said, "I know where the records are, and I'll get them the next time you come." When they discovered a discrepancy, they didn't report it. The company doesn't want to let the DEA know that they were so lax that some punk stole for five years and they didn't know it. So they kept it a secret. (PharmD, age 41)

Addicts hide these drugs strategically so they can easily access them. A pharmacist kept a large stash in his car's trunk.

> On one occasion I was working for three different pharmacies, and one Saturday night a woman came in with a prescription for Dilaudid. She needed four milligrams for her mother, who was a terminally ill cancer patient. They were going away for the weekend. It was late at night, and nobody else was open, and we had only a couple of tablets in the safe. The woman was upset, and I said, "Hold on. Let me see what I can do." I went out the back door, went to my car, and filled her prescription from my car. I had 100 or more from one of the other stores. I remember thinking to myself, "See, patient care still comes first." (PharmD, age 38)

Easy drug availability attracts some drug users into pharmaceutical careers. "Pharmacy is a nice profession, a good career," one acknowledged, "but I chose pharmacy not just for these reasons. I thought to myself, 'Wow, what a great way to get all of these things that make you feel so terrific!'" (PharmD, age 45).

A pharmacy student discovered that he could trade stolen drugs for anything he needed. "While in school, I worked in the pharmacy and could steal cough syrup with codeine and a little meprobamate or other drugs and sell it to the junkies in the neighborhood for marijuana. We had a little exchange" (PharmD, age 47).

Others barter sex for drugs.

> When I first got to nursing school I went to this obstetrician who gave me a drug for cramps. He never said, "I will give you this drug if you give me sex," but it worked out that way. I would call him for frequent refills because it made me feel good and got me up in the morning. I would always make my appointment with him the last of the day. I felt very powerful in doing this.   (RN, age 42)

OTHER PROFESSIONALS

Many attorneys have the contacts and the funds to buy drugs. "Everywhere I went, it [cocaine] was there," an addicted lawyer said (Silas 1987, p. 13). Attorneys who defend drug dealers are particularly at risk. "My source for cocaine was a guy from Colombia who decided it would be a good idea to have a lawyer on retainer. If you do criminal work like I do, you have easy access to drugs" (JD, age 49).

Sometimes large drug caches from drug raids are available.

> I woke up one morning after a blackout and found a valise in front of me with thousands of pills in it. I frankly didn't know how they had got there. First I thought that a dentist friend of mine had felt sorry for me and brought me these pills. I finally figured out where the pills came from because some of them were in little evidence pouches to be used in evidence in court. I had taken them from the property room at the county court house when I was in a blackout. Every time I saw a judge of that court, he would ask, "How'd you get into my property room?" The room has a very, very complicated lock, and you aren't supposed to be able to get in, and I don't know how I did, but I did.   (JD, age 47)

He was arrested when the judge noticed him "bouncing off the walls." "They called me in, the police came over, and in about two hours they had their man. A real easy crime to solve, but they are still trying to figure out how I did it." Using temporary insanity as a defense, he was found not guilty by a jury when his attorney convinced them that a proficient trial attorney would never participate in such a crime unless he was crazy

Alcohol is easily accessible to pilots. "In the state where I lived," one reported, "I had to drive 45 minutes from my home to get a bottle. So when I laid over in D.C. I would buy it by the case. I've had many FAA inspectors ride on my jump seat sitting on three cases of booze clearly evident in a plain brown wrapper and not realize what it was. I told them it was some very expensive books I was taking to the university library" (pilot, age 57).

Passenger aircraft provide an easy source of alcoholic drinks. "It's very easy for a flight attendant to bring up a little bag with a couple of miniatures in it," one pilot (age 57) explained. "It used to happen quite often. If a layover was to be an extended one, it was the cabin attendants' function to steal as much as they possibly could so that we didn't have to buy any."

Some pilots plan their flight schedules around their alcohol access. A pilot (age 54) who had served in Operation Desert Storm reported, "We had an airplane take off from Saudi at the end of the war, a 747 with some 400 troops who had been down there for almost a year. When they blew an engine right after takeoff en route to Rome, the captain said, 'Where to now?' 'Where do they have the beer?' Someone said, 'Cairo,' so they flew to Cairo. You can be sure they weren't going back to where there wasn't any beer."

Pilots who fly internationally can purchase drugs that require a prescription in this country. "I was a daily drinker, and my anxieties were a problem. But I found a cure for that in Europe; they sell medications over the counter that include Valium and Librium. It was a great way to get over a case of the shakes" (pilot, age 53).

Pharmacological Optimism

Most Americans, accustomed to "miracle drugs," accept drug therapy uncritically. "Much of our population is conditioned to think that the first moment of mental, physical or emotional discomfort is a signal for instant pharmaceutical treatment," a pharmacist remarked (Spierer 1986). "I grew up believing the Du Pont slogan, 'Better Living through Chemistry,'" said another pharmacist. "I thought that knowledge of chemicals was the answer to everything. If I knew how to use chemicals, they would help me, and I could achieve anything I wanted" (PharmD, age 47).

In his book *The New Industrial State*, economist John Kenneth Galbraith (1971) pointed out that, with the rise of twentieth-century industrial capitalism, the economic sequence changed. Previously a company first determined which products were wanted by the public, and then produced and advertised those products. Now giant corporations reverse the sequence. They first determine which products represent maximum long-term profitability, and then develop the product and conduct mass-media advertising campaigns to stimulate a public perception of need for those products. The pharmaceutical industry is a prime example. During the 1950s and 1960s this industry created psychotropic drugs and then marketed them. Ever-expanding advertising budgets produced geometrically increasing sales.

Prescription drugs are a $21.2-billion-a-year industry. Today's clinician can prescribe 400,000 different drugs (Furtado 1992). For the past thirty years the drug manufacturers of the Fortune 500 have enjoyed the fattest profits in big business. Drug companies funnel hundreds of millions of dollars into research and development (typically 15 percent of revenues) and spend up to twice as much on sales and marketing. In 1990 Americans paid some $50 billion for prescriptions, compared with $150 billion for cars and $100 billion for computers. The rest of the world paid $120 billion for prescription drugs (O'Reilly 1991, pp. 48, 50).

If miracle drugs like sulfa and penicillin can eradicate devastating diseases, new "wonder drugs" may alleviate vicissitudes of daily life. Bernstein and Lennard (1973) call this marketing approach "medicalization of the human condition." "People are less and less willing to accept pain and anguish as natural concomitants of living, and have come to expect medicine to end all personal suffering." Drug manufacturers have convinced the public that human suffering is a medical disease. Clinicians and the public have been persuaded to think first of chemical solutions—sedatives for sleeplessness rather than social or psychological help, laxatives for constipation rather than diet change, and so on. Once a problem is considered a "disease," the next step is to think of drugs as a cure (Bernstein and Lennard 1973). Interestingly, the National Institute on Alcohol Abuse and Alcoholism (NIAAA) supports research leading to pharmacological solutions to alcoholism (Gordis 1995).

Pharmacological companies woo and propagandize physicians, "gatekeepers of the legal drug industry" (Seidenberg 1971), through frequent mailings and visits by pharmaceutical representatives and free samples. Each year the pharmaceutical industry spends upward of $5 billion to market drugs to U.S. doctors—about $8,000 apiece (Whitaker 1991). The pharmaceutical industry realizes that physicians determine whether their products profit or perish.

The success of this marketing strategy is phenomenal. Wholesale prices for new drugs are three to six times the manufacturing cost; a yearly supply of a drug that costs only $50 to produce may be sold to a druggist for $300. Marketers estimate that if a pharmaceutical representative calls on about forty physicians, and one puts a single patient on a given drug, the profits will cover the salesperson's salary (O'Reilly 1991).

Questionable selling practices also occur. In 1987, for example, American Home Products offered physicians points for airline tickets to prescribe Inderal, a medication for blood pressure, when far cheaper generic drugs were available. Critics dubbed it "the Frequent Prescriber Plan." In December 1990 the American Medical Association issued guidelines that discouraged doctors from availing themselves of costly gifts from pharmaceutical companies (O'Reilly 1991).

Medical students are also marketing targets. Sharfstein (1993) points out that "the pharmaceutical industry spends hundreds of thousands, if not millions, of dollars each year for medical students." He describes the "goodies" they provided at a 1993 American Medical Student Association meeting, from luggage tags to free meals.

The industry makes taking drugs easy and enjoyable. In 1994 a pharmaceutical company produced a raspberry-flavored Fentanyl "lollipop." Twenty or 30 times more potent than morphine, this FDA-approved Schedule II narcotic is primarily used as a preoperative medication. It is also the most popular drug for addicted anesthesiologists (Public Citizen Health Research Group 1994a).

During the 1950s and 1960s, when many currently practicing health professionals received their training, psychoactive drugs were used in hospitals to keep patients content. "I went into nursing in the 1950s, when we used a lot more narcotics than we do today. It seemed like no matter what the patient would say, there was always a medication ordered. Drugs were used to make them comfortable. This affected my thinking through all the years that followed" (RN, age 56).

An anesthesiologist learned the importance of keeping patients comfortable.

During my sophomore year in med school we spent mornings at the hospital in physical diagnosis and pharmacology. Four of us were talking one day with the professor about the differential diagnosis on a patient. The interns and residents wouldn't tell us the diagnosis, and we were supposed to figure it out for ourselves. He asked if we had given the patient any medicine to keep him comfortable. We said, "No, we wouldn't do that." He said, "Look, the patient doesn't give a damn about what's wrong with him, he just wants to be comfortable; you have to give him something." That was the attitude taught in medical school: keep your patients comfortable. That's what I carried away from medical school. (MD, age 75)

Seeing patients benefit psychologically from drugs, emotionally taxed clinicians may take the next step and self-administer. "If I am giving medication and it helps the patient," a nurse reasoned, "then I can take it myself, because it will help me too" (RN, age 42). Another nurse said, "We are taught that drugs are a cure for physical and emotional problems. So if you are hurting at work, the cure is right there available to you. Before you know it, you are addicted" (RN, age 70). According to a pharmacist, "I'd see these people come into the pharmacy every week or so to get 100 Percodan, and I would rationalize, 'They're taking it, and look at them, they're doing alright.' So I figured it was alright for me too. What I didn't admit is that they had terminal cancer and I didn't" (PharmD, age 46).

But self-treatment and rationalization escalate. "If one will work, then two will work better," a nurse reasoned (RN, age 56). "I had a fool for a doctor and a fool for a patient," admitted a self-medicating physician who called himself "Doctor Feelgood" (MD, age 38).

Some drug-prescribing professionals inadvertently addict their family members. "My mother was a doctor and treated me with amphetamines," a physician reported, "and for 25 years they allowed me to function the way I thought I should" (MD, age 60). A nurse working in her physician husband's medical office became chemically dependent with her husband's "help."

At the office one evening we had 23 patients stacked in the waiting room and I had an extremely bad migraine. Every time the phone rang, I threw up. My husband said, "You can't leave now, because there's no one else to fill in for you. Come on back, and I'll give you something." He took me into a treatment room and gave me 100 milligrams of Demerol IV. Needless to say, my headache went away and I felt great! I felt immediate euphoria. I completed my work and didn't think anymore about it. Later I woke up one morning with no pain but told him that I needed a shot of Demerol. It was like my life depended on it; I couldn't think of anything else. The only way I could function was if I could have a shot right now! I got it, and the need became greater and greater. He was an unwilling supplier, and we had terrible arguments. He gave it to me just to shut me up. I started stealing it from him, and it got very, very difficult for us both.   (RN, age 56)

Ignorance and Misinformation

Surprisingly few professionals understand the dynamics of addiction, and this naiveté may contribute to the addiction of some. Although it debilitates so many of their clients and colleagues, most receive little or no training about substance abuse. "Believe it or not, they teach medical students and nurses more about the diseases in Africa than they do about addiction and alcoholism. It's beginning to change, but it's far from there" (RN, age 56). "Everything I've learned about addiction, I've had to learn the hard way," a nurse commented. "I didn't get any training at all. When I spoke to alumni of the recovery center and told them that they know more about addiction than the average doctor coming out of medical school, it blew them away" (RN, age 40).

Typical undergraduate nursing programs provide only two to four hours on addiction, and some offer no information at all.[2] "Substance abuse education?" a nurse asked. "We never had any of that; I didn't even know what it was" (RN, age 56). "I don't remember ever hearing any mention about this in my classes," another lamented (RN, age 67). Said another: "They promote the view that nursing students don't need to know this sort of stuff" (RN, age 42).

Correct information about drugs, especially alcohol, might prevent some from escalating into chemical dependence. "Alcohol was doing a lot of damage to me, but I wasn't aware of it," a nurse said. "If I had known that alcohol was a drug, I might have been a lot more careful. I regarded it like Coca-Cola" (RN, age 70).

Ignorance also pervades other professions. Most dentists practicing today received no instruction on addiction.[3] "We had absolutely nothing," one complained. "Nothing like this was available when I was going through. It was total ignorance. If it had been available, it would probably have changed a number of us before we got into the active phase of the disease" (DDS, age 45). "It definitely would have helped me," another remarked (DDS, age 37); "I would have known what to look for and to see what I was falling into." (See also Tucker, Gurnee, and Sylvestria 1988; Spencer-Stachen 1990.) Uninformed professionals fail to recognize addiction's developmental signs and symptoms in themselves. "I never thought I was a drug addict," another dentist explained. "It never even crossed my mind. I thought if I had a problem, I could handle it by switching drugs. I'd just switch if I thought I was getting addicted" (DDS, age 37).

Pharmacists likewise receive little training on addiction. Typically what instruction they do get takes the form of an occasional lecture sandwiched into another demanding course. Such arrangements convey the impression that the topic is of peripheral or no significance. "The topic is critically important," a pharmacist declared, "but we just had a smattering of it. It's important not only for the pharmacist as a pharmacist, but for him/her as a person as well" (PharmD, age 49).

Until recently, medical education mostly ignored substance abuse (Lewis et al. 1987). "Contrary to what may be expected," Miller and Gold (1988, p. 46) state, "education and curricula in medical schools are gravely and dangerously inadequate regarding alcohol and drug problems."[4] Consequently, many physicians share society's negative stereotypes of drug abusers, reinforced by unpleasant emergency room experiences with chronic late-stage alcoholics of the "skid row" variety. "The way substance abuse was presented to me as a medical student," a physician recalled, "was that addicts and alcoholics are low-lifers, not diseased people" (MD, age 50). Attending physicians and house staff make pejorative comments about "junkies" and "winos." "Alky-bum," "yellow-bellied sapsucker," "yellow balloon," and "pumpkin" are a few of the slang terms used by physicians to refer to alcoholic patients (Coombs et al. 1993).

"This marks the thirtieth anniversary of my graduation from one of the top medical schools in this country," Canavan (1983) remarked.

> In the four years I spent there, I cannot remember a single lecture on the subjects of alcoholism or drug addiction . . . It became increasingly apparent to me that most of my fellow physicians were just as ignorant as I had been for this very same reason. The world's most sophisticated system of medical education "missed the boat" in preparing its students to understand, accept, recognize, and to treat the diseases of substance abuse.

An expert pilot examiner, a physician with 30 years of clinical and administrative experience with addicts, described his do-it-yourself training.

> I hadn't learned anything in medical school, so I tried approaching it from a common sense point of view. As an intern, I came into the ER urging those who were drunk to quit drinking, and they all promised to. I concluded it was very easy working with alcoholics. Next weekend, though, they were back in the ER drunk again and in worse condition. I had read in that great medical journal, *Reader's Digest,* that AA is a good organization, so I went there to learn what I could. At my first meeting I came in my white uniform and noticed people milling around a coffee urn in the corner of the room in the basement of a church. They didn't look like the alcoholics I'd seen in the ER, so I thought it was a Bible class. Someone noticed me standing at the door and asked if I was an alcoholic. I said, "No I'm not" in the same tone of voice my patients use when I ask them that question. I thought to myself, "Maybe you are an alcoholic and don't know it. You've been drunk at frat parties and New Year's Eve." So I listened very carefully—and it was a turning point in my life. I realized addiction is a whole field that I knew absolutely nothing about. I kept going back to learn.

Few pilots have more than a street knowledge of alcohol and its effects.[5] "I didn't have a good understanding of alcoholism," one pilot (age 50) reported. "Like the general public, I used to believe that addiction was a lack of moral character. In my heart of hearts, I believed that anybody with an ounce of guts could quit drinking if he wanted to."

Moreover, pilots have little faith in their flight surgeons' knowledge. "They get one afternoon of education in six or eight years of training, and if they slept through that one, they missed it all," a pilot (age 45) complained. "If they saw any drunks in medical school, they were ones that came off the streets. They never sat down with an alcoholic who has a white shirt and tie. Yet they think they can play a critical role with pilots. In my view, all flight surgeons should be addictionologists trained in this field and receive continuing education in addiction medicine to keep their licenses."

Most recovering addicts feel that there should be better professional school education. "They ought to have a law school course dealing with alcohol and drug problems," an attorney asserted. "My thinking is, the further upstream we can put this message out, the better off we will be" (JD, age 41).

Students often seem more open to instruction than their professors. "There are a lot of egghead professors out there," an attorney observed, "who really don't want to hear anything about personal behavior because they think they have the right to be alcoholic or drug dependent. When I go into their schools, some of them challenge me. I tell them that they aren't doing their students a favor by belittling this message" (JD, age 44). "A lot of the older nurses don't want to hear about chemical dependency," a nurse agreed. "Last year I spoke at a national convention where there were 185 nurses in the room listening to the previous speaker. When they announced my topic, about 100 of them got up and left. When I speak to student nurses and tell them about alcoholics and drug addiction, the students listen, but we need to get our older nurses to listen" (RN, age 70).

In Perspective

Professionals are exposed like others to societal influences that glamorize and normalize the use of alcohol and other drugs. But because they have very easy access to drugs, a lifestyle that encourages overwork, and an indoctrination process that promotes drug solutions to most human problems, they are more at risk of abusing substances. We expect professionals to be better informed about addiction than others, and to use their knowledge to assist and protect us, their clients and patients, as well as themselves. But until recently, professionals have been no better informed or educated about addiction's dynamics than those they serve.

Professionals are waking up to the need to educate their students.[6] In 1990 the American Bar Association's Commission on Impaired Attorneys recommended that a substance abuse lecture be part of the continuing education of each bar and the curriculum of each law school (Spilis 1995).[7] However, an attorney commented, "Because law professors are neither trained nor comfortable on how to do this, it rarely gets taught. What they ought to do is several times a year bring in professionals who are recovering to give concrete information and tell real-life stories" (JD, age 54).

And indeed, this approach is increasingly being used in law schools and other professional training centers. A pharmacist reports, "My wife and I do a two-hour presentation to the second-year pharmacy students, and many of them say that this is the first time they've been exposed to this. Their evaluations are extremely positive, and they want more information about the subject. It's really important for them to get some information along these lines" (PharmD, age 44).

Drug education often prevents abuse. When the University of Kentucky College of Dentistry implemented a 16-hour curriculum component on alcoholism and other drug dependencies, participating students, especially those at high risk, significantly reduced their drug use. The program had a positive impact on all participating students, but it had the greatest impact on those with a positive family history of alcoholism (Sammon, Smith, and Cooper 1991).[8]

The time is long overdue for the professions to take a leadership role with regard to drug problems in America.

FIVE

Developmental Stages

"The doctor prescribed Vicoden for headache. The damn things would sing to me from the drawer!"

(JD, age 41)

"I had a full-time job as nursing supervisor in charge of 30 positions and was responsible for patients' lives. Then when I came home I was supposed to be a super wife and a great mom. I didn't do a very good job of it, so I drank to escape. On the way home I stopped at a small grocery store, bought a pint of vodka, and went to the country club parking lot. I leaned under the dash so I wouldn't be seen and drank out of the paper bag. It would hit me by the time I came home. Toward the end, every night was a blackout."

(RN, age 37)

"At first alcohol was my ally that kept me from being overwhelmed by my practice. Actually it was just the opposite, but I didn't realize it. In the end it doublecrossed me; it turned on me. I thought alcohol was my friend, my buddy; but it turned into my enemy"

(JD, age 56)

Addiction never springs into full-blown existence at first use; physical and psychological dependence evolve developmentally. The typical stages are initiation, escalation, maintenance, discontinuation, relapse, and recovery (Coombs, Fry, and Lewis 1976; Coombs 1981a; Coombs and Coombs 1988). Some addicts relapse many times, while others bypass relapse altogether and remain clean and sober.

Initiation

Drug initiation typically involves three realities (Coombs 1981a). First, experimentation usually begins in adolescence—during junior and senior high school or the first years of college. Second, it is almost always a social experience; initiates rarely use drugs alone. Third, use of alcohol, marijuana, and tobacco—called "gateway drugs"—typically precedes the use of so-called hard drugs.

The interviews conducted for this book confirm these generalizations. Only 11.9 percent of the professionals began using before age 12; the large majority (84.1 percent) began in early or late adolescence. Only a few late bloomers (4.0 percent) did not begin until professional school.

Alcohol was the first drug for nearly everyone. Many were first exposed to alcohol in their parental homes and were initially given alcohol or other drugs by their parents, family, or friends as a gesture of interpersonal warmth and sociability. A friendly gathering, at home or with peers, was the most likely setting.

INITIATION AT HOME

Some naive parents encourage their children to use alcoholic beverages. "My parents thought it was a nice novelty to give the kids a little drink and watch them get silly, not realizing the potential hazards and dangers," a pharmacist commented (PharmD, age 45). "My parents promoted it," a nurse recalled. "There was a lot of alcohol in our house, and they told me, 'If you are going to drink, drink at home.' So we did" (RN, age 37).

Through gradual exposure, such children may develop a taste for alcohol. "When I was six or seven my father gave me little sips of beer," an attorney said. "I clearly recall liking the taste" (JD, age 37). Another attorney explained:

> I come from a family that always has alcohol available. I can remember being in my bed and knowing that I liked the taste of beer very much. I remember listening for my father to go down the hall with a bottle of beer and timing my cry so that he would come in, pick me up, take me into the living room, put me on the couch between him and my mother, and give me sips of beer. Of course, he had no knowledge that this was in any way harmful to me.   (JD, age 41)

Serving alcoholic drinks at family socials and holidays reinforces the pleasure of drinking. "I had my first drink—wine—as a very young child at Thanksgiving dinner," recalled a pharmacist. "I thought it was a very grown-up thing to do. Saturday night, the big dinner meal of the house, was very traditional, very dysfunctional, and very alcoholic" (PharmD, age 49).

Wine served at religious holidays and ceremonies adds mystique to the encounter with drug use. A pharmacist reminisced, "When I was six or seven I had a glass of wine at a Passover seder, and I remember the feeling, 'Boy, this is wonderful!' It allowed me to feel free, to get outside of myself and to just be like other folks there. It made me feel really giddy and silly, and I just loved it" (PharmD, age 45).

The medicine cabinet is another drug source. "My mom had quite a few prescription drugs, and that was my access," a nurse remarked (RN, age 40). "She didn't know I was using them until she found me 'meditating' flat on my back on the floor."

Some parents inadvertently launch their children's drug careers by medicating them. "When I was a child between the ages of 5 and 10, my parents gave me phenobarbital to sleep," a dentist recalled. "Later, when I got to dental school, I used to take a stiff drink before bedtime to help me sleep" (DDS, age 55). Health professionals, likely to have drugs around the house, may unwittingly teach their children to rely on chemicals to solve problems. "We always had drugs around because my mother [a nurse] would bring them home from the hospital. If you had pain or wanted to sleep, there was always a pill available" (RN, age 42). A dentist described his introduction to narcotics:

> My father, a physician, gave me Demerol for pain when I had a root canal. After the shot, I had an out-of-body experience in which I was totally elevated and the pain was completely gone. It left a marked impression on me. Later he gave me an injection of Demerol after nose surgery, and I had the same profound experience. It made me feel good about myself, and I hung on the buzzer to get more narcotics. Later, in college, I was able to get my friend, a pharmacist, to give me Demerol tablets. They made me euphoric, gave me a warm glow that was highly pleasurable.   (DDS, age 49)

The most extreme case of parental involvement was reported by a dentist who, at age 17, used cocaine with his father. "I used to freebase with my dad. He was a physician who had lost his license because of his drug addiction. We used to freebase together, shoot drugs together. We were a pretty sick family" (DDS, age 37).

INITIATION WITH PEERS

Drinking with friends is common during adolescence. Parties during junior and senior high school and college typically include alcohol and other drugs. Teenagers often perceive drugs as the key to popularity. One noted: "The only people at my school who were popular and who everybody knew, were people who were using" (Smith 1994, p. E1). Self-conscious youngsters' worst fear is to be socially ostracized and to stand out as different. Joining in with peers who use alcohol and other drugs helps adolescents fit in. "Everybody else was drinking, and I wanted to be part of that and to belong," a nurse explained. "It was important to let my friends know that I could drink" (RN, age 35). At this stage, the social high that comes from being accepted by peers is much more important than the chemical high that comes from the drug's effect. "The thing I liked best about it was fitting in with the crowd," a pharmacist recalled. "I had been going to dances for 6 or 12 months by myself and standing against the wall. So when some guys said they were going out to get beer I said, 'Sure, what the hell.' It wasn't the buzz I enjoyed as much as the feeling of being part of the gang" (PharmD, age 26). This need to fit in, to appear "cool," was cited over and over again by professionals recalling their earliest experiences with drugs.

Those emotionally wounded by pathological parenting quickly learn that alcohol numbs their battered self-esteem. "I had a hard time feeling that I amounted to much, and alcohol took away that feeling," a dentist explained (DDS, age 67). As if by magic, alcohol transforms acutely self-conscious and introverted teenagers into outgoing, gregarious, confident people. "I was a shy kid, and alcohol let me be funny, witty, and part of the crowd," an attorney recalled (JD, age 37).

Drug-using activities also provide adventure. Drinking parties offer fun and excitement. "Boredom was the trigger for me most often," an attorney recalled. "I was always looking for something to make me happy" (JD, age 48). A nurse said, "I enjoyed the challenge of not getting caught, sneaking cigarettes and so on" (RN, age 42).

Demonstrating independence from parental control is another motivation for teenage drug use. "My home life was one of religious rigidity," a nurse complained. "Lots of rules, and lots of discipline. I was eager to get away from it, so I went as far away as I could for college. That's where I had my first real exposure to alcohol" (RN, age 42).

Collegiate social life, centering upon alcoholic beverages and other drugs, can introduce those not already exposed to the drug scene. "I was a latecomer to alcohol," an attorney reported. "My folks didn't drink, and it wasn't until I was in college that I had much exposure" (JD, age 61). "My first exposure was when I started college and drank at fraternity parties," a pharmacist recalled. "I was away from the family and had the freedom to drink. I had the feeling that this was the answer, and I drank at every opportunity" (PharmD, age 46).

Escalation

Looking back on the course of their addiction, professionals perceive initiation not as a single point in time, but as a period during which they used drugs only occasionally. Escalation—increasing use of and preoccupation with different drugs and association with other users—does not begin immediately after first use, but when use becomes more frequent.

As in the initiation stage, drug use occurs mostly in social settings. As favorable attitudes toward drugs develop, so does physiological tolerance. "The first time, I drank I was very ill, and I thought to myself, 'I don't like this and I'm not going to do it again,'" an attorney remarked. "The second time, though, I was not as sick" (JD, age 42). "I gradually progressed to doing hallucinogens and smoking marijuana. Initially it was just on the weekends, but as my comfort level grew, I allowed myself to have fun with it and could do more and more during the week. I got over the initial fear that this is wrong or I might get caught; it just didn't matter." Once escalation began, nine out of ten (89.4 percent) of the 66 professionals who provided this information were addicted within 10 years—more than half (56.1 percent) within 5 years, 33.3 percent within 6 to 10 years, 7.6 percent within 11 to 15 years, and 3.0 percent within 16 to 20 years.

The escalating nature of addiction is readily apparent. One pharmacist recalled, "It started off in small quantities from time to time and increased to daily and to larger quantities until it brought me to my knees" (PharmD, age 43). Usually drug escalation is gradual.

"It was just a natural progression," another pharmacist said, "a linear development that went up in a stepwise manner a notch at a time. Each year it got worse and worse" (PharmD, age 45).

The variety of substances ingested also escalates. "When I was in college I didn't drink every day," an attorney commented, "but in law school I started drinking every day—a quart of beer, a six-pack, everyday stuff. On an ascending scale, I used first beer, then liquor, and later on barbiturates and/or amphetamines" (JD, age 47). "I started doing drugs as a teenager by smoking pot," a physician reported.

> The dishwasher in the restaurant where I worked as a busboy turned me on to speed. It was perfect because it helped me work faster. From there it was one drug after another; I progressed to acid, barbiturates, amphetamines. When I got to college I discovered "ludes," and when the FDA got wise and dried up the "ludes," I started drinking again. I became a walking garbage can, taking anything I could find. I took PCP, heroin, coke, and even some "brain solvent" that I found out was chloroform. I did everything; you name it, I tried it. Then when I became a doctor, it got *really* bad.   (MD, age 38)

Clinicians' access to drugs facilitates experimentation with a wide variety of substances. "I had a license and insisted on trying every drug I gave to my patients," a dentist said. "I tried Percodan, Demerol, Halcion, Xanax—whatever I gave a patient. I wanted to make sure I experienced what they would experience" (DDS, age 37).

PERCEIVING DRUG USE AS NORMAL

At this stage users regard drinking and drugging as entirely normal behavior, a healthy recreational outlet. A pharmacist observed, "I didn't think there was anything abnormal about drinking and using marijuana during evenings and weekends because that's what the people I was associating with were doing" (PharmD, age 41). "I disdained those who didn't drink as prudes," an attorney recalled (JD, age 41).

Intoxication is admired in some circles. "When I began drinking," a physician remembered, "I didn't realize you weren't supposed to get intoxicated. I thought everybody got intoxicated every time they drank and that was the reason they drank. I had no idea that alcohol was only part of the event. For me it was *the* event, and it didn't matter where I was or what I was doing" (MD, age 46). A pharmacist explained, "In my first year of pharmacy school I didn't really think anything was wrong with a pharmacist's drinking, smoking pot, doing cocaine, and dropping acid and using mushrooms. I can remember at the time thinking, 'When am I going to grow out of this? When am I going to chill out?' Then I decided, 'I guess it's not going to be now, so I won't worry about it' " (PharmD, age 26).

At this stage, drug users feel little or no concern for how substances might impair them and damage their future. "I can remember becoming intoxicated with a number of physician friends," a doctor recalled. "We all thought that if we separated our personal from our professional lives it would be okay to go out and get drunk. We convinced ourselves that it was appropriate behavior" (MD, age 45).

SEEKING SOCIAL REWARDS

During the initiation stage, users discover that alcohol and other gateway drugs relieve inhibitions and discomfort. During escalation they increasingly use them to help succeed socially. "Socializing and being with friends was a major problem for me in high school," a dentist commented, "but when I drank it allowed me to feel at ease in situations where I normally wouldn't have felt that way" (DDS, age 43). Drug-using activities also provide participants with a conversational topic, a social ritual they can discuss. "It enabled me socially by giving me something to talk about and do," an attorney remarked (JD, age 40).

In the escalation stage, social rewards greatly outweigh the unpleasant consequences of using. Participants simply keep trying until they "master the art of social drinking," as one put it. "When I was at a college party," he reported, "I was deathly afraid to try drugs. But my need to be part of the crowd compelled me to try them. My absolute horror and fear was outweighed by the social need" (MD, age 35).

A pilot who experienced a blackout after his first drinking experience at a teenage beach party avoided drinking for a while. But he kept trying. "I was a member of the college crew team, and we used to return from rowing to a big refrigerator filled with beer. I would have a beer and get sick, but I was determined to learn how to drink" (pilot, age 62).

A variety of other drugs are used at professional schools. "All through law school, we smoked a lot of reefers and hashish and drank wine," an attorney recalled (JD, age 49). "In medical school we had great nitrous oxide parties," a physician said. "It was a lot of fun; all the auditory and visual distortions made us laugh. When we used coke I felt like Superman, like I could jump over a house. It was the best feeling I ever had in my life" (MD, age 41).

SEEKING PSYCHOLOGICAL REWARDS

"Magic," a term used to describe a drug's initial psychological benefit, entices users to try it again and again. A pharmacist recalled, "The first time I used the drug and magic was there, was after I graduated from pharmacy school. I tried a new morphine tablet that made me feel euphoric. I don't know any better way to explain it than to say that the magic was there" (PharmD, age 45). "When I discovered cocaine," a nurse reported, "I just went crazy. It was wonderful! I thought I had gone to heaven" (RN, age 40).

Escalating users increasingly turn to chemicals to feel adequate, to mask unhappy feelings, to impart energy, to facilitate valued activities, and to foster feelings of success. A pilot (age 48) explained, "It was like a tranquilizer for my emotions. Instead of dealing with the problems that I had and was afraid to handle, I drank."

More and more, escalating users become psychologically dependent on these chemical "friends" to help them deal with life's challenges. "It was a nice lubricant for my social scene and got me through law school," an attorney said. "I would study three, four, or five hours a day and then reward myself by having a few beers. But at the end of law school I was studying for a couple of hours or less and drinking for several hours—many hours" (JD, age 47).

At this stage, psychoactive drugs begin to offer other "benefits." Stimulants help beleaguered students increase their energy and facilitate their work performance. "When I went to college," a physician recalled, "it was no challenge at all. So I wouldn't study until the last week of the semester. Then I'd buy as much speed as I needed to get through, hole up in a study cubicle for a week, and cram like crazy. I aced everything and ended up magna cum laude and Phi Beta Kappa" (MD, age 38). Drugs are also used to induce sleep. "My drinking accelerated when I couldn't sleep," a pilot (age 50) commented. "I stopped drinking socially and started drinking alone and for a purpose—to go to sleep at night. But I built up an immunity to the chemical and needed more and more of it to get the job done."

A physician escalated his use when he learned that drugs relieved his physical pain and gave him an emotional boost.

> The last three months of my residency was a very uncomfortable, very worrisome time. When I took this medicine, not only did my headache and backache go away; I was unshakable. I could have patients crashing in the unit and every other kind of problem, but I was cool and didn't worry about my ability or my patients. The thing that was missing from my life had been found. I figured that everyone else felt this way naturally. After a while, I was taking the liquid equivalent of 70 milliliters of pain medication a day. I was writing prescriptions for myself all over town.   (MD, age 35)

Maintenance

When addiction occurs, all other life activities become secondary to drugs. Psychologically dependent addicts, obsessively preoccupied with and compulsively driven by drugs, often resort to deceitful behavior and coverups. As drug tolerance increases, the addict's goal shifts from feeling high to just feeling normal. The fabric of life unravels as the drug becomes betrayer.

Addiction can occur at almost any age. In our study population it ranged from ages 14 to 50. Of the 74 professionals interviewed who provided this information, 17.1 percent became addicted before their twenty-first birthday; 23.7 at age 21–25, 26.3 percent at age 26–30, 22.4 percent at age 31–35, and 7.9 percent at age 36–40. In addition, one became addicted at age 43 and another at 50.

LIFE FOCUS ON DRUGS

At this stage professionals use drugs not for recreation, but to function. A survival mentality replaces the fun-and-games attitude. "As my tolerance began to increase," an attorney said, "I enjoyed it less. More and more, it was becoming something that I needed, not something I did for fun" (JD, age 57). "Alcohol was a drug that I had to have every day to survive," another attorney admitted (JD, age 61). Other concerns shrink in importance. "I was drinking 24 hours a day, seven days a week, and couldn't stop," said a pharmacist. "It didn't matter if it was eleven in the morning; I didn't care if I was just opening the pharmacy, hadn't eaten, or had pissed in my pants" (PharmD, age 49).

An attorney explained, "A maintenance drinker is addicted and needs to maintain a certain level of alcohol in his bloodstream 24 hours a day, seven days a week" (JD, age 38). Drugs are an addict's first concern day and night. "My first thought in the morning," a physician recalled, "was 'Where's the stuff?' " (MD, age 35). And this preoccupation continues through the night, as this physician related:

> I was ingesting large amounts of Vicodin [codeine], and it got to the point where I could not make it through the night; I would wake up sick and withdrawing. I remember waking up at three in the morning in bed in a cold sweat thinking about where I could get some Vicodin. So I ran into my backyard naked and rummaged through my car to find some. After I drank it I ran back into the house and crawled into bed without my wife knowing.   (MD, age 35)

Despite all the hard work invested in a career, professional activities now become primarily a means to get drugs. But no matter how much money a professional makes, the drug habit can quickly deplete it. "I went from making $14,000 as an intern to $42,000," a physician said. "In the 1970s that was a fortune for a 24-year-old, much more than I knew what to do with. But when I started buying coke, $42,000 was not enough."

> I was fully addicted, physically and psychologically. I had a closet with maybe fifty shirts, and every night I would put my coke in a different shirt pocket, and half the time I would wake up in the morning and forget which shirt pocket I put it in. Then I would search frantically. I would wake up by 6:00 A.M., and by 6:30 A.M. I was at my dealer's house. Every day I would stop by the money machine, take out $200, go to the dealer's house, wake him up—he was so pissed off because he was hung over from the night before—and he would give me a couple of grams. I would come to work, snort all day, and then at 6:00 or 7:00 P.M. I would stop using coke and, because drinking was acceptable, I drank until 10:00 or 11:00 P.M. Then, after my girlfriend went to sleep, I would snort coke for a couple of hours until I passed out. The next day the cycle started all over again.   (MD, age 38)

STASHES, SECRETS, AND COVERUPS

At the maintenance stage, the social context of drug use usually shifts to solo use. "I drank for nine years, mostly at home, the closet-drunk type stuff where I would drink until I passed out," a pharmacist reported (PharmD, age 44). Concealing compulsive drug use from others contributes to social isolation. "I started drinking secretly because I was afraid my law partners would find out," an attorney remembered. "My best friend from law school had already been disbarred, and I figured that was where I was headed, and I just wasn't going to tell anybody. It was a hard burden to bear" (JD, age 41).

Psychologically dependent addicts go to great lengths to hide their drugs. They feel they cannot face life without them. "I had stashes hidden in various places all over the house, so that when I got up the next morning or the middle of the night, I could just get out of bed and find my amphetamines and narcotics," a pharmacist explained (PharmD, age 41).

This behavior is carried into the workplace. "I hid booze in a closet in my office," a physician said. "I would pour it into my coffee cup in the morning and in the afternoon pour it into a cup of Pepsi" (MD, age 50).

Fanciful excuses and deceit are common, as this physician reported:

> I started using drugs during the day, whatever samples the drug men happened to bring—mostly cough syrups and codeine. When I slurred my words and dropped things, the clinic administrator was told. No one said anything directly to me, though a couple of times when I lost my balance and dropped things, people expressed concern that I was having neurological problems. I told them I was having little spells every once in a while. I saw a neurologist and had an MRI [magnetic resonance imaging] when I knew full well that it was the drugs. I wanted to have others think that I had some sort of physical problem.   (MD, age 34)

Ingenious excuses are legion. For example, a pilot was excused from a drunk-driving ticket when he told the judge that he was applying to the National Space Administration to be an astronaut. "The judge said, 'No problem, we will overlook this' " (pilot, age 48).

Staying one step ahead of trouble becomes a way of life for the addict. Some relocate. "They couldn't take any punitive action against me because I moved out of the state," a pharmacist admitted (PharmD, age 50). "I started taking an annual geographic cure," an attorney said. "I would just move away from the environment. I would find a reason such as they weren't paying me enough or I wasn't handling the kind of cases I deserved to handle. I moved to several different cities, and in each city I had three or four different offices" (JD, age 41).

STRUGGLE TO FEEL NORMAL

Early in their addiction some professionals experience considerable success in managing drug effects. "There were only one or two times I lost control, but other times I could reach a point when I was happy, euphoric, ambitious, had a lot of motivation, and was never sloppily stoned" (PharmD, age 46). Others, like this physician, find they cannot control drug effects. "My goal was to get to feeling good and then stay there—just coast. But I never could do that even once. I would go right through to oblivion" (MD, age 50).

Although some professionals remain faithful to one substance—typically alcohol—most become cross-addicted, often through trying to balance drugs—using one drug to minimize the unwanted effects of another. The goal is "to always control the ups and downs and be straight-line mellow," a nurse explained (RN, age 40). "Alcohol was not always working anymore," an attorney recalled, "but I found that I could work all day on pills and drink at night, so I started doing Valium pills in the morning to smooth myself out" (JD, age 41)

The usual pattern is to balance depressants with stimulants. One pharmacist called this balancing act "habit substitution." "I found that supplementing the narcotic use with a little bit of amphetamines or amphetamine derivatives offset the lethargy caused by the codeine. It created a euphoric feeling that I liked and somehow made everything feel okay" (PharmD, age 41).

Many addicts become skilled at titrating—mixing this with that, "taking just enough to maintain the feeling that I wanted to achieve" (PharmD, age 41).

> I was titrating everything I had. When I took my final bar exams and was taking Dexedrine, I almost counted the tiny pillettes inside the capsule. I needed enough to really perform well but not be so excited that I would go over the edge and flop. I was titrating all the other drugs, too, including Valium in significant amounts and smoking reefers and drinking to take the edge off the cocaine I was doing. (JD, age 49)

As it becomes increasingly difficult to maintain control, the addict's life inevitably becomes more and more complicated. It is impossible to stay "a master of cross-addiction," a dentist found (DDS, age 46). "When I was getting high each day," a physician said, "I used alcohol, caffeine, Soma, Robaxin, Haldol, Benadryl, Darvon, Tenuate, chloralhydrate, and marijuana—about eight drugs" (MD, age 46). With so many substances, it is virtually impossible to control the variety of chemical effects. "I was doing everything and anything," a pharmacist noted. "I was falling asleep on the way home at night when the upper effect wore off and the downer effect would take over. I'm amazed that I am not dead or stuck on somebody's grille. It got to the point where my family thought I was crazy and stuck me in a psychiatric ward. At the time I was probably doing 40 to 50 grains of codeine a day along with a handful of other things; I can't really say" (PharmD, age 46).

THE MAGIC DISAPPEARS

The addict's lifestyle evolves through a typical sequence: a quest for euphoria, followed by a desire just to feel normal, and finally, a struggle to survive. A dentist described his evolution from pleasure to panic: "I didn't know how to enjoy myself unless I changed my consciousness. For a long time alcohol was just big fun, but during dental school I slowly and subtly switched over to needing chemicals. I crossed over a line where I couldn't deal with the pain and fear that was inside me. In the end even the chemical serenity was fleeting" (DDS, age 46).

Addicts feel betrayed when their trusted drugs stop working. "Alcohol, my best friend, turned on me," an attorney remarked (JD, age 67). Another explained, "My friend [alcohol] ended up grabbing me so that I couldn't give it up; I *had* to drink. I thought that it was a friend, but before I knew it, I drank not because I wanted to, but because I *had* to; I could not *not* drink" (JD, age 65).

Only during recovery do psychologically dependent addicts realize they have been seduced by the illusion that drugs can solve problems. "I thought chemicals were my close companion and support, but there they were killing me," an attorney reflected (JD, age 70).

LIFE'S FABRIC UNRAVELS

Life during the later stages of addiction becomes "a horrible slide," "a nightmare." "My drinking wasn't fun anymore. It made me physically sick, and I looked horrible" (JD, age 37). Another attorney said, "I simply came to the point where I couldn't continue to exist. I couldn't eat or do anything to function, so my wife called a psychiatrist and admitted me to a hospital. At that stage, I didn't give a damn" (JD, age 50).

Escalating problems—withdrawal symptoms, desperation, and panic—engulf addicts. An anesthesiology resident recalled, "I was so desperate for drugs that I searched through the 'sharps boxes'— the big red boxes where needles and dangerous things are disposed of—looking for glass vials of narcotics. It was a dangerous and reckless thing to do! Who knows, there may be hepatitis or AIDS on those needles, but I was in an absolute panic sorting through these sealed boxes hoping to find half a cc of narcotics left over in a vial" (MD, age 34).

Physical health deteriorates rapidly. An addicted nurse was so badly "wasted" that, though 5'6" tall, she weighed only 98 pounds. "I looked like a survivor of Auschwitz. Others thought I was dying from cancer and would send me get-well cards and ask me if I was seeing a doctor" (RN, age 40). A pharmacist's health deteriorated like this:

> I had had so many opiates—Percodan in particular—that it burned my stomach. I would mix and drink a cocktail that had Xylocaine, an anesthetic, and Maalox. It would numb my gut, burn, and cause bleeding. I would go to a bar and throw down shots and beers and then go to the men's room and vomit red projectiles into the urinals, wash them down, wash myself off, go back to the bar, and drink. I knew that I had high blood pressure, but I didn't care. In my mind I would be dead in a couple of years anyway. One morning at work my stomach perforated, but, being a professional, I stayed there. I just dosed up real well and continued working, closing the store that night. My stomach puffed out like I was seven months pregnant. When I got home my wife rushed me to the doctor, who rushed me to the emergency room saying I was in walking shock.   (PharmD, age 47)

Staying out of trouble with the law takes effort. A wealthy attorney went to jail. "I got convicted of stealing money that I didn't need from an insurance company. At the time I had a very successful practice and was a millionaire. This doctor and an insurance guy schemed with me, and we stole $312—just a crazy thing. It took us two days to do it, and I wound up going to jail" (JD, age 61).

Relationships with professional colleagues deteriorate. "I would invite very important people in my profession over for a party or something and then pass out before they got there. It was unpredictable, uncontrollable, and *very* embarrassing," a pharmacist commented (PharmD, age 42). Professional censure and job loss often ensue. An attorney who lost a tenured professorship at a prestigious law school was thrown out of his house. "For a short time I lived in my car. I lost everything. I descended to the bottom" (JD, age 64).

Profound guilt and shame engulf addicts. Regarding the pain he inflicted on his family, a physician remarked, "I married a really lovely woman who put up with me much longer than she should have, but I absolutely destroyed her life. I hurt her so badly that she still can't forgive me. I found that unless I'm sober an straight, I'm not worth a plugged nickel to anyone—my family, friends, or anyone" (MD, age 50).

Discontinuation and Relapse

The length of time addicts remain at the maintenance stage varies widely—from 1 to 41 years among the professionals interviewed for this book. Some die from an overdose or other drug-induced health problems. Others stop their self-destructive use, regain their health, and establish effective relationships at home, work, and elsewhere. One in five (18.0 percent) of the 72 professionals who provided this information discontinued within 5 years after becoming addicted, one-fourth (26.4 percent) quit within 6–10 years, 20.8 percent quit within 11–15 years, and 22.2 percent within 16–20 years. Of the remainder, 5.6 percent stopped within 21–25 years, 4.2 percent (3 addicts) within 26–30 years, and 2.8 percent (2 addicts) at 32 and 41 years.

Among the 76 professionals who provided this information, 40.8 percent relapsed at some point. Of this group, 61.3 percent did so only once. The rest relapsed repeatedly—some as many as six or seven times.

How does a professional move from maintenance to discontinuation? What events or circumstances provide sufficient motivation?

OVERDOSING

Death through overdosing—intentional or accidental—ends drug use abruptly.[1] A pharmacist who deliberately overdosed recalled,

"I had had blackouts that lasted months and only eight dollars in my pocket and my clothes in two grocery bags. I had heavy financial problems, the IRS was after me, my mother was in a nursing home, my wife had left me, and I didn't dare go back to my pharmacy. I was scared to death" (PharmD, age 49). A physician told of a prominent colleague who died from a cocaine overdose: "He was a highly successful physician who excelled in his practice, a pivotal person in the city and well known in the region and state. He was incredibly addicted to cocaine, using it on a 24-hour-a-day basis. He went out to get Chinese food for his family but never returned. They found him dead in his Mercedes behind a small shopping mall out by the garbage cans. He was in the car with the cocaine and the food with the engine running" (MD, age 37).

Death may seem desirable. A study of 100 addicted female physicians and medical students found that 73 percent experienced suicidal ideation before recovery, 26 percent after the drinking ended. Thirty-eight percent had made overt suicide attempts, 15 percent more than once (Bissell and Skorina 1987). "I had a suicide pact with myself," a physician admitted. "I felt so very hopeless, I said, 'I'll try this AA thing, and if it doesn't work, I'll kill myself.' I just didn't care about death anymore" (MD, age 34).

An anesthesiology resident barely escaped an accidental death by injecting what he thought was Fentanyl—a very strong, short-acting narcotic—but it was Ketamine, a highly potent animal tranquilizer. Unknown to him, an unidentified addict had used the Fentanyl and replaced it with the other drug. "I know the tricks that come to mind like this when you are a drug-abusing doc," he explained, "In the OR you give the patient a drug that mimics the effect and keep the narcotic for yourself" (MD, age 34). This resident injected himself with the Ketamine solution remaining in the 5 cc vial, expecting a narcotic rush.

> It was 1:30 A.M. when I injected in the bathroom and woke up with the room spinning. I couldn't see, and I was hallucinating wildly. I knew that I had overdosed. It took me a while to find the doorknob and get out. One shoe was off where I had injected myself, and I hobbled and crawled to the front desk of the OR. I told the nurse that I was having a nervous breakdown. She got some other residents out of bed who put me on a gurney and rushed me to the ER. I had fallen several times, and my swollen face was black and blue. I thought I

was permanently blind. They shot me up with Narcan, a narcotic antagonist, and it put me in instant withdrawal. It was horrible. Yet, as bad as this was, I was relieved. "Okay, good, I can't keep this secret to myself anymore. It's over. I can't hurt myself anymore." (MD, age 34)

The physician who treated this resident tried to protect him by disguising the truth. "They worked me up for a heart problem or a seizure. But I started crying, 'No, it's not a seizure, I overdosed and need help.' He kept trying to smooth it over, saying I wouldn't get into trouble. But I didn't care. I had lost everything. It's all over! I surrender!"

Besides suicide, what options remain? A dentist explained, "I reached this jumping-off period when I was sick and tired of being sick and tired and sat in my garage with a 9-millimeter automatic in my hand. I was using narcotics in the quantity of 100, 200, 300 milligrams of morphine a day but could not justify it anymore, even in my demented state. I was going to blow my brains out, but I couldn't do it. So I went to see a counselor who got me going to Narcotics Anonymous meetings" (DDS, age 49).

EXHAUSTION AND DESPAIR

The downward spiral of loss and adversity takes its toll. "I remember going into the bathroom between cases shaking and in an absolute panic hurrying to tie up my arm and get the vein. I looked in the mirror and saw a monster. It was like being outside myself watching a skull-and-bones movie. 'Who is this creature?' I could see that in my addiction I had become a pitiful monster, and all ahead of me was blackness—but I couldn't do anything about it" (MD, age 34).

An academic physician who gave up a tenured professorship at an elite university recalled, "I resigned because I was full of despair and hopelessness. I saw that I was going nowhere, and I didn't know where to go except out" (MD, age 57). An attorney said, "The next step down for me was living on the street or dying—literally. I realized that I had no choice. I was depressed and worried that I would lose my law license and end up in the penitentiary" (JD, age 41).

Despite strong, habitual denial mechanisms, bitter experiences bring some addicts face to face with their pathetic circumstances. An attorney recalled:

> I had become a totally unethical and immoral person. I was writing bad checks and had been evicted from the place I was living. I was incapable of working and fortunately didn't have any client trust funds to steal. I was overwhelmed with feelings of guilt. My license had been suspended for nonpayment of dues. Having nowhere to live, I went around from place to place. I had no money, couldn't stand myself, and didn't know what I was going to do. The only place I could go was an alcoholic recovery unit. I had reached the end of my ability to wheel and deal. So I signed myself in—and the longer I stayed sober, the more I realized that booze was not going to help me.   (JD, age 55)

The moment of truth for a physician came as he concluded a successful three-day seminar. He was supposed to celebrate with executives who had employed him to plan and conduct the conference.

> At 10:20 P.M. I thought one drink couldn't possibly do any harm, but by 11:00 I was sound asleep, intoxicated. The next day I was unable to get up in time for the wrap-up session of my own workshop. They started without me at 8:00 A.M., and I got there at 9:20, hung over, ashamed, and discredited. I had dismantled all the good things that had happened, and they wouldn't even speak to me by the time I left.   (MD, age 57)

The decision to seek help comes when all other options fail. "When my wife pressured me into going into a hospital, I felt like I was in prison," a dentist recalled. "This is hell! I hate this place! Get me out of here! I can't stand it!'" Despite his anguish, he remained, because, he said, "I knew that I couldn't go back out there and use. The only thing that kept me there was wanting to keep my life" (DDS, age 37).

LEGAL PRESSURE

Discontinuation may be forced on professionals by drunk-driving arrests or other legal problems. "I was reported to the Board of Dental Examiners and the county well-being committee when I was arrested for driving under the influence of Valium, codeine, cocaine, and marijuana. I was charged with a variety of felonies and for the past two years have been in their diversion program," a dentist said (DDS, age 53).

Being involved in automobile accidents while intoxicated brings some professionals to the turning point. "I had a major, major traffic accident in which I broke my hip and almost rolled the car into the river," a pharmacist said. "I had some Vicodin in my purse and didn't have a script for it, so I was reported to the board and had to surrender my license. I've been sober ever since" (PharmD, age 42).

Legal intervention interrupted this dentist's addiction.

> I staggered into a drugstore one morning to have a prescription of Hycomine [cough syrup] filled and happened to have the bad luck—the good luck I now realize—to wander into a pair of DEA [Drug Enforcement Agency] agents who were surveying the pharmacy. They asked the pharmacist about me and he said, "Oh, he's the dentist from across the street; he apparently has a severe cough because he gets a lot of this stuff!" They came across the street to see me, and that was the end of that. They confronted me and asked if I was using this stuff. Then they came to my house that night and asked me to relinquish my narcotics license voluntarily, which I did. They turned me over to the board of examiners and put me on probation for five years.   (DDS, age 55)

Those arrested for felonies must deal with their drug problems. "I was picked up for shoplifting at a drugstore," a pharmacist confessed. "You do all kinds of crazy things when you're using drugs. They found a polyethylene baggy in my sock with Percodan and Methadone and reported me to the state bureau of narcotic enforcement, which already had a file on me. I was put on leave from my work and went into a treatment program. I stayed the whole course, and since that time I haven't used" (PharmD, age 45).

JOB PRESSURE

Sometimes pressure from associates forces professionals to discontinue. An employer's ultimatum leaves little choice. "I went to treatment solely to save my job," admitted a pilot (age 57).

A confrontation with one's boss can be highly motivating, as this attorney indicated:

> One Monday morning the senior partner of my firm came into my office and read me the riot act. The previous Friday I had missed an

appointment, which was becoming a regular event. The senior partner didn't know what was wrong with me, but he told me that I had better get my act together or get out of there. I was scared by this guy, whom I respected a lot, and the incident shattered my illusion that nobody knew. So I got hold of one of my clients who had gone to Cocaine Anonymous, and I haven't had a drink or a drug since. My partner's ultimatum really motivated me!   (JD, age 37)

Called into the department chair's office, an academic physician was told:

"We aren't going to talk about your fringe benefits, so please sit down. The last month you have created about as much turmoil as we can tolerate; we have a notebook here with all the complaints that have been filed against you by patients, their families, coworkers, and hospital staff. People can't stand you anymore. Your behavior is beyond tolerance. People around you are frightened that you will throw your instruments in the OR and you are too quick to blame others. We have complaints against you that may result in malpractice suits. One of the men on staff believes you are an alcoholic. Whether you are or are not, you have seen your last patient here until you do something about it!"

I asked him what he meant, and he said, "We recommend either of two places for you to get treatment: one for alcoholism and the other for psychiatric problems. Take your pick." They had arranged for travel to both places. I picked up the ticket for the alcohol program, had a friend take me to the airport, and within a few hours was in treatment. The director of the program met me at the airport, and as I walked from the airport gate to the lounge I was met by my father, my mother, and my sister. I insisted that I didn't belong there; it was a big mistake. Then a phone call came from my good friend at work, who told me, "You realize you won't have a job to come back to if that is how you feel."   (MD, age 61)

Other professionals cannot salvage their jobs. A pharmacist's employer had him arrested as he left the store. "He thought I was stealing and booted me out that night. I figured that I'd be selling cars for the rest of my life. But a fellow who was on the advisory board of a treatment center, someone who delivered commodities to my home, referred me to the treatment center" (PharmD, age 46). A physician's partners forced him out of their group practice. "At first they made me sign a contract that they could pull a urine test on me at any time and if it was dirty they could throw me out. Three months later they called me into the office, said they had changed their locks on the door, and ejected me from the practice" (MD, age 38).

PRESSURE FROM FAMILY AND FRIENDS

Family influences, ranging from threats of divorce to gentle encouragement and education, can play an important role in helping addicts stop. A dentist reported, "I don't know what would have happened if my husband hadn't been around. He's the one who said, 'You have to do something about this now!' He was very firm about it. The last night I drank I was in a bar and had no idea where I lived or how to get home. I passed out and was taken to the hospital. I called him and angrily told him that I was leaving treatment. He said, 'If you leave, I won't be home when you get here' " (DDS, age 48).

A law student's mother motivated him to action. "When I came home after an altercation one night, my mom suggested I go to AA. I had been in a bar and had a black eye and was wondering if maybe I had some kind of problem. It was obvious to my mother that I did, so I called them, and someone came to my house to pick me up, and we went to a meeting" (JD, age 34).

Friends who say the right thing at the right time are also influential, as this pharmacist recounted:

> My housemate said, "Hey, you are really losing it on drugs. Why don't you try to deal with it?" It was 5:00 P.M. I had overslept from the night before and missed an important exam. Not exactly a smart thing to do. At that point suicide became an option, a thought that went through my head on numerous occasions. What he said caught me at the right moment, and I said, "Yeah, you're right." The next day I was on my way to a rehab to deal with my cocaine habit.   (PharmD, age 26)

At a social event, an attorney told his friend, a psychiatrist, " 'Gee, Frank, I think I'm an alcoholic.' When Frank said, 'Yeah, I know,' it wasn't what I wanted to hear. The next day he referred me to another psychiatrist, and I didn't drink for a year" (JD, age 57).

Religious leaders may play a role. "I went back to church reluctantly, kicking and screaming and leaving in the middle of the service," a physician reported. "But a priest who was a recovering alcoholic picked me out and knew what I was going through. He very carefully and gently let me know he could help. It was the turning point. He gave me a book to read about a woman alcoholic, and I had the last drink. I thought, 'I sure will miss you, old girl.' I could see that if I lost this opportunity to stay sober, I would lose it all. I'd already lost my self-esteem, my husband, my business, and my hope" (MD, age 49).

Strategically planned group confrontations—motivational interventions—help addicts grasp the need for change.

> My sister suggested to my wife that she contact the physicians' health program in my state. She talked to the doctors I work with and the clinic administrator, who contacted an interventionist to orchestrate things. They asked me into the administrator's office, where doctors, nurses, my wife, and the interventionist were sitting. The interventionist started by saying how all the people here love you very much and they have some things they went to tell you. Then they took turns telling me about my problem. My M.D. colleague said that he had noticed that cough syrup samples were gone and he was pretty sure he had not given them to his patients, that kind of thing. They said that I had to go into treatment, and there were no options. I asked them, "What if I decide not to go?" They said they'd report their findings to the state licensing board. They had my bags packed in the trunk of the car and wouldn't let me go home. I felt very trapped and betrayed. I was pissed as hell at my wife for calling the authorities on me. But I went into the inpatient program.   (MD, age 34)

QUITTING INDEPENDENTLY

Some professionals come to recognize their problem and take appropriate action on their own. A pilot was influenced by "one of those fortuitous events" that he said "I still don't understand. I woke up one morning after a bad evening with lots of booze and put in a call to my airline pilots' association representative. It is really strange that this phone number was somehow available in my head. It was not somebody I had called previously, and to this day I still don't know how I got the phone number. They made an appointment with their EAP people and got me into treatment" (pilot, age 53).

A stranger forced this addicted attorney to face reality.

> At that time my wife was as addicted to alcohol as I was. I had lost my first wife, my children. "Ain't no matter," I thought, I needed to drink. As a matter of course I puked every morning. Believe it or not, I was living in the back seat of an abandoned car in a very small

junkyard—I knew the guy who owned it—and showering in the car wash, then going to work trying to practice law. I had had multiple convulsions and broke my back during one of them. But all that didn't stop me from drinking because alcohol gave me a way to cope with life. But when I took my wife into rehabilitation to get her some help, somebody said to me, "You're an addict." They used these offensive words for the first time in my life. "Alcoholic" is one thing, but "addict" is something else. An addict is somebody who's in the gutter, someone on skid row. Not me! (JD, age 65)

Her daughter's attempted suicide shocked a physician into confronting her own self-destructive behavior. "I realized that my own alcohol use was the equivalent of suicide," she said. "This led me to stop drinking, and I've never drunk since" (MD, age 60).

Recovery

Recovery begins when an addict discontinues use of psychoactive drugs. Among the 74 addicted professionals who provided information about their recovery, this period ranged from 10 months to 27 years. One-third (32.4 percent) had been clean and sober from 10 months to 5 years, 41.9 percent for 6–10 years, and 17.6 percent for 11–15 years. The remaining 8.1 percent had not used drugs for 17 years or longer.

Denial, the defense mechanism that keeps addicts from recognizing their enslaved condition, must be overcome, as it was with this desperate nurse. "I came to the point when I was willing to do *anything* to not drink or use again; I'd do *anything*. I was willing to get up at 4:30 in the morning to go to AA meetings at 6:00, or whatever else was needed" (RN, age 42).

Physical recovery occurs before emotional growth. "I spent the first year after I stopped drinking and taking pills just getting the chemicals out of my body and learning how to be a human being again and not a zombie," a nurse recalled. "And then life really hit me with a bang" (Barde and Pick 1993). One does not overcome years of emotional neglect in a hurry. "It took me a full year before I started even to hear the messages in my AA meetings," a pharmacist recalled. "I understood intellectually, but it didn't have any meaning to me. But when I started hearing them, things started turning around for me. I started to understand how to handle day-to-day situations the way rational and normal people do. The lessons I've learned have helped me deal with my work and my re-lationships at home—with everything" (PharmD, age 43).

As they progress in their recovery, addicts, like this aviator, may rejoice in the idea of never drinking again. "The difference is in *me*," he enthused. "I look forward to all the years of my life that are left and the opportunity to spend them sober. It just makes me feel good inside, and that's the difference. I no longer have to take it one minute or day or week at a time. Now I don't even think about drinking" (pilot, age 50).

It is a gross understatement to say that life in recovery is better than it was before. A pilot described his exhilarating recovery: "This ten years has been a euphoric ride. Look what I'm able to do now. I know where my car is, my wallet has gotten fatter, and things just keep getting better and better. More and more things are opening up to me, and I'm examining and learning more about myself and becoming the kind of person I want to be: more loving, more un-derstanding—in truth, a person I like" (pilot, age 58).

RECOVERING PHYSICAL HEALTH

Recovering addicts rejoice as their health and physical appearance improve. "I don't even resemble the person I was," a pharmacist exclaimed. "I'm healthier now than when I was 22 years old. I look better than I've ever looked in my life" (PharmD, age 47). "I used to be at the doctor's a lot," an attorney recalled, "but during the seven and a half years I've been sober, I've had only one cold. I've finally been sober long enough that I can get life and health insur-ance. I'm well all the time and feel good" (JD, age 41).

Some work harder at improving their health than others. "I watch my health and my diet carefully and do exercises every day," an attorney reported (JD, age 44). Others bring it along more slowly. "There are a lot of heavy-duty 12-steppers still smoking cigarettes," a physician observed. "They sit on their butts getting fat and dying of heart disease and tobacco-related illnesses. Lung cancer and em-physema are the number-one killers of recovering alcoholics" (MD, age 46).

EMOTIONAL GROWTH

Addicts who replace old ways with drug-free lifestyles must learn healthy ways to deal with anguish and pain. "I started feeling better slowly," a nurse said, "but it didn't occur without great struggle. It took years to overcome destructive habits; healthy ones didn't begin overnight. I had to confront all the old emotional pains that were covered up by drugs" (RN, age 70).

A sudden transition to life without drugs—"clawing oneself back to mental health" (JD, age 44)—can be terrifying. "It was pretty scary when I took that last pill," a Valium addict recalled. "I walked around terrified for a long time, tied up in a knot and really anxious; I felt all wired up and overwhelmed" (RN, age 40). "When I look back on it, I shudder," a dentist said. "I went through some pretty rough times. But now I see that I have accomplished something, and these experiences help me help others going through it. Most people generally admire me for having stopped and gone through all this" (DDS, age 47).

Recovering addicts learn that chemical solutions are like Band-Aids covering a malignancy and that by addressing the underlying problems they can find genuine relief. "I used to subscribe to the philosophy that 'life is a bitch and then you die,' " an attorney recalled. "But after my first real experience in my treatment group talking about my drinking and drugging history, a huge burden was lifted. It was a bright and sunny day, and I experienced a wonderful relief after weathering a terrible storm" (JD, age 41).

Although addicts may be intellectually and clinically competent, their emotional growth atrophies through lack of exercise. Like intellectual and muscular development, emotional growth occurs only through challenge; one must struggle, as this physician did.

> I had an assignment in a 12-step treatment program to play every day because I worked compulsively. Whenever I felt bad, I would go buy a 1,000-dollar toy and then feel better for a few hours. They gave me $10 and told me to go buy a toy and play with it in a Beverly Hills park. So I bought a watergun, a yo-yo, and a Batman kite. Here I was, an overachieving professional who had always done everything perfectly, trying to fly a $2.50 kite—and I couldn't even get the damn thing to fly. I felt so foolish; every time I would get it up it would crash.
>
> After 30 to 40 tries, I felt like everyone in the park was watching me. "Why am I doing this stupid shit?" Then I got the kite up a couple of hundred feet in the air and it stayed a few minutes, and I became totally lost in the activity. The joy I felt was that of an eight-year-old. At that moment I realized, "I have a right to be in this world like anybody else, and who in the hell cares if I am flying a silly kite in my suit and tie? Everyone else in this park is so involved in their own

lives they probably don't even notice that I'm here, and if they do, who cares? I'm probably never going to see them again." I realized that God meant for me to enjoy this life just as much as anyone else. It was kind of silly, but it helped bring me back to life. I now have a very different attitude.   (MD, age 38)

These professionals repeatedly emphasized the priority of inner peace over external possessions and achievements. "I'm making as much money now as I've ever made in my life," an attorney said, "but I've learned that if I have to choose between losing physical things or emotional things, I'll lose the physical things" (JD, age 64).

A pilot (age 50) explained the difference between the peace and serenity that comes from healthy living and its chemical counterfeit:

> I was chasing peace and serenity from alcohol; it was instant and absolute. I had a sense of calm with no problems. It was chemical serenity. But it's dawned on me since my recovery that most of my time I now have peace and tranquility without chemicals. I've still got a lot of worries, but I have a sense of serenity. This last year and a half hasn't been real good, but I'm dealing with it and going to meetings and staying in recovery trying to help other people.

Emotional growth comes from facing up to stressful events and consistently trying to improve. "When I find my insides getting uncomfortable," an attorney explained, "I immediately begin to look for what it is I am avoiding; that's the key. I figure that God is talking through my guts and intuition. If I listen to that and other people, it works. Instead of overriding my feelings, I listen and learn." (JD, age 55).

Self-care, neglected in professional training, fosters a healthy affect and self-esteem. "I've learned it's okay to take care of myself," said an attorney (JD, age 55). "I now have confidence in myself!" a nurse exclaimed. "I like me! I like me today!" (RN, age 37).

SPIRITUAL AWAKENING

For some professionals the entire recovery experience is miraculous. "It's a spiritual experience to be able to go one day without a drink, let alone a month, a year, or in my case 13 years," a nurse marveled. "It's a miracle! Early in my recovery I was leery about talking about God and thought AA was a religious cult, but I don't worry about that now" (RN, age 67).

Physician Sam Naifeh, speaking at a California Society for Addiction Medicine meeting, called alcoholism a spiritual illness and cited Carl Jung, who noted that the craving for alcohol is the equivalent of spiritual thirst. Psychiatrist Garrett O'Connor noted that to be deprived of spirituality, courage, and hope is to become despairing, disheartened, bewildered, disordered, and alienated. The paradox of spirituality, observes O'Connor (1992), is that peak spiritual experiences can occur when a person reaches the depth of despair.

Many addicted professionals describe recovery as a spiritual awakening. "Those who get into recovery discover that it's a spiritual journey," a dentist said. "Maintaining our spiritual condition day by day is the number-one thing. I work with a lot of newcomers, and those who don't get this concept have recurring problems" (DDS, age 46). A nurse explained: "We get sick spiritually first, then emotionally or mentally, and then get well in the opposite way. First we get physically better, then emotionally and mentally, and finally spiritually" (RN, age 67).

Spiritual experiences are not easy to describe.

> Getting sober is getting spiritual, and the more spiritual awakening I have—brushes with angels' wings or however you want to describe it—the easier it is to stay sober. But it's a private thing, and I don't know how to talk about it except to say that spiritual experiences are always uplifting. I'm unable to explain except to say that spiritual experiences come from the heart. It's a gift from God, it's grace or whatever words you have to describe it. It is an awareness of a higher power, a connection between God and your heart that takes away your compulsion to drink.   (JD, age 44)

Organized religion, anathema to some, can interfere with true spirituality. "My spiritual feelings are not like those that sometimes come in organized religions," an attorney explained. "They are not control mechanisms or guilt trips. I get the most spiritual feelings when I get out in the country, in the mountains, oceans—those sorts of places" (JD, age 37).

Those who don't reject organized religion replace harsh religious concepts with benign ones. "I don't believe in an evangelical God anymore," a nurse said (RN, age 70). "Now that I believe in a kind and loving God, my life has become freer and happier." "My religion has improved because of my spirituality," another nurse commented (RN, age 42).

Recovering addicts who haven't experienced dramatic happenings also attest to the importance of spiritual growth. "I've never experienced a lightning bolt or seen a burning bush," a dentist said, "but I've had a spiritual awakening" (DDS, age 49). "My spiritual experiences haven't been blinding flashes," an attorney commented, "but I've had a series of small ones that gradually increase my spiritual feelings" (JD, age 37).

Such experiences were described by a pilot as "a gift from heaven. I don't know how it works or why it works. I don't care, just as long as it works. There have been many minor miracles in my recovery, and they happen every day. They're not like the ocean parting or time standing still or anything like that, but it's just too much and too often to be coincidence. I've stayed sober for as long as I have because of God and because I want to continue flying airplanes" (pilot, age 57).

After gentle probing in our interviews, some professionals described dramatic spiritual experiences that had profoundly enhanced their recovery. "I was working the AA step where you ask the God of your understanding to accept you with your faults and help you eliminate your shortcomings," a pharmacist reported. "I was dwelling on that, asking Him to take away some of my faults, when, in the middle of the night, I saw a bright light come through the window. I don't tell many people this—but it was a warm and loving feeling that made me believe that there was something else out there helping me" (PharmD, age 43).

A drunk pilot jailed for hitting a policeman had this experience:

I thought they were going to kill me. They told me in no uncertain terms, "You are not coming out of here except in a box." Man, I was absolutely coming unglued in that rubber room in the jail. So I prayed. I've prayed a lot when I've been in trouble, but this time I honestly prayed to God to let me die. A very calm and comfortable feeling came over me—a totally peaceful feeling of serenity. It was the first time I had been able to find that except in alcohol.   (Pilot, age 50)

An attorney's prayer of desperation resulted in this experience:

I was withdrawing from heroin in a state hospital—a really grim place—in emotional and physical agony. I couldn't even push my glasses up on my face because I couldn't get my hands or legs to work. I was also in psychological torment because the enormity of what I had done had sunk in. It was the most severe pain I have ever felt, much worse than the pain I had as a child during open heart surgery. Much worse. In my agony I cried out to God, "I can't take this anymore." It was a cry that came from deep within me. And I had an experience that was similar to what Bill Wilson describes in the AA book. I was flooded with a subjective presence of light in the room to the extent that the walls and ceiling appeared less defined. I felt an overwhelming sense that everything was the way it was supposed to be—everything was fine. I can't articulate the feelings; I can only say that it was an overwhelming sense for the first time in my life that everything was going to be okay. I didn't think or guess; I *knew* that everything was going to be okay. It was a sudden transformation—in an instant everything changed. Since then my whole life has been different, and I've never had another craving for drugs or alcohol. It's been seven years, and although my child was sick and damn-near died—I sat and slept in the hospital by her side for 28 days—and I had no insurance to pay for her care, it never once occurred to me that a drink or a drug would make it better. Even with all that pressure it didn't cross my mind.   (JD, age 41)

FAMILY MENDING

Family life improves dramatically when professionals discontinue drug use. "I've made peace with the family members who hated me," a grateful attorney exclaimed. "And I'm close as hell to my kids and wife now. They came back!" (JD, age 60). "Since I've been in recovery, *all* my relationships are better than before," a nurse said. "I'm more accepting and patient, less critical and judgmental. I'm God-centered now rather than drink-centered, and have a better sense of humor. In all my relationships, I am a kinder, gentler person" (RN, age 42).

But it takes effort to turn unhealthy family patterns into healthy ones. "I found that relationships are the biggest stressor and the hardest thing I've had to handle in sobriety, much more so than my work," another nurse confided (RN, age 45).

Painful events must be reviewed and repaired.

Today I have a marvelous relationship with both my children because I was able to go to them and apologize. I said, "I'm sorry; I know what has happened to you, and it was wrong." It took several sessions of my doing that before they stopped yelling at me. It was very painful, like walking over spikes, but it was something I had to do. My daughter has written powerfully about her dysfunctional family. When I hear these things I think, "Oh my God, this is me she is talking about." The pain is incredible!   (DDS, age 48)

Although family members benefit greatly from the addicted professional's sobriety, they must make major adjustments. The recovering addict acts so differently that it takes some getting used to. "My family have certainly benefited, but they aren't totally comfortable yet with the new me," a pharmacist observed (PharmD, age 42). Some, like this physician, are uncomfortable with the new family patterns: "I still have a hard time accepting love from my wife and kids because it's just given so tenderly and innocently," he confessed (MD, age 35).

Little children, the quickest to adjust, bring great joy to recovering addicts.

> When I was drinking, my two-year old daughter would run from me when I would call, "Come to Daddy." I couldn't understand what was wrong, and it bothered me. After I'd been sober and dry for about two or three months, she came up to me and put her arms around me . . . [long emotional pause] That was about 21 years ago. And the only thing that was different in my life was that alcohol was out of it. She knew that something was different, and that was my reinforcement to stay in AA.   (JD, age 56)

A physician described the difference in his marriage before and after abstinence: "We used to be at each other's throats, and the love wasn't there much. We had knock-down-drag-out-fights and drifted away from each other. But now it's great; it would be hard to be much better than it is now" (MD, age 34). "It's much better than I could even explain or even imagine," a pilot (age 61) said.

Continued participation in family-oriented programs such as AA and Al-Anon facilitates family recovery. "I go to AA meetings where we focus on family issues," an attorney remarked. "It basically provides us a safe place to discuss our family problems" (JD, age 41). When the damage has been too great for couples to survive, recovering addicts often find new partners.

WORK SUCCESS

Success at work is particularly sweet for those burdened with unhappy memories of less successful times. A physician recalled:

I'll never forget the tremendous feeling of abandonment when my colleagues told me they wanted nothing to do with me. I didn't have a friend to turn to and came close to committing suicide. It was pretty awful. I was a real go-getter type of guy who made things happen, a pretty heavy hitter who had been riding high in the medical community. I'd been president of the surgeon center, started a medical building, and been a managing partner. But I nearly lost it all.   (MD, age 50)

The transition back to work can be awkward, as this nurse found out:

When I went back to work on the surgery floor, they put me on probation for three months, and I didn't have a narcotics key during this time. I had to give weekly urine samples and be clean and sober for 90 days before I could administer any medication. They worried that I would cross over the line and watched me a lot. I figured, "What the hell. I have to make a living." But every time the drug count was off at the end of the shift, I got real nervous. I always made sure that everybody signed when they took out the drugs and didn't leave until I was certain the record was correct.   (RN, age 40)

After an initial struggle, job performance typically improves. A pilot found that although at first the airline company wouldn't let him fly as captain, things eventually got better.

They let me come back to work as copilot serving with people a lot junior to me, and I resented that. After six months I went back through the entire schooling again and made the best grades I ever did in ground school. The FAA inspector who gave me the oral said that I was the best-prepared applicant he had ever examined. The inspector who rated me on the simulator said the same thing. After a year I was flying very happily again. I just applied the principles I had learned in the treatment program and in the 90 AA meetings I attended, and now I really, really enjoy my work!   (Pilot, age 57)

Some recovering addicts are pleasantly surprised to find a high level of support from their associates when they return. "When I got out of the recovery house," a nurse recalled, "I went back to the same hospital, got hired, and tried to make amends. At a reception luncheon at the hospital, a lot of people who knew I had been an active user—the supervisor, the director of nursing, old head nurses—came up to me and said they were so proud of me! I had done this sober, and it was hard and I was elated!" (RN, age 40).

Surprisingly, adversities sometimes become assets. "When I was hired," a pharmacist recalled, "they informed me that they were very positive about people in recovery because, company-wide, they have had very good experiences. Now, because my work performance has been so good, they are even more willing to hire others in recovery" (PharmD, age 42).

Self-confidence quickly develops as recovering addicts prove to themselves that they have overcome one of life's most difficult challenges. Against formidable odds, a dentist started an entirely new practice. "I have the only cold-start practice that's been successful in town in twenty years," he reported. "Things have gone so well for me that it has paved the way for other recovering addicts" (DDS, age 48).

Thinking and performance also improve. "My thought processes are a hell of a lot more clear," remarked a physician. "I don't miss very much anymore, and I trust my intuitive feelings now. I'm more sensitive to other people's problems." He added, "It's amazing now that fewer of my patients get a second opinion than they did when I was drinking" (MD, age 50).

Recovery makes professionals like this physician more sensitive and compassionate:

> My bedside manner is as different as night and day. Before, I was not at all compassionate about the human condition and what it means to suffer. I would see people in the emergency room in physical and emotional pain, but had no feeling for them. I'd tell parents of a kid injured in a motorcycle accident, "Your kid was injured and will never be the same; he will be a vegetable." Then I would leave the room and let the pastoral-care counselor deal with the family. Now I know what it means to suffer. My suffering was self-inflicted, but it has made me more compassionate to others; my heart goes out to those who are down and out.   (MD, age 38)

These newly developed skills directly benefit clients and patients, as this physician explained: "When I was using, I missed a lot of important information. Now, I concentrate much, much, much less on solving the patient's problem and concentrate much, much, much more on hearing what the patient is telling me. I try to put together the little things they drop and try to understand them. I find that this is much more effective in primary care" (MD, age 35).

NEW ASSOCIATES AND SERVICE OPPORTUNITIES

The focus of informal relationships shifts radically during the recovery stage. Whereas social life previously centered around drinking and drugging, it now focuses on more wholesome activities.

> I no longer like going to parties where the point is alcohol and drugs. I don't like being around people who escape through using. I find them boring. I love getting together with old friends, but now I don't meet them in a bar for happy hour. For me the point is conversation and seeing how people are doing. In the bar it is always loud because people don't want to communicate, they just want to drink. So when I go to a social event, I ask, "Are people going to communicate, or is this just an encounter for people to get together so they can ignore each other and get drunk?"   (JD, age 40)

Addicts who use drugs in isolation may have few intimate friends, and filling this void is rewarding. "My using was a pretty solitary thing," a physician said, "but now I have a whole new set of friends, activities, and things to do" (MD, age 36). "I have a ton of friends now!" a pharmacist enthused (PharmD, age 38).

Friendships often develop with other recovering addicts in recovery programs. "I don't see a lot of the people I used to," an attorney observed.

> I have a very active social life, and most of my friends are in recovery. We do a lot of things together. We run, play bridge, play golf, go to movies, have parties. We just don't have the alcohol involved. Whenever I'm in a gathering that has drinks, I hold onto my club soda. I never put it down so that it doesn't get confused with someone else's. I come late and leave early and never depend on anyone else there who might be drinking. No longer do I need drugs to have fun. I'm also very active in politics.   (JD, age 38)

Professionals benefit greatly when they reach out to colleagues. "I give freely the gift that was freely given to me," a dentist explained. "This approach is an insurance policy on my own sobriety" (DDS, age 49). "Recovery all boils down to love and service," an attorney remarked (JD, age 42). Recovering addicts widely acknowledge that helping others helps them too. "Everybody in the AA program says the reason you help another alcoholic is not just for his sake, but your own. It will save *your* soul," a physician said. "Bill Wilson, the AA founder of Alcoholics Anonymous, is a good example. After working six months in a sanatorium trying to keep drunks from drinking, he felt like a failure, since none of them had quit. His wife pointed out with a smile that he hadn't had a drink in six months" (MD, age 46).

Service opportunities assigned in recovery programs at first seem trivial, but once they experience the social and emotional rewards, many recovering addicts make service a lifelong habit. "I spend a lot of time helping other people, but I get much more out of it than I give," an attorney explained. "If anybody else tried it and got as much satisfaction and pleasure from it as I do, they would do it too! It reinforces itself" (JD, age 41).

In Perspective

Addicted professionals evolve through fairly predictable developmental stages. Although drug initiation typically begins in adolescence in peer settings, some get an early start in their parental homes. Regardless of social setting, alcohol and other drugs are first offered as a gesture of friendliness. Initiation is almost always a social rather than a solitary happening; young people rarely use drugs alone.

Escalation, the period of transition from initiation to full-blown addiction, occurs as developing addicts experiment with a variety of drugs and become increasingly preoccupied with them and other users. At this stage, social rewards such as peer approval are typically more motivating than the drugs' euphoric effect.

During the maintenance stage the focus shifts from having fun to serious business; obtaining and using drugs takes precedence over all other activities. At this time drug use typically shifts from group settings to isolation. Friendships change, too—from expressive roles providing social and psychological rewards such as acceptance and support to instrumental roles such as helping the user obtain drugs. Addicts, relying on drugs to cope, stash them at strategic locations and become adept in covering their use. Work associates and family members who have an investment in the professionals' careers often enable them to maintain these evasive tactics. When the addict's body stops responding as drug use increases, life becomes frantic and frenzied.

Those who realize that drugs are the cause of their problematic symptoms—rather than the solution—and have other coping strengths (Type 3 and 4 users) discontinue drugs when they realize what is happening. However, those who are psychologically dependent (Type 5 addicts) rarely stop using without outside help, and some intentionally overdose. Even those threatened by prison or loss of professional license may continue use.

When detoxification discomforts fade and the mind clears, the addict is better able to comprehend the complex nature of dependence. At that point the difficult phase of emotional struggle begins; addicts must go back where they left off in emotional growth and learn how to deal with life's problems without the chemical crutch. Steinglass describes recovery as "turning off one hundred switches, one switch at a time" (quoted in Scriven 1994). When each chemical "switch" is turned off, it must be replaced with a new, more healthy one.

The process of emotional development, though taxing and frightening, can also be exhilarating. "Be drug-free, and you will find your strength within you in places you have not dared to visit," a recovering addict advises ("What's So Great about a Drug-free Lifestyle?" 1991). With great satisfaction, a now-sober attorney said, "My happiness now comes from within me" (JD, age 55).

III

BREAKING FREE

SIX

Recovery Tools

"Recovery takes a long time—a *long* time! It doesn't happen overnight. So, if somebody's looking for a quick fix, forget it. It doesn't exist."

(DDS, age 37)

"In recovery, you climb out of the pit one step at a time each day trying to see the light that is so far away."

(DDS, age 47)

"I came to understand that there wasn't something really wrong with my character—I was just sick."

(DDS, age 48)

A variety of therapeutic tools, used singly or in combination, are available to help addicts free themselves from chemical dependence. Some tools have a long history and are routinely utilized by treatment personnel. Others are relatively new or unfamiliar even to those who work with addicts. Few recovery programs utilize all these tools, and currently there is no place where clinicians can receive comprehensive training in all techniques.

Motivational Intervention

Conventional wisdom presumes that addicts cannot be helped until they "hit bottom" and ask for help. In the 1960s, however, drug counselors began experimenting with a way to get drug users into treatment sooner. In a 1973 book, *I'll Quit Tomorrow*, Vernon Johnson, an Episcopalian minister from Minnesota, described a method designed to "bring up the bottom." Called "intervention," this approach, "a lifeline in the tunnel of despair" (Bernard 1988), was widely popularized six years later when Johnson conducted a successful intervention with former First Lady Betty Ford. Now interventionists train professionals to conduct successful confrontations with their addicted colleagues. A caring group of family, friends, and other associates, all carefully rehearsed, surprise the addict in a meeting in which they tell him or her how the addictive behavior adversely affects them (Bernard 1988).

From 1975 through 1990 the Georgia Impaired Physicians Program assessed and treated 2,100 physicians. Of these, Talbott and Gallegos (1990) estimate, one-third entered formal treatment as a result of a planned confrontation. Until the secret is broken, most addicts, like this dentist, continue to hide their problem, even from themselves: "I didn't see myself as an alcoholic or addict until I quit. I knew I had a problem, but I thought I was immune to that" (DDS, age 43).

Professional training and status often reinforce the tendency to deny and rationalize personal problems. For example, because pilots carry such heavy responsibility for others' safety, they rarely acknowledge personal weakness. "We always feel we are a cut above others," said one. "Since I was a fighter pilot selected to be a defender of the nation because I was strong, I couldn't be a weak alcoholic like those on skid row" (pilot, age 57). "I've never had a chemically dependent pilot pick up a phone and call me directly for help," an airline EAP director recalled.

Reluctance to confront an addicted colleague, friend, or family member may have grim consequences. Regarding a deceased colleague a physician noted, "Tragically, there were lots of people who saw the signs and symptoms of his cocaine use, people who a year before his death had contacted our state's physicians' health service but were unwilling to testify or be involved in an intervention. None were willing to risk anything personally. If they had, they probably would have saved his life" (MD, age 39).

Intervention experts now contract services to lead interventions (Storti 1994). They first screen potential participants to make sure they have no ulterior motives (for example, a desire to air other problems) or addictions of their own. Then they teach them how to express distress about the addict's behavior with love and concern free from threats and hostility.

Planned confrontations vary with the specialist's style and the addict's circumstances. Most are done in the spirit of advocacy, but sometimes consequences—an "emotional hammer"—are emphasized. An airline EAP director recalled, "I was in an intervention where the captain said, 'Either you do everything the EAP director tells you to do, or you will have all hell to pay in this office from me!' That intervention worked."

A chemically dependent nurse described her intervention:

> I was so drunk I couldn't hold my head up when at 6:00 A.M. there was a knock at the door and I thought, "Who could that be?" When my mother walked in first, I thought my dad had passed away. Then behind her came the whole procession—relatives, friends, and two docs from work. The specialist who walked in last said, "Hi. You don't know me, but we're here to help you." I knew what they were there for, and I backed into the stove saying, "No! No!" (I probably left a dent in the stove.) At 7:45 A.M. I was in the car going to the treatment center.

"It was a very loving experience," she recalled. "They all told me that they loved and cared about me. They had recorded messages from my father and two brothers who couldn't make it and gave me 40 letters from aunts, uncles, and cousins with instructions not to open them until I got to the treatment center" (RN, age 37).

The group meeting can be so emotionally charged that, to keep to the plan, participants are asked to write what they intend to say and to bring their notes (yellow pads are used with attorneys to lend an air of legal certainty).

Group confrontations need to be well documented. "If you don't have sufficient evidence, forget it," an EAP representative emphasized. "What work best in helping pilots overcoming their denial are the toughest, hardest, facts that you can deliver, sledgehammer facts, observational facts that cannot easily be refuted." In addition, arrangements are made before the confrontation to transport the addict immediately to a treatment program. Of one interventionist's 397 cases in three years, 94 percent of those confronted in this way went immediately into treatment, and of those who did not, 80 percent received treatment one day to three years later (Storti 1990). "It was a big relief when my office staff confronted me," recalled one physician. "I was scared to death that someone would find out, see me using or acting funny. My life was like being chased by a tiger. I had run so long, when I finally got caught it was a relief, a rest" (MD, age 40).

Although confrontations ideally involve a preplanned group of caring associates—preferably 12 to 15 people, according to Storti (personal correspondence)—some groups are much smaller and less rehearsed. A physician, for example, described how a less formal family meeting got him into treatment:

> It was strictly a family meeting, but I didn't know it was coming up. My wife, our son and two grandkids (ages 17 and 20), and other relatives came for a barbecue. I had the silver fizzes all ready for breakfast, but before I started drinking they all joined in saying they were concerned about my drinking. My grandkids said they didn't like being around me anymore. I used to take them on three-day fishing trips, and the last time we went I had taken 72 cans of beer plus hard liquor, and they had to drive home. One grandson said the reason he didn't drink was because he didn't want to act like me. I said, "Hell, I'll take care of that," and dumped the jug of fizzes into the sink. They said, "Oh, you quit before." But I haven't had a drink since. They arranged for the medical director at the treatment center to call, and I tried to convince him that my drinking wasn't as bad as everyone said it was. He got me into the outpatient program, and I made a commitment that I kept. I haven't had a drink since. It scared the shit out of me and was the greatest thing that ever happened to me.   (MD, age 75)

Confrontation by a single contact, even a phone call, can also work. "The simplest intervention I ever did," said an airline executive, "was when I received information from two plane mechanics about a pilot who showed up for his flight at 0700 smelling of alcohol. I sensed that he was in deep trouble and called him on the phone, saying, 'It's time to go to treatment.' He said, 'Yes!' I asked him to appear in my office in the morning, and he did."

Information about motivational interventions is increasingly distributed by professional organizations. In addition, some lawyers' assistance programs, like those in Illinois, offer statewide training sessions four times a year. Procedures for carrying out confrontations in hospitals and other health-care settings are now standardized (Pauwels and Benzer 1989).

Detoxification

Detoxification, the transition from chronic drug dependence to a toxic-free physiologic state (Kleber 1994), involves gradually reduced dosage of the abused drug or, if such a strategy is safer, a drug from the same general pharmacological class.[1]

Withdrawal symptoms are generally the opposite of the drug's acute effects (Schuckit 1995c). For those addicted to depressants (alcohol, benzodiazepines, and barbiturates), the withdrawal symptoms include insomnia, anxiety, tremors, and increased heart rate, pulse, respiratory rate, and body temperature. Withdrawal from opiates such as heroin or prescription pain killers includes pain, coughing, runny nose, and diarrhea. Withdrawal from stimulants like amphetamines, cocaine, and prescription diet drugs involves depression, sleepiness, and increased appetite. These symptoms are sometimes preceded by marked agitation, hallucinations, and explosive violence.

The withdrawal time is likely to be three to five days for relatively short-acting drugs like alcohol, heroin, and cocaine, but two weeks or longer for very long-acting drugs such as benzodiazepines (for example, Valium and Xanax) or methadone (Schuckit 1995c). Several studies indicate that both acute and subacute protracted withdrawal symptoms persist for several weeks. Central nervous symptom hyperexcitability persists long after the removal of the drug (*Alcohol and Health* 1990).

In earlier times, detoxification was the only treatment used (Mann 1991). Clinicians treated the toxic condition, managed existing medical complications, and then discharged the patient. The pain and discomfort of the detoxification experience were regarded as an advantage, the reasoning being that aversive conditioning might make drug use less attractive. This assumption proved to be faulty; many addicts choose to endure the pain and discomfort of another detoxification rather than discontinue drug use. "When I was going through all this pain, a guy told me that it was a good thing because the pain would teach me a lesson. He said, 'You will remember and won't want to get high again.' Although the pain was tremendous, the withdrawal in itself wasn't enough to keep me sober without a follow-up program" (DDS, age 49).

Those who went through detoxification programs in the 1960s and 1970s report distressing experiences. Psychiatric hospitals, where detoxification programs were usually located, were "drying-out places where you could smell the formaldehyde" (JD, age 61). "They put me in a psych ward in a hospital because I was depressed—that is pretty much all they could come up with in 1976. Then they sent me up to this new unit for alcoholics, and no one tried to bring me down, and no one had any insights. They were brand-new at this, and nobody knew much" (JD, age 47). Those forced to detoxify "cold turkey"—without medical aid or social support—such as those in jails or prisons report even worse experiences. (The term "cold turkey" came from heroin addicts who noticed that one side effect of detoxifying is having goose bumps and clammy skin, like a turkey stripped of its feathers (Shaffer and Jones 1989, p. 129). A dentist hooked on narcotics, "crank" (a street form of methamphetamine), and other drugs recalled: "They kept me in maximum security for about a week. I had great physical pain, cramps, and diarrhea. But worse than any physical pain was the emotional pain. I wished I could die. While I was crying there, I promised God, even though I was an atheist, that if he would get me out of this one, I'd never fix again or take another pill" (DDS, age 46).

Some try with varying success to detoxify on their own. "I tried to white-knuckle it for three weeks," a physician said, "but when this didn't work, I went into a 28-day recovery program that began with detoxification" (MD, age 46). An attorney reported, "I detoxed pretty much on my own at home. I shook a lot, had hallucinations, and couldn't eat. That went on for about a week, and I kept going to work and faking it. Since most of my work was in the courtroom, I would go to the office, grab an empty briefcase, say I was going to court, go right back home, and go to bed" (JD, age 64).

It is usually futile for Type 5 addicts to try to detoxify themselves without aid. "I was always attempting to detoxify myself, using every vacation that I was eligible for," a pharmacist explained, "but I was never able to get off. Though I cut them down half, way down,

I had horrendous withdrawal and eventually ended up spending 21 days in detox and 68 days in treatment" (PharmD, age 47). An attorney's cold-turkey detox was made possible by a network of supportive friends who literally stood by her throughout the ordeal:

> It was almost a full-time job for me to sober up and recover. There was no place to admit me, and they didn't want to take me to an emergency room. This was back in the 1980s. So my AA sponsor, who was recovering herself, stayed with me for hours and hours and hours. For the the first 2 or 3 days she made sure I wasn't left alone. I was really, really sick! But after 7 to 10 days all the hallucinations left. Whenever the thought occurred to me to drink again, I remembered how very, very sick I'd been and how bad that last drunk was, and that's helped keep me sober! (JD, age 44)

Without a follow-up program, experience has shown, detoxification has limited long-term benefits; most patients quickly relapse. "I was in detox for 10 days," a pharmacist recalled, "and as soon as they let me out, I knew I would drink again" (PharmD, age 49). Such programs become little more than revolving doors that help addicts lower their drug tolerance and reduce the financial cost of their habits. Fortunately, detoxification is now regarded as the first phase of an extended program of therapy.

The attitude of treatment personnel has shifted from an aversive-conditioning stance to one of making the detoxifying addict as comfortable as possible during this ordeal and then following up with the next phase of treatment. "Drug 'em, don't bug 'em" is the prevailing attitude, notes a methadone maintenance practitioner.

Some addicts reportedly experience no serious medical complications during withdrawal. For others, withdrawal and detoxification can be life-threatening. Severe nutritional deficiencies may require immediate treatment with intravenous solutions to remedy or prevent seizures or circulatory collapse. The use of Valium or Librium to detoxify alcoholics was a medical breakthrough; before its use, as many as one-third of those undergoing hospital withdrawal reportedly died. Now it is rare to hear of a withdrawing addict dying. An essential treatment plan for helping any addict withdraw from any drug includes a good physical exam, education, reassurance about the temporary problems of withdrawal, and adequate nutrition and vitamin supplements (Shuckit 1995c).

Disease Education

Redefining themselves as sick rather than as moral failures profoundly affects addicts' recovery. "The disease concept is the most powerful thing," a nurse emphasized. "When I got fired the first time the head nurse told me, 'You are a terrible person, and I never want to see you again.' But when a compassionate person told me in a caring way that I was a sick person who needed help, not a bad person, I went into treatment. I went home and started calling hospitals" (RN, age 40).

Early in the nineteenth century, Benjamin Rush, founder of the American Psychiatric Association, wrote a paper declaring alcoholism a disease (Miller 1991). Not until 1945 did the American Medical Association formally accept this definition. Since then the disease model has become the dominant rationale for treating chemical dependencies and has been officially endorsed by the World Health Organization, the American Psychiatric Association, the National Association of Social Workers, the American Public Health Association, the National Council on Alcoholism, and the American Society for Addiction Medicine. The disease model defines substance abusers as people who are ill or unhealthy, not because they have an underlying mental disorder, but because they have the disease of chemical dependency, which manifests itself in an irreversible loss of control over alcohol and other psychoactive substances. The disease may go into remission, but because there is no known cure, complete abstinence is the treatment goal. The disease is progressive and, without abstinence, often fatal.

The disease model profoundly benefits Type 5 addicts. Haaga and McGlynn (1993) point out that getting addiction labeled a disease was an essential prerequisite to incorporating drug treatment into standard mental health practice and making treatment reimbursable. Calling addiction a disease provides, as Vaillant notes, a "ticket for admission" into the health care system ("New Insights into Alcoholism" 1983). Beginning in the 1970s, private health insurance plans increasingly provided benefits for substance-abuse treatment, in many cases restricted to particular settings such as inpatient treatment or medically supervised care. They also usually carried limitations on length of care (typically 28 days). These disease-oriented reimbursement programs motivated addicts to submit to medical treatment for their "disease" and to view the recovery process as "healing" (Haaga and McGlynn 1993). The disease model also softens the public's harsh attitude toward drug users, as a surprised pharmacist learned when his addiction secret was inadvertently revealed. The editor of the local newspaper, a former schoolmate, asked him to write an anonymous article about his addiction experiences, but his name was mistakenly published with it.

> I nearly died when I opened the paper and saw my name in print! But when I went to the pharmacy that day, people were saying, "Hey, Frank, I loved your article!" I got phone calls all day. (Later the editor called and apologized.) Ten years ago it would have been a disaster, but thank God the country is changing. We now look on alcoholism and drug addiction as a disease that can happen to anyone. (PharmD, age 41)

Most important, the disease model offers recovering addicts hope. "It helps when you realize that you are a sick person trying to get well, not a bad person trying to get good," said an attorney (JD, age 64; see also Stammer 1991, pp. 286–287). On the other hand, having a disease implies responsibility for taking care of oneself, for seeking treatment and thereafter maintaining a lifestyle that keeps the disease in remission. Self-care is emphasized rather than self-control.

> I remember a very wise man who said to me early in my recovery, "John, let me tell you something. You aren't responsible for your disease, but you are responsible for your recovery." It's just as if you were born with diabetes, high blood pressure, or anything else. It's not your fault. Now it *is* your responsibility to get well, and that's what I've been trying to do ever since. (PharmD, age 45)

The disease approach defines relapse as a process, not as an event. "Addiction is a chronic illness, and relapse is part of that condition," a treatment expert explained. "The expectation that somebody will come into treatment and be struck sober is totally unrealistic." The state director of an impaired physicians' program added, "It's a long-term planning process. A lot of physicians and nurses have the idea that once they've been through treatment, they're cured. They think, 'Hey, I'm okay now.' The most common time for relapse is immediately following the end of the monitoring contract. Unless the professional realizes that he has a chronic condition, the relapse sneaks up."

Despite its usefulness, the disease model remains controversial.[2] Social and behavioral scientists tend to dismiss it outright when it is presented strictly as a single, incurable, all-or-nothing disorder caused exclusively by biological abnormalities. According to Miller (1993), four assumptions underlie the biogenic disease model. The first is that alcoholism/addiction is a unitary disease; that is, there are two kinds of people in the world—addicts and nonaddicts.

The second assumption is that only physical abnormalities cause addiction. "Alcoholics become addicted because their bodies are physiologically incapable of processing alcohol normally," Milam and Ketcham (1983, p. 12) assert. "Psychotherapy," they argue, only "diverts attention from the physical cause of the disease, compounds the alcoholic's guilt and shame, and aggravates rather than alleviates his problems" (ibid., p. 14).

Third, addicts are assumed to be powerless to control their reactions to alcohol and other drugs. "The alcoholic's drinking is controlled by physiological factors which cannot be altered through psychological methods such as counseling, threats, punishment or reward" (Milam and Ketcham 1983, p. 42).

Fourth, addiction/alcoholism is considered irreversible. Because the addict's biogenic disease is physiologically based, the condition can be arrested but never cured. Once an addict, always an addict. Total abstinence must be the treatment goal, and no substitute drugs (for example, methadone) are prescribed beyond the acute withdrawal period (Milam and Ketcham 1983, p. 146).

Critics of this biogenic perspective assert that this model leads to treatment and prevention programs that are extremely limited in focus (Miller 1993, p. 135). "If alcoholism is just a hereditary anomaly, then there is no point in trying to prevent it among people who don't have a drinking problem" (ibid., p. 133).

The Institute of Medicine (1989) proposes a broader definition that includes both nature and nurture. Drawing on a public health perspective, this model identifies three classes of etiologic factors: (1) *agents*—the psychoactive drugs; (2) *hosts*—individuals who differ in their genetic, physiologic, behavioral, and sociocultural susceptibility to various kinds of harm from the chemical agents; and (3) *environment*, which influences the supply of and demand for the agents through actions such as increasing taxes on tobacco and alcohol, tightening advertising restrictions, increasing licensing regulations and warning labels, and promoting prevention and treatment.

The public health perspective encompasses the variety of factors identified by research as contributing to drug abuse, and its interdisciplinary nature requires cooperative expertise from such fields as epidemiology, medicine, psychology, and sociology. It incorporates research on genetic predispositions, biologic risk factors related to deficiencies in various neurochemicals, and various psychological and psychosocial factors (Wallace 1990). It also includes spiritual aspects.

Miller (1993, p. 134) considers hypertension a useful analogy, since it allows for progressive stages: "People differ along a continuum of systolic and diastolic blood pressure, and it is somewhat arbitrary where one draws the line between normality and hypertension. Hypertension contributes to a range of physical diseases. It has various causes and courses and is genetically influenced yet quite responsive to psychosocial factors. A number of potentially effective treatment options exist, depending on the nature and severity of the problem. Prevention and treatment blend into each other along the continuum of severity."

Regardless of definition, an addictionologist asserts, work sites and training centers need policies stating clearly that addiction will be treated as a disease, not as a moral failure.

> The department chairman at the school of medicine has a good way of putting it. He tells all the new residents, "I want you all to know my policy. Addiction is a disease, and we treat it like any other medical illness. If you come to me and say, 'I have the illness of addiction and need treatment,' we'll give you a leave of absence just as if you had broken your leg and needed to be in traction for a while. But if you keep it a secret and endanger your health and the lives of your patients, you're out on your ass!"   (MD, age 34)

Spiritual Development

This educational approach teaches addicts that a more powerful source of life energy than oneself exists, and that it can be accessed to improve health, happiness, and peace of mind. Addiction is viewed as a symptom of a spiritual impoverishment, and the chemically dependent person is urged to seek this higher power actively by humbling himself, adopting a clean lifestyle, and serving others. Addicts learn that abuse of the body renders one insensitive to spiritual forces, that ingesting psychoactive substances is akin to putting corrosive chemicals on a sensitive instrument designed to receive and transmit vital energy, and that only by keeping the instrument clean is one able to access these real but imponderable forces.

The spiritual approach to addiction contrasts with secular humanism—the philosophy that human beings are in control of their own lives and that human reason is the highest form of self-determinism. Rather than a *mechanistic* view (that is, people are nothing more than the sum of their biological parts), the spiritual approach presents a *vitalistic* view (that is, people have a vital force within themselves that cannot be explained by the five senses). "The soul needs an intense, full-bodied spiritual life as much as and in the same way that the body needs food," psychotherapist Thomas Moore (1993, p. 77) explains. "The soul—the seat of our deepest emotions—can benefit greatly from the gifts of a vivid spiritual life, and can suffer when it is deprived of them. The soul, for example, needs an articulated world-view, a carefully worked-out scheme of values and a sense of relatedness to the whole" (ibid., p. 28; see also Moore 1992).

Spiritually vital people live longer, are healthier, and have happier lives. Studies by McCormick and Schmidt (1989, 1991), for example, focused on 180 older men and women in San Francisco, Hawaii, and Arizona to determine the significance of spirituality in healthy aging and concluded that spirituality is a major health determinant. They found three elements among those who live long healthy lives: spirituality, a good psychosocial environment with strong interpersonal relationships, and active participation in preventive health programs. The investigators observed that spirituality and religion are two different things. Hawaiian men age 80 and older who felt a love for living things and an interconnectedness with the earth were as a group healthier and avoided hospitalization more than other groups. (See Dossey 1993 for a review of prayer and healing.)

Many professionals credit spiritual development as the primary energy in their recovery. "Part of my recovery," one explained, "was learning that I'm not necessarily the only one in charge, the one who has to make everything happen and has to fix everything" (PharmD, age 43). A treatment expert (Khouzam 1993) cites a 52-year-old opiate addict who had been treated sixteen times in different states for morphine dependence. "I would do anything to have a morphine fix," he confessed, including faking heart attacks in a hospital emergency room. After unsuccessful treatment with clonidine transdermal patches, methadone maintenance, and naltrexone maintenance, he had a spiritual experience that removed his drug craving. Seven months later he wrote a pamphlet, hoping to help others recover. "My desire for heroin was completely gone. I thought that this was just a temporary period of tiredness but three weeks passed and I could not bring myself to use any heroin" (Anonymous n.d.).

Not everyone experiences "doors opening or clouds parting or anything like that," a surgeon explained. "Spirituality is my weak side, but I've learned that it's an important side of my recovery. It's not an automatic reflex, but I pray and get outdoors into the mountains and that kind of thing" (MD, age 40).

Surrendering to a strength greater than self is easier when addicts hit bottom and realize that they can no longer manage their personal affairs. These "bottoms," frequently mentioned in meetings of recovering addicts, occur when users are confronted with overwhelming evidence of their personal failure and inability to cope. At such times, a pharmacist acknowledged, surrender, even to another human, is more likely. "For the first time in my life I realized that could no longer control my own life. My recovery began when I began to realize that I needed to surrender. So I said, 'Here I am, do what you will.' So my counselor, Frank, acted as my first higher power. It felt really good, wonderful, to let someone else take control" (PharmD, age 45).

Paradoxically, by humbling themselves to a higher power, many addicts experience an elevated, more healthy concept of self. One physician reported, "I have come to the point where I feel like a deserving creation of God" (MD, age 38). Another physician also reported an enhanced self-image:

I no longer need to resort to chemicals to believe in myself. I now enjoy living and looking forward to tomorrow. I don't have to hide from it; I'm not afraid of the telephone ringing or what might be on the other end. I'm no longer frightened by a letter that comes from an attorney's office, because I'm comfortable with me as a person. I was having trouble accepting myself. I believed in God but didn't think that God wanted any part of me.   (MD, age 61)

Although some experience dramatic spiritual experiences—especially during moments of crisis—for most, spiritual growth, like intellectual development, is slow and requires sustained effort. According to psychologist David G. Myers (1992, pp. 191–193), "The march forward begins with a step back." When an AA member stands up and says, "My name is Joe, and I'm an alcoholic," he is liberated from his arrogance. In the struggle for self-worth, there is an ancient and paradoxical road, Myers asserts. "Take a step back . . . face your spiritual poverty and emptiness." He explains, "People who have this idea of God—as loving, accepting, caring—tend to enjoy greater self-esteem." Self-acceptance comes by eliminating pretensions. "No longer is there a need to define our self-worth solely by our achievements, material well-being, or social approval. To find self-acceptance we needn't be or do anything. We need simply to accept that we are, ultimately and unconditionally, accepted."

Peer Support

Emotional support from colleagues and friends is critical in recovery. There is "overwhelming research evidence that the quality of one's social network is a crucial determinant of whether or not relapse will occur," Barber (1992, p. 157) asserts. A nurse explains, "Treatment programs that offer closeness, companionship, acceptance, and unconditional love provide an atmosphere and environment that has been lacking in the person's life until that time" (RN, age 42).

Support groups are powerful therapeutic tools because they allow professionals to share experiences and feelings. A dentist recalled, "I started going to a group for doctors in recovery, just 12 guys who shared, and it provided the only place that I could discuss my personal issues. A support group helps you realize 'Hey, I'm not alone; there are other people here that are experiencing the same problems.' It is tremendously helpful in getting away from the isolation that professionals have. Now dentists call me all the time and say, 'Is there a group where dentists meet?' " (DDS, age 47).

Chemically dependent attorneys in a Texas community get together in a large and highly successful informal gathering. "I've been very active in a group called Lawyers Concerned for Lawyers that meets every Thursday for lunch at one of the churches downtown. Anywhere between 50 and 75 guys come, and there are always 3 to 4 new ones. It's a good feeling to help these guys who are in deep, deep, deep trouble and tell them, 'Hey, you aren't a criminal, you're an alcoholic.' To see these folks listen and then give it a shot is a great feeling!" (JD, age 37).

Support groups give addicts associates who understand them and provide a reality check for them in recovery. When addicts begin to feel isolated and think that their struggles are unique, others like them give them insightful feedback and remind them of the potential consequences of relapse.

The unconditional acceptance and support given newcomers is a welcome relief from the rejection they often experience. Hearing others' personal experiences gives them hope, since group members have passed through similar adversities. They also hear potential solutions to their own problems and learn (or relearn) basic interpersonal skills.

A "big brother" or "big sister" assigned by the support group to watch over a participant between meetings plays a critical role in providing ongoing encouragement and continuity. Some of those who recover, like this dentist, credit such a person with saving their lives. "My AA sponsor actually kept me alive. He let me live with him and gave me $20 a week to keep me going. It was really bleak for me. It's hard for people who have never experienced such a relationship to understand what a sponsor does for us and how selfless they are" (DDS, age 46).

The relationships that develop between recovering addicts and sponsors often continue as lifelong bonds of affection. "A saint was sent to me who became my sponsor," an attorney said.

> He rescued me and saved my life. When my terror reached a point that I thought I was going to die, I wandered very drunk into an AA meeting; I had been drinking most of the night. I will never forget when he came up to me that night . . . He shook my hand and said,

"You've been drinking." I said to myself, "What a perceptive guy!" He took me under his wing and told me about AA. I haven't found it necessary to have a drink since that day. He was a marvelous, marvelous person, and I still can't believe how it happened, but it did happen!   (Anonymous 1993)

The recovery process is much more difficult without a supportive network. Addicts surrounded by judgmental and disapproving associates who regard drug abuse as a moral weakness or character deficiency are much more likely to be secretive and to suffer in silence. An anonymous nurse wrote this letter to the editor of a nursing journal:

I was dismayed but not surprised to read of attitudes of nurses towards impaired colleagues. As a recovering alcoholic for four years, I have long known that negative attitudes exist towards substance abuse. However, that 25% of the nurses surveyed would not support a return to work is quite disheartening. I wonder if they would feel the same way about colleagues who are plagued with cancer . . . I have chosen to go underground with my disease, rather than face the judgmental attitudes of my peers.   (Anonymous 1988)

Her anguish is shared by other addicted nurses. "Addicted nurses are a professional embarrassment," one commented. "I know the system exists to serve patients—and I accept that—but we *treat* people who are sick, we don't punish them. People are still very prejudiced against health professionals who have a history of addiction" (paraphrased from Nagel 1992).

To extend their helping network, some professional organizations divide their states into regions, organizing members to help those who are less advanced in their recovery. Peer-support networks are advertised at professional meetings and supplement newsletters encouraging addicted colleagues to come forward and accept the help of supportive associates. Well-publicized help-line phone numbers allow addicted practitioners to phone anonymously, receive advice, and find support. (See the Appendix.) Another nurse availed herself of this program with good results:

When I finally phoned for help, they asked me if I wanted someone to come by my house to talk to me. I said, "Gee, isn't that nice, sure." I was expecting some bums, but these two very nice ladies came to my door who were well dressed and happy. I thought, "They don't even send alcoholics out to talk to alcoholics." But I let them come in, and the first thing they told me is that I had a disease called alcoholism. I told them, "I'm a nurse, and if I had a disease, I would know it." I blew it right there because I didn't want them to know that I was a nurse. But I learned that these ladies were nurses also! Talk about a higher power sending me the right people!   (RN, age 70)

Peer support is also promoted by organizational efforts to educate and improve the attitudes of nonaddicted colleagues. Employee assistance programs, for example, have profoundly influenced colleguial perceptions, changing them from prejudice to advocacy and in doing so have facilitated the recovery of countless individuals (Peterson 1988).

Drug Screening

Urine, blood, or hair testing for illicit drug use reduces the likelihood of relapse (Anglin and Hser 1991). There is considerable evidence that urine screening, a common practice among treatment programs, is effective in controlling drug use when linked to sanctions (Anglin, Deschens, and Speckart 1987). The combination of legal supervision and urine testing significantly suppresses both narcotic use and concurrent property crime among addicts.[3]

The Federal Aviation Administration requires commercial airlines to randomly test pilots, flight attendants, air traffic controllers, and maintenance workers for drug use. When a San Diego airline pilot launched a legal challenge to the FAA rule, citing Fourth Amendment prohibitions of unreasonable searches, the Supreme Court let stand the FAA rule requiring a "comprehensive anti-drug program"—including random, unannounced urine tests ("Drug Testing for Highflyers" 1991).

Acknowledging that drug-using pilots are unlikely to reveal their chemical intake, an FAA executive said, "Although a pilot may say, 'I'm the Virgin Mary,' I reply, 'You may be, but I don't believe you. We know you use drugs, and in this profession you shouldn't be using at all.' " Then he explained, "Drug-abusing pilots think using is normal and the FAA are a bunch of jerks who make up their own rules. They think they can get away with it, but when they learn they will be caught, they regretfully give up their use. If they don't it will cost them a lot—maybe their career" (FAA treatment specialist).

Urine testing helps motivate addicts to avoid drugs. "It is a constant reminder to our recovering colleagues that 'Big Brother' is watching," Canavan (1984, p. 66) asserts. An excellent warning system to indicate when a client slips, drug testing also reliably documents a professional's drug-free state when she applies for relicensing (Canavan 1984). Results protect the professional from suspicion and provide objective data to enhance employer confidence.

Recovering addicts extol the benefits of drug testing. "Urine testing should be mandatory for relicensing," a dentist asserted. "Drug screening is very helpful to a recovering professional. If nothing else, it tells me I damn well better keep my nose clean—because there's a hammer hanging over my head. If I don't want the hammer to fall, I'd better not use" (DDS, age 55).

Test results proving that an addict is "clean" are exhilarating. "Initially, drug screening was a little scary," a nurse explained. "But I felt good when I got the lab reports saying, 'Negative,' 'Negative,' 'Negative.' I'm clean and can prove it because I have tangible proof in my hand!" (RN, age 40). "A positive result makes me feel good," a surgeon agreed. "If something goes bad in the OR and they say I screwed up, I can now give a urine and say, 'I'm not using any drugs.' It protects us and provides positive feedback" (MD, age 40).

A pharmacist recovering from cocaine addiction posted the testing certificates on the refrigerator door.

> Because I lied to my family for 10 years—God only knows the things I've told them—they're not too trusting of me, and I don't blame them. Until their trust is built up, the urine screens are nice to have. They help me gain acceptance from my family. I need them for my credibility—for evidence that I'm clean. I need to show my employer and my family and say, "Gee, here are my screens, and you can see that I'm clean." Although they are very costly—I pay for them myself— I'm going to sign another contract for random urine tests after this one runs out. I just want to have it for my own benefit, for my family and my employer. Plus it allows me to keep my license.   (PharmD, age 41)

Although testing procedures are carefully monitored to prevent cheating, addicts devise ingenious methods to escape detection (Coombs and West 1991). For example, a female clinician ran a feeder tube down through her buttocks. By leaning back against a urine-filled bag, she got the expected urine stream. A young anesthesiologist filled a small polyethylene bag with clean urine, palmed it, and, by squeezing the sides together, delivered the appropriate specimen in the appropriate arc when observed by testing personnel. At first his wife provided the specimen, but when she later refused, he substituted his dog's urine. "We didn't realize we were analyzing the dog's urine until later when he told us" the testing director remarked.

A urologist catheterized his own bladder, removed his urine, substituted clean urine, and urinated clean urine under close supervision at the testing site. "This tells you how devious and sick these people are," said the testing director. "No one in their right mind would catheterize themselves." Random urine screening typically includes (1) the development of a random time schedule, (2) the presence of same-sex monitors who directly observe the specimen collection, (3) examination of the urine for color and temperature, and (4) test for acidity.

All addicts try to beat this system, but health care professionals develop the skill to an art form. When a pharmacist who had obviously relapsed consistently tested negative for drugs, a suspicious colleague investigated.

> His behavior and attitude told me that he was using, but his lab results were always insignificant; nothing positive—no dirty urines were ever reported. This puzzled me, so I called the lab doing the testing and asked them to test some of the other variables such as PH, creatine, and specific gravity. They checked and said, "They are all identical at *every* testing." Amazingly, this pharmacist was concocting his own urine. He took an IV solution, added vitamin B, obtained the proper PH and creatine, and filled up the cup at testing time with this pharmacy-made urine! (PharmD, age 41)

Hair testing has recently been promoted as a better screen for drugs. Since the mid-1980s, the rising popularity of cocaine has lent urgency to developing better ways to measure drug use. Cocaine and opiates are water-soluble and quite rapidly excreted—generally within 48 to 72 hours. Only marijuana, which is fat soluble, has a slow, relatively long-term urine excretion rate; regular and heavy marijuana users can test positive for weeks.

Studies show convincingly that radioimmunoassay of a single

hair specimen detects more drug exposure—especially cocaine—than is self-reported or detected by a single urine test. The only practical difficulty is collecting specimens from subjects with short or no head hair at all (Mieczkowski et al. 1993). However, hair testing cannot detect drug use shortly after drug intake, whereas urinalysis can. Therefore, hair testing will not replace urine screening but is considered a viable supplementary technique (Gropper and Reardon 1993).

Behavioral Contracts

A recovery contract defines what is expected of the addicted professional in order to remain in school or retain a license to practice. It specifies the negative consequences of continued drug use—loss of license, job, or school status—and counteracts the addict's euphoric image of drugs with negative realities. "They help extinguish positive expectations that users have about what drugs will do for them," explained a New York treatment expert. "Although the addict may think 'Drugs are wonderful,' the contract specifies that something really awful is sure to follow if there is a positive urine."

The contract specifies that the participant will not use alcohol, illicit drugs, or mind-altering prescription drugs. An inpatient treatment program and/or weekly meeting with a profession-specific diversion group (see Chapter 8) may also be required, as well as regular meetings each week in Alcoholics Anonymous or a similar group (Ikeda and Pelton 1990).[4] A number of people may participate in the treatment contract: the recovering individual, the employer or school representative, a monitor, and any other parties deemed necessary. All receive lab results of drug screenings, and the monitor routinely follows up on all expectations specified in the contract.

Routine monitoring meetings are held for 3–5 years to facilitate communication of progress and problems (Smith and Starnes 1988). The motivational power of the contracts depends on the client's stage of addiction. Asked how the potential loss of his license would affect him, a pilot (age 58) replied, "At one point in the development of my disease I would have told them to shove it; I wanted to drink. I didn't care about going to work or being a pilot; I was pretty sick." Later, however, when confronted he admitted, "I'd rather stop drinking than lose my job."

Motivated by a news magazine reporting a 90 percent chance of sobriety one year after putting one's license on the line, a physician who had "hit bottom" went to a counselor and said, "I want to do what this article says. I'm giving you a signed letter to put in your safety deposit box and ask you to mail the letter if I relapse." The letter read: "Dear Board of Medical Examiners: I'm an addict. If you receive this letter it means I've relapsed. Please take my license away. Put me in treatment and do anything you have to do to save my life" (MD, age 38). He also asked the counselor to check his urine three times a week.

Not only do contracts keep addicted professionals off drugs; they also forestall retaliation from colleagues. "I was very nervous about telling some people at my hospital, especially the chief of staff and some people in the OR. But the contract required me to, and I now realize it's a good thing. The contract forces you to be honest" (MD, age 40). In former days, a pharmacist explained, the prevailing attitude toward an addicted colleague was "Lock him up and throw away the key. They were blackballed and ostracized from the profession." He added, "It was pharmacy's loss. In the past this was necessary, there was no better solution available" (Dickinson 1988, p. 216).

In the past, employers, who understandably wanted to protect themselves, refused to hire recovering addicts. Now, with encouragement from professional societies, employers utilize return-to-work contracts. These become effective tools for monitoring the employees' behavior and a positive influence in recovery (Smith and Starnes 1988; Crosby and Bissell 1989, pp. 195–196).

The value of contracts becomes evident when monitoring ends. At this time, an aviator observed, some addicted pilots drop out of sight. "Once the monitoring is over, guys slip back and go back into use, usually alcohol. After retirement they tend to slip. Monitoring isn't ongoing, the peer group isn't there, the salary and status incentives are not there, the image of the pilot fades from their minds. Once their ticket is clean and there is no more monitoring, they feel they can handle this themselves" (pilot, age 57).

Individual and Group Therapy

Individual and group therapy, traditional components of drug treatment programs, have a colorful and varied history (Golden, Khantzian and McAuliffe 1994; Woody, Mercer, and Luborsky 1994).

These interventions range from Freudian psychoanalysis, in which individual patients recline on a couch recalling childhood and other memories, to "attack therapy" (the Synanon Game) practiced in "therapeutic communities" (TCs), in which 10 to 12 addicts tear into another addict's behavior, shouting insulting comments as she occupies the "hot seat."

In TCs, addicts, defined as sociopaths who lack social conscience, are resocialized by breakdown of their ego defenses, followed by rewards of higher status within the "family" (the community of ex-addicts) as they mature. Those who endure this emotional abuse rise in rank until, as "elders," they administer discipline to newer arrivals. Needless to say, most addicts "split," and of those who complete these programs, the vast majority relapse. In my own study (Coombs 1981a) only 9 of 208 participants (4.3 percent) remained drug-free more than 18 months after leaving, and each of these credited AA with their continuing sobriety.

Psychoanalytic therapists try to help addicts uncover unconscious emotional conflicts that predispose them to addiction. But controlled outcome studies of addicts show this approach to be ineffective (Institute of Medicine 1989). Well-meaning but unsophisticated therapists contribute little if anything when clients do not want therapy. Consider this pharmacy student's experience:

> The dean of students offered me a medical leave if I promised to get into an outpatient treatment program. So I set up counseling with the county substance abuse program and lied my way through six months of counseling. I told him everything he wanted to hear, then got the piece of paper saying I was clean, had my goals in place, and all this other bullshit. These people who treated me didn't really understand the disease. It scares me that others are going to see this counselor and get some real crappy advice.   (PharmD, age 26)

Certified as rehabilitated, he returned to school and continued using cocaine, marijuana, and alcohol. "Nothing changed. I was using full steam, drugs, booze—the whole works."

Vaillant (1983) found that one-on-one psychotherapy is a remarkably ineffective treatment for active alcoholism. Only 2 of 26 subjects who received a combined total of 5,000 psychotherapy hours attained sobriety, and one of these had relapsed and joined Alcoholics Anonymous.

Some office practitioners, like this psychiatrist, recognize their limitations and refuse further office appointments: "He felt that to continue seeing him was a waste of time for both of us, so he fired me as a patient. Today I am grateful to him for that. I was looking for someone to enable me, and I would have let him; I would have accepted any diagnosis other than addiction or would have taken any kind of pill he wanted to give me—I would have done anything to not face what my problem was" (RN, age 40).

On the other hand, clinicians trained in chemical dependence can have a beneficial effect. "When I was in the hospital," a dentist related, "I met a psychiatrist I really hated at first. He was a no-nonsense kind of guy who became my therapist for over a year. It was really rough, but I had more progress with that guy than with anybody else" (DDS, age 47). Psychotherapy is very useful in aftercare support (Kilburg, Nathan and Thoreson 1986). It helps clients uncover persistent and unproductive behaviors, develop problem-solving skills, and gain new insights about personal characteristics that contributed to their addiction. A physician commented, "Therapy helped me get in touch with my emotions. I had suppressed a lot of feelings, but when I let them out, it was like a balloon lifting off with all the pain. It was a very freeing feeling." He added, "Therapy also helped me learn that I didn't need to use drugs to feel good" (MD, age 40).

Group therapy is usually much more effective than individual therapy for addicts who are still using (Rounsaville and Carroll 1992; Washton 1992). "Groups work best for chemically dependent people because we need other addicts to call us on our stuff," a nurse explained (RN, age 40).

Group therapy energized this surgeon and helped him gain insights about how his dysfunctional family contributed to his addiction.

It was a big emotional thing when this guy was talking about being left alone by his parents. I instantaneously went back to being a young kid and my brother beating the crap out of me. I had to pay him 25 cents a week for life insurance, and like the real companies, he was always canceling my policies. I used to have to hide in the bushes outside until my parents came home at six, so he wouldn't beat me up. It was dark, and I was cold. He'd strip me down, tie me up, and then bring in a girlfriend from across the street to see me naked—

some pretty crazy stuff. My mom and dad hated each other—the worst match-up you could ever imagine. It was a pretty crazy life. When I got to college and got my marijuana, it was peace, man. It helped me keep "hiding in the bushes." Before group therapy I thought my life was normal. I didn't realize that my family was emotionally abusive and it had affected me. But in group I was able to get in touch with it. When that guy expressed his pain on the porch, I was back in the bushes in my pain. I learned that I was trying to be Superman to find acceptance and to compensate for my abuse as a kid. I didn't *feel*, I just *did*; and I did it with extraordinary effort. When this guy cried, the group leader had us all gather around at one time and embrace him in a group hug. All this energy was going into the center of this person and then coming back, and I felt that it was for me too, back there in the bushes. It was a very emotional thing—very healing!   (MD, age 40)

BEREAVEMENT COUNSELING

Drugs may be valued so highly that they take priority over all other things, including human relationships. Some addicts experience profound loss when they relinquish them—not unlike the grief reactions of any person when a beloved family member dies. Grief over this loss contributes to the protracted withdrawal symptoms addicts experience—tightness in the throat, shortness of breath, loss of appetite, loss of sleep, emotional waves that may last from a few minutes to an hour, exhaustion, and an altered sense of reality. Mourning may also account for some of the depressive feelings recovering addicts often experience (Jennings 1991, p. 223). Other people may unwittingly exacerbate psychic pain by celebrating the addict's rejection of drugs and failing to recognize his mourning. Supportive individual and group therapy can play an important role in helping the grieving addict make the transition to a life without his once-trusted and beloved associate—his drugs. Bereavement counseling may help recovering addicts cope with painful feelings of loss and helplessness.

WOMEN'S ISSUES

Gender issues are another potent focus for therapy. A survey of the Association of Junior Leagues found that women make up about 30–40 percent of patients in treatment centers for chemical abuse (Sheffield 1992; see also Wilsnack, Wilsnack, and Hiller-Sturmhofel 1994). Although women use illicit drugs less frequently than men, those who do suffer from more acute and chronic problems. Chemically dependent women suffer health problems earlier in their addictions than men, their families disintegrate more often, and their babies suffer from fetal alcohol/drug syndrome.Because of gender differences in body-water content, women experience higher blood-alcohol concentrations with a lower alcohol intake, and long-term problem drinking takes a greater health toll on women and disables them longer than men. Women alcoholics are also more likely to die from suicides, alcohol-related accidents, circulatory disorders, and cirrhosis (Galbraith and Lubinski 1992). In addition, many more addicted women than men have experienced physical, sexual, and emotional violence as children and in their adult relationships.

Women, twice as likely as men to be lifetime abstainers, are less likely when they drink to be involved in alcohol-related violence, legal problems, or work problems (Schuckit 1995b). Because society considers it more shameful for women to be alcoholics/addicts, they tend to conceal the illness more often and longer (Galbraith and Lubinski 1992). In America's traditional double standard, men are more likely to be regarded with humor or compassion—"the poor guy can't help it"—but an alcoholic woman is "disgusting." Unlike men, women who drink to excess are never considered funny, especially a drunk mother.

Moreover, 70 percent of psychoactive drugs are prescribed to women, and women are more likely to use alcohol in combination with other drugs, particularly psychoactive drugs. Compared with men, alcoholic women have a 50–100 percent higher death rate. Women are disadvantaged in outreach and intervention strategies because treatment services have been developed for white males. Programs are seldom directed to meeting the needs of women. Few programs, for example, accept addicted women who are pregnant (Galbraith and Lubinski 1992). Although the medical community now has the resources to address physician impairment, Steindler notes, "there has been a reluctance to recognize the addiction problems of women physicians" (1987, p. 2954).

The recovery process is also more difficult for women because there are few treatment centers exclusively for women, and few provide child care. Women in treatment need to focus on such issues as low self-esteem, sexual abuse, battering, and child abuse, questions not easily discussed in coeducational settings. Women in coed groups tend to take a back seat, allowing men more time to talk. A nurse asserts:

> Every program needs to have some women-specific groups. Women need a place to talk about mental issues, parenting issues, and career issues. It's much harder for a woman to reenter the work force. Society is much more judgmental toward women than toward men, especially mothers who may have crack babies or fetal alcohol syndrome babies. We've kept women hidden in the closet or under the carpet; nobody wants to talk about Mom's problem. Women have such tremendous shame about sexual behavior that happened under the influence, things they probably wouldn't do when clean and sober. Drunk women have been raped and not talked about it because society calls them "slut" and "whore." "It's a woman's own fault," they say, "she shouldn't have got herself into that situation. It shouldn't have happened." There's still the old double standard.   (RN, age 40)

Lack of family support is another issue; many more women than men leave treatment facing divorce and acute financial problems. Women more often arrive at AA meetings alone and rarely have the support most men take for granted: someone to clean their clothes, provide supper and child care while they attend to personal needs, and so on. Willis (1992, p. 271) points out, "It may not be 'convenient' to have mom in treatment if she cooks, cleans, does household shopping, and holds down a job which contributes significantly to household finances. Treatment or sobriety may be inadvertently or subconsciously sabotaged if a woman focuses on home, work, and family instead of herself in recovery."

Coping-Skills Training

Just as Walt Disney's Dumbo the elephant believed he needed to carry a magic feather in his trunk to fly, so addicts believe they need a drug to perform adequately in stressful situations (Marlatt 1985b, p. 76). They do not know if they can cope without it.

Coping-skills training, developed by behavioral psychologists G. Alan Marlatt and Judith R.Gordon (1985), rests on the premise that using psychoactive drugs to ameliorate unpleasant situations reinforces maladaptive coping and eventual negative consequences for health, social status, and self-esteem (Marlatt 1985a, p. 10). This approach teaches users that they will most likely relapse within the first 90 days following initial cessation and will most likely do so in high-risk settings, situations in which the drug has previously been used extensively to cope (Marlatt 1985b, p. 76). When a drug user decides to eliminate the drug habit, these high-risk situations become even more stressful.

Three primary high-risk situations account for three-fourths of all relapses (Marlatt 1985a, p. 37). The first (35 percent of relapses) are times of unpleasant emotions—frustration, anger, anxiety, depression, or boredom. The second (16 percent) occurs after interpersonal conflicts with family members, friends, or work associates; and the third (20 percent) happens when others exert social pressure, either directly (for example, verbal persuasion) or indirectly (for example, being present when others are using). Obviously, these categories may overlap.

Clients learn to recognize high-risk situations and practice new coping skills in response to them. Several strategies help addicts cope with urges and cravings in high-risk situations. Labeling the urge when it occurs is key. Another strategy is "urge surfing." The mass media in our society constantly bombard us with stimulating messages of "drink me, smoke me," and when the messages call up pleasant memories of past drug behaviors, the user is flooded with cues that excite craving. Clients are forcefully reminded that to give in to an urge will actually strengthen its intensity and increase its probability of recurrence (Marlatt 1985c, p. 241). If craving responses are not reinforced by subsequent drug consumption, they eventually subside through a gradually diminishing interest, the psychological process of extinction. Like an ocean wave, the urge starts small, builds to a crest, and then breaks in intensity. Marlatt teaches the user to imagine surf-riding the urge like a wave until it subsides.

Clients practice the new coping responses, such as how to say no when offered drugs, and they practice alternative behaviors, such as exercising rather than going to a bar during high-risk periods (Rawson et al. 1993). At later stages of training, clients go to real-life settings such as a tavern or bar where they can practice their new skills, surrounded by other people actively modeling the undesirable behavior. Then clients discuss their reactions and provide each other with support. For example, after 40 trips to their favorite pubs to observe others drink—"cue overexposure"—clients eventually report little or no desire to drink.

Clients are shown "choice points," forks in the road that led them closer to the brink of relapse. Such "cognitive road maps" help clients picture a road with various choice points along the way, some leading directly to the high-risk situation and others providing escape routes—"U-turns" and "bypasses" (Marlatt 1985a p. 46). The user learns to view cues as "highway signs" calling for a change of direction. In some cases clients can avoid risky situations altogether by "taking a detour" (ibid., p. 56).

This journey metaphor, complete with stages—preparation, departure, and journey markers—helps users imagine successful progress. At "departure," the point of greatest risk, clients keep an ongoing record of urges or craving experiences. They gain a feeling of mastery and control by rating the intensity and duration of the urge. Although all journeys involve minor setbacks, frustrations, and disappointments, clients learn to prevent a slip from evolving into a total relapse. "Travelers" are encouraged not to give up, blame themselves for setbacks, or assume that all is lost—the road is not a dead end (Marlatt 1985c, p. 244).

Clients learn that slips can result in growth. Instead of saying, "I blew it, it's all over," the user asks, "What went wrong? Did I take a wrong turn? What can I do to fix the problem?" Through the application of behavioral and cognitive "brakes," the initial lapse does not "spin out" into a full-blown relapse. "Reminder cards" list "emergency procedures" to be followed when slips occur, and "relapse drills" are practiced (Marlatt 1985a, p. 51).

When an addict succeeds in high-risk situations, he develops "self-efficacy," a confident expectation that he can cope successfully with the next challenging event. Research confirms the effectiveness of this approach.[5]

Lifestyle Planning and Monitoring

To expect to eliminate something meaningful—drug use—from one's life without a replacement is unrealistic. Lifestyle monitoring addresses this issue by helping chemically dependent persons replace bad habits—ones that are self-defeating—with good ones—ones that are self-enhancing (Marlatt and Barrett 1994). Although bad habits (for example, gambling, adultery, debt spending, drug use) may at first be rewarding, they invariably have negative consequences. In contrast, good habits (for example, exercising, taking classes, and saving money) require effort up-front but later yield positive long-term benefits (Marlatt and Gordon 1985, p. 299).

As their addiction progressed, addicts increasingly excluded activities that brought long-term physical, mental, emotional, and spiritual benefits—relying instead on short-term gains that undermine these qualities. Each time an addict felt uncomfortable, she habitually looked for a "quick fix." The negative after-effects became cues for the next use. Each repeat strengthened the bad habit, reinforcing a vicious addictive cycle (Marlatt and Gordon 1985, p. 286).

Replacing bad habits with good ones reverses this downward spiral. "I now get natural highs from the positive things that I do," said a physician. "This includes exercise and nutritious food, hobbies, making friends, getting involved with groups, and doing charitable things" (MD, age 46). "Everyone needs pleasure," Zackon and colleagues (1993, p. 109) observe, "and giving up drugs should not mean giving up fun. In fact a person whose mind, body, and lifestyle are no longer addicted can have more fun in more ways than ever before. Most drug-free pleasures, however, require effort. With drugs it was automatic: Take drugs—feel good. A person who has mainly relied on drugs for fun, and whose nervous system has been accustomed to a very abnormal stimulation, has to adjust."

An imbalanced daily lifestyle increases the risk of relapse. Marlatt (1985a) defines balance as the degree of equilibrium in one's daily life between demanding activities—"hassles" ("I shoulds")—and those perceived as pleasures—"I wants." A lifestyle dominated by "I shoulds" can engender feelings of self-deprivation and a desire for indulgence and gratification. "I owe it to myself to have a drink; I deserve a break," the professional rationalizes after a hard day (Marlatt 1985a, p. 47).

How is a balanced lifestyle achieved? Clients record stressors and positive experiences—called "uplifts"—that give pleasure and relief from tension or agitation—recreational activities such as reading for pleasure, listening to music, or attending movies. Also assessed are activities that affect physical health, such as nutrition, exercise, and the use of other drugs like caffeine. The quality of interpersonal relationships is considered. How much time is spent alone in self-reflective activities—meditating, praying, spiritual reading, keeping a personal journal, and getting in touch with nature and one's inner being? "Spiritual pursuits and addictive behaviors often share a common element in that they are frequently associated with an altered state of consciousness quite different from the ordinary waking state of mind," Marlatt and Gordon (1985, p. 298) explain. "For some clients, the need to experience this altered state with drugs or other addictive activities may mask an underlying need for a deeper and more satisfying spiritual life."

Once the assessment is complete, counselors help the client develop new habits. Because it is difficult for those long accustomed to immediate gratification to overcome inertia, changes begin with small, easily accomplished goals. Most important, Marlatt and Gordon observe (1985, p. 302), the new activities must belong to the "I want" rather than the "I should" category. Otherwise, these activities simply add to the client's list of life stressors.

Zackon and colleagues (1993) compare recovering addicts to immigrants, strangers in a new land who need gradual assimilation into the new lifestyle. The old ways must be replaced with new ones. "In recovery, filling the voids of weekends, off hours, and holidays is one of their biggest challenges," Zackon notes (p. 49). "A healthy schedule of social recreation reduces boredom and loneliness, helps manage stress, and provides occasions for new fun and satisfaction—all needs that, if unmet, pose major threats to abstinence."

A softball enthusiast testified to the "highs" that this activity creates for him. "On the softball field there is socialization and camaraderie. This is one way to learn to live in a normal world and not isolated in 12-step meetings." Commenting on his drinking, which had become unmanageable, he said, "It was crazy. If I didn't stop I would have ended up dead or in jail. But I love playing softball; it makes being sober so much more fun" (Malaman 1993, p. 3).

According to Glasser (1976, p. 93), quality self-time activities meet these six criteria. They are (1) noncompetitive and can be done in an hour a day, (2) easily done and without a great deal of mental effort, (3) not dependent on others, (4) beneficial physically, mentally, or spiritually, (5) subject to improvement with persistence, and (6) done without self-criticism.

McPeake, Kennedy, and Gordon (1991) point out that addicted clients can achieve desired states of altered consciousness (ASC) by increased physical activity, relaxation training, meditation and prayer, cognitive therapy, and art/aesthetic experience—just as they did when taking alcohol or other drugs. In so doing, "the patients are accessing the same neurohormonal and brain pleasure-pain centers that they did when drinking or drugging, only now they are doing so without substances" (p. 80). Patients become enthusiastic, McPeake and colleagues (1991) note, when they learn that they can initiate an ASC by bringing these neural systems under voluntary control through daily practice. Failure to address a recovering addict's need for achieving ASC is, they assert, a major reason for relapse.

Marlatt's studies show that taking regular timeout periods to relax, even short periods each day, is associated with significant reduction in drinking rates (Marlatt and Gordon 1985, p. 327). "If I only had known what was there for me—the joy, beauty, and love that are available to me—I would have stopped a long time ago and would have avoided a lot of suffering," a dentist enthused. "It was a lot harder getting sober than staying sober. Now I spend an hour and half in the gym every day and spend time with my child. I have a lot of activities, and I'm not bored. What I have now is so much better than what I ever had in the past: the joy of a great relationship, financial success, respect from other people, friends. And I really love working with people" (DDS, age 49).

Family Education and Counseling

Addicts whose families participate in treatment have better outcomes than those treated alone (Nyman and Cocores 1991, p. 885). Treating the patient as an isolated entity almost guarantees a poor response (Mann 1991, p. 1208). Ignoring family members is, as one addictionologist explained, "like taking the addict out of a muddy puddle, cleaning him up, and then throwing him back into the puddle."

An analysis of 500 physicians followed for four years after receiving treatment found that the relapse rate was higher when the spouse was uninvolved and untreated (Talbott 1987). Physicians who achieve sobriety do so with their spouses' help. Thomas and colleagues (1986) found a 57 percent increase in the number of addicts who continued in long-term treatment after being detoxified once a family program was instituted that included behavior contracts with the spouse. (See also Noel et al. 1987; *Alcohol and Health* 1990, pp. 263–264; Kaufman 1994; and Steinglass 1994.)

Family input is critical to gaining an accurate picture of the problem. "When I see a pilot for evaluation," a pilot examiner reported, "I always have the spouse attend because I get a much better idea about the problem than from the pilot alone. I'm also able to evaluate the spouse's role in being supportive or destructive."

Family education and counseling identify and eliminate family patterns that undermine recovery. "Little white lies" covering the addicted behavior are a way of life in the addict's family. Rationalizations, partial truths, and conscious omission of information distort the truth and mislead others. "Everybody in the whole family was in total denial," a nurse recalled. "We were all too ashamed to talk about it; nobody discussed the problem openly. Nobody" (Barde and Pick 1993). "As loyal members of this family system we protect our own at all costs," Crosby and Bissell note (1989, p. 37). "We lose our ability to know what reality is—what the real truth is. Worse, we learn to devalue truth."

"Codependency" and "coaddiction," interchangeable popular terms, refer to unique psychological and behavioral attributes of family members who live with an addict (Nyman and Cocores 1991). "A codependent," states one physician, "is a person who denies that her spouse really has a problem and makes excuses for him. She fixes the car when he smashes it and doesn't require him to face the consequences of his own actions" (MD treatment practitioner). Bombarded with personal attacks from the irrational addict, codependents typically feel guilt-ridden and worthless. They often feel responsible for the destructive behavior and wonder how they went wrong. Sometimes they question their sanity (Nyman and Cocores 1991).

Not surprisingly, codependent family members tend to develop significant, stress-related illnesses such as ulcers, colitis, and migraine headaches (Nyman and Cocores 1991). Also common are personality disorders characterized by excessive denial, emotional constriction, depression, hypervigilance, compulsions, anxiety, and substance abuse. Yet angry, disappointed, guilty, and anxious family members tend to resist participation in a recovery program, since, by the time treatment begins, relationships are typically severely strained (Mann 1991, p. 1208). "It was suggested that my wife have counseling," a pilot (age 58) reported, "but she rejected it, saying it was my problem and she didn't need any help."

Some treatment centers routinely include multifamily group sessions, individual family therapy, couple therapy, and week-long family programs, including a variety of family strengthening methods. Family participation enhances the therapeutic leverage in managing resistant addicts by dismantling the enabling systems, clarifying boundaries, enhancing self-esteem, and reducing the co-addict's potential for sabotaging the addict's treatment (Nyman and Cocores 1991). "I was in a 21-day program when my wife was asked to come to a family meeting," a physician (MD, age 50) recalled. "She said she was getting a divorce—I'd heard that song before—and would come one time only. She came the night we had a psychodrama, and it was really emotional. It was a turning point for her, and she got into the program with both feet. We did everything and later played a big part in forming an alumni group [those who complete the treatment program]."

A nurse had a similar experience:

> I sat through an entire day of the family program at the center where my husband was in treatment. When they did the "sculpting" of the family portrait, bringing people out of the audience to enact different family roles—the caretaker mommy, the withdrawn kid, the clown, the mascot, the hero—I was so moved by it I had to fight back tears. When I went up to the instructor afterward she said, "It sounds like you have some personal issues to deal with." So I went home, phoned my father, and unloaded 32 years of resentment. About 6 or 8 months later he called me from a treatment center asking me if I would mind if he came for a visit when he got out. When he came we went to some AA meetings together, and things started working out pretty well between us.   (RN, age 40)

Family-oriented self-help programs like Al-Anon and Adult Children of Alcoholics also have a therapeutic impact. Al-Anon, the oldest family program, was started by Louise Wilson, the wife of AA Founder Bill Wilson. While the men were having their meetings, the wives began to see how they were affected and needed support. In 1950, 87 of these family groups asked AA to print their meetings in the AA directory. When AA refused, these women started their own organization (Schulz 1991).

Adult Children of Alcoholics (ACA) helps adults raised by alcoholic parents (Schulz 1991). Functioning much like AA groups, they provide insight about the codependent lifestyle and support during times of crisis and difficulty and address the denial, humiliation, and shame that arise in an addictive family. Educational materials, including films and lectures, offer basic information about addiction, codependence, and recovery. Some family members are referred to long-term comprehensive treatment that includes intensive group and individual counseling (Nyman and Cocores 1991, p. 886). "I'm a great believer in Al-Anon and in family therapy," an airline treatment expert observed. "They can greatly help family members come to terms with their role in the whole addiction process. There's a lot to repair."

Prior to treatment, the family unit centers upon the addict's self-defeating behaviors, with family members playing well-defined roles. Without drug-using behavior, the entire family structure must be reorganized and the script discarded. The process inevitably creates confusion and feelings of loss (Swift and Williams 1975).

The family of an addict is often rewarded in strange ways for its long-suffering. For example, relatives and neighbors may praise the family for enduring the difficulty of living with an addicted person. When the addict recovers, the praise ceases. Also lost is the family scapegoat—the family role commonly played by the addict—who provides an explanation for all kinds of frustrations and problems. When the bills aren't paid, for example, it's the addict's fault. However, once the addict becomes responsible, each family member must assess his own responsibility when things go wrong.

When addicts enter treatment, threatened codependents, full of anxiety and feeling irrelevant and left behind, may consciously or unconsciously undermine recovery (Nyman and Cocores 1991). "One of my first patients in the early 1960s was an alcoholic pilot, who brought in his wife," a treatment expert noted.

> It was clear they were fond of each other, and she was working two jobs to support their family. I saw him regularly once a week in psychotherapy, and he made a fantastic recovery. He went to AA six times a week, got his job back, and everything was fine. At the end of the year he wanted to celebrate his year's sobriety and repay his wife for her support by taking her out to dinner. When I reminded him, "Remember, you can't drink," he assured me, "Don't worry, I'm a good

AA member." When he didn't show up the following week I called his home, and his wife answered in tears. John had gotten drunk that weekend and was in detox. He was so embarrassed that he didn't want to come to see me. Later, when he explained what happened, he said that his wife was so grateful to him for his sobriety that she brought him a gift—a bottle of scotch. I was furious with the wife. (MD pilot examiner)

The wife subsequently sought help from another psychiatrist. "It turns out that she had resented giving up her two jobs. Being bread-winner in the family was gratifying to her, and though it had been a chore she unconsciously wanted to restore the status quo. Now that her two children were grown up, her husband was drinking, he was her baby."

Pharmaceutical Agents

The medical model for treating addiction utilizes one drug to ame-liorate addiction to another; it considers addiction a physical crav-ing that can be interrupted by chemical means. For decades psy-chopharmacologists have searched for analgesics and treatments that are safe, effective, and nonaddictive—or less addictive (Green-stein, Fudala, and O'Brien 1992). Many psychiatrists and addiction-ologists, especially those with hospital-based practices, subscribe to this model. "Medication plays an increasingly important role in the treatment of alcohol and other drug addiction, in part because many patients do not respond to existing psychosocial treatment alone," Gorelick (1993, p. 141) explains. Just as in the 1910s heroin was in-troduced as a cure for "morphine addiction," methadone is cur-rently used to get addicts off heroin, Valium to get alcoholics off alcohol, and amphetamines to control calorie "addiction" (Cum-mings 1991, p. 510).

Inspired by western medicine's history of chemical break-throughs—medical miracles like sulfa and penicillin—scientists search for new pharmaceuticals to cure substance abusers. Phar-maceutical companies and government agencies finance clinical tri-als to assess the potential of various chemical agents.

The past decade has witnessed an increase in pharmacologic re-search to identify recovery aids (Fulco, Liverman, and Earley 1995). In 1990 Congress established the Medications Development Division in the National Institute on Drug Abuse with a budget of $36 million, a full-time staff of 33, and a mission to encourage the development and marketing of new medications for the treatment of drug addiction (Institute of Medicine 1994, pp. 1–4). Although no panacea has been found, pharmacologic agents are currently used to reduce cravings and help make treatment more efficient and successful (Kaufman and McNaul 1992). Although it is generally recognized that pharmacologic agents alone are unlikely to produce long-lasting solutions, a majority of private practitioners prescribe pharmacologic agents for treatment of alcoholism (*Alcohol and Health* 1990, pp. 266–268). Prescriptions are issued in accordance with three strategies: symptomatic treatment, agonist substitution, and antagonist treatment (*Drug Abuse and Drug Abuse Research* 1991).

Symptomatic treatment utilizes a medication whose pharmacologic action is unrelated to the abused drug but whose effects might ameliorate emotional or physical symptoms related to drug abuse (for example, tranquilizers for insomnia or anxiety).

Agonist substitution is treatment with a medication having pharmacologic actions similar to those of the abused drug (for example, nicotine chewing gum for tobacco dependence). Agonist substitutions are used either for short-term detoxification, with progressively decreasing dosages while helping suppress withdrawal symptoms, or for long-term maintenance, such as administering methadone to replace illicit street drugs.

Methadone maintenance, a common form of agonist therapy for opiate addicts, involves administering stable dosages of methadone as an oral substitute for heroin and other narcotics (Senay 1994). Under federal guidelines, methadone is given only to people who have unsuccessfully attempted drug-free treatment and cannot function without chemotherapeutic support (Anglin and Hser 1991). Research consistently shows that such addicts significantly decrease in opiate use and criminality and show improvements in general health and social functioning (Ward, Mattick, and Hall 1994). A three-year field study of 506 methadone patients at six clinics in three eastern U.S. cities found that, of the 76 percent who remained in treatment for one year, 71 percent discontinued their illicit intravenous (IV) drug abuse. Substantial reductions also occurred among those who did not completely discontinue IV drug use. Eight of 10 (82 percent) of the methadone treatment dropouts relapsed to IV drug abuse within a year (*Drug Abuse and Drug Abuse Research* 1991).

However, addicts in methadone maintenance often find it difficult to hold a regular job because, according to federal regulations, they must come to the clinic each day for their methadone. Many also fear that they will lose their health insurance if their employers learn of their drug problem. Moreover, some still have ethical objections to its use, despite its record of helping thousands of opiate addicts for more than 25 years.

A neurological model of addiction assumes that cocaine-seeking behavior results from a deficit or imbalance of neurochemicals (neurotransmitters and neuromodulators), particularly dopamine. Pharmacotherapies seek to substitute or restore dopamine, but these solutions sometimes cause new problems. For example, Bromocriptine reduces cravings within minutes after administration, but its side effects include headaches, sedation, tremor, vertigo, and dry mouth and may itself lead to drug dependency. A second substance, amantadine hydrochloride, reportedly has fewer side effects but sometimes causes Parkinsonian symptoms, such as muscular rigidity or impaired reflexes. A third, levodapa, can produce hallucinations (Blum, Trachtenberg, and Kozlowski 1989).

Antagonist treatment utilizes pharmaceuticals to block the chemical effects of the abused drugs (O'Brien 1994). For example, since the 1950s disulfiram (Antabuse) has been widely used as an aversive medication to treat alcohol dependence. It inhibits one of the major alcohol-metabolizing enzymes, and the user gets nauseous when he drinks. Clients, however, are not always motivated to use antagonists. Studies have shown reduced drinking among those who use aversive agents, but sustained abstinence is rare and poor compliance typical. "When I was discharged from treatment I went back to the same job and place," a nurse commented. "I was the same me; no change. They gave me a bottle of Antabuse and told me that I should take it—for what, though, I didn't know. I took it for a while and then stopped. Then I started drinking again" (RN, age 71).

Aversive agents are most effective when, like drug screening, they are mandated by authority. Administered to an unwilling patient or without professional monitoring, aversion therapy doesn't work. "I prescribe it only for those who request it or when the diversion program requires it," a treatment practitioner explained. Otherwise, as another physician observed, such treatment is futile and lacks common sense.

> I had the opportunity to observe aversion training with alcoholics in the former Soviet Union. A psychiatrist at one treatment center had a group of patients sit in a circle, each with a bowl in front of them. They were each given an injection of Ipecac followed by a drink of whiskey. Then they all threw up simultaneously. The psychiatrist then told them about the terrible consequences of drinking. That kind of technique isn't effective, because people aren't stupid. They know that when they go into a bar, they will not be injected with an aversive agent and throw up.

In January 1995 the director of the National Institute of Alcohol Abuse and Alcoholism announced U.S. Food and Drug Administration approval to publicly dispense Naltrexone, the first new drug to treat alcoholism in 47 years. "This is the beginning of a new era . . . in alcoholism treatment," he asserted (Maugh 1995, p. 14). Results from ongoing clinical trials show that, when combined with counseling, Naltrexone cut the rate of relapse by about half. Those who received naltrexone reported less craving for alcohol, fewer drinking days, and less severe alcohol-related problems than did patients treated with a placebo (Gordis 1995). Naltrexone affects the brain receptors that produce feelings of pleasure when heroin or other opiates bind with them. But unlike psychoactive drugs, it is not habit forming (Maugh 1995). As good as this sounds, however, some are unimpressed. "Patients don't like it," said a physician who treats alcoholics.

Despite practical problems, the search for agents to attenuate drinking and drugging continues. Several compounds with specific effects on neurotransmitters have been found to reduce alcohol consumption in experimental animals. But as David Freedman (National Institute on Drug Abuse 1993) points out, "there will never be a magic bullet that will cure drug addiction . . . People will be helped by medications, but they still need to learn how to change their behaviors."

Holistic Care

Holistic medicine considers health in the context of the entire person and her community. Each person's health and illness can be understood only in reference to his or her total functioning—physical, psychological, social, and spiritual. The whole organism is always more than merely the sum of the parts (Jaffe 1980, p. 5).

Holistic care does not fragment patients by focusing only on a particular organ or other structure; nor is it a reductionistic approach that treats only specific diseases. Ask any holistic clinician if he treats cancer (or any other malady), and he will reply, "No, but I treat people who have cancer." This distinction between treating the disease versus the whole person defines holistic care (Bliss et al. 1985; see also Jaffee 1980 and Miles 1985).

Balance is the basis of good health, and uncovering an imbalance is the key to healing the whole person, said David Luce, a Harvard-trained physician.

> When a patient comes in I ask myself, "What combination of physical and emotional events produced this person's problem?" I'm interested in knowing who he or she is in terms of physical body, psycho-emotional self and spirit. I look at all the factors that make up that person's life, that produce balance or imbalance. I try to get them to reflect on their life and to see their illness in the context of their whole life. Then I try to help them find a vantage point from which to change and bring more balance to their life.   (Quoted in Arnold and Finn 1994, p. 14)

Three approaches from the holistic tradition—acupuncture, meditation, and nutrition counseling—are increasingly used to help addicts recover. (See Apostolides 1996 for a discussion of other holistic techniques used to treat addicts.)

ACUPUNCTURE

Acupuncture reportedly facilitates detoxification by reducing cravings, ameliorating withdrawal symptoms, and mitigating the anxiety, pain, and hostility that usually affect users when they stop using drugs. Then they are reportedly more receptive to counseling (Finn and Newlyn 1993).

A Hong Kong neurosurgeon, H. L. Wen, discovered acupuncture as a way to help addicts overcome chemical dependence by chance in 1972. When he used acupuncture to anesthetize a patient who was in heroin withdrawal, the withdrawal symptoms ceased. Wen replicated this occurrence and documented results with at least 10 publications (Wen and Cheung 1973; Brumbaugh 1993; "Alternative Medicine" 1994).

Dr. Michael O. Smith, director of a methadone program at New York City's Lincoln Hospital, read Wen's results and hired Chinese doctors to provide acupuncture treatment for heroin- and cocaine-addicted patients. Smith learned that when acupuncture points in the ear were stimulated, withdrawal symptoms and craving abated within minutes. In 1985 he founded the National Acupuncture Detoxification Association (NADA) to provide training, consultation, and certification for treatment personnel throughout the world. NADA outpatient clinics have a simple focus: addicted clients do all they can for themselves—for example, cleaning their ears (the site of needle insertion) with alcohol, selecting their needles, and perhaps removing them after treatment. Clients may drop by without an appointment; they are not coddled, questioned, lectured, or confronted; and conversation about drugs is discouraged. After the 45-minute session, clients receive herbal tea to help them relax or sleep (Brumbaugh 1993).

In New York City, Yalisove (1993) observed that patients who receive acupuncture report less craving for alcohol and relief of depression, anxiety, and other withdrawal symptoms. Of 175 consecutively admitted patients, 70 percent completed six or more treatments, 51 percent reported alleviation of withdrawal symptoms, and 46 percent reported reduced cravings for alcohol (p. 2).

Lincoln Hospital, located in New York City's South Bronx, daily treats about 250 addicts with acupuncture; in a six-year period more than 10,000 addicts participated in the program either voluntarily or by court order. The supervising physician reports that 50–75 percent participated for at least three months and were clean by then. Nearly 400 U.S. and European detoxification programs now utilize this approach ("Alternative Medicine" 1994).

In 1989 Florida Judge Herbert M. Klein developed a comprehensive plan including acupuncture treatment, education, and job placement assistance to help addicts recover (Finn and Newlyn 1993). Dade County implemented this program for nonviolent defendants accused of drug possession. Informally called "the Miami

Drug Court," it offers daily detoxification, case management, and education as an alternative to prosecution; successful participants have their criminal charges dismissed. During the first four years (1989–1993), about 4,500 defendants entered the program, 60 percent of whom graduated or continued to be involved. Only 11 percent of the graduates were rearrested; the typical recidivism rate is up to 60 percent. The average cost per client per year is only $800, roughly what it would cost to jail him for nine days. The county collects fees from participants on a sliding scale according to ability to pay.

Clinical experience demonstrates that acupuncture detoxification is safe and also acceptable to addicts in withdrawal. In 1993 Washburn et al. conducted the first controlled evaluation of acupuncture as a treatment modality for heroin addicts. In a single-blind design—the subjects did not know which group they were in—addicts were randomly assigned to either auricular acupuncture treatment for addiction or to a "sham" acupuncture treatment that used points near the standard points. Although attrition was high for both groups, those receiving actual acupuncture came for treatment more days and stayed in the program longer than those in the sham treatment. Those who reported lighter drug-use habits attended most frequently.

Despite these results, critics allege that acupuncture is "based on primitive and fanciful concepts of health and disease that bear no relationship to present scientific knowledge" (National Council Against Health Fraud 1991, p. 273). Undeterred by critics, however, acupuncture treatment proponents point out many advantages: it is more effective than pharmaceutical programs, relatively inexpensive, and effectively administered on an outpatient basis. Moreover, large numbers of clients can be treated simultaneously by only two or three staff members, and the treatment allows patients to "taper off" from drugs. Another benefit is that the client need not initially admit to being alcoholic or addicted (Yalisove 1993).

As the Miami Drug Court program indicates, acupuncture works best in combination with other recovery tools. It is especially useful as an entry point to treatment because it produces euphoric feelings. Endorphins, the body's natural pain killers, are released when thin, sterile, disposable needles are inserted at specific acupuncture points on the outer ear. The pleasurable feelings contrast markedly with aversive aspects of some other programs (Finn and Newlyn 1993).

Brumbaugh (1993) asserts that acupuncture may be particularly beneficial to pregnant women, since medication used for detoxification may harm the fetus. Regardless of gender or health status, however, acupuncture can support a client during withdrawal and ameliorate the shock of sudden abstinence.

MEDITATION

Meditation, a spiritual discipline about 5,000 years old, contrasts sharply with most current treatment philosophies. Chopra (1991, p. 161) explains: "typical programs for treating addicted people employ highly confrontational tactics, emphasizing the need for constant vigilance to guard against the possible return of the all-powerful habit. 'The monkey is on your back,' the addict is told, 'and he'll be there for the rest of your life.' The rationale for this insistence is that compulsive addicts will never be cured until they are turned into compulsive abstainers."

Meditation advocates assume that addicts will abandon their drugs when offered greater satisfaction through meditation. "We hold that the source of addiction is a search for satisfaction," Chopra elaborates. "Alcohol, cigarettes, and drugs cause untold damage, but their users derive some kind of pleasure from them, or at least relief from the massive stress that they would otherwise feel. Addicts maintain their habits for want of a way out" (Chopra 1991, p. 162). "But by exposing their minds to a greater source of satisfaction, the natural tendency would be to head away from the addiction, because the greater satisfaction is more appealing."

Studies in the early 1970s showed that anxiety levels and use of psychoactive substances decreased among addicts who learned to meditate. A review of 24 studies (Gelderloos et al. 1991) consistently showed that transcendental meditation (TM), for example, has a beneficial influence on drug-program participants and prisoners with drug-abuse histories without harmful side effects. TM subjects developed enhanced ability to produce and process serotonin, a mood-elevating chemical produced by the brain, a possible cause of enhanced psychological well-being and increased ability to cope with stressors. Meditators' lower blood cortisol and plasma lactate levels result in reduced anxiety, Gelderloos and colleagues note (1991).

Practiced by a variety of techniques—including TM, Tai Chi, and Yoga—all meditation has a common goal: to quiet the mind by entering a state of consciousness that goes beyond, or "transcends," normal thought processes (Schafer 1987, p. 318). The meditator learns to clear his mind of distracting thoughts by directing his attention to a single stimulus. Rather than focusing on the content of each thought, the normal process, the meditator develops a capacity to observe the ongoing process of experience, one of the most significant benefits of regular meditation (ibid., p. 319). "The meditation that I learned to do in treatment," said a physician, "helped me get my mind quiet, center on here and now—the sounds, the feelings, and the temperature—and get out of my narcissistic self-involvement. It helped me come into contact with my surroundings" (MD, age 34).

According to Benson (1975, p. 27), "all techniques involve four essential elements: (1) a quiet environment; (2) a mental device such as a word or phrase which should be repeated in a specific fashion over and over again; (3) the adoption of a passive attitude, which is perhaps the most important of the elements; (4) a comfortable position . . . appropriate practice of these four elements for 10–20 minutes once or twice daily should markedly enhance . . . well-being." Schafer (1987, pp. 304–305) elaborates: "Thousands of careful studies have been conducted on various forms of deep relaxation, especially Transcendental Meditation and the Benson Meditation method (sometimes called the Relaxation Response). Specific benefits include better 'mental health' (decreased anxiety, depression, aggression, and irritability, and increased self-esteem and emotional stability) and reduced drug abuse" (see also Benson and Stark 1996).

NUTRITION COUNSELING

In 1990 the American Dietetic Association (ADA) published a position paper asserting that "nutrition intervention, planned and provided by a qualified nutritional professional, is an essential component of the treatment and recovery from chemical dependency" (Beckley-Barrett and Mutch 1990, p. 1274). "Nutrition counseling is needed in all stages of treatment," the authors assert. "Nutrition intervention must begin during detoxification . . . During detoxification, the body experiences tremendous physical stress. Without drugs, the body begins withdrawal, exhibiting many physical and psychological disturbances, including nausea, vomiting, and diarrhea, which contribute to fluid, electrolyte, and caloric imbalances. The diet should be planned to minimize the symptomatic discomfort of acute withdrawal" (pp. 1274–75).

An NIAAA publication summarizes how alcohol impairs healthy nutritional functioning. "Alcoholics often eat poorly, limiting their supply of essential nutrients and affecting both energy supply and structure maintenance. Furthermore, alcohol interferes with the nutritional process by affecting digestion, storage, utilization, and excretion of nutrients" (*Alcohol and Nutrition* 1993, p. 1).

Drug rehabilitation requires nutrition therapy to restore metabolic balance, correct nutrient deficiencies, and prevent or minimize alcohol and food cravings. According to Biery, Williford, and Mc-Mullen (1991, p. 466), "To reduce cravings, a well-balanced, high-complex-carbohydrate, nutrient-dense diet is recommended, including vitamins and mineral supplements, if indicated; caffeine and sugar intake should be reduced; and frequent eating should help normalize blood glucose levels." In effective nutritional intervention, a dietician assesses the client's nutritional status, then develops and implements a nutritional care plan that fits his particular lifestyle and monitors results (Visocan 1983).

When Biery, Williford, and McMullen (1991) studied 38 alcoholics to assess the effects of nutrition counseling in a traditional rehabilitation program, they found significant improvements among alcoholic subjects who received specially modified menus and nutrition counseling compared with those who did not. The former experienced significantly fewer hypoglycemic symptoms, lower sugar intake, less alcohol craving, a greater nutrient intake, and fewer relapses. Reduced craving, the investigators suggest, reflects the improved neurotransmission and brain function resulting from differences in intake of sugar and complex carbohydrates, vitamin and mineral availability and utilization, greater stability of blood glucose levels, and more-efficient serotonin and B-endorphin synthesis. (See also Carey 1989; Beckley-Barrett and Much 1990.)

Nutritionists claim that metabolic disorders persist in the many who discontinue alcohol and other drugs but continue to use other

addictive substances—coffee, cigarettes, and sugar—to satisfy continuing cravings. "I can get the same effect from certain foods that
I could from drugs," a nurse explained (RN, age 40). An internist
agreed. "I can go up and down with them. When I first got sober I
ate every sweet I could find because I was looking for a fix; the
sweet gave me the high. Then the insulin kicked in and I went back
down" (MD, age 34). Malnourished addicts are vulnerable to these
"hidden addictions," nutritionists agree. "There are trigger foods
for alcoholics," an addicted physician explained. "Some go to 'near-
beer,' others become addicted to nicotine or caffeine. You have a
coffee break, get a spike of energy, and then start to wind down"
(MD, age 34).

Sugar, "the world's most insidious, widespread, and unrecognized addiction," Finnegan and Gray (1990, pp. 20–21) assert, contributes to the addictive process. Two hundred years ago the average U.S. citizen used less than a pound of sugar a year. By contrast
he now eats or drinks 130 pounds annually—one-third of a pound
daily.

Those trained in western medicine typically resist the nutritional
approach. But a physician who had once been hooked on cocaine
spoke from his own experience. "Everything I have learned medically tells me that there is no such thing as a sugar addiction. It just
doesn't exist; it's a carbohydrate and is metabolized in such a way
that you can't go through withdrawal syndrome. But if it looks like
a horse, sounds like a horse, and feels like a horse, it must be a . . . "
Then, commenting on his own addiction, he added, "I've learned
that if I stay away from sugar, I lose my craving for it. But if I eat
it, I lose control, and it affects my emotions; my mood gets depressed, and I get physically lethargic. I can't defend it medically,
but I now identify myself as a sugar addict" (MD, age 40).

In Perspective

The arsenal of overlapping recovery tools has an interesting history.
From the beginning, individual and group counseling have been
popular techniques, as has western medicine's medication approach—agonists, antagonists, and detoxifying pharmaceuticals.
For decades Alcoholics Anonymous and its derivative 12-step organizations demonstrated the efficacy of peer support, disease ori-

entation, and spiritual development. More recently, psychologists have added coping-skills training, lifestyle planning, behavioral contracting, and family therapy. In addition, alternative therapies are available in the forms of nutrition counseling and the ancient eastern practices of acupuncture and meditation.

Of course, none of these tools will be useful if the addict is unwilling to participate—and Type 5 addicts are motivated only by the most extreme circumstances. Motivational intervention and drug screening dramatically address this problem. The former breaks through the addict's defensive denial and gets her into treatment, and drug screening, an invaluable technique for monitoring recovery, helps reinforce motivation, especially when linked to a behavioral contract.

Few clinicians are trained in all these techniques, and there is a tendency to disregard or minimize unfamiliar ones. Moreover, practitioners trained in western medicine's biological model generally reject acupuncture and other alternative approaches. Although some pursue a medicinal cure, others think it folly to substitute one form of drug dependence for another (for example, methadone for heroin). Moreover, those focused solely on a biologic view of addiction sometimes reject treatment based on social-learning theory (coping skills enhancement and lifestyle approaches), and vice versa. Meanwhile, the debate continues about the importance of spirituality and whether addiction is a disease.

Regardless of training and ideology, most treatment experts embrace personal, group, and family counseling, peer support, behavioral contracting, drug screening, and motivational confrontations. Eventually training programs may become more comprehensive and practitioners less territorial and ideological. Addicts will be much better served by clinicians skilled in the full range of treatment tools available.

SEVEN

Self-Help Recovery

"When I hit bottom, I thought, 'This is crazy! This is insane!' But I can remember thinking, 'Who the hell can I call?' I didn't know anybody to call for help."

(JD, age 41)

"The best monitor of how an addict is doing is another addict. They can't fool each other."

(FAA treatment expert)

"Some days the compulsion comes back when something happens or a smell hits me. So, I make a phone call to [my volunteer group], a network of people like myself who help each other."

(PharmD, age 47)

Self-help programs differ from other recovery programs in that they lack a professional cadre of employed staff to direct and supervise activities. Alcoholics Anonymous, the oldest and most impressive of these recovery programs, spawned a variety of similar self-help programs. Others, put off by AA's emphasis on spirituality, formed 12-step substitutes that retain AA program features but omit reliance on "a higher power." Grass-roots mutual-help programs, usually in conjunction with AA, have proliferated among the professions; some of these are sponsored by professional organizations. Most Type 5 addicts trace their recovery to such programs.

Twelve-Step Programs

Alcoholics Anonymous (AA) and its derivatives—Narcotics Anonymous, Pills Anonymous, Cocaine Anonymous, Al-Anon, Alateen,

Adult Children of Alcoholics, Codependents Anonymous, and so on—have an impressive record.[1] AA began in 1935 when an alcoholic New York stock broker (Bill Wilson) and an alcoholic surgeon (Dr. Bob Smith) in Akron, Ohio, realized that their ability to stay sober was related to the amount of help and encouragement they gave other alcoholics. The new movement, nameless and without descriptive literature, grew slowly at first. The beginning groups, established in Akron, were soon followed by autonomous groups in other parts of the country and then around the world. Current AA membership is estimated to number more than 2 million participants in 134 countries.[2] "I've attended AA meetings all over the world," a pilot (age 54) reported:

> It's very stimulating. I've met in Rome and even in a bomb shelter in Tel Aviv! Even when they speak in French, Korean, or whatever, there's still an aura that's the same everywhere—a feeling of camaraderie. Though the format may be a little different, the meetings themselves are extremely similar. I was at an AA meeting in Paris one day with a television personality and discovered we were on the same flight going back to New York. It was great fun when I got on the plane in my captain's uniform. He was excited when he saw me and said, "Wonderful!"

AA relies on participants' sharing firsthand experiences of suffering and recovery. The only requirement for participation is the desire to stop drinking/using. Administratively, AA has no officers or executives with authority over members, no hierarchical bureaucracy with decisionmaking at the top. Local groups are autonomous except in matters affecting other AA groups or the fellowship as a whole. The General Service Office, in New York City, serves the United States and Canada with a staff (mostly AA members) who print and distribute literature, organize the annual conferences, and respond to requests for information (Makela et al. 1996).

Each new AA participant can purchase at minimal cost *Alcoholics Anonymous,* known as the "Big Book." Originally published in 1939 and revised in 1955 and 1976, it recounts the recovery stories and principles of 42 early members. Those in recovery refer frequently to the insights and inspiration found in this and other AA publications.

In 1994 there were reportedly 1,127,471 members of AA in the United States. A typical member attends three meetings a week.

About 50,000 groups meet in the United States and around 89,000 worldwide; 2,085 meetings are held in correctional institutions. Every three years AA's General Service Office conducts a random survey of members. The 1992 survey showed that of the 6,723 members polled, 65 percent were men, except in the age-30-and-under category, where the proportion dropped to 57 percent (Alcoholics Anonymous General Service Office 1995, 1996). In 1995 between 70,000 and 80,000 members from 87 countries attended an international convention in San Diego, California, celebrating 60 years of AA (Perry 1995).

Financially self-supporting, AA accepts no contributions from nonmembers. Although there are no dues, participants may donate small sums to cover meeting expenses—no more than $1,000 a year per individual.

AA does not keep membership records or case histories or engage in research (except the membership surveys). Nor does it offer religious services, medical or psychiatric prognoses; dispense medicines or psychiatric advice; or provide housing, food, clothing, jobs, money, or any other welfare or social services. It does not provide domestic or vocational counseling or letters of reference to parole boards, lawyers, court officials, social agencies, employers, or the like. AA does, however, sign off on attendance sheets as required by the courts. "One of its most attractive features for the newcomer," Bissell (1992, p. 74) notes, "is the promise of anonymity. There is never a need to give one's full or even accurate name. There are no records, no promises made to be broken or regretted."

Some meetings are limited to members, who discuss problems that are best understood by other alcoholics/addicts. The discussions are informal, and all members participate. New members are encouraged to ask questions. Nonaddicts are welcome at open meetings, but are instructed that sharing during the meeting is for alcoholics and other addicts and that what is said in the meeting is confidential and not to be discussed elsewhere. Most meetings conclude with refreshments and informal socializing. "Somebody shows up early and makes the coffee, sets the tables, cleans the ashtrays, and wipes the floors," reports an attorney. "Each group is autonomous, and everyone gets a job. I made coffee for three years, and it helped me meet lots of people. Then you rotate through various jobs" (JD, age 64).

Getting to the initial meeting is often the most difficult part. "Going to my first meeting was terrible," a nurse acknowledged. "Amazingly hard!" (RN, age 42). A physician agreed: "I used to have nightmares about going to AA and sitting with these guys with fecal stains and wine bottles sticking out of brown paper bags in their back pockets singing praises to Jesus. I had no idea what it would be like. It scared the hell out of me." His wife took him to a psychiatrist who "lined me up with a temporary sponsor. 'Show up at this address, and we'll go together,' he said."

> When we got there I thought, "Wow, if I walk through that door there may be no way back." Much to my relief I found that there were three or four other doctors there. I'm not the only one! I thought I was the only alcoholic physician in the whole country! I didn't realize that the medical profession was so well represented. I felt relief because I had a tremendous amount of shame about being an alcoholic doctor.   (MD, age 50)

AA rituals and socials acknowledge those who reach recovery milestones. In some groups, newcomers receive a purple poker chip and are encouraged to keep it in the same pocket with the money used to buy alcohol. The chip reminds them to stay sober for just that day. After a month's sobriety, a white chip replaces the purple one, and so on. Other groups give medallions with duration of sobriety engraved on one side and the "Serenity Prayer" (see page 218) on the other. Anniversaries of one's first day without a drink are usually celebrated with a cake or a party.

Slogans and acronyms remind addicts of basic principles. "First things first" emphasizes that staying sober is the most important priority. "One day at a time" encourages focus on the here and now. "Easy does it" reminds them to be patient, not to become frustrated or discouraged or try to accomplish everything at once. "Keep it simple" encourages them to do the simple things: go to meetings, read the Big Book, work the steps, and reach out to others who suffer from chemical dependence. "HOW"—standing for Honesty, Openness, and Willingness—reminds AA members to be honest in sharing what they feel and experience, open in considering new ideas, and willing to look at and change their destructive habits. "HALT" warns alcoholics to avoid becoming Hungry, Angry, Lonely, or Tired, since an excess of any one may lead to relapse.

AA defines chemical dependence as a progressive illness that can never be cured but, like some illnesses, can be arrested. Although it is not shameful to have this illness, it must be faced honestly and dealt with appropriately. Recovery tools include disease education, spiritual enhancement, peer support, and family support. Though not formally designated, 12-step groups often incorporate the basic principles of group therapy, coping-skills enhancement, meditation, and lifestyle planning and monitoring, but they emphasize that today is the focus of activity; nothing can be done about yesterday. Even the worst drunks, they say, can go 24 hours without a drink. Thus members learn to postpone the next drink/drug for the next hour, even for the next minute. One attorney recalled:

> When I told my sponsor that I'd been using again, he said, "When did you use last?" And I said, "About noon today." He said, "Okay, you will have a new sobriety date starting tomorrow." I wanted to scream. "Don't I get any credit for the rest of the day?" He made me commit to going to meetings for the next 30 days. I had to sit and listen to people in great pain and trouble and watch them get fixed by a power greater than me. It was very impressive, very powerful. (JD, age 49)

AA does not require any particular religious belief as a condition of membership. Though endorsed by many religious leaders, its participants include agnostics and atheists. Each member is free to interpret AA's spiritual values or not to consider them at all. To maintain sobriety, AA recommends that addicts accept the existence of a power greater than themselves. Some participants define this power as God, as individually understood by each person. Definitions of higher power may vary from a divine being to the state licensing board. "Those who have a great deal of difficulty with the God concept," explained a dentist, "find other entities outside themselves to trust in" (DDS, age 55). AA members agree that while it is not necessary to believe in a personal God, it is important for alcoholics to realize that *they themselves are not God!* That is, they are not the center of the universe, nor are they running the show.

Agnostics, relying on the strength of the group rather than on a divine being, learn that group members working together have a strength transcending that of isolated individuals. "If nothing else works for you," a physician remarked, "make the AA group your higher power. Rely on us. Get our phone numbers and, when you have a problem, call us up!" (MD, age 46).

For some, like the AA founders, developing trust in a higher power begins with an extraordinary experience. For others, spiritual awakening comes gradually. "The turning point in my recovery came when I really realized that there was a higher power," reported a physician. "But it took years, not months or weeks" (MD, age 50). "Developing my own spirituality has made the difference in the long term," a pharmacist said. "Just going to AA meetings is not enough to keep me sober; it's what comes beyond that that counts" (PharmD, age 42).

The "Serenity Prayer," slightly revised from theologian Reinhold Niebuhr's original, is recited in concert at each meeting: "God grant me the serenity to accept the things I cannot change, the courage to change the things I can, and the wisdom to know the difference."

AA's 12 steps are:

1. We admitted we were powerless over alcohol—that our lives had become unmanageable.

2. Came to believe that a Power greater than ourselves could restore us to sanity.

3. Made a decision to turn our will and our lives over to the care of God as we understood Him.

4. Made a searching and fearless moral inventory of ourselves.

5. Admitted to God, to ourselves and to another human being the exact nature of our wrongs.

6. Were entirely ready to have God remove all these defects of character.

7. Humbly asked him to remove our shortcomings.

8. Made a list of all persons we had harmed, and became willing to make amends to them all.

9. Made direct amends to such people wherever possible, except when to do so would injure them or others.

10. Continued to take personal inventory and when we were wrong promptly admitted it.

11. Sought through prayer and meditation to improve our conscious contact with God, as we understood Him, praying only for knowledge of His will for us and the power to carry that out.

12. Having had a spiritual awakening as the result of these steps, we tried to carry this message to alcoholics and to practice these

principles in all our affairs. (Alcoholics Anonymous World Services 1976, pp. 59–60)

"Spirituality comes by working the steps," an attorney concluded.[3] "It helped me change my focus from 'What's in it for me?' to 'How can I help other folks?' It's a great thrill when I look over at a meeting and see a guy I've sponsored put his arm around another person he's never seen before. It's obvious that he's sharing from his heart. Then I feel that he's going to be okay" (JD, age 64).

Peer support, an extraordinary recovery tool, comes to each new member from a sponsor, someone of the same gender who has been in AA for a longer time—a personal contact who can be called upon 24 hours a day. "When you are new, you are like a traveler in a strange country," an attorney explained. "You're trying to get away from where you were but have no idea where to go or how. So when you're given a sponsor, you have a travel guide and mentor who knows the territory. You stick close to him for the first couple of years, just like he's another parent, and you ask him, 'Should I do this or that?' " (JD, age 64). The commitment and energy offered by sponsors are remarkable. "We talked every day on the phone for 20 minutes!" exclaimed a pilot (age 52). "He asked me what AA materials I was reading, what kind of meetings I went to, about my weekly visits with the psychiatrist, my airline pilot's association representative, my special health-services person, and my monthly meeting with my chief pilot. He was a longtime member who stays in AA to work the twelfth service step. He was very helpful to me."

Stories of selfless service and devotion abound. One pharmacist on the brink of relapsing was kept so busy by his AA associates that he didn't have time to drink:

> I was flirting with relapse by going to bars but not drinking; I just drank sodas. When my AA group found out, the old-timers stayed with me after the Friday and Saturday meetings for the next six months until three or four in the morning. They more or less kidnapped me. They kept that up until I was back in school and had been nine months clean and sober. They encouraged me to go back to pharmacy school, where I had been booted out twice. (PharmD, age 26)

Another pharmacist was invited to live with his sponsor:

> It was classic AA. He took beginners into his house fresh out of treatment and did a lot of 12-step work there. When I lied to them and hid

drugs all over their place, they voted on whether I could stay or not (there were two other beginners with me). It was snowing outside, and I had lost my own apartment and was afraid that they would put me out in this heavy snowstorm. Fortunately the vote was three to one, with the sponsor's wife voting against me. They said, "If you want to live here, you go to meetings every day, and that's all you do." So for the next 14 months I went to at least three meetings every day, and through the grace of God and these wonderful people I became sober.   (PharmD, age 47)

Sometimes the sponsor relapses and the roles are reversed. "Now I sponsor two of the doctors who helped me," a pharmacist reported. "My sponsor cried when I relapsed. When he relapsed nine years later I sponsored him again" (PharmD, age 47).

AA members learn that by helping others they also help themselves. "The twelfth step is a wonderful tool kit and has become an active part of my life," a dentist said. "I work with other people as much now as I can and have had wonderful experiences, such as having an addicted anesthesiologist live in my house. I was able to give away freely the gift that was freely given to me. I consider it a little insurance policy for my own sobriety" (DDS, age 49).

Family education and support, another program feature, is implemented by inviting family members to AA activities such as open meetings to hear AA speakers and share in the fellowship with other families; social events—suppers, dances, picnics, and other activities held regularly for AA members and their families; and weekend conferences at resorts and hotels. Al-Anon and Alateen meetings for family members are often held concurrently at these conferences.

Psychologist Stanton Peele (1989, 1992) and others (for example, Kaminer 1992) assert that these programs promote authoritarianism, conformity, disempowerment, and evasion of personal responsibility. To assess these criticisms, sociologist Paul Scriven (1994) attended over 100 meetings at more than a dozen locations and concluded that much criticism comes from those who apparently have attended only a session or two, if any, and whose interpretations do not appear to reflect sincere attempts to understand the process (see also Bissell 1992). Instead of an ideological program that promotes religious conformity and evasion of personal responsibility, Scriven found AA to be just the opposite: "When twelve-step meetings are researched firsthand, the impressive stories of recovery combined with the sincerity of the participants and the range of uses the twelve-step meetings are convenient for, an entirely other sort of portrait of the meetings emerges. Twelve-step meetings provide a genuine community service" (Abstract). He adds, "The meeting, rather than being ideological, is intimate and familiar with trust and voluntary cooperation the core" (p. 16).

Psychiatrist John N. Chappel, a nonalcoholic member of AA's General Service Board, suggests that clinicians can learn much by attending 12-step meetings and discussing their experiences with a seasoned AA contact. "I have learned much about the power of sharing personal thoughts, feelings, and experiences," he explains. "This has been of particular value in relating to my family and friends" ("Two Psychiatrists View AA" 1995, p. 2).

How effective are the 12-step programs in helping addicts recover? William E. Mayer, M.D., onetime director of the federal government's Alcoholic, Drug Abuse and Mental Health Administration, states:

> AA by and large works better than anything we have beenable to devise with all our science and all our money and all our efforts. AA has shown the way and presented us with a model of long-term care that is really not care. It is participatory self-management. It is an assertion of the autonomy of the individual. Instead of his thinking of himself as a victim, a helpless person . . . AA gives a person a kind of sense of self-worth and along with it the kind of humility and reality testing that are absolutely essential in the management of alcohol problems.   (Alcoholics Anonymous World Services 1982)

Steven Hyman, director of Harvard University's Mind, Brain, Behavior Initiative, explains that "addiction is a form of adaptation" (Delbanco and Delbanco 1995, p. 61). In the context of individual vulnerability, adaptation occurs in the brain's reward circuitry in response to the psychoactive drug. He adds, "I suspect that if I could compare scans of the brain of an alcoholic person before and after treatment in a twelve-step program, you would see clear changes. Of course, the altruistic activity affects the brain as much as the drug does" (p. 62).

Recent studies indicate that those who complete one month of residential drug treatment and continue to attend AA-type meetings regularly are almost twice as likely to remain off drugs as those who do not attend follow-up support sessions (Gerstein and Harwood 1990).

The satisfaction of AA participants is high. For example, 100 successfully rehabilitated physicians treated in the Georgia Impaired Physicians Program ranked AA as more effective in their recovery than all other treatment components: hospitalization, halfway-house programs, personal counseling, family therapy, and urinalysis. All espoused belief in AA and felt an intense cohesiveness with other 12-step members (Galanter et al. 1990).

In 1994 seven directors of the nation's drug control policy from five presidential administrations held a symposium to review what has and should be done about the drug problem in America. Robert L. Du Pont (from the Nixon administration), regretting his slowness in realizing the worth of the 12-step program, called it "the secret weapon in the war on drugs. It is completely free; there is no bureaucrat involved; there is no hungry mouth to feed; it can't be cut out of anybody's budget; it can't go out of fashion; and it is accessible to every single person all of the time" ("Reflections of the Drug Czars" 1995, p. 118).

Interviews with drug-impaired professionals overwhelmingly confirm these observations. Although some come to AA "kicking and screaming," the personal benefits are profound. One pharmacist contrasted it with many previous years of ineffective therapy:

> Before I found AA I had seen seven psychiatrists, five psychologists, and four drug and alcohol counselors. I had done transactional analysis, Jungian, Reichian, and Freudian therapy. I had tried transcendental meditation, biofeedback, hypnosis, and self-hypnosis. But in all those 12 years of therapy, I never breathed a sober breath. I now refer to myself as a survivor of the mental health system. Unfortunately, no one ever mentioned to me 12-step programs such as AA or NA until the very end, when I began my recovery. The therapists thought that I drank because of my behavior and my mental illness. They always had the cart before the horse.   (PharmD, age 47)

The professionals interviewed for this book credited AA more often and more enthusiastically than any other recovery program. "I've become a hard-assed, unreconstructed believer in AA," an attorney volunteered. "AA saved my life, and it will save anybody's life if he is willing to do what AA tells him to do" (JD, age 64).

Of course such unqualified enthusiasm is not universal. "There are those who preach it [AA], and that's all they do," a dentist observed. "Then there are people like me who don't buy every single thing. I go to meetings and try to take from them what is helpful. I try to practice the principles and not go out and use, but I will never be the ideal AA member. It's very important to me, but I don't eat, sleep, and breathe it, and I never will. I simply try to integrate it as best I can. So far I have five years of sobriety" (DDS, age 37).

Even hard-core resisters often lose their preconceived notions and stay to benefit. A law student was relieved to find that AA participants were not "the pious hypocrites" she had expected (JD, age 34). Experimenting is believing, an attorney explained. "When they told me to pray, I said, 'I don't believe that works.' But they said, 'We don't care, just try it.' They also told me to read this book that I thought was stupid, but I read it anyway. Being willing to try brought great blessings into my life" (JD, age 64). Another attorney reported: "The day I wrecked the car, passed out at my desk, and got thrown out of five bars, I went to an AA meeting and thought, 'Possibly I can fit in here; maybe these people will not reject me or insist that I believe this way or that or the other thing.' That meeting saved my life! I just hung around with these people until I found out that it did work, and I stayed sober" (JD, age 34).

Many professionals report that they are energized, not worn out, by all the meetings. "At the end of the work day I'm so exhausted and empty from giving so much; I go to AA meetings, and it fills me up again. When I don't get to my meetings—usually two to three a week—I don't feel good. It provides fulfillment in my life" (JD, age 41).

Twelve-Step Alternatives

Addicts from oppressive, punitive religious backgrounds are usually uncomfortable with AA and other 12-step programs. "The God stuff," as one called it, conjures up images of smug piety. "I have difficulty believing in God," a dentist said, "so my higher power is the state boards" (DDS, age 37).

Acknowledging that AA has helped millions of addicts, Ellis and Schoenfeld (1990, p. 459) claim that "even more millions of addicts have turned away from AA because of its sectarian emphasis on

Higher Power." Noting that 6 of the 12 steps make reference to God, they assert that it can be destructive to the treatment process to tell addicts they can recover only by direct intercession of a higher power. "For alcoholics to 'humbly' ask God to remove their short-comings seems to us self-denigrating, a real cop-out," they state (p. 465). "Alcoholics and other addicts need to learn that with hard work and practice, they can significantly change their lives and not believe they are such weaklings that *only* a supernatural being can help them" (p. 464).

Ellis and Schoenfeld recommend that AA jettison its spiritual emphasis and adopt behavioral psychologist Skinner's (1977) "Humanist Alternative 12 steps":

1. We accept the fact that all our efforts to stop drinking have failed.

2. We believe that we must turn elsewhere for help.

3. We turn to our fellow men and women, particularly those who have struggled with the same problem.

4. We have made a list of the situations in which we are most likely to drink.

5. We ask our friends to help us avoid those situations.

6. We are ready to accept the help they give us.

7. We earnestly hope that they will help.

8. We have made a list of persons we have harmed and to whom we hope to make amends.

9. We shall do all we can to make amends in any way that will not cause further harm.

10. We will continue to make such lists and revise them as needed.

11. We appreciate what our friends have done and are doing to help us.

12. We, in turn, are ready to help others who may come to us in the same way.

Alternative programs, recently formed to help those who reject AA's approach, define themselves in contrast to AA. The state director of a physicians' health program reported that most of the addicted physicians she deals with find a place in AA. "For those willing to go for six months, about 80 percent will feel that AA works for them." On the other hand, "If somebody has been going to AA for six months because it's been required as part of their monitoring program, and nothing has changed, it's time to recognize that it probably won't work for them. At that point we need to look for alternatives such as individual counseling or some other type of group, such as Rational Recovery."

Alternative programs provide choices for the many AA dropouts. A study of AA attendees found that 68 percent quit before 10 meetings (Brandsma, Maultsby, and Welch 1980). Court- or employer-mandated AA attendance results in poor prognosis (Emrick 1989; Walsh et al. 1991).

Four organizations currently offer alternatives to the 12-step program: Women for Sobriety, Rational Recovery, Secular Organizations for Sobriety, and Moderation Management.

WOMEN FOR SOBRIETY

Although many women alcoholics achieve and maintain sobriety through AA (Beckman 1993; Katsukas 1994), sociologist Jean Kirkpatrick failed to do so (Kirkpatrick 1977). In 1975 she founded Women for Sobriety (WFS), a self-help alternative to AA for women alcoholics. Since then WFS has grown to about 5,000 members in 250–300 groups in various U.S. cities (Kaskutas 1989).

The principal tenet of WFS is that women alcoholics in recovery have fundamentally different needs from men in recovery. Largely as a result of harsh societal judgment of women alcoholics, many feel a deep sense of inadequacy and guilt. AA's spiritual approach seeks to neutralize the alcoholic's egocentricity, but WFS members believe that the issues women alcoholics face are less about self-centeredness and more about self-esteem. Kirkpatrick (1977) argues that women require a positive program that reinforces positive thinking about one's ability, instills independence, and focuses on the future. She sees AA as negatively emphasizing the sins of past drinking and encouraging dependence on a higher power, on one's sponsor, and on lifelong attendance at AA meetings.

Based on principles of cognitive therapy, WFS teaches that "faulty thinking" initiates and reinforces drinking and that by changing their thinking women can avoid self-destructive behavior (Kaskutas 1994). WFS meetings differ from AA in structure, format, and philosophy. Instead of being led by an elected secretary, the usual practice at AA, WFS meetings are led by a certified moderator. Drinking stories are not told at WFS meetings, on the grounds that they keep women from forming a positive image of themselves. Instead, women talk about positive things that occurred in their past week. Furthermore, whereas AA advocates lifelong membership, WFS does not (Kaskutas 1994).

Women for Sobriety's "Thirteen Affirmations" emphasize four themes: no drinking, positive thinking, belief in one's own competency, and spiritual and emotional growth:

1. I have a drinking problem that once had me.
2. Negative emotions destroy only myself.
3. Happiness is a habit I will develop.
4. Problems bother me only to the degree that I permit them to.
5. I am what I think.
6. Life can be ordinary or it can be great.
7. Love can change the course of my world.
8. The fundamental object of life is emotional and spiritual growth.
9. The past is gone forever.
10. All love given returns two-fold.
11. Enthusiasm is my daily exercise.
12. I am a competent woman and have much to give life.
13. I am responsible for myself and my actions.   (Kaskutas 1994, p. 188)

Advocates assert that the safety and comfort of WFS meetings provide women, possibly for the first time in their lives, with a nonmasculine and nonthreatening setting devoid of competitive, aggressive, and domineering behavior. About one-third of WFS participants also attend AA meetings as an assurance against relapse (28 percent), for its wide availability (25 percent), and for sharing (31 percent) and support (27 percent) (Kaskutas 1994). But because some women cannot accept the AA way, "WFS should be recognized as an appropriate and relevant option" (ibid., p. 194).

RATIONAL RECOVERY

Rational Recovery (RR), formed in 1986, "is for people who are not interested in spiritual life," says its founder, Jack Trimpey. Trimpey asserts that AA promotes a "victim mentality," "ritual affection," and "forceful indoctrination," encourages a perception of individual powerlessness, and crams the higher-power concept "down people's throats" (Mehren 1992). The spiritual component is not the only thing about AA that troubles Trimpey. "AA's cycle of guilt, blame, and denial" encourages regular attendance at meetings to maintain sobriety. By contrast, RR "teaches that alcoholics can conquer their addiction in a relatively short time, perhaps in no more than 6 to 12 months . . . an occasional backslide is not tantamount to total failure" (ibid.).

A licensed clinical social worker, Trimpey established RR in his hometown of Lotus, California, after trying "lots of AA." After nearly two decades of dependence on alcohol, he attended his last AA meeting when another participant related how valuable his 20 years of AA meetings had been to him. "I felt like a truck was parked on my chest," Trimpey says. "Twenty years?" (Mehren 1992).

AA's insistence that an addict is powerless over his dependency is, Trimpey asserts, "almost like a curse. It took me a couple of years to realize that I was entirely recovered. I kept waiting for the other shoe to drop—until I realized that there was no other shoe" (Mehren 1992).

Trimpey became abstinent through his own determination and Albert Ellis' rational emotional therapy (RET). The guiding principle of RET, he says, is the belief that "you feel the way you think." A change in thought will produce a change in feelings and in actions. Anyone can self-correct who utilizes this technique. "There really is no great mystery here" (Mehren 1992).

To publicize RR, Trimpey and his wife made a three-month trip across the country in 1991. They stirred up discussions with AA advocates in each state and left printed RR material saying, "It's alright to just say no to AA." In 1992 RR sponsored meetings in 350 cities, including at least 25 in southern California. RR has an official manual called *The Small Book*, playing off the informal title of AA's "Big Book."

A national study of 433 RR members in 63 RR groups reported that most participants were college-educated men who had previously attended AA (Galanter, Egelko, and Edwards 1993). The study's comparison of RR members with a probability sample of other Americans polled by the Gallup Poll Organization found that "RR members scored much lower than other Americans with regard to belief in God and the importance of religion in their lives" (p. 508). Among those who had attended RR for six months or more, 58 percent reported at least six months of abstinence (p. 499). Galanter, Egelko, and Edwards suggest that RR may be more appropriate for some alcoholics who are uncomfortable with the spiritual concepts of AA, since it is important to frame treatment "in a way that expresses values similar to those of the patient" (p. 508).

In early 1995 the RR board of directors split with Trimpey and established SMART Recovery (Self Management and Recovery Training) as a nonprofit option emphasizing Albert Ellis' RET (1962). SMART uses a four-point program: (1) building motivation, (2) coping with urges, (3) problem solving, and (4) lifestyle balancing (Kern 1996).[4]

SECULAR ORGANIZATIONS FOR SOBRIETY

Secular Organizations for Sobriety (SOS), established in 1987, is "a non-profit network of autonomous, non-professional local groups dedicated solely to helping individuals achieve and maintain sobriety." SOS takes "a reasonable, secular approach to recovery and regards sobriety as a separate issue from religion or spirituality. It credits the individual for achieving and maintaining his/her own sobriety without reliance on any higher power" (Secular Organizations for Sobriety 1993a). Its organizer, James Christopher, during a 17-year battle with his own addiction, turned to AA but was repelled by "more dogma, more repression, and more of organized religion's judgmentalism" (Hernandez 1993).

Like AA, SOS regards addiction as a chronic, progressive, and fatal disease and recognizes total abstinence from alcohol and other mind-altering chemicals as the prime requisite for a healthy and sober life. Claiming to have the best that AA offers—friendships, support, and peer networking—SOS is a recovery program for those who place more faith in reason than in spiritual guidance— although some hold religious beliefs (Secular Organizations for Sobriety 1993b).

Headquartered in Buffalo, New York, SOS hosts an annual national conference and publishes an international newsletter that offers brief feature articles and news, lists publications and videotapes for sale, and gives locations of affiliated groups. SOS brochures emphasize that it is not opposed to or in competition with any recovery program, nor is it a spinoff from other groups. "We are not competing with AA," its leader points out. "Long may it wave." But SOS members maintain that religion corrupts and merely shuffles alcoholics from one cult (alcoholism) to another (AA) (Hernandez 1993).

MODERATION MANAGEMENT

Moderation Management (MM), founded by Audrey Kishline in 1993, is a program designed for "problem drinkers" (Type 3 and 4 users) that prescribes 30 days of abstinence followed by a moderate drinking regime. Not intended for chronic alcoholics, severely dependent Type 5 addicts, it does not ask users to admit that their lives are unmanageable, as AA does. "Most problem drinkers," Kishline (1994, p. 51) explains, "have not reached that point—their lives are still manageable." MM encourages users to seek help "when you *first* become aware that you are getting close to the edge of the cliff."

Since alcoholics like to think of themselves as social drinkers and rarely admit that their use is unmanageable, the MM approach may sound attractive to Type 5 users. But it is not designed for them. Indeed, David Smith, president of the American Society of Addiction Medicine, cautions that a controlled-drinking message "just about killed a guy I know. He's an alcoholic who tried to moderate, then lost control and landed in the hospital. You tell a drunk he can drink again and you're risking his life" (Carey 1995, p. 80). MM advises those who experience serious withdrawal symptoms or have other conditions made worse by alcohol to go to an abstinence-based program (Kishline 1994).

Kishline recalls that she initially drank chiefly out of habit. Eventually, however, the drinking affected her health and work, and she was driving intoxicated. Depressed, frightened, and lonely, she sought help and was diagnosed as "alcoholic"; "their 'diagnosis' was predetermined by the traditional, black and white, either-you-are-an-alcoholic-or-you-aren't model of alcohol abuse" (1994, p. 4). Checking into a 28-day treatment program, she was told she must attend AA meetings or she would not be certified as a program graduate and her insurance would not cover her treatment. If she didn't attend AA meetings for the remainder of her life, they said, she would be dead, insane, in jail, or in the gutter. Yet she experienced few withdrawal symptoms when detoxified. "My physical dependence on alcohol was not severe—a point either ignored or considered irrelevant by treatment personnel" (p. 5).

Kishline never felt comfortable in AA meetings, even after hundreds of meetings with "honest, sincere, kind, and warm-hearted people with strong convictions. But I did not relate to the severity of their drinking stories . . . Although I tried desperately to belong in the beginning, I never really did belong. It took me years to figure out why" (1994, p. 6).

After marrying, having children, taking college courses, and developing new hobbies, interests, and friends she returned to moderate drinking. "I am comfortable with the role that alcohol plays in my life now. When I choose to drink, I drink in moderation and responsibly . . . And alcohol no longer stops me from doing more important things with my time, like living every day to its fullest" (1994, p. 7).

Kishline began the MM program in the hope that other problem drinkers "could benefit from a moderation-oriented layperson-led (and therefore free of charge) support group *when they first realize that they have a drinking problem*" (1994, p. 8). After learning about moderation-oriented programs in Great Britain, Sweden, Denmark, Norway, Germany, Australia, and New Zealand, she established MM "to provide a supportive environment in which problem drinkers who want to moderate their drinking behavior can come together to help each other obtain their common self-management goals" (p. 10).

Who is a moderate drinker? A moderate drinker does not experience personal or social pathologies and has no alcohol-related problems affecting family, employment, health, or well-being.

A moderate drinker considers an occasional drink to be a small, though enjoyable, part of life; has hobbies, interests, and other ways to relax and enjoy life that do not involve drinking alcohol; usually has friends who are moderate drinkers or nondrinkers; generally has something to eat before, during, or soon after drinking; usually does not drink for longer than an hour or two on any particular occasion; usually does not go over the .055 percent moderate BAC [blood alcohol content] limit; usually does not drink faster than one drink per half-hour; feels comfortable with his or her use of alcohol (never drinks secretly and does not spend a lot of time thinking about or planning to drink. (Kishline 1994, p. 110)[5]

Kishline identifies six characteristics of people likely to be successful in moderating their drinking: (1) a short history of problem drinking (about 5 years)—"people who have had drinking problems for over 10 years do less well with moderation"; (2) relative youth—"with the exception of those whose problems begin later in life, significantly fewer people over the age of 40 successfully moderate their drinking level"; (3) relatively few negative consequences from drinking (arrests, lost work days, marriage problems, and the like); (4) personal, social, and economic resources (family and friends, stable jobs, and education); (5) a conviction that moderate drinking is possible and freedom from negative self-labels ("alcoholic"); and (6) little or no previous contact with AA. What such people have in common, Kishline emphasizes, is that "they take action to change their behavior in life *sooner* than those who are less likely to be able to return to moderate drinking" (1994, pp.69–70).[6]

Colleagues Helping Colleagues

Until recently, professional organizations ignored chemical dependence in their members, were lax in peer review, and protected themselves and their colleagues by maintaining silence (Gualtieri, Cosentino, and Becker 1983). Now, however, as a result of efforts by recovering addicts in their ranks and an erosion in public confidence, professional associations are addressing the problem.

Most progress has come from efforts by recovering addicts within their respective professions. Working behind the scenes and in conjunction with AA, they educate professional societies about the drug problem among their members and the need for help rather than punishment. Organized informally, they sponsor their own rehabilitation programs, some of which are now incorporated into established societies.

PHYSICIANS

International Doctors of Alcoholics Anonymous (IDAA), the first such informal professional organization, was established in 1949 in the upstate New York garage of Dr. Clarence P. Attended by physicians from the United States and Canada, IDAA has held annual meetings at locations throughout the world. One physician recalled, "I didn't think there were a lot of docs around who had this problem, but when I walked into my first IDAA meeting there were 268 people talking. I couldn't believe it. I thought to myself, 'This organization has gone out and hired circuit speakers to act like doctors' " (MD, age 50).

The organization supports itself through the contributions of its members. According to a pamphlet, "The only requirement for membership is the doctor's desire to belong" (International Doctors of Alcoholics Anonymous n.d.). The international meetings, usually held at exotic sites, serve as vacations that support sobriety and strengthen families. Al-Anon meetings offer concurrent small-group sessions dealing with couples' communication and other family issues. Continuing medical education credit is offered for those who attend preconferences on alcoholism and allied diseases.

Administered by a volunteer steering committee, IDAA provides "scholarships" to help new members early in recovery attend annual meetings. In 1993 it awarded 80 scholarships totaling $30,000. IDAA now numbers over 2,500 women and men who have, or are preparing for, doctorate degrees in the health-care professions.

In 1973, spurred by a growing awareness of the critical need to recognize and treat impaired physicians, the American Medical Association's Council on Mental Health urged physicians to report debilitated colleagues. Two years later the AMA sponsored its first Impaired Physicians Conference. Convened biennially until the mid-1980s, these conferences stimulated state and county medical societies to implement their own impaired-physician programs. By 1984 all 50 state medical societies had impaired-physician committees (Platman and Llufrio 1990). Although many are fully functioning, some exist only on paper. "Some have aimed at being little more than cosmetic; others have fallen into disrepair and, if present, are inactive" (Hester 1989, p. 8).

PILOTS

Birds of a Feather International, founded in 1976, is an IDAA clone for pilots that meets annually at a range of locations worldwide. Members attend with their spouses and significant others. "We have two or three AA meetings a day, a business meeting, guest speakers, and a banquet. We meet once a year as a group in the United States,

Germany, Iceland—all over," reported the chair of one such meeting (pilot, age 54).

Affiliate groups—"nests"—hold weekly meetings in major U.S. cities. "You name it, and there's probably one there. Two to 14 pilots get together from all strata of aviation—all age groups, from retired airline and military pilots right down to young student pilots who recognize that they have a problem. We meet to discuss our problems, with anonymity closely guarded" (pilot, age 54).

A newsletter, *Bird Word,* circulates news and information and personal notes from members. Begun in 1981, *Bird Word* connects highly mobile members with other pilots in recovery. A sample entry reads, "If there are any readers in Long Island interested in meeting, please call me at [phone number]." Cities, contact people, and phone numbers of different nests are listed, as are organizational officers—"trusted servants."

The mental health significance of colleague support is illustrated by this *Bird Word* note: "Sometimes I get so wrapped up in my school here, where I am working on an aviation degree, that I nearly forget how fortunate I am to be alive and have my sobriety. Thank God for the meetings and my friends who help keep me humble and appreciative of this wonderful gift of life."

As an indirect outgrowth of these informal activities, in 1991 the Air Line Pilots Association (ALPA) negotiated a contract with the Federal Aviation Administration to reactivate a former FAA-financed program. Called Human Intervention and Motivation Study (HIMS), the HIMS II project provides seminars and materials to train airline management, airline human resources and employee assistance personnel, pilots, and physicians about addictions and recovery. The first major seminar was held in November 1992.

ATTORNEYS

Addicted lawyers formed a number of informal organizations in the 1970s. "The Other Bar" began spontaneously in 1971 as an effort to help an incarcerated fellow attorney on a court-sanctioned work-furlough program. "They let me out every morning with a sack lunch to go to work," he recalled. "But they had no AA program or anything else to help me stay sober."

> I wasn't allowed to go home to launder my things or anything else. The minute I finished my work it was back to jail. A couple of attorneys said to me, "We'll create a meeting for you." So every morning

when I left the jail they met me at the coffee shop. They brought the Big Book, and we would have an AA meeting there. That got us thinking that there must be a lot of other lawyers with a need to talk to others in the profession and share how it has affected them. So in 1971 one of the guys, a presiding judge, said, "Let's get together one night with those of us who are lawyers or former lawyers and share our experience." At that time there was still a lot of stigma attached to lawyers' coming to AA meetings, because we were afraid that our clients would see us. So we created our own little group, and everybody liked it so much we kept doing it on a regular basis. We spread the word around that anybody who was having trouble with alcohol could call this number. When we got calls they would ask, "Is this an AA meeting?" and we would say, "No, it's not. We are just a bunch of lawyers who are sober and get together." It was a bridge into AA. Soon the *New York Times* did an article on it, and we started receiving phone calls from guys all over the place—New York, Canada, you name it—and we started communicating with each other. It just sprang up.   (JD, age 61)

Thousands of lawyers now belong to the Other Bar. In California 25 groups meet weekly, with 18–22 newcomers monthly (McCarthy 1994).

Following the example of IDAA, in 1975 a group of attorneys founded the International Lawyers of Alcoholics Anonymous (ILAA) in Niagara Falls, Ontario, attended by 20 lawyers. Today membership exceeds 500. Before 1975, "there was nowhere for a lawyer to turn for confidential assistance," a founding member recalls.

Sometime before July 1969 I realized that I was in trouble with alcohol, but where could I go? Who would find out? Would my practice and reputation suffer? All of these things ran through my mind long before I had my back to the wall and achieved my dry date. So, after the 1975 meeting of the International Group, we each brought back to our respective states the idea of forming vestibule groups. At that time there were no Lawyer's Assistance Programs (LAPs).   (Anonymous 1993)

The ILAA-inspired plan initially met with resistance from officials in the various state bar associations: "Getting those ideas across took a lot of education, but finally in 1984 we were able to get a full-time executive director in our state for a Lawyer's Alcoholism and Drug Abuse Committee, someone who would go out and conduct a confrontational intervention and really help the lawyer who was in trouble. Now we have them in 50 states!" (Anonymous 1993; see also Lawyers Concerned for Lawyers n.d.).

In 1988 the American Bar Association, recognizing that it was lagging behind, formed a Commission on the Impaired Attorney. "I was fortunate enough to be a founding member of that commission," an attorney said. "Through this effort . . . LAPs in the individual states now receive the dignity that they really deserve" (Anonymous 1993).

"Business is booming" in California, according to the LAP director there. Within an hour a toll-free telephone number puts 500–800 callers a month in touch with a recovering alcoholic volunteer attorney (McCarthy 1994, p. 4). An LAP director underscores the value of such services:

> Very often you get a phone call from someone (it may be a secretary) who wants help, saying that the boss is out of his mind, he doesn't come back after lunch . . . he misses appointments and telephone calls, et cetera. Since he rarely will come in for help, we phone him in the morning (not a good idea to call after lunch). The conversation goes like this. "Good morning, my name is ——, and I'm with Lawyers Assistance Program here in New York. A very dear friend of yours, a person who is very concerned about you, asked me to call you because they think you may have a problem with alcohol." I must tell you that in all my experience I've never had a person on the other end jump through the phone and say, "Thank God you called!" That's never happened. But I will tell you they have never hung up, and 90 percent take my phone number because they know that I'm their lifeline. They know inside that they're in trouble, so they say, "Let me have your number and thank you for calling." I can't say what percent call back, but I can say that I see them in the rooms of AA within the next year or two. You plant a seed and let them know there is help out there and it isn't a fellow with a brown bag sitting on the curb. It's your professional colleague in AA that wants to help you get into treatment so that you can straighten out your life. (Anonymous 1993; see also Goff 1987; Texas Young Lawyers Association 1990; Pitulla 1992; Oregon State Bar Association 1991, 1993)

State LAPs also sponsor "sobriety contracts" with professionals in recovery who agree to sign a written contract to remain sober and attend so many meetings within a certain period. These contracts may also include a monitoring agreement. "Monitoring can be a rather thankless job," an LAP director said, "but it is something that gives the courts confidence in what we do in the LAP" (Anonymous 1993)

The ABA's commission sponsors a two-day convention immediately before the ILAA meeting. It helps LAPs by providing speakers, articles, information, a national directory, and advertising openings for full-time LAP state directors. The commission also encourages law schools and providers of continuing legal education to incorporate ethics and substance-abuse programs into their curricula. In addition, it explores ways that bar associations can sponsor health-insurance programs that provide for addiction rehabilitation treatment, and tracks innovative approaches to handling attorneys with substance-abuse problems.

PHARMACISTS

An informal organization for pharmacists—the Impaired Pharmacists Program (IPP)—began with a Pennsylvania pharmacist reluctant to admit in an AA meeting that he was a health professional. "I was ashamed that I was a pharmacist," he recalled.

> A slew of us got together to help get through our problems. I'm now in contact with other impaired pharmacists on a weekly basis, sometimes daily. This group sets up speaking engagements for me where I can go around and tell other pharmacists who are still in their addictions and working that they can come forward and say, "I need help." I tell them my story and let them know that they don't need to lose their licenses.   (PharmD, age 41)

International Pharmacists Anonymous (IPA), a mutual support group for pharmacists and pharmacy students in recovery, now has more than 200 members. IPA was founded in 1987, and confidential membership is open to any pharmacist or pharmacy student who belongs to or is seriously considering joining a traditional 12-step program.

IPA keeps a list of pharmacy recovery support group meetings to help addicted pharmacists find peer-group meetings wherever they are. IPA has no local chapters and requires no dues or fees (Williams 1994). Not affiliated with any disciplinary or regulatory body or agency, IPA is "a fellowship of pharmacists-in-recovery who share their experience, strength, and hope with each other so that they may solve their common problems and help others recover from addictive disease" (ibid., p. 1).

A similar informal recovery group, the Caduceus Group, also helps pharmacists and other health care professionals. "It did more for me than anything else," a pharmacist reported:

> It was a very tight network of professionals who monitored each other. In 1987 I had a friend take me to one of the meetings. This was a bunch of physicians, and they sort of adopted me and gave me a contract to sign. I scratched out where it said "M.D." and put "pharmacist." They called it a sobriety contract and offered to monitor me and do urines on me and maintain my meeting attendance. When I tried to explain to them that I wasn't an addict, they told me I was nuts and explained the disease concept to me. (PharmD, age 41)

In 1982 the American Pharmaceutical Association (APhA) officially recognized chemical dependency as a problem within its ranks. That year the APhA's House of Delegates committed to support the establishment of state-level programs for counseling, treatment, prevention, and rehabilitation for addicted pharmacists and trainees.

Following APhA's lead, in 1983 the American Society of Hospital Pharmacists (ASHP) adopted a policy "to support the APhA's program of activities to assist impaired (chemically dependent) pharmacists." APhA annually cosponsors the Pharmacy Section at the University of Utah School of Alcoholism and Other Drug Dependencies, publishes a handbook on planning and implementing state programs for impaired pharmacists, assists in the development of state programs, and networks with more than 300 persons concerned about impaired pharmacists (Talley 1988).

An outgrowth of the Utah School section has been the development of APhA-endorsed regional Pharmacists Recovering Network (PRN) meetings (American Pharmaceutical Association 1994). In 1994 the PRN launched a recovery contact service of consultants and speakers, a list of volunteer member pharmacists in recovery familiar with 12-step programs. They provide information, talk to pharmacists in recovery, or attend meetings or classes. PRN also publishes a quarterly newsletter called the *PRN Memo*.

DENTISTS

Before 1985, when the first National Conference on Alcoholism and Chemical Dependency in the Dental Professions met in Chicago, there were only a few state programs in place,[7] and addicted dentists were on their own (Bowermaster 1988). Early, informal volunteer efforts are hailed today as breakthroughs. "Our first meeting was in 1983 with 12 of us," a dentist recalled. "There was a book there, and everybody signed it. Now it's in the archives or something" (DDS, age 47).

Volunteer groups that met in the early 1980s, such as Dentists Concerned for Dentists, are credited with saving careers. "I met with a private group of dentists, all in recovery," one recalled. "We held regular meetings once a month and then, after the business meeting, held an AA meeting. I went through hell in dental school trying to maintain my sobriety and protect my anonymity, and that group was incredibly important to me. I probably would have dropped out of school without it" (DDS, age 48).

In 1986 the American Dental Association House of Delegates adopted the following five-part policy statement on chemical dependency:

1. The ADA recognizes that chemical dependency is a disease entity that affects all of society.

2. The ADA is committed to assisting the chemically dependent member of the dental family toward recovery by education, information, and referral . . .

3. The ADA encourages those institutions responsible for dental education to allocate adequate curriculum on substance use, misuse, and addiction.

4. In meeting the needs of the public and the profession, the ADA also encourages ongoing liaison between constituent society chemical dependency committees and their state boards of registration.

5. The ADA recognizes the need for research in the area of chemical dependency in dentistry.   (Peters 1987, p. 513)

State and regional dental associations now sponsor a variety of programs to assist chemically dependent dentists (Crosby 1996). Many offer confidential hotlines, as this dentist explained:

I volunteer to answer calls on the confidential physician/dentist hot line three or four days a month. It's an assistance line not connected with the state board. All we do is give information and explain available resources. For example, a gal called recently about her brother, an anesthesiologist. We did a conference call with the whole family and gave them a picture of what an intervention is, how they could do it, and how to get involved with their hospital well-being committee. They connected up with the latter, did an intervention, and got the brother into treatment. (DDS, age 47)

Some state dental associations now sponsor educational workshops and well-being programs at meetings of dental societies. In the California Dental Association's presentation, each participant receives a workbook containing information about confidential assistance, telephone help lines, intervention techniques, treatment programs, references, films, and publications relating to dentistry and chemical dependency.

Many states, like New York, offer all-day seminars on topics such as "New Beginnings—Hope for the Addicted Dentist" (Crosby 1995). These programs discuss what is being done nationally and at the state level to help drug-addicted dentists and explore the latest concepts in identifying, intervening with, and treating chemically dependent dentists (O'Connell 1989).

NURSES

Before formal recovery programs were available for nurses, informal groups emerged spontaneously, as this nurse recalled:

> I participated in a Nurse to Nurse group founded by a recovering nurse who recognized a need for nurses to support each other. Doctors really enable other doctors; their colleagues will cover for them. But nurses on the other hand will shoot each other. Nurses can be very punitive and critical. Their attitude is "You are bad; we don't want you; get out." To a certain extent it's the way we were trained in school. We have a "Saintly Syndrome"; if we use drugs we are not only bad nurses, we're bad people. (RN, age 40)

In 1983 one nurse formed a support group for addicted nurses and organized a program of strategic confrontations. In addition, she wrote a "Memorandum of Understanding" to the state nursing association, the state board of health professionals, and the state nursing board, prodding them to make it a policy that chemically dependent nurses should not lose their licenses until they have had an opportunity for treatment (RN, age 70). Now a number of states have diversion programs.

Nurses lagged behind physicians in acknowledging and addressing chemical impairment in their profession. Not until 1982 did the

American Nurses' Association (ANA) House of Delegates adopt a policy stating that treatment was to be offered before disciplinary action for chemical dependency or emotional illness. The ANA set up a task force to collect information and to help state nurses' associations develop programs for chemically dependent nurses. The first ANA Conference on Impaired Nurses was held in 1985 (Sullivan, Bissell, and Williams 1988).

Today a variety of hospital employee assistance programs (EAPs), state diversion programs, and peer assistance programs help addicted nurses recover and resume their careers. International Nurses Anonymous, begun in 1988 as an unaffiliated network of nurses in 12-step recovery programs, serves as a resource for those looking for a nurses' support group. Although there are only about 450 current members—compared to 5,000 in the IDAA (Secretary-Treasurer of International Nurses Anonymous 1995)—this number does not suggest a shortage of chemically dependent nurses. "There is a tremendous problem in our profession," said the secretary-treasurer of INA. "Doctors have more resources than nurses. Nurses usually can't afford the conventions in expensive places, and they are more often single parents with child care responsibilities."

Solo Recovery

Some addicts put an end to their chemical dependency without self-help programs, professional therapists, or formal treatment. The number of these spontaneous, natural, or untreated recoverers is unknown.

Some think the number who quit by willpower alone is very small. Others disagree, claiming the number exceeds those who seek professional help. Among the former is an informal network of 12–15 California physicians who specialize in chemical dependency, the Los Angeles Physicians Aid Network (LAPAN). "We gathered informal information from friends, families, AA associates, patients in private practice, anywhere we could find them," one recounted. "We accumulated data and tracked all known addicted physicians to see if they were in treatment. In 1975 we knew of only 3, but by 1994 we had identified 201 chemically dependent physicians in the county." Asked how many of these became sober without program aid, he replied, "A few do exist, but they are very difficult to find because they maintain anonymity. They aren't active in any program and don't share their experiences openly with others. But they are there. I can think of a surgeon who didn't get active in a program who stayed sober by compulsively flying his plane."

A literature review by Shaffer and Jones (1989) documents that some addicts recover without assistance. Though few in number, "all of these studies find some evidence for the existence of spontaneous recovery" (1989, p. 91).

Those who think the number who recover by themselves is very high call it "the elephant that no one sees" (American Sociological Association 1994). They cite as evidence heroin-addicted Vietnam veterans who discontinued their drug use without formal treatment upon returning to the United States. They also point out that 90–95 percent of cigarette smokers who quit do so without assistance. (This percentage sounds remarkably high, but according to the Centers for Disease Control and Prevention [1993], only 2.5 percent of daily smokers quit smoking permanently each year.)

Granfield and Cloud (1994, p. 16) assert that "there is considerable evidence from additional research to suggest that this population [those who recover without help] is quite substantial." According to some estimates, "as many as 90 percent of problem drinkers never enter treatment and many recover without it" (ibid., p. 1).

To locate "natural recoverers," Granfield and Cloud used a snowball sampling technique—a chain-referral method—to identify hard-to-find individuals. They interviewed 25 men and women who had quit using drugs for at least a year (an average of 5.5 years) without relying on formal treatment or self-help programs. Ranging in age from 25 to 60 (a mean of 38.4 years), all had been drug dependent for at least a year (an average of 9.1 years), and all had a history of extended periods of daily use, frequent drug cravings, and personal problems resulting from using drugs. Addicts with less than two weeks of hospitalization were included if they had had no follow-up outpatient treatment, as were those with less than one month's exposure to self-help groups such as AA, Narcotics Anonymous, or Cocaine Anonymous. A few of the 25 had attended one or two self-help meetings, but the majority had avoided treatment programs and self-help groups altogether.

Most of Granfield and Cloud's respondents did not regard themselves as addicts or ex-addicts (1994, p. 9). Although all admitted their earlier addiction, nearly two-thirds refused to identify themselves as currently addicted, as recovering, or even as recovered. Several reacted strongly to the idea that addiction is a disease, fearing that such a permanent label would hinder their growth. "I'm a father, a husband, and a worker," one explained. "This is how I see myself today. Being a drug addict was someone I was in the past. I'm over that and I don't think about it anymore" (p. 8).

Only 2 of the 25 claimed ignorance of self-help groups like AA; their decision not to seek help was a conscious decision, although several said treatment programs and self-help groups had helped addicted friends and family members. They typically rejected the ideological underpinnings of these programs, particularly the idea that they were powerless over their addictions, a belief they felt was counterproductive and demeaning. "In contrast to the poor success rates of formal treatment programs and self-help groups, the overwhelming majority of our respondents reported successful termination of their addictions after only one or two attempts" (Granfield and Cloud, 1994, p. 12).

Granfield and Cloud conclude that addicts who have "a stake in conventional life" can more readily change their drug-taking behavior than those who do not. They have "not yet burned their bridges" and have friends, family, and other associates to help them adjust to a drug-free state. These communities make it unnecessary for them to affiliate with "artificial communities that are found within the self-help groups" (1994, pp. 13–15). In addition, these subjects often build new support structures by joining recreational, sports, and religious organizations. Some return to school, get involved in civic organizations, or undertake new hobbies that bring them into contact with drug-free associates. As they build new lives, they typically hide their drug-using past, fearing that exposure will jeopardize their status in the new groups. Some subjects relocated to a different part of the country to avoid their former drug-abusing associates. Some pregnant women left addicted boyfriends because of a sense of responsibility to their unborn child (ibid., p. 16).

Other studies have also identified solo recoverers. Using newspaper, radio, and television solicitations, Tuchfeld (1981) found 162 people in a southeastern city who had resolved their chronic drinking problems by themselves. The 35 men and 16 women who agreed to answer questions had abstained for at least a year without participating in treatment of any kind or self-help organizations such as Alcoholics Anonymous. However, Tuchfeld concluded, "Few, if any, cases in this study could be characterized as 'spontaneous' in the sense of developing without apparent external influence" (p. 638). The reasons given for discontinuing alcohol, ranked by frequency, were:

> (1) personal illness or accident, (2) education about alcoholism, (3) religious conversion or experience, (4) direct intervention by family members, (5) direct intervention by friends, (6) financial problems created by drinking, (7) alcohol-related death or illness of another person, (8) alcohol-related legal problems, and (9) extraordinary events including personal humiliation, exposure to negative role models, events during pregnancy, attempted suicide, and personal identity crisis; humiliating events were frequent precursors.   (P. 632)

Tuchfeld and others, assuming that large numbers of addicts recover without help, challenge the widely held belief that chemical dependence is an irreversible disease requiring extensive treatment and aftercare. "If such persons exist at all," they argue, "they are a small minority of those who have destructive patterns of alcohol use, and . . . most persons 'naturally' resolve such problems without any exposure to treatment" (Tuchfeld 1981, p. 627; see also Peele 1996).

Shaffer and Jones (1989, p. 4) agree that "some drug abusers are resilient and—left solely to their own devices, without intervention—recover from addiction." They conclude that the current perception of addiction and treatment—"clinical fundamentalism"—is like the treatment of mental illness in the 1930s and 1940s. "During this time, the prevailing wisdom dictated that the most effective treatment for many mental illnesses was psychosurgery; that is, lobotomy and electric shock treatment"—practices that are now considered "primitive, excessively invasive, unethical, and medically clumsy" (p. 2). Citing jaw-wiring for the treatment of obesity and brain surgery for compulsive gambling or alcoholism, they assert that "similarly 'interventions' are a part of the prevailing wisdom of our drug treatment time" (p. 3).

"The conventional wisdom of 'once an addict, always an addict' is a myth," Biernacki (1986) asserts. His results from 101 heroin addicts who discontinued this drug without assistance "run counter to scientific theories of opiate addiction. Most, if not all, theories of addiction are extremely pessimistic and do not even consider the possibility that at least some addicts can recover on their own, without the benefit of treatment" (p. 41).

Locating and interviewing a heretofore-hidden population of solo recovers—Type 4 addicts—provides invaluable data, but these data do not nullify well-documented findings that Type 5 addicts cannot overcome drug dependence without massive aid. Type 5 addicts depend on drugs to cope. When drug use is no longer "fun," they do not simply abandon the substances, as Type 4 addicts do; instead they frantically titrate and search for other substances to feel "normal". All too often the results are disastrous. Over and over again Type 5 addicts credit others, usually those in AA programs, with literally saving their lives. For them solo recovery is not an option.

Although none of the investigators who identified solo recoverers differentiates between Type 4 and 5 addicts, evidence of both can be readily inferred from descriptions of their research populations. For example, Waldorf, Reinanman, and Murphy's (1991) study of cocaine addicts includes some who quit without assistance; more than half had successfully stopped using on the first try, although it was not easy. However, others had tried unsuccessfully to quit, one so often that he lost count—40 unsuccessful attempts, by his own account, was a low estimate (p. 203). Shaffer and Jones's (1989, p. 98) study group also includes two types of quitters: (1) those who did not experience serious dislocations in their lives as a result of using cocaine, who "saw the light" and decided to quit; and (2) those who found themselves in desperate circumstances because all aspects of normal life had disintegrated.

In some solo recovery studies, certain subjects were free from one substance but still using others. For example, in Biernacki's study (1986), a widely cited report of 101 heroin addicts who quit heroin without formal help, some had simply switched drugs—from opiates to alcohol or Valium (p. 138). The author fails to see this as a continuing manifestation of chemical dependence. Similarly, in Waldorf's (1983) study of "naturally recovering" heroin addicts, more than one-third were still chemically dependent. In forsaking heroin, they switched to more socially acceptable drugs—41 percent reported heavy drinking during the first six months to cope with life without heroin, and 37 percent reported using marijuana 1,000 or more times as a heroin substitute.

Pharmacologic substitutions—switching from cocaine to alcohol or other drugs—also occurred among the cocaine users interviewed by Shaffer and Jones (1989). The authors report that one-fifth of the addicts drank more alcohol after quitting than they had before. One of their subjects said, "I started drinking like a fish, although gradually. Two years later I am now coming to terms with alcoholism" (pp. 140–141). An unspecified number also used marijuana after discontinuing cocaine (p. 216).

Clearly, some addicts can quit without help from a recovery program. In my view, this is because they are Type 4 addicts: they do not need the drug to cope; they are not psychologically dependent. They use drugs for pleasure, but when drug-related problems begin to outweigh the benefits, they grasp the reality and quit. Typically these physically dependent addicts have meaningful social ties and activities that provide "natural highs." These users perceive recovery programs not only as unnecessary, but also as a potential threat to their reputation and self-esteem.

Just as it is faulty for treatment personnel to claim that all addicts require massive assistance, it is unwarranted for ethnographic researchers to conclude that, because they have searched out Type 4 addicts, few addicts need assistance. Most of those interviewed for this book—Type 5 addicts—desperately searched for chemical solutions to their problems as their lives spiraled downward. Self-correction through rational insight and willpower was completely beyond them. "Nothing motivated me until I was desperate for help," said one attorney. "If anyone had said I needed to alter my lifestyle—do this, that, or the other—I would have said, 'To hell with you; get out of here.' But when I became absolutely desperate, I sought help" (JD, age 50).

In Perspective

There are about 750,000 self-help and mutual-support groups in the United States, with an estimated 15 million members (Christenson and Jacobson 1994). Although outcome research on self-help participation is in an embryonic stage, it is obvious from the interview testimony gathered here that most progress in rehabilitating addicted professionals can be credited to volunteers, most of whom, once addicted, are now sober.

Recovering addicts can cut through others' denial and effectively monitor sobriety. Having experienced suffering, recovering addicts are also the most compassionate and willing to help, and in so doing they sustain their own recovery. Progress by professional associations in reaching out to impaired colleagues can be largely credited to the efforts of once-addicted members, mostly AA participants. No informed person can dispute the powerful impact that AA's twelfth step—service—has had on countless thousands.

Type 4 addicts, those who are physically but not psychologically dependent on drugs, can quit using without relying on AA and or other support. But for Type 5 addicts, those who have come to rely on drugs to cope, self-help programs—as well as the formal ones described in the next chapter—are essential. For many, they literally save lives.

EIGHT

Formal Recovery Programs

"I woke up fighting and telling them I didn't belong. I told them how important and busy I was and how many clients I had. How could I be in detox with no phone privileges when I had all these people to contact? They said, 'This is the way it is here. You can leave if you want to,' but I had no place else to go."

(JD, age 55)

"I was relieved that [in treatment] they didn't tie me down, put me in a smoky room, and make me vomit or do electric shock to the genitalia. It was a 12-step approach with lots of meetings and individual and group counseling."

(MD, age 34)

"The only thing that made me stop using was the threat of losing my license and my livelihood. That's what made me go in and get help. Everything else could have gone out the door and I wouldn't have cared; but the thought of losing my license kept me clean."

(DDS, age 37)

Self-help recovery programs rely on member-volunteers working individually and collectively within a loosely defined structure of sponsorship and sharing of their own experience, strength, and hope. These people are qualified by personal experience with recovery from chemical dependence and by their desire to stay sober and to help others achieve sobriety as part of their own recovery program. New members are encouraged to seek out and model senior members whose relational style and approach to recovery would work for them.

Formal programs, both more structured and more restrictive, are staffed by trained professionals and have specific agendas that go beyond helping addicts and alcoholics achieve sobriety and amend their lives. Operating in a clearly defined hierarchy, the professional staff may or may not have personal experience with chemical dependency. Some formal programs—inpatient, outpatient, and office practice treatment—operate for profit. Work-site and training programs seek to minimize organizational losses and embarrassment caused by drug-debilitated professionals in their ranks. Diversion programs monitor and rehabilitate selected professionals, and state and federal control programs protect the public by investigating complaints and enforcing standards.

Inpatient Treatment

Although the disease concept of alcoholism was presented in AA's "Big Book" in 1939, publicized in various periodicals, and accepted by the AMA in 1956, organized medicine mostly ignored chemical dependency until the late 1960s and early 1970s, when the current system of inpatient drug treatment began. Until then, addiction was usually regarded as a symptom of underlying psychiatric problems (Mann 1991). Treatment consisted of identifying these problems and applying the appropriate therapy. No major U.S. health plan reimbursed substance-abuse treatment, although the medical consequences of alcoholism, such as cirrhosis of the liver, were covered. The well-to-do masked their alcoholism as a medical condition and paid out of pocket to dry out at deluxe private facilities. Middle-income alcoholics who could afford it also paid out of pocket to stay in small motels or guesthouses run by recovering alcoholics, with minimal medical help (Cummings 1991).

Chronic public inebriates, the most visible addicts, were usually consigned to the criminal-justice system. A few states provided hospital programs and enforced abstinence in locked wards. Some programs tried to condition alcoholics to avoid drinking after their release by giving them a drug called Antabuse, followed by cocktails in rapid succession in simulated barrooms; the combination of Antabuse and alcohol induces vomiting and intense physical discomfort (Cummings 1991).

Significant expansion of drug-treatment programs began in the mid-1960s (Haaga and McGlynn 1993). A 1968–69 National Institute of Mental Health survey of organizations that operated drug-treatment programs identified only 183, and more than 75 percent of these had operated five years or less. Before 1965, specialized drug treatment outside of the federal prison system existed mainly in large cities, notably New York (Haaga and McGlynn 1993).

In 1929 the federal government opened U.S. Public Health Service hospitals in Lexington, Kentucky, and Fort Worth, Texas, where addicts could enter for heroin withdrawal under an assumed name. Most of them used these programs to decrease the daily quantity of heroin needed to get high when their habit had become too expensive. Rarely did they intend to discontinue drug use altogether. (See Musto 1987 for a history of narcotic control in America.)

Professionals who had lost their licenses occasionally participated in these early hospital programs, but little was accomplished beyond detoxifying (Poplar 1969). "I went into the hospital for a week and dried out under supervision," an attorney remembered. "After they gave me a little counseling and recommended AA to me, I left the hospital and thought I was fine; I could eat again and felt good, better than I had for some time. But I left with the idea that drinking wasn't evil, I was just drinking too much. I still didn't understand that an alcoholic can't drink at all. So I was quickly back where I started" (JD, age 50).

In some cases, treatment centers became "shooting galleries"— places where addicts gathered to use. "Long before treatment centers were available," a nurse reported, "I went into a little outpatient program where they didn't know how to help; there was no drug testing and no specific guidelines to follow. There were eight of us in this program, and right in the middle we'd go to the bathroom to use. One after the other, we'd each go to line up a line of cocaine or shoot up behind the patient's curtain. It was almost an enabling situation" (RN, age 40).

Forced into a mental hospital after being arrested, a lawyer had this outlandish experience: "They decided I was clinically depressed and gave me an antidepressant that made me feel awfully strange. When I walked around like a zombie, it reinforced their idea that I was a mental patient." Admitted a second time to the "psych ward," he was again diagnosed as having an affective disorder. "Depression was all they could come up with," he said. "Eventually, in 1976, they sent me over to an inpatient unit that had just opened for alcoholics. I don't think they knew an awful lot, because no one tried to bring me down or give me any insight. Nobody knew what to do. After that they sent me to prison for 20 months" (JD, age 47).

Life on a locked psychiatric ward could be especially traumatic for professionals. "I was at the height of my career in cardiology almost 25 years ago," a physician reports, "and there was no place for me to get help. I went to numerous hospitals and psychiatric facilities, and none of them seemed to work. Finally my wife had to have me committed to the state hospital, where I was placed on a locked ward. When the inmates found that I was an M.D., they severely abused me verbally and physically. I remember saying that if I ever got well, I would find a place for the healer to be healed" (KCET Video Lifeguides 1991).

Amazingly, some professionals found sobriety in such places. "I got sober in a recovery house," said a pilot (age 50). "I had been in a never-ending spiral downward in and out of places like this before, but this time something good happened. They made me the 'house mother.' It turned out to be a good thing. Here I am sober for like a week, and I'm deciding who comes in and who doesn't. You wouldn't believe it."

Treatment of chemical dependency advanced swiftly in the mid-1960s and the 1970s as health insurance plans began to include mental health and chemical-dependency treatment benefits. When third-party payers accepted addiction as a disease, treatable by standard medical and mental health practice, treatment became reimbursable. At about the same time Congress developed "diagnosis-related groups" (DRGs) as a way to contain Medicare and Medicaid expenses (Cummings 1991). This strategy reduced hospital reimbursement for more than 300 DRGs to a limited number of days, and the occupancy of medical and surgical beds dropped dramatically. Faced with financial disaster, hospital administrators, realizing that DRGs did not apply to mental health and chemical-dependency problems, converted empty beds to chemical-dependency units. Hospitalization had been primarily for medical detoxification, rarely for rehabilitation. These new insurance benefits created a new industry in the 1980s: hospital chemical-dependency programs—usually 28 inpatient days—dovetailed with general indemnity benefits (Haaga and McGlynn 1993). Many of these 28-day programs, modeled upon the Hazelden approach in Minnesota, actively involved participants in working through AA's 12 steps (Hester 1994).

By 1986 most hospitals aggressively advertised new programs. "I saw thousands of advertisements on TV about hospital chemical-dependency treatment programs," recalled a pharmacist (PharmD, age 46). The response was immediate. The average amount spent on chemical-dependency treatment in the United States increased by more than 40 percent for each of the next four years and became a $40-billion-a-year "treatment industry" (Cummings 1991). The accompanying flagrant profitseeking angered this pharmacist: "I went along with their stuff for 37 days because I had 40 days of insurance. I should have finished the program in 21 days, but they kept me around unnecessarily for a couple of extra weeks for the insurance. I still feel resentful about this" (PharmD, age 44).

Although relatively few people initially applied for inpatient benefits, employee assistance program (EAP) counselors encouraged employees to use their chemical-dependency hospital benefits. During the 1980s, EAPs mushroomed (Haaga and McGlynn 1993; Roman and Blum 1994).

Now as then, most of those entering treatment drop out before finishing their program. A national study of 41 selected treatment programs assessing the recovery progress of 11,750 drug-abusing clients who undertook treatment in 1979–1981 found that "treatment works" (Hubbard et al. 1989). The results, however, refer only to clients who remained in treatment for more than three months. At that point 55 percent of those in inpatient programs had dropped out, compared with 64 percent from outpatient programs and 32 percent from methadone treatment.[1] About two-thirds of alcoholic clients who stay through completion show favorable outcomes at three-month follow-ups, but this rate drops to one-fourth or less after a year (Miller 1992).

Despite these unpromising figures, it is cost-effective to treat addicts as inpatients (Weiss 1994). Researchers at Rutgers University's Center of Alcohol Studies reviewed the costs and consequences of untreated alcohol-related illnesses and injuries, as well as future "cost-offsets" when treatment is provided. Studies show that untreated alcoholics' health care costs are usually 100 percent higher than those of nonalcoholics, even many years before a severe health crisis. Furthermore, during the 12 months immediately preceding a medical emergency, health care costs for alcoholics escalate to almost 300 percent higher than those of nonalcoholics. After treatment and over time, however, health care costs decline to near the level of the nonalcoholic population (Langenburcher et al. 1993; Langenburcher 1995). "If treatment is done appropriately," observed the chief executive officer of a drug treatment center; "everybody wins: the patient wins, the family wins, the employer wins, the insurance company wins financially—everybody benefits for as long as the person stays sober."

Miller and Hester's (1986) review of 26 controlled studies found no advantage of inpatient over outpatient treatment (see also Institute of Medicine 1989). However, a more recent report (Walsh et al. 1991) reveals that alcoholic inpatients are likely to stay abstinent longer than those who only attended AA or chose other recovery options.

Participation in a self-help program following treatment increases the probability of continued sobriety. A 10-year follow-up of 158 randomly selected patients who completed a 12-step-oriented treatment program in 1973–74 found that 61 percent had been sober for at least three years before the survey and 84 percent had stable families, employment, and residence (Cross et al. 1990). Continued involvement in AA after leaving treatment greatly facilitated continued sobriety and stability; 91 percent of those who sponsored other AA members during the follow-up period were still sober.

Compared with the general population, addicted professionals show a spectacular recovery rate. In the few rigorous studies conducted, treatment centers report extraordinarily high recovery rates. For example, the director of Michigan's Physician Recovery Network (Skuter 1990) reports a 95 percent recovery rate for physicians two years after treatment. Kliner, Spicer, and Barnett (1980) report that 51 (76 percent) of the 67 physicians completing treatment at Hazelden—a residential facility for alcoholism treatment—were abstinent one year after release. A follow-up study of 250 physicians who completed treatment in the Georgia Impaired Physicians Program—4 months of supervised treatment plus 20 months of community aftercare—found 73.9 percent completely abstinent at least two years after treatment began. When those who relapsed shortly after treatment but had subsequently recovered were included, the total increased to 77.3 percent. The latter were back on their personal recovery program in AA or NA, usually without another admission (Gallegos and Norton 1984).

Treatment programs for other professionals also report astounding success. Eugene F. Willis Jr., the director of Georgia's Impaired Dentists Program, who has been involved with the treatment of 230 dentists from 29 states and three Canadian provinces, estimates the recovery rate to be "about 90 percent" (1990). Similarly, Spicer and colleagues (1978) found that a year after discharge from treatment at Hazelden, 91 percent of the professionals remained free of mood-altering drugs; 74 percent were attending AA meetings once a month or more often. Spicer noted that professionals as an aggregate showed more improvement than nonprofessionals.

Ninety-two percent of 199 United Airlines pilots involved in in-patient alcohol treatment from 1973 to 1989)—usually for 28 days, followed by an aftercare program of AA meetings and mandatory attendance at company-sponsored meetings—were recertified as commercial airline pilots. An additional 3 percent were awaiting recertification after successful completion of the program. One hundred seventy-four (87 percent) returned to flight duties (Flynn et al. 1993).

What accounts for these remarkable results? Professionals are usually highly educated, high functioning, heavily invested in their careers, and with access to personal and professional resources. The importance of their services, highly valued by society, requires that they not be "turned loose" after their initial treatment lest they be a danger to the public. If they want to return to their career, they must participate in aftercare monitoring, which usually includes regular attendance at mandatory meetings, ongoing screening for drugs and alcohol, and periodic evaluations of their progress.

The best outcomes for impaired physicians occur for those who undergo random urine monitoring. An eight-year follow-up of 63 impaired physicians found 75 percent stable and improved. The proportion rose to 96 percent for those monitored after treatment and dropped to 64 percent for those not monitored (Shore 1987). In California, diversion-program specialists follow addicted physicians for three to five years. To retain their licenses and continue practicing during this probationary period, they must submit to random drug testing and participate consistently in other aftercare activities such as biweekly diversion group meetings supervised by a professional facilitator, and numerous 12-step meetings. This rigorous long-term monitoring greatly improves long-term recovery rates (Ikeda and Pelton 1990).

However, professionals rarely make easy clients.[2] According to Modlin and Montes (1964), "The physician addict shares many characteristics with the general addict population . . . his capacity for rationalization, simulation, vacillation, subterfuge, and prevarication is infinite" (p. 362). Like all other addicts, they precipitate stormy encounters—exploitation, manipulation, angry and hostile outbursts—and experience periods of hopelessness and despair (Johnson and Connelly 1981, p. 256).

Professionals are usually independent, intelligent, and resourceful. Accustomed to being in charge, they dislike restrictions on their freedom. Nevertheless, many are able to put aside old habits, take their rehabilitation seriously, accept program requirements gracefully, and participate sincerely, if not wholeheartedly. Many gratefully acknowledge that the program saved their lives. Others remain defiant and resentful and merely maintain a facade of compliance in order to "graduate." "I got out of there by being the star, the perfect patient, the good boy," a pilot (age 58) recalled. "I did my penance, jumped through the hoops, and got the hell out of there."

A dentist who came in "kicking and screaming" resisted every effort. "I consented to go into the hospital to save my marriage, but it was a horrible experience. I felt like I was in prison. They had so many rules and regulations I couldn't stand it. If I had to piss, somebody had to come with me—things like that. So in a few days I said, 'I'm out of here.'" When the program staff told him he couldn't leave, he took a cab. Upon his arrival home his wife told him she was getting a divorce.

> I told her to go for it; I wasn't going to hang out in one of those places. But after a couple of days—I was so lonely and depressed—I thought, "It's not worth it, I'll do it." So I went to a different hospital where nobody knew who I was. I woke up every morning saying, "I hate this place; get me out of here; this is hell; I can't stand it." I cussed her out every morning on the phone and every night. But I was trying to salvage our relationship and keep from being reported to the state board. I wanted my life. But after seven days I quit. They told me that

when I went back out there I'd start using—but I didn't. The thing that kept me sober was I wanted to keep my life.   (DDS, age 37)

What happens in inpatient programs? A typical day might go like this:

We have wake-up, do meditation, and go to breakfast. You can work out—they had a running track on 23 acres and trees—and I would run and exercise most mornings. Then we have a lecture or go into group therapy for two hours; a lot of group—big-time. Then lunch, another lecture, then group, then a meeting every night. No TV except Saturday afternoon and Sunday. No visitors except on Sunday. No phone calls for more than 10 minutes—which we all thought was crazy—but that isolates you and gets you to think about what is going on.   (MD, age 40)

Confinement in a structured environment helps addicts focus on their problems. Temporary removal from daily life interrupts behavior patterns and provides physical and psychological healing. "The completely controlled environment subjected me to a lot of introspection and interaction with others who have the same problem," a dentist remarked (DDS, age 55). It also isolates addicts from their drugs and drug-using associates. "Drugs are always close by," a pharmacist acknowledged, "and being an addict and a great manipulator, I can go into any pharmacy and without their knowing, steal half their stock. It helps being physically away from that" (PharmD, age 41).

The inpatient experience, a 24-hour-a-day reality shock, brings participants face to face with their addiction. It is hard to remain in denial when constantly confronted with "righteous peer pressure" from staff and other addicts. "The 28 days I spent were well worth it," the pharmacist above recalled, "not only to start feeling better physically, but to have the constant support of recovering people in the same position. It was good to have a support system of people who a few days ago were out on a bender, shooting up, or popping pills."

Inpatient treatment also guarantees supervised detoxification. "In my case," a pharmacist commented,

inpatient rehab was a benefit. After ten years of daily drug use, my body was totally toxic, and there was quite a heavy psychological addiction also. Believe me, detoxing was not pleasant. They kept me in a hospital room and monitored me for seven days. They watched me, took my blood, and made sure my body was withdrawing okay. It gave me time to realize where I was—"I'm an addict in an addiction hospital: what happens next?" It took me 7 to 10 days before I actually felt decent enough to go upstairs to a meeting or attend class. (PharmD, age 41)

Effective treatment programs utilize a variety of therapeutic tools. Besides constant confrontation and support, many contemporary inpatient programs, especially those modeled upon the Hazelden approach, combine disease education, encouragement for individualized spiritual development, individual and group therapy, family education, and counseling and aftercare follow-up. The combination of techniques used is tailored to the needs of the individual.

Repeated educational sessions about the biogenic aspects of chemical dependence motivate addicts to fight "the disease" and overcome their denial and guilt. "After a week I was relieved to find out that I had a disease and I could be treated. As a pharmacist I could really understand that" (PharmD, age 46). A pilot (age 58) agreed. "After about four days listening to talks and whatnot, I started getting the picture. They were talking about me. I began to understand that the way I used alcohol was abusive and I was addicted. I wasn't very happy about those thoughts, but I decided, 'Well, this is okay.' "

The majority of current treatment programs in the United States and Canada use the AA model. The description of the program at the Betty Ford Center, in Rancho Mirage, California, furnishes an example: "Treatment is the attempt to focus the addict/alcoholic on the consequences of the addiction. We do this most effectively by using peer groups led by trained addiction counselors. Treatment is really simple. You teach the patients about the 12-step method of recovery" (Sipe 1993, p. 2).

Sponsors play an important role, as this pharmacist related: "About four days into treatment, a great big monster of a guy walked in and told me that he was a pharmacist, had been clean three years, and if he could do it, I could too. It was a wonderful starter. It impressed the poop out of me and kept me there" (PharmD, age 46).

Daily group therapy with other impaired professionals helps dismantle the facade of omnipotence, uniqueness, and professional immunity (Talbott et al. 1987). It also focuses participants on their emotional problems. "I had to realize that I was there to work on me and get healthy," a pilot (age 56) explained. "I had to face inadequacies and insecurities. I assumed that there was something wrong with me because my father didn't want anything to do with me and couldn't show feelings. But I learned that he was emotionally handicapped and there was nothing inherently inadequate about me. Once I learned this, some really good things started happening."

Personal counseling with an assigned staff member individualizes treatment. But a counselor who makes the addict confront his problems is rarely popular.

> My counselor was a bald-headed, mousy kind of little fellow. I couldn't stand him. We went around and around and around for about two weeks. When I complained to another guy about him, he said, "Man, you've got the best one here. His story is in the back of the Big Book. Have you read it?" I went to my room and got the Big Book and realized, "My God, that little bald-headed runt is mean enough to shoot somebody. He was in prison and all that. Maybe I better pay attention to what he's telling me." (Pilot, age 57)

Despite the confrontational nature of these relationships and the behavior of the occasional abusive or excessively harsh counselor, clients often remember the majority of the staff as "caring, people who are interested in assisting you—the most effective part of inpatient programs" (pilot, age 53). "They had a very loving approach," a nurse remembered. "They told me that they loved and cared about me" (RN, age 37).

Commenting on program staff, a pharmacist said:

> The 30 days I spent in the inpatient treatment center were the most enlightening of my life. I used to be a very passive, doormat-type person. I was invisible and would go right into the wall if confronted—I hid from my problems. But they wouldn't let me do that. They made me announce myself before groups, meetings, and whatnot. When I intellectualized that I was a pharmacist, not a street addict, they had me walk wherever I went for three days between two street junkies while they kept calling me "junkie"—real loudly. "You think you're better than we are." I walked out of there realizing that I was as low as anybody and as high as anybody. It did wonderful things for my self-esteem. (PharmD, age 46)

Family involvement during the inpatient experience also helps clients resolve vital issues. Talbott and Martin (1986) regard family problems as the single most important contributing factor to relapse. At the Betty Ford Center, for example, family members, housed in a nearby hotel, spend a 40-hour week in family education and therapy. The Ridgeview Institute, in Smyrna, Georgia, offers monthly three-day family workshops.

Before leaving the recovery center, participants develop a "spiritual road map" by working through the first four or five steps and being assigned to a sponsor to help make the transition to AA or NA in the community. A pharmacist remarked, "The spirituality of the program made a big difference to me" (PharmD, age 42).

Aftercare services, usually consisting of weekly or biweekly support-group meetings facilitated by treatment staff, continue for one or two years following discharge from most contemporary treatment programs. Also encouraged are 12-step programs and support groups for professionals. A 10-year study of individuals treated for alcohol and other addictions found better recovery rates among those who remained in contact longer with self-help groups and appropriate professional services (Hoffman 1993; see also Pakull 1990).

Outpatient Treatment

Outpatient centers developed in the late 1970s and proliferated rapidly in the 1980s. Some are located in hospitals as day or evening programs, others at residential treatment centers, and still others function independently. Outpatient treatment offers a variety of therapeutic approaches: methadone maintenance,[3] behavioral, 12-step oriented,[4] or some combination of these[5] (Hester 1994).

Unlike addicts in residential treatment, most outpatients maintain their daily routines during treatment, which usually occurs in the evenings after work hours. A nurse described her outpatient experience:

> I spent four nights a week for six weeks at a recovery center connected with the hospital where I worked. It was convenient, and insurance paid for most of it. It allowed me to continue working without having to tell my supervisor. Four hours a night I attended lectures and participated in group therapy. I kept a journal of my feelings and had

assignments to call at least two peers every day for reinforcement. I had written assignments to do the 12 steps and was in a grief recovery group. Then on Friday nights there was a mandatory social life: all of us in the outpatient recovery group went out to dinner and then to an AA meeting. The objective was to give us experience in socializing again in a sober atmosphere and to have normal interactions outside a formal, lecture-hall setting. The weekends were free. During this time I continued to work full-time five days a week.   (RN, age 42)

Outpatient programs, less costly and more readily available than inpatient programs, offer structured evening programs to addicts, usually those who have not yet suffered addiction's most severe consequences. Although they experience difficulties at work and home and may have minor legal problems, these problems are usually not yet irreparable.

Inpatient and outpatient programs each have their advantages and disadvantages. Inpatients must leave home, discontinue social activities, daily routines, and responsibilities, and adjust to a stressful new environment—albeit one sheltered from alcohol and other drugs and the stresses and strains of ordinary life. Outpatients, having access to alcohol and other drugs during their treatment, must resist the temptation to socialize with friends who use substances, who will sometimes insistently repeat invitations to drink or use. On the other hand, outpatients are able to practice drug resistance in actual social situations, rather than contrived ones in residential settings (Harrison, Hoffman, and Streed 1991).

Inpatients have more time with staff—typically extending 12 hours a day, seven days a week—and can interact with peers at meals and other times. Outpatients' time with staff is limited to 60–120 hours over a four-to-eight-week period—and there is comparatively less unstructured time for informal interaction with peers (Harrison, Hoffman, and Streed 1991). But the friendships that develop among outpatients provide a real-world network of peer support. "The 14 of us who went through outpatient together got our one-year anniversary chips together," a physician remarked, "and after several years we still have eight of us together" (MD, age 75).

Many inpatient and outpatient treatment programs, similar in content and format, reflect the Hazelden model of treatment grounded in AA principles. Total abstinence from all psychoactive drugs is considered essential, and much time is spent in lectures and group therapy sessions. Twelve-step meetings are held weekly at the facility during all phases, and clients are encouraged to participate. A ceremony celebrates the completion of treatment and launches aftercare follow-up.

Outpatient treatment works very well for those, like this nurse, who are motivated. "I learn best through lectures," she said. "I'm very left brained and took notes down on everything they taught us. I took directions, followed instructions, opened up emotionally, and did everything asked of me during the six weeks. It was very effective and set the foundation to continue in my recovery through the 12-step programs" (RN, age 42).

Less motivated participants like this physician benefit if they stay long enough.

> After my family confronted me, I called the medical director at the Betty Ford Clinic and tried to convince him that I wasn't as bad as everyone said I was. He put me in the outpatient program for six weeks. During my physical exam on the first day he told me that my liver was enlarged. After being half-asleep the next three weeks, I finally woke up and realized that I had to do something about it. I thought, "Hell, I'm going to die of cirrhosis." It scared the shit out of me, but it was the greatest thing that ever happened to me. I made a commitment and haven't had a drink since.   (MD, age 75)

But the dropout rate is high: many outpatients leave treatment in the first four weeks (Hubbard et al. 1984). Within three months, 60 percent have dropped out, transferred, or otherwise discontinued treatment (Simpson 1993). Using data on 12,697 outpatients, ages 12 to 80, Mammo and Weinbaum (1993) concluded that being female, unskilled, less educated, and young makes dropping out more likely.

Most relapses occur within the first six months following treatment. In one study from the general population, 9 of 10 patients who stayed abstinent during the first six months maintained a drug-free status for a full year. Older clients had better outcomes than younger ones, as did married compared to unmarried ones. Those abusing alcohol had better outcomes than those abusing other drugs. Participation in an aftercare program and weekly attendance at peer-support group meetings also predicted successful recovery (Harrison, Hoffman, and Streed 1991, p. 1190). Utilizing urine testing in aftercare also enhances program success. Rawson et al. (1993) report that urine and breath testing are crucial to client accountability and measuring program effectiveness. (See Coombs and West 1991 for an overview of drug testing in the United States.)

Office Practice

Most office practitioners are poorly trained to manage addictive patients. Very few of the physicians who treated our interviewees diagnosed their addiction and referred them to an appropriate recovery program. "I went to a psychiatrist and told him that I was depressed and that I thought I was drinking too much," a nurse reported. "But he didn't say much of anything and didn't tell me there was a nice organization like AA or recovery homes or anything of that nature" (RN, age 54).

Minimizing drug problems is also common. "I went into the hospital for a severe back problem and told my doctors that I was concerned about my drinking. They asked me how much I drank, and I told them that I never drank huge quantities but I was concerned that I was drinking too much. They did a liver enzyme test and told me that I was fine. I really, really wanted help at that point, but nobody was willing to give it to me. The message they gave me was, 'Okeydokey, it's alright to continue what you are doing' " (MD, age 41).

Naive clinicians often exacerbate drug-related problems by dispensing psychoactive drugs. "I found a doctor who treated alcoholism as a Valium deficiency," an attorney related (JD, age 48). A pharmacist reported a similar experience: "The doctor put me on some Valium to relax my muscles. From then on it was 'Welcome to the Valley of the Dolls!' Where the alcohol hadn't taken me, the Valium did. The progression was very, very rapid from then on" (PharmD, age 59).

Addicts manipulate physicians to obtain drugs. Seeing an addicted nurse crying at work, an attending physician asked what was going on. "When I told him I'd been going through a divorce and things were piling up on me, he said, 'Here, I want you to go home and take some of these pills.' They were Valium. I said, 'Okay! Yes!' I stopped on the way home and got a beer and popped a couple of Valium" (RN, age 40). Eventually, however, most clinicians realize what is happening. "I started thinking that I had to get another connection for Valium," said a nurse,

> so I went to a family-practice doctor and told him that I wanted to quit drinking, and asked if he could give me some tranquilizers. He gave me a month's prescription for Librium that I took in about eight days. I called him again and told him I had lost my prescription and was feeling really anxious, so he wrote me another one, and in about three weeks I called again and told him I had taken all those pills and was feeling really anxious and could he please give me some more pills. He told me to come into his office, and when I did he told me that he thought I had an acute drug withdrawal problem, that I was a drug addict, and he never wanted to see me ever again. I got up and left, pissed off.   (RN, age 40)

Mental health therapists are no more sophisticated than other clinicians in treating addiction. "She had no clue," one physician said of his therapist (MD, age 35). Even when psychotherapists accurately diagnose the problem, talking therapy tends to be ineffective. "I bounced back and forth between a lot of therapists," a pharmacist with 12 years of psychotherapy recalled. "One of them told me that my problem was the way my mother nursed me, another blamed the neighborhood I grew up in, and another the relationship with my brother. One said that all I needed to do was just take Valium and not drink or use those other drugs. They put me on psychotropic and antidepressant drugs that added to my existing list" (PharmD, age 47).

When addicts at advanced stages of addiction become depressed, psychotherapists tend to treat the depression but not the addiction. "My psychiatrist knew nothing about chemical dependency and thought that I was using because I was depressed," a physician recalled. "But I was depressed because I was using" (MD, age 41). An addicted pediatrician had this experience:

> I saw two psychiatrists at different times for depression. I told each of them during the course of therapy that I thought I was taking too many drugs. The first psychiatrist said, "You're taking too many drugs because you're depressed. I'll have to treat your depression before we can get you off drugs." He put me on Mellaril and Tofranil. The second said, "You're depressed because you have too many unresolved conflicts. We need to talk about these. Cut down on those other drugs you're taking." He put me on Elavil. Surely they would have told me if I were a drug addict.   (Rogers 1995)

Such outcomes may reflect in part physicians' reluctance to antagonize income-generating patients. Pilots fault flight surgeons for "conveniently overlooking" their drinking problems. "Since they make their living by treating pilots," a pilot (age 54) observed, "they don't want to be known as whistle blowers." Another pilot (age 57) said, "They don't want to get in the patient's face; they don't want a confrontation. The patient is their customer."

The problem worsens when the clinician is also chemically dependent. "We had an alcoholic flight surgeon who was put in charge of the drug and alcohol program on base," a military nurse said. "This guy was just 'lit' when he came in to lecture everybody about drug abuse. One day I told him that I was having anxiety and tension and he said, 'You need to try some of these pills; they're great!' He said that he used them. He wrote a prescription for 100 10-mg Valium. I thought these were the greatest things that had happened. I ate them like candy the four years I was in the service" (RN, age 40).

These accounts are compelling arguments for better training of office practitioners. A breakthrough in this regard came in 1967 with the national organization of the American Medical Society on Alcoholism, renamed in 1989 the American Society of Addiction Medicine (1992). In June 1990 the AMA Board of Trustees designated addiction medicine as a practice specialty. ASAM established the first certification program in addictive medicine and, as of May 1992, certified 2,320 of its members as knowledgeable in alcoholism and other drug dependencies. ASAM's membership increased 150 percent in six years, and by 1993 17 states had organized chapters. ASAM now hosts an annual Medical-Scientific Conference and a Medical Conference on Adolescent Addictions. The society, headquartered in Washington, D.C., publishes the *Journal of Addictive Diseases.*

Some physicians working out of their offices successfully treat addicts. Three-fourths (46 of 60) of the patients treated for alcohol and drug dependence by one ASAM specialist "experienced major or full improvement" (Galanter 1993, p. 251). To achieve these impressive results, he organizes a social network of the patient's associates (Galanter 1994). A spouse or close friend attends the first meeting with the client and therapist, helps break the addict's denial and rationalization, and helps the therapist obtain an accurate history and develop a viable treatment plan. Many patients initially resist having this person present because they realize that the latter's alliance with the physician will hamper their drug use (Galanter 1991, 1993, 1994).

The doctor then forms a support network of caring individuals to monitor and handle most day-to-day problems. The therapist functions as a task-oriented team leader, not a purveyor of psychological insight. During the first weeks, especially during detoxification, he schedules appointments one to three days apart. As abstinence increases, so do the intervals between sessions. The network group meets with the therapist every three months for the duration of the patient's therapy (Galanter 1991). When emergencies arise, the therapist consults with members of the support group by phone. Information about the addict is kept confidentially within the team.

Galanter (1994) mobilizes the network team to encourage the patient's involvement with a 12-step program until she becomes comfortable in the group meetings, adopts the treatment ethos, and expresses a commitment to abstinence. He notes that this commitment rarely comes from patients who experience psychotherapy only. When the patient is actively involved in the 12-step program, the therapist addresses issues such as marital conflict, lifestyle adjustments, and coping skills. In short, as the addiction gradually becomes less compelling, treatment increasingly resembles the traditional one-on-one psychotherapeutic model.

Diversion and Control Programs

When an addict's activities bring him under the jurisdiction of a governmental agency, two contrasting responses are possible. The criminal-justice response, experienced by the general public, metes out punishment depending on the violation and the court's attitude toward alcoholism and addiction (Dowell 1988). The second response, diversion from the court system to a treatment program, is available to addicted professionals unless harm to clients or major criminal violations are involved (the criteria vary from state to state).

The punishment response has disastrous consequences. In California, for example, a suicide "epidemic" occurred among physicians when a licensing board utilized a punitive instead of diversion approach. The same thing happened in Oregon. Dr. Roy Lusch, co-chair of Oregon's Impaired Dentist Committee, reports, "Ten years ago, the Board of Medical Quality Assurance put 42 physicians on probation because they were under investigation for substance abuse. They also published their names in the newspaper. Six of the 42 physicians committed suicide within a year" (Moffit 1986, p. 28).

An addicted physician described his situation before his state developed a diversion program:

> The attitude was "Off with his head!" "Get rid of the bad apples!" I'm here to tell you that many of those bad apples come from pretty good trees that can yield good fruit. But organized medicine, my loving colleagues, turned their backs on me. I was alone and very lonely. Rather than addressing my underlying problem, their way of dealing with it was throwing me off the staff of two hospitals. I lost everything, and there was nowhere to get help.   (MD, age 50)

Diversion programs changed that. Now encouraged or sponsored by professional societies, they seek to rehabilitate impaired practitioners and prevent malpractice. State licensing boards, increasingly responsive to the needs of the helping professions and the public, protect the integrity and public image of their profession by diverting impaired colleagues from the legal system to effective treatment alternatives and monitored aftercare services.

Diversion programs managed by state regulatory boards are clearly coercive. Some regulatory boards rigorously monitor addicted professionals and allow them to practice if they undergo treatment and keep their recovery agreements. In other states compliance removes all records against their licenses, but if a relapse occurs, the license to practice is suspended or revoked (Green 1989). Most state programs are managed by state professional societies instead of by state boards.

Although state regulatory and disciplinary boards were initially skeptical, results have been overwhelmingly positive in rehabilitating addicts and protecting patients and clients. Other unexpected benefits have occurred. First, those who successfully complete recovery programs improve relationships with their patients, clients, colleagues, and families. Second, recovering health professionals can better diagnose and assist chemically dependent patients. Third, recovering addicts reach out to help others with chemical dependencies. Fourth, a professional's recovery frequently forces family members to deal with their dysfunctions, and as a result family members often begin to develop strong recovery programs of their own (Ikeda and Pelton 1990). A fifth benefit is that professionals in recovery often step back and take a hard look at how their profession enables addictive behavior in its practitioners, and then broaden that perspective by recognizing that the profession reflects or even magnifies pervasive cultural patterns.

Diversion programs benefit the public at large, notes a past president of a state board of dental examiners. "The tax monies saved by returning these practitioners to practice is immense when you think of direct tax support of their training through government-supported schools, tax-deferred donations to private schools, and the income and other taxes paid by the average professional" (Oberg 1994). Of 117 physicians in the California Diversion Program during one year, for example, 109 (93 percent) continued their medical practice while undergoing treatment (Gualtieri, Cosentino, and Becker 1983). More important are the savings in human suffering.

Notwithstanding these positive results, traditionalists still argue for a criminal-justice approach. Since some drugs are illegal, they reason, users must be punished; rehabilitation purportedly rewards drug-abusing individuals, puts them in a favorable light, and gives them the excuse "drugs made me do it" (Powell 1991). "I chair the pharmacists' recovery program in our state," a pharmacist related,

> and we have been fighting with officials in the department of health who still hold to a willful-misconduct model. Their chief investigator is a former FBI agent who conducts his investigations in that way. When they try to obtain our hospital records to discover the identity of the people we work with, we refuse, telling them they have no right to such confidential information. They have gone to the extent of posing as medical students in our hospital to obtain them. That's the kind of thing we are dealing with. I've even gone to the governor, but thus far without success.   (PharmD, age 44)

As of 1990, nine states had legislatively mandated diversion programs for physicians administered by state medical boards, state medical societies, or independent organizations through contracts with medical boards. The first diversion program began in California in 1980. Administered by the same state agency that disciplines physicians, it has an impressive record. Within a 14-year period (1980–1994), 479 physicians participated, and 78 percent successfully completed the program (Ikeda and Pelton 1990; Medical Board of California 1995). Success, assessed by a five-member Diversion Evaluation Committee, is defined as being free from alcohol and other drugs for more than two years and demonstrating a lifestyle consistent with future sobriety.

Diversion removes fear of legal discipline and its attendant publicity. A physician recalled:

> I was the sickest I have ever been and knew in the innermost part of my soul that I was going to die. I went back to the hospital where I worked and told them that I still had problems but wanted my job back. "What can I do to get it back?" I asked. They said, "Join diversion." So I did; I signed up for the state diversion program. It is totally confidential; the state board doesn't know a thing about me unless I screw up. They require me to give urines, go to two meetings a week with others in the program, and attend lots of AA meetings.(MD, age 46)

In signing the diversion contract, the incoming candidate agrees to abstain from all mind-altering drugs, including prescription medications. An inpatient treatment program may also be required and, upon successful completion, weekly attendance at two diversion group meetings, and not less than two AA or NA meetings. Most contracts are for five years, but many professionals successfully complete the program in three. State law in California mandates that each hospital have a well-being committee, and participating physicians must notify their hospital committee of their involvement in state diversion.

A case manager, a paid staff member, monitors each program participant for compliance with the agreement and orchestrates activities. A facilitator conducts group meetings. A surgeon described his group facilitator:

> Our facilitator is the closest thing to God you'll ever find. He's very understanding and really cares. He has 44 years of sobriety and can answer any question and can immediately spot weird behavior. He is very giving and kind, but can be very tough when he needs to be. Like a good father, he will kick your butt when you need it. You believe what he says, and when he has something to say, you listen! He can foresee when bad things may start to happen, but he doesn't try

to fix everything for you. He is supportive and lets people grow. (MD, age 40)

Meeting exclusively with peers has many advantages. When first introduced to her group of six other addicted nurses, an alcoholic felt "a tremendous release because for so long I had thought, I'm the only nurse in the whole world that has this problem" (Barde and Pick 1993). Openness in discussion also becomes easier. "Diversion is an extremely safe place where you can talk about anything because there are only doctors there," a physician said. "It's a safe environment to tell about when you gave a patient the wrong medicine or made a mistake in a surgical procedure" (MD, age 40). Sharing such accounts in AA meetings can be threatening. Those outside the professions can be harsh critics, even though they themselves may have brutalized or abandoned their families, defrauded or destroyed businesses, or recklessly endangered innocent strangers while driving under the influence. "I've heard all kinds of wild stuff," a physician recalled. "One guy wanted to blow up the hospital with a bomb because they wouldn't let him on the staff; another guy was using two grams of Demerol daily; a dentist was on the nitrous tank for 17 hours; others have been to jail. These things couldn't be talked about in AA meetings" (MD, age 40). He added:

> I realize that we're all supposed to be equal in AA— we're all addicts—but we're not. Others hold us to a higher level of expectation and are shocked when we tell our stories. "Did you hear that!? Can you believe that doctor!?" But in a professional group I can be more open and not worry about being sued for malpractice. I'm not afraid of running into a patient or someone who knows me. In AA groups you get a better slice of life, but in my diversion group I can talk about certain things that laymen can't relate to. Doctors are kind of screwed up in a certain way and need our own little space.

Strong friendships developed in such fellowship reinforce recovery. "We have very good peer support. I used to hate one of the new doctors who came into the group, but now we're good friends. It's been very healing for me to sit there and talk with him, because he felt really bad about coming into this group. That kind of peer support is helpful. A supportive group is crucial" (MD, age 40).

Other professions have also developed diversion programs. The California Board of Dental Examiners, for example, reports that of the first 210 dentists to participate in its diversion program when it began in May 1982, 109 were self-referrals (TenBroeck 1995). One dentist credited diversion with keeping him out of jail: "I was sentenced to five years in prison, but it was suspended. They revoked my dental license, put me on five years' probation with the board, and had three probation officers look after me. I had to surrender my DEA [Drug Enforcement Agency] license. If I had slipped, I would have had to do five years in prison. So by the end of the first year I completely dedicated myself to my recovery because I realized that it was my only salvation" (DDS, age 46).

Diversion programs are also available for pharmacists,[6] nurses,[7] attorneys,[8] and pilots.[9] Three other government programs seek to protect the public from impaired practitioners: the Federal Aviation Administration tracks airline pilots,[10] the National Practitioner Data Bank tracks impaired physicians and dentists who move from state to state,[11] and the Drug Enforcement Agency monitors drug prescriptions.[12]

Work-Site Programs

Increasingly, hospitals, pharmacies, law firms, and airline companies are implementing work-site programs for employees whose performance is diminished by alcohol and other problems. These programs took hold in the mid-1970s in major American businesses as an alternative to firing impaired employees. About 85 percent of employees with debilitating personal problems can return to productive work via employee assistance programs (EAPs).[13]

Based on the assumption that timely intervention with impaired employees reduces turnover and increases performance, EAP services are usually offered free or at minimal charge. The company absorbs all or most of the financial expense and recovers costs in savings from reduced absenteeism, decreased use of health benefits, and improved job performance. EAP managers train supervisors to spot absences, substandard performance, strained or disruptive interpersonal relations, chronic alcoholism, anxiety, and depression. Once identified, the employee is referred to the EAP staff, who function as knowledgeable "purchasing agents acting on the clients' behalf" (Haaga and McGlynn 1993, p. 23). John Adams, the director of a consulting and training organization, estimated that a "well-supported EAP" could save a company "on the order of 40 percent in lost time, 60 percent in accident and sickness payments, 50 percent in grievances, 70 percent in accidents, and 75 percent in alcohol rehabilitation" (1988, p. 47). "A lot of EAPs contract with companies and serve as feeder operations for treatment centers," an attorney noted (JD, age 61).

AIRLINE COMPANIES

The airline industry launched EAPs in 1974, when the Air Line Pilot Association established its Human Intervention and Motivation Study (HIMS) treatment program. During the early years, airline EAPs experienced growing pains, and since then progress has waxed and waned. "We didn't have a full-time EAP, just had a part-time designated EAP rep, and she was really a flight attendant. The only services she provided were referrals," one pilot (age 50) recalled. Another pilot (age 51) observed, "Eventually TWA developed an excellent program. The EAP rep I talked to in New York was very, very helpful in finding money so that I could go through treatment the third time—but since then it [the EAP] has regressed to the point that it is even worse than it was in 1979."

Once EAPs were established, airline personnel realized that alcoholic colleagues would not be summarily fired, and they were less willing to cover up for them. A now sober pilot explained, "Once they return and are back on line, they start telling other pilots that there is help from the company and that this help is beneficial. By word of mouth, the EAP has become known as an agency that helps rather than harms" (airline treatment expert). Consequently, five of every six pilots in the ALPA program have been reported by fellow pilots, flight attendants, supervisors, and wives.

EAP programs that identify alcoholic pilots early prevent the deterioration of flying skills and judgment that threatens flight safety. "When there is a good EAP in place, the alcoholic has no place to hide. They go looking for *you*. The numbers trickle in at a steady rate" (FAA treatment specialist).

The disease orientation has been crucial to the development and expansion of such rehabilitation programs. For example, TWA's orientation manual on alcoholism describes the result of the 1975 decision by the airline's group health insurance carrier to designate alcoholism as "a fully covered disease on par with other illnesses.

This step . . . tended to reduce the stigma surrounding alcoholism. It gave all concerned a chance to deal with the disease honestly and openly. There was no longer a need to conceal the diagnosis" (Trans World Airlines n.d., p. 3b).

Careful long-term monitoring greatly improves the chances of recovery. "The major accomplishment . . . in our airline pilot program," according to an FAA executive, "is our emphasis on aftercare. We monitor pilots with continuous therapeutic contact. By talking frequently with a pilot, we help him work through it while he is only *talking* about going back to drinking. We help him stay sober."

An EAP representative described his monitoring role:

> I'm the one who is there when they have their confrontive intervention and refer them to treatment. I visit them in the treatment center and get ongoing clinical reports about how they are doing. These experiences help me bond with them. They see me as the representative of the company and the one person who really wants them to do well and get back to work. Once they are out of treatment—and perhaps out of the state—I monitor them with weekly phone calls and make sure they go to their support-group meetings, AA or whatever, until they get back to work. Combined with phone calls from their ALPA rep and their treatment provider, they may have three different monitoring phone calls a week. Once they are back at work I have monthly reports from them and from the treatment provider. Initially a pilot sees me once a week, and then we move it back to once a month. I monitor them for a full two-year period—it's pretty thorough.

An FAA executive, a psychiatrist, described effective EAPs as "an extra pair of eyes and hands for the monitoring system."

> If the flight surgeon doesn't have a lot of expertise in alcoholism, he is smart if he has the EAP staff do the legwork in checking up on the pilot to see how well he's doing. It requires a lot of compulsive energy, calling up aftercare programs to make sure the guy is going, finding out if he is seeing the right people, and so on and so on. Because the EAP people know a lot more about alcoholism than the flight surgeon, they do a much better job in that regard. Moreover, the EAP program implies that the company has a commitment to uncover and help the alcoholic.

A pilot's experience verifies this observation: "I knew that having to see the EAP people was going to be stressful, so I took some Valium. Although the company doctor thought I was no worse than any other pilot, the EAP person nailed me right then and there, telling me I needed to be in treatment. So off I went" (pilot, age 53).[14]

How effective are these programs? A 1984 study of medical records by the FAA and the ALPA for 587 alcoholic airline pilots found an 85 percent success rate in being medically certified and returned, with active monitoring, clean and sober, to active flight duty. One-fourth (23 percent) sought treatment voluntarily, 60 percent were referred by the ALPA, their employers, or both, and the remainder (17 percent) by their families or other sources such as courts or counseling centers (Russell and Davis 1985). And these impressive statistics are improving. An airline executive asserts, "We've found that about 95 percent recover when monitored in the ALPA HIMS program. The recidivism rate among noncommercial pilots is quite a bit higher than among commercial pilots because they don't have the motivation or the commercial pilot's status and finances."

Airline executives report that EAPs save money. An EAP cost-effectiveness study at the McDonnell Douglas Corporation found that, over a five-year period, employees who received EAP assistance for chemical dependence were absent 29 percent fewer days than employees with similar conditions who did not receive assistance. Medical claims for EAP clients were an average of $7,150 lower than those of impaired employees who did not use an EAP. "I don't think we can overemphasize the effectiveness of the EAP in any industry, but particularly in the airline industry," an EAP executive acknowledged. "It's an incredible cost-saving measure to any company. As you know, it's a particularly sensitive, safety-sensitive industry, and having a very solid EAP program that is highly publicized and recognized and has credibility with the union makes it very effective for prevention, identification, and early intervention."

LAW FIRMS

Law firms are taking a more proactive approach to chemically dependent partners, trainees, and staff. A law firm partner admits, "The professions are more reluctant than industry to come to terms with the fact that employees have substance abuse problems" (Samborn 1990, p. 26).

Large law firms implementing EAPs report great success (Elzea

1989). The chair of one firm's EAP partnership responsibility committee asserts, "We feel that we not only have saved some lives, but have regained lost productivity and ensured profits for the firm" (Samborn 1990, p. 26). Although EAP-sponsored treatment costs the firm an average of $33,000 a year for about 500 employees, it is less expensive than not providing services: "in the long run it saves firms hundreds of thousands of dollars because they gain back efficient, productive attorneys" (ibid.).

Encouraged by state bar associations, other firms now contract with EAPs to offer administrative and professional services to their partners and staffs (*Rhode Island Bar Journal* 1991). One interstate EAP, a private organization, provides contracts in 28 states to more than 90 companies, municipalities, and professional peer organizations, assisting more than 86,000 employees and their families.

The ABA is now urging firms to develop formal, written policies similar to those that govern workers in many offices and factories. Resistance to implementing such policies arises from several considerations, including the ethical dilemma of reporting a colleague and the possible loss of income to the firm. Lack of a formal written policy allows a firm to retain its options to fire an unproductive drug-abusing associate while keeping another who, though alcoholic, is succeeding financially (Samborn 1990).

In 1995 the ABA Commission on Impaired Attorneys created a model lawyer-assistance program to help state and local bar associations develop and maintain programs to identify and assist attorneys and law students impaired by chemical abuse, chemical dependency, or mental health problems. This program will also provide monitoring and other services (Keegan 1995).

The 300-lawyer firm of Hale and Dorr, with offices in Boston, New Hampshire, and Washington D.C., adopted the ABA guidelines even before they were adopted by the ABA in August 1990 (Huie and Spilis 1991). Formerly, the firm's reaction to chemical-dependency-related problems was to ignore them in hope they would go away. If that didn't work, the firm handled each situation on an ad hoc basis. When one of the partners, a recovering alcoholic, encouraged the firm to develop a comprehensive policy, his suggestion fell on deaf ears. But when, in 1988, a senior partner showed indisputable evidence of alcoholism, the firm established a task force to design a drug- and alcohol-abuse policy offering compassionate assistance. Members included a cross-section of senior and junior partners, associates, administrators, paralegal assistants, and secretaries. After the task force adopted the ABA guidelines, which discourage punitive action and recommend early discovery, treatment, and recovery, several individuals came forward seeking help (Huie and Spilis 1991).

HEALTH CARE CENTERS

In hospitals, clinics, and other health care centers, the last frontier for the EAP movement, resistance has been formidable. "Resistance stems from professional pride. Physicians and some other health professionals don't consider themselves employees—even when their wages are paid by a health care institution, and they may regard EAP personnel—usually social workers, addiction counselors, or psychometricians—as having lower professional status and less-lengthy and less-intensive training (Solursh 1989). Health professionals may also worry about a paper trail—applications, medical records, and claims to insurance carriers—and the potential humiliation of being a patient. Even the most desperate health professional tends to be unwilling to risk being seen in a busy waiting room with patients who may know him.

A pharmacy assistant who was working at a prestigious university medical center during the mid-1970s, when drug regulations and procedures first tightened, described the potential for widespread drug theft and abuse.

Before drug regulations got really severe, you could walk into the pharmacy, and right on the shelf and available for anyone were two bottles of Dexadrine containing 255 mg. Soon thereafter they were put behind a cage in a locked-in area. But this didn't matter to me, because I was a supervisor; so every day I helped myself to 5 mg of Dexadrine and, if I felt the need for it, 5 more in the afternoon. I had the keys to the cage, and in there was one kilogram, or 2.2 pounds, of 99 percent pure cocaine. There it was, so I began helping myself to it. For a number of years in that pharmacy up to 5,000 pills of uppers and downers would be lost every month, and also ounces of cocaine. It wasn't all me; I wasn't addicted that much. And if you look at the people who used that pharmacy, not a one of them looked like a drug user—they were all very professional-looking people, very neat, very straight looking. You wouldn't imagine that these people collected thousands of pills and ounces of cocaine every month. And it continued because the pharmacy was part of a university system, and since it was in the state constitution that no other state bureaucracy could regulate school systems, we had these losses month after month.   (Pharmacy assistant, age 38)

Lacking effective EAPs emphasizing prevention and rehabilitation, hospitals sometimes resort to draconian measures to deal with escalating drug problems. To investigate the theft of drugs, one hospital hired a company to install a hidden video camera. "That might be abhorrent to some people, but the cold, hard facts of life are that here we have drugs going out the door," lamented a security company official (Uboise 1992).

Mandatory drug testing for all hospital clinicians is ineffective and regarded as an invasion of privacy. Called "chemical McCarthyism" (Gillespie 1987), it casts a wide net to catch a relative few. Such programs collapse under their own weight. For example, the controversial Johns Hopkins Hospital mandatory drug-testing program was eventually scaled back to new employees only. EAPs are less inflammatory, more cost effective, and more beneficial in the long run.[15]

U.S. hospitals have recently been forced by bad publicity and lawsuits to recognize that it is in their best interests to identify and deal effectively with impaired clinicians who adversely affect patient care (Fisher and Weisman 1988). The courts now reflect a growing and deep-seated belief that hospitals are accountable for their clinicians' mistakes.

As a result of legal liability and the encouragement of state and national organizations, physicians'-aid committees have been implemented in many hospitals. Their primary mission is to identify cases of physician impairment as early as possible. Preferring a non-punitive approach, most hospital committees safeguard patients from harm while supporting the recovery of the chemically impaired professional. They detect emerging impairment, offer support to the physician and family, and encourage early treatment.[16]

Trainee Programs

Until recently, administrators and faculty at professional training centers gave scant attention to the substance-abuse problems of trainees and faculty. Counseling services, the usual remedy, are now typically offered by professional therapists and, more recently, by trained classmates. The availability of counseling services sends a message that it is acceptable to seek help.

A model counseling service, the UCLA Mental Health Program for Physicians-in-Training (MHPT), addresses trainee reluctance to seek help by maintaining an off-campus facility with independent administrators (Borenstein 1985; Pasnau and Stoessel 1994). Trainees are encouraged to regard counseling as a healthy remedy when the stresses of training become overwhelming and to seek it as a first resort rather than as a last, desperate one. Borenstein and Cook (1982) note that most trainees assume they are too busy for such self-indulgence. Those who seek help early in their careers can learn to function better and establish more empathic and satisfying relationships with patients and clients.

Borenstein and Cook (1982) point out the cost-saving benefits of counseling services. If the training institution absorbs all therapy expense, they say, even at private rates the cost will be less than 10 percent of the investment the school makes for each incoming trainee. If treatment is successful in only half the cases, the institution will reduce its economic losses from dropouts by 80 percent. Savings in human costs, however, far outweigh financial benefits. Obvious immediate and long-term losses result from substance abuse, emotional disorders, and suicide.

Some training centers augment professional counseling with peer-assistance programs, in which trained students with professional backup assist troubled classmates. At the University of South Carolina, for example, a peer-advocacy committee teaches interested students how to reach out to fellow students before severe problems develop. Although program effectiveness ebbs and flows as students enter and leave, the concept of collegial assistance is constant (Johnson 1990). A similar program at Wake Forest University's Bowman Gray School of Medicine certifies peer counselors to work with substance abusers. Training continues throughout medical school (McGann 1990).

A consortium of more than 20 medical schools, organized to identify and intervene with substance-abusing medical students, was developed in 1982 at the Memphis branch of the University of Tennessee and called Aid to Impaired Medical Students (AIMS). A similar program was adopted in 1993 by the American Association of

Law Schools (Association of American Law Schools 1993). The AIMS program emphasizes that trainees have an obligation to report an associate's impairment. "Once colleagues become impaired, they may literally be unable to help themselves," trainees are told (*AIMS* n.d.). Reminded that chemical addiction will eventually ruin health and careers, students are encouraged to show concern by identifying and assisting impaired classmates. When a student is noncompliant, the council, as a last resort, will inform the dean.[17]

A student member of an AIMS committee related her experience:

> I was nominated and elected by the second-year class. The committee—one male, one female per class—met once a month with two faculty representatives. We'd spend 15–20 minutes on some topic—a film, an interview with a recovering addict, a role-play or a mock intervention—and then bring up cases. We tried to educate people that our program was an aid, not a policing system, but there was not a lot of forthrightness in coming forward; there's still such a stigma about reporting a classmate. But it helped some. One case was so severe that everyone recognized it. He was suspended and went to a rehab center—by force, not choice. Others were less obvious. For example, I got a phone call from a classmate about a friend who didn't want to reveal her name. I listened until I understood, then told her, "I'll get back to you." I called a faculty member who gave me a list of places she could call. The contact was made, and the person said, "Thanks for your help."

Because confidentiality is a great concern to law students, only 10 percent said they would unquestionably seek assistance from the law school or university substance-abuse program. An additional 41 percent said they would do so only if assured that bar officials would not have access to the information. Asked whether they would refer a troubled classmate to counseling or treatment, 19 percent said yes unreservedly, and 47 percent said they would do so only if bar officials could not gain access to the information (Association of American Law Schools 1993, pp. 23–24). Bar admission policies should not impede school efforts to get students into counseling and treatment. "The need to protect the public from impaired lawyers and the need to encourage attorneys to seek treatment present conflicting policy considerations" (ibid., p. iii).

In 1990 the American Association of Law Schools formed a Special Committee on Problems of Substance Abuse in Law Schools and charged it with developing recommendations to assist law schools in dealing effectively with substance-abuse problems. After two major surveys—one of law school administrators and one of law students—the committee made a number of recommendations about forming and implementing a drug-abuse prevention and intervention policy (Association of American Law Schools 1993, pp. 2–3).

In 1990 the federal government encouraged substance-abuse policies and programs in training institutions with the Drug-Free Schools and Communities Act Amendments. As a condition of receiving federal funds or participating in federal student loan programs, each institution of higher education must certify that it has adopted and implemented a program to prevent the use of illicit drugs and the abuse of alcohol by students and employees (Association of American Law Schools 1993).[18]

Such programs can have a profound effect. "On our campus," a professor of pharmacy declared, "we get about 9 or 10 students into recovery each year. Isn't that wonderful? I've been involved in most of their interventions. I coordinate with others in a state program and help set up a contract and monitoring program so they can return to school" (PharmD, age 47).

In Perspective

Attitudes diverge widely regarding the appropriateness and efficacy of drug treatment in America. Peele (1996), for example, contends that our country needs to recover from its "all-or-nothing approach." Abstinence appeals to something "deeply American" in us, Peele says, because of our temperance heritage from nineteenth-century revivalist Protestantism. He objects to what he sees as a "one-size-fits-all" treatment system dominated by AA, its 12-step philosophy, and the notion that addiction is a disease. "America's alcohol-treatment industry attacks the idea of self cure, saying people who believe they've recovered on their own are in denial" (p. 41).

As Peele correctly notes, some addicts—Type 4 users—quit without participating in formal treatment programs. What is generally not understood by those who emphasize self-cure, however, is that other addicts—Type 5 users—cannot turn their lives around without formal treatment programs.

How beneficial are formal recovery programs for Type 5 addicts? Far better than the alternatives—despair, harm to others, and even death. Although conduct norms at work sites may discourage "snitching," none of us should stand by waiting for an addicted associate to self-cure.

Existing recovery programs should constantly analyze their successes and failures and make modifications to improve effectiveness. During the past decade, for example, much progress has been made in reducing attrition and relapse. In my own study of heroin addicts in the early 1980s—all of whom completed an intensive nine-month residential treatment based on the harsh and punitive Synanon therapeutic-community model—less than 5 percent remained clean and sober 18 months after discharge (Coombs 1981a). By staying in contact with the clean ones for several years thereafter, we learned that, without exception, those who remained abstinent did so by attending AA or NA meetings several times a week. Now, thanks to better tools—motivational interventions, contracts, drug testing and monitoring—more than three-fourths of professionals who enter recovery programs remain abstinent.

Punitive approaches, such as those routinely experienced by addicts who are not professionals, yield dismal results. Clean and sober professionals demonstrate that recovery through self-help or formal programs is not only feasible; it also costs much less than criminal-justice measures—in both monetary and human terms.

Epilogue

Psychoactive drugs are an integral part of American life. Magic elixirs—widely advertised and everywhere available—promise social well-being and relief from psychic discomfort. Tobacco and alcohol, the most widely used drugs, though legal cause more misery than all illicit drugs combined. Giant profit-seeking corporations saturate the media with the message that alcohol and tobacco enhance popularity, romance, adventure, achievement, and sex appeal. And now there is a growing trend to market "look-alike" products to children and adolescents: bubble gum is shredded to look like chewing tobacco, and soft drinks are bottled to look like beer. Thus in 1995 Royal Crown Cola was introduced in long-necked amber bottles with "draft" printed prominently on the label. A television commercial for the product was set in a bar, with "draft" flashing on a neon sign, reinforcing the implied equivalence with beer (Gellene 1995).

As long as youngsters are exposed to such messages, they will be more susceptible to drug use—and abuse. And as long as pharmaceutical companies advertise that there are chemical solutions to seemingly every human problem, people of all ages will flock to clinicians for prescription medications for whatever ails them. Clearly, the drug problem in America cannot be solved by criminalizing users of illicit drugs and at the same time advertising, glamorizing, and subsidizing legal drugs.

Addicts come from all walks of life. For many, drugs seem to promise solace from emotional or spiritual impoverishment during childhood. Many professionals, deluded by notions of their own immunity to addiction, focused on intellectual attainment and careers at the expense of other aspects of life, look to drugs as a way to deal with the demands of work. Whatever their social circumstances, Type 5 addicts compulsively rely on drugs to cope with life, and their lives spiral downward until someone else intervenes.

Addiction's estimated annual cost to society is $150–200 billion (Langenbucher et al. 1993, p. i). Among the highest-cost consumers of health care, alcohol and other drug abusers fill 10–50 percent of hospital beds, constitute a large share of emergency-room admissions and consume up to 15 percent of each American health-care dollar (Langenbucher 1994).[1] Nearly half of all hospital trauma beds are occupied by patients injured while under the influence of alcohol (Gentilello et al. 1995).

Currently, federal drug policy is aimed at ferreting out and punishing addicts. (For an overivew of drug policies, see Kleiman 1992; Bertram 1996.) This approach has proved to be both costly and ineffective. From 1981 to 1993 federal drug-control spending increased more than eightfold—from $1.8 billion to $12.3 billion (Drugs, Crime & Campaign '94 1994, p. 14). From 1981 to 1995 federal and state governments spent $100 billion on drug-related programs (see also "Projecting Future Cocaine Use" 1995). Warehousing drug users in prisons costs $6.1 billion a year (Lewis 1995). Yet a 1994 survey of Americans' attitudes toward drug problems and the federal policy found that 7 in 10 saw drug abuse as a greater problem than it had been five years earlier and that one-half expected the problem to be even worse in another five years. Nearly half of those surveyed knew someone who had become addicted to drugs, and 4 in 10 said that drugs had forced them to change the way they lived: they were staying in at night and trying to make their homes more secure (Drugs, Crime & Campaign '94 1994, p. 12).

A more effective approach would focus on prevention and treatment (for a comprehensive plan, see Coombs and Ziedonis 1995). The ideal solution would be societal: the implementation of policies promoting healthy, nurturing families and healthy, strong communities. Lacking these, we can at least pursue prevention through education. People can be told about the developmental dynamics of addiction. They can also be taught that personal growth comes only through successful struggle with life's problems, that drugs interrupt this process, and that there are no short cuts to emotional and spiritual maturity.

An emphasis on prevention and treatment also makes good economic and social sense. Every $1 spent in this country for substance-abuse treatment saves $11.54 in other social services, such as hospital and emergency-room care ("Elected Officials Endorse Treatment" 1992, p. 2). Every $1 spent in treatment returns $2 to $10, depending on treatment, intervention stage, and other such factors (Langenbucher et al. 1993). And the ratio of benefits to expenditures increases further when reductions in criminal-justice costs, drug-impaired babies, and HIV incidence are taken into account.

A cost-benefit analysis of drug treatment efficacy, based on a survey of 1,900 Californians representative of the 150,000 in drug treatment from September 1992 to March 1994, found that the cost of treating the survey group—$209 million (less than half from public funds)—yielded $1.5 billion in benefits to taxpayers, an average of $7 dollars for every $1 invested (Mecca 1994).

The personal stories of addiction and recovery in this book show clearly that many addicts can recover and become productive. With a more enlightened public policy, many more addictions could be prevented altogether. Such a policy would quietly divert addicts away from the legal system and into treatment. Carefully monitoring them with drug testing and contracts would allow them to contribute to society and maintain their livelihoods instead of draining scarce resources. These relatively inexpensive treatment alternatives—typically available to professionals but not to laypeople—have already proved their effectiveness. It is time to generalize the benefits of these enlightened and proven methods to *all* addicted individuals.

Self-Assessment Tests / Resources
Notes / References
Acknowledgments / Index

Self-Assessment Tests

CAGE Test

Please answer "yes" or "no" to each of the following questions:

- Have you ever felt the need to CUT DOWN on your drinking/drug use?
- Have you ever felt ANNOYED at criticisms of your drinking/drug use?
- Have you ever felt GUILTY about something that's happened while drinking/using drugs?
- Have you ever felt the need for an EYE OPENER?

One "yes" response raises suspicions of an alcohol/drug use problem. More than one is a strong indication that a problem exists.

First published in the American Council on Alcoholism's *ACA News* (July/August 1994).

Johns Hopkins University Hospital Test

Are You An Alcoholic?

To answer this question ask yourself the following questions and answer them [yes or no] as honestly as you can.

1. Do you lose time from work due to drinking?
2. Is drinking making your home life unhappy?
3. Do you drink because you are shy with other people?
4. Is drinking affecting your reputation?
5. Have you ever felt remorse after drinking?
6. Have you gotten into financial difficulties as a result of drinking?
7. Do you turn to lower companions and an inferior environment when drinking?

8. Does your drinking make you careless of your family's welfare?

9. Has your ambition decreased since drinking?

10. Do you crave a drink at a definite time daily?

11. Do you want a drink the next morning?

12. Does drinking cause you to have difficulty in sleeping?

13. Has your efficiency decreased since drinking?

14. Is drinking jeopardizing your job or business?

15. Do you drink to escape from worries or trouble?

16. Do you drink alone?

17. Have you ever had a complete loss of memory as a result of drinking?

18. Has your physician ever treated you for drinking?

19. Do you drink to build up your self-confidence?

20. Have you ever been to a hospital or institution on account of drinking?

If you have answered YES to any one of the questions, there is a definite warning that *You may be an alcoholic.*

If you have answered YES to any two, the chances are that *you are an alcoholic.*

If you have answered YES to *three or more, you are definitely an alcoholic.*

Short Michigan Alcoholism Screening Test

1. Do you feel you are a normal drinker? (By normal we mean you drink less than or as much as most other people). [No = 1 point]

2. Does your wife, husband, a parent, or other near relative ever worry or complain about your drinking? [Yes = 1 point]

3. Do you ever feel guilty about your drinking? [Yes = 1 point]

4. Do friends or relatives think you are a normal drinker?[No = 1 point]

5. Are you able to stop drinking when you want to? [No = 1 point]

6. Have you ever attended a meeting of Alcoholics Anonymous? [Yes = 1 point]

7. Has drinking ever created problems between you or your wife, husband, a parent, or other near relative? [Yes = 1 point]

8. Have you ever gotten into trouble at work because of your drinking? [Yes = 1 point]

9. Have you ever neglected your obligations, your family, or your work for 2 or more days in a row because you were drinking?[Yes = 1 point]

10. Have you ever gone to anyone for help about your drinking? [Yes = 1 point]

11. Have you ever been in a hospital because of drinking? [Yes = 1 point]

12. Have you ever been arrested for drunken driving, driving while intoxicated, or driving under the influence of alcoholic beverages? [Yes = 1 point]

13. Have you ever been arrested, even for a few hours, because of drunken behavior? [Yes = 1 point]

Total Score:
Seltzer [definition]: 0–1 = nonalcoholic; 2 = possibly alcoholic; 3 or "yes" to 6, 10, or 11 = alcoholic
Ross [definition]: 5 = alcohol abuse

First published in *Journal of Studies on Alcohol* (1975) 36.

Resources

The following organizations can provide anonymous help-line telephone numbers in each state. Nurses should call their state nurses' association.

Attorneys
Commission on Impaired Attorneys
American Bar Association
541 N. Fairbanks Court
Chicago, Illinois 60611
Telephone: 312-988-5359

Commercial Airline Pilots
Air Line Pilots Association
14707 E. Second Avenue, #200
Aurora, Colorado 80011
Telephone: 303-341-4435

Dentists
American Dental Association
211 E. Chicago Avenue
Chicago, Illinois 60611
Telephone: 800-621-8099, ext. 2622

General Public
National Council on Alcoholism and
   Drug Dependencies
12 W. 21st Street
New York, New York 10010
Telephone: 212-206-6770

Pharmacists
American Pharmaceutical
   Association
2215 Constitution Avenue, N.W.
Washington, D.C. 20037
Telephone: 202-628-4410

Physicians
Department of Mental Health
American Medical Association
515 N. State Street
Chicago, Illinois 60610
Telephone: 312-464-5066

Notes

1. The Secret Sickness

1. Prescription drug dealing is extremely difficult to trace. California and six other states use computerized systems to track prescriptions for the most potent medicines, used mostly in hospitals. Doctors must use state-issued triplicate forms to prescribe those drugs. The physician and pharmacist each keep a copy, and one is mailed to the state office. A book of 100 forms lasts most doctors a lifetime. When officials detect a suspiciously prolific prescriber, they can try to make an undercover purchase. But the cases are hard to win in court, because the doctor typically argues that he diagnosed a real patient or was fooled by an addict.

2. An earlier study of lifetime prevalence in three cities (New Haven, Baltimore, and St. Louis) found that alcohol abuse or drug dependence affected between 11 and 16 percent in each city. The abuse of other drugs was less common, affecting between 5 and 6 percent at some time in their lives. Adding alcohol and drug abuse/dependencies together, researchers found that 15 percent in New Haven, 17 percent in Baltimore, and 18.1 percent in St. Louis had experienced a substance use disorder (Robins et al. 1984). A more recent study of five U.S. cities by some of the same investigators found a lifetime prevalence of alcohol abuse or dependence among 23 percent of white males (Regier et al. 1988).

2. Addiction's Defining Nature

1. A psychoactive drug is a pharmacologically active substance that has a distinctive chemical impact on the functioning of the central nervous system (CNS)—the brain and spinal cord—which governs states of consciousness, perception of sensation and emotion, memory, reasoning, and judgment. The CNS also monitors and regulates the activities and interactions of all tissues, organs, and systems, voluntary and involuntary, from basic

life functions such as respiration and digestion, to complex behaviors involving abstract reasoning and imagination.

Psychoactive drugs also affect the autonomic nervous system (ANS), which mediates changes in states of consciousness and governs involuntary processes such as glandular secretion, the regulation of the cardiac and respiratory pumps, and the activity of involuntary muscle in the iris (which controls the size of the pupil,) blood vessels, airways, and the digestive tract. The ANS has two divisions: the sympathetic nervous system, which mediates alert wakefulness and the "fight-or-flight" stress response via neurotransmitters such as norepinephrine; and the parasympathetic nervous system, which mediates relaxation, pleasure, and sleep via neurotransmitters such as the endogenous opioids. The drug, an exogenous chemical (originating outside the body), works by mimicking endogenous chemicals (those synthesized by the body).

2. Nicotine, ingested through tobacco use, is a CNS stimulant and involves specific nicotine receptors and also dopaminergic pathways. At the same time, it produces skeletal muscle relaxation and a decrease in the deep-tendon reflex ("knee jerk") through its effects on the spinal cord. Its benefits to the user include increased alertness, enhanced attentiveness and memory, skeletal muscle relaxation, and decreased appetite and irritability.

The detrimental cardiovascular effects of nicotine occur with any mode of ingestion. Pipe smokers and snuff users also risk mouth cancer. Inhaled tobacco smoke carries nicotine suspended on particles of "tar" and contains many other harmful constituents, such as carbon monoxide. Cigarette smoke can cause serious cardiovascular and pulmonary diseases, and the risk is cumulative.

The health risk is dose-dependent. Each cigarette increases the chances of developing serious disease; quitting decreases the chances because the body has a chance to recover and "undo" some of the damage. Nonetheless, as with any addiction, it is very difficult to quit, especially without help. For some, the withdrawal syndrome is extremely unpleasant. It may include nausea, headache, gastrointestinal distress, difficulties concentrating, insomnia, and extreme irritability and hostility. There are a number of programs available to help smokers break this legal but deadly addiction

3. Caffeine is a xanthene, a CNS stimulant, popular since ancient times and found in plants all over the world. Its benefits include increased alertness, enhanced concentration, increased capacity for muscular work, and decreased reaction time. Regular use leads to tolerance of its effects. It can cause the heart rate to be rapid or irregular, leading to mild discomfort in some users, and potentially dangerous cardiac dysfunction in others. It increases acid secretion in the stomach, and thus has the potential to cause irritation, bleeding, or ulcers, and aggravates fibrocystic disease of the breast. Individuals vary in their response and sensitivity to caffeine. Some react to a large dose with anxiety, insomnia, and tremors. Withdrawal produces transient headaches and decreases alertness and concentration.

4. CNS depressants, the most widely abused class of drugs, are the "down-

ers," the sedative/hypnotics and the anxiolytics. This group ranges from alcohol and over-the-counter remedies for sleeplessness; mild Schedule IV sedatives, including benzodiazepines (such as Librium, Xanax, and Valium), nonbenzodiazepines (such as Nortec and Placidyl); to more potent Schedule III drugs such as glutethimide (Doriden) and Schedule II drugs, including the barbiturates.

Depressants sedate and reduce anxiety. Responses to increasing dosages range from disinhibition, sedation, and hypnosis (sleep) to general anesthesia, coma, and death (Bushman 1993). In a society that eschews pain and discomfort, these psychic painkillers are in great demand.

Sedatives slow heart rate and lower blood pressure. Some progressively depress the central and autonomic nervous systems, resulting in poor judgment, impulsive actions, lack of motor coordination, somnolence, and eventual respiratory arrest. Commonly abused sedatives are Amytal, Seconal, Nembutal, and Quaaludes. "In general, these drugs cause significant metabolic tolerance, definite psychic dependence, and a severe withdrawal syndrome. Withdrawal from high-dose abuse results in delirium with disorientation and hallucinations, *grand mal*–type seizures, and possibly fatal hyperthermia" (Young 1986, p. 546).

Benzodiazepines, found in abundance in medicine cabinets today, reduce anxiety, cause sedation, hypnosis, amnesia, and act as anticonvulsants. Inhalants (glue, paint, and vapors such as aerosols) relax smooth muscles, decrease blood pressure, and act on the CNS to produce euphoria and anesthesia. Nitrous oxide, another inhalant, is widely abused by dental and medical professionals as a result of its availability and therapeutic use in practice (Willis 1992; see also Schuckit 1995a).

The most widely used CNS depressant is formed by the fermentation of sugar reacting with yeast. Alcohol is the major active ingredient in wine, beer, and distilled spirits. Depending on the amount and the manner of consumption, ethyl alcohol, the kind found in alcoholic beverages, can produce feelings of well-being, sedation, intoxication, or unconsciousness. Like other CNS depressants, it causes slowed reactions, slurred speech, and sometimes even unconsciousness. It can alter moods and become habit-forming. Alcohol is particularly dangerous when used in combination with other depressants or with narcotics.

5. Narcotics are divided into two groups: opium alkaloids extracted from the opium poppy, such as heroin, morphine, and codeine; and synthetic narcotics such as methadone, Demerol, Lomotil, Darvon, Talwin, Nubain, and Stadol. Narcotics relieve pain, suppress coughing, and treat diarrhea. They affect the CNS, causing euphoria, sedation (calm relaxation, drowsiness) and analgesia (pain relief) (Bushman 1993). Users typically develop both psychological and physical tolerance and dependence. When the effects wear off, the user craves more.

The signs and symptoms of narcotic use include drowsiness, nausea, itching, respiratory depression, and constricted pupils. Withdrawal signs and symptoms are tremors, panic, insomnia, nausea and loss of appetite, muscle cramps, sweating and chills, watery eyes, running nose, and yawning. Results of narcotic overdose include convulsions, coma, shallow breathing, rapid heartbeat, elevated blood pressure, clammy skin, and pinpoint pupils (Center for Substance Abuse Prevention 1991b). Demerol can cause convulsions even when the user does not overdose.

When narcotics are self-administered by injection, overdose is only one of the dangers to the user; endocarditis (inflammation of the heart muscle and valves), blood poisoning, abscesses at injection sites, bronchiectasis (destructive abscesses in the lungs), hepatitis, and AIDS are other possible complications. Users of injectable street drugs are at particularly high risk for these complications because the potency and purity of street drugs are variable, the street drug may be contaminated with toxic chemicals or infectious agents, and the paraphernalia used to prepare and inject it are not sterile. Sharing needles, a common street practice, is particularly dangerous and has resulted in an AIDS epidemic among intravenous drug users.

Those who self-administer intravenous drugs, even professionals with access to pharmaceutical supplies, put themselves at risk. But for physically and psychologically dependent addicts, the risks are greatly outweighed by the perceived benefits.

Heroin is considered to have the highest abuse potential of all the narcotics because the pleasure, or "rush," it gives upon injection is the most intense. It is not legally obtainable in the United States. However, all narcotics are habit-forming because they affect the CNS to produce both a pleasurable sensation and physical and psychological dependence, which lead to a repetitive pattern of seeking and using the drug that becomes habitual and increasingly destructive, taking precedence over every other aspect of the user's life.

The combination of narcotics with other narcotics, CNS stimulants, or CNS depressants, including alcohol, increases their potential for harm and accelerates their debilitating effects on the addict in every sphere of life: physically, mentally, emotionally, spiritually, and socially.

6. Stimulants ("uppers") range from the seemingly innocuous drug caffeine—in the form of coffee, tea, cola, and chocolate—to Schedule II drugs such as cocaine and the amphetamines, also called "speed." Cocaine is used medicinally as a topical anesthetic and as an astringent (to control bleeding). The other stimulants are used as diet pills to reduce appetite and also as part of the pharmacological management of certain forms of depression and of attention-deficit disorder, with or without hyperactivity.

Low dosages of stimulants increase behavioral activity, energy, and alertness, reduce the appetite, enhance mental functioning, elevate mood, and produce a false sense of well-being. These effects appeal to students and professionals who must meet deadlines; the drugs enable them to work longer hours with greater energy and efficiency.

Users exhibit symptoms such as uncharacteristic confidence and elation, excessive or rapid speech, restlessness, anxiety and irritability, elevated blood pressure, rapid heart rhythms, xerostomia (dry mouth), dilated pupils, and facial twitching. High doses and prolonged continuous use can produce anorexia and weight loss, extreme anxiety, compulsive or repetitive behavior, mood swings, violent conduct, and toxic psychosis.

Depression and fatigue result when the drug effect, or "high," wears off or is diminished through continual use and user exhaustion. Mental functioning is impaired until the user rests and recovers. Users withdrawing from higher dosages may experience intense cravings, extreme agitation, paranoia, and hallucinations.

Cocaine, the most popular stimulant, may be ingested in the form of a fine powder formed into "lines" or held in a tiny spoon, then snorted or inhaled into the nostrils, where it is quickly absorbed through the nasal mucus membranes, immediately producing a marked but brief euphoria. It may also be taken orally or sprinkled on a marijuana cigarette and smoked as a "cocoa puff." Chronic use can result in nosebleeds and eventual significant tissue damage to structures inside the nose, causing, for example, a perforated septum.

A much more intense "rush" is produced when the drug is injected intravenously or smoked by "freebasing." Freebase cocaine is produced by a chemical process that converts the "street" compound to a pure base by removing the hydrochloride salt and some of the cutting agents. Since cocaine is not water soluble, smoking is the only way to get it into the system. Freebase cocaine reaches the brain within seconds, resulting in a sudden and intense high. But the euphoria quickly disappears, leaving the user with an enormous craving to freebase again and again in a vain effort to achieve the intensity of that first hit.

"Crack" is the street name for freebase cocaine that comes in the form of small lumps or shavings. The term refers to the crackling sound produced when it is smoked or heated.

Cocaine's physiological effects include accelerated heart rate, constriction of blood vessels, and elevated blood pressure. Ingested through the lungs, the drug may irritate the airways, causing them to constrict and inducing severe respiratory distress. Mucus membranes become dry, pupils dilate, and body temperature rises. These physical changes may be accompanied by facial twitching, seizures, cardiac arrest, respiratory arrest, or stroke. Users often report feeling restless, irritable, and anxious while under the drug's influence, and feeling depressed when they are not using the drug. They often resume use to alleviate further depression.

Despite its potentially toxic effects, cocaine has been popular among affluent and upwardly mobile professionals who enjoy its euphoric rush and instant relief from fatigue and boredom. Cocaine acts directly on the pleasure centers in the brain. The cocaine high is so intense and euphoric that some users are at a loss for words to describe it.

By allowing brain chemicals, the neurotransmitters norepi and dopamine, to remain active longer than normal, cocaine produces euphoria followed by an intense craving for more of the drug. But the high lasts only about 30 minutes, and users frequently find that they need more and more cocaine to generate the same level of stimulation. A cocaine user follows the same addictive path as the alcohol abuser but deteriorates much more rapidly, with early signs of grandiosity and paranoia, and severe reality distortion (toxic psychosis).

7. Hallucinogens, which include peyote, mescaline, mushrooms, psilocybin, LSD (lysergic acid diethylamide), DMT (dimethyltryptamine), DET (diethyltryptamine), marijuana, and PCP (phencyclidine, also called "angel dust" and "peace pill"), blur the distinction between imagination and reality. If hallucinogens are taken regularly, tolerance results, requiring greater amounts to obtain the same effect. Psychedelics, phencyclidine, and marijuana are the most commonly abused hallucinogens. Psychedelic drugs such as like LSD alter perception and cognition. Usually taken orally, LSD produces symptoms similar to those of stimulants.

PCP is dangerous because its effects are unpredictable; it can stimulate or depress, and because its purity is uncertain the user may accidentally overdose. Chronic PCP use may also lead to a psychotic state lasting months after discontinuance. Chronic users are often violent, hostile, and unmanageable. Those who take even the lowest dose suffer impaired attention, disorganized thought, and emotional instability.

Marijuana, widely used by people of varying ages and socioeconomic backgrounds, affects the brain, heart, and lungs. A difficult drug to classify, marijuana, like hashish, has some long-term depressant characteristics that modify mood and alleviate anxieties. Even small doses can impair brain function; they distort perception, hamper judgment, interfere with memory, and diminish motor skills. Observers in clinical settings note increased apathy, loss of ambition, loss of effectiveness, diminished ability to carry out long-term plans, difficulty in concentrating, and a decline in school or work performance.

8. Analogues ("designer drugs") are created by underground chemists who modify the chemical structure of certain substances to create drugs that have structures similar to those of medical or illegal drugs but are altered enough to make them different from controlled substances monitored by the Drug Enforcement Administration. Examples of designer drugs are an analogue of methamphetamine (commonly known as Ecstasy) and an analog of Fentanyl, a narcotic (Wharton 1989; Schuckit 1994). Another example is "cat" (methcathinone), recently concocted by a drug dealer in his apartment. Resembling cocaine in appearance and potency, it "spread like wildfire" in the Midwest once the formula was shared with others. Although the DEA outlawed its manufacture, the drug is reportedly produced in about 40 underground laboratories in the Midwest ("New Law Attempts to Stop Spread of CAT" 1994). Chemically dependent people are usually cross-addicted: they use a variety of drugs, and when the effect of one drug fades, or their supply runs out, they switch to another.

The Drug Enforcement Administration lists 171 narcotics, depressants, stimulants, and hallucinogens (Peters 1990b). At advanced stages of addiction, many addicts trying to function and feel normal combine whatever psychoactive drugs are available.

9. Schedule I drugs include heroin, hallucinogens, marijuana, methaqualone (Quaalude); Schedule II drugs include opium or morphine, codeine, synthetic opiates such as meperidine (Demerol), barbiturates such as secobarbital (Seconal), amphetamines, methylphenidate (Ritalin), and phenmetrazine (Preludin); Schedule III drugs include aspirin with codeine, paregoric, methyprylon (Noludar) and PCP; Schedule IV drugs include chloral hydrate (Noctec), ethchlorvynol (Placidyl), flurazepam (Dalmane), pentazocine (Talwin), chlordiazepoxide (Librium), propoxyphene (Darvon), and diethylpropion (Tenuate); and Schedule V drugs—those perceived as having lowest abuse and highest usefulness—include narcotic-atropine mixtures (Lomotil) and codeine mixtures (less than 200 mg) (Schuckit 1995c).

10. Rosenberg (1993, p. 129) calls these users "problem drinkers." "The term *problem drinker*," he says, "is usually reserved for persons who display few if any signs of dependence, although problem drinkers often drink excessively (e.g., more than 21 standard drinks of 0.5 oz. of alcohol per week) and suffer one or more alcohol-related problems such as drunken driving arrests, occupational or social dysfunction, and health problems."

11. Management of the signs and symptoms of withdrawal during detoxification is discussed in Chapter 6.

12. See Schatzberg and Nemeroff (1995) for additional information about the psychopharmacology of substance abuse.

4. *Vulnerabilities*

1. Research indicates that a family history of emotional abuse during the personality's formative years is highly correlated with drug abuse during adulthood. There are at least 10.5 million alcoholics in the United States, and 76 million Americans have an alcoholic family member; nearly one in five (18 percent) spent their childhood with an alcoholic (Schoenborn 1991). An inordinately high percentage of health professionals come from such families (Peters 1990a). A South Carolina study of nurses, social workers, and medical students, for example, found that 22–30 percent had been raised in families dominated by alcohol abuse (Peter N. Johnson 1990). A New England survey of about 500 physicians and nearly equal numbers of medical students, pharmacists, and pharmacy students revealed that 22 percent of the physicians and 27 percent of the medical students had family histories of substance abuse, as did a similar share (22 percent and 25 percent, respectively) of pharmacists and pharmacy students (McAuliffe et al. 1987).

2. Several phone calls to nursing organizations resulted in scant information about substance-abuse education in undergraduate nursing programs. The American Association of Colleges of Nursing told us they have no figures

on this subject. The Dean's Office at the UCLA School of Nursing said that such a course was "not directly part of the curriculum, but usually comes up at scattered places in various courses" (Dean's Office 1995).

3. A 1986 survey of all U.S. dental schools found that about one-fourth gave no substance abuse instruction. About half offered a maximum of three lecture hours. Only one school offered formal instruction in all four years (Sandoval, Hendricson, and Dale 1988). A few years later, when 36 of the 52 dental schools responded to another survey, 23 reported having a formal chemical dependency curriculum in their programs, and 3 others offered seminars and other types of training (Crosby 1995).

4. A telephone survey sent to a nationally representative sample of 500 physicians (family practice, internal medicine, and general practice) by the Hazelden Foundation found that two-thirds (63 percent) had spent less than 20 hours in medical school hearing about addiction. Among these, 36 percent had devoted fewer than 10 hours, and 5 percent could not recall any instruction on the topic.

5. A national sample of licensed pilots found that although they recognize the risk of combining alcohol and flying, they are surprisingly uninformed about the 0.04 percent blood-alcohol count (BAC) rule. Survey results indicated that moderate and heavy drinkers, compared with abstainers and infrequent drinkers, made more judgment errors in the number of drinks that resulted in a given BAC and the amount of time it took for BAC to decay (Ross and Ross 1990).

6. In 1971 NIDA and NIAAA developed the Career Teacher Training Program in the Addictions to improve the quality and quantity of substance abuse training in U.S. medical schools, and in 1977 the Association for Medical Educators and Researchers in Substance Abuse (AMERSA) was organized (Pokorny and Solomon 1983). Lewis (1986, p. 827) notes that these innovations helped move the educational deficiency "from almost total neglect to general inadequacy."

In 1989 the federal government's Center for Substance Abuse Prevention (1994) initiated the Faculty Development Program by providing 3-to-5-year training grants to improve clinical teaching about alcohol, tobacco, and other drug abuse. The purpose is to develop a cadre of academically based health professionals who will lead drug abuse training within their clinical specialties and departments. By 1994 35 institutions—16 schools of medicine, 11 schools of nursing, 7 schools of social work, and 1 graduate psychology department—had received funding to train 3 to 5 postdoctoral fellows.

In 1989 the Addictions Nursing Certification Board (ANCB) was established to raise the standards and quality of nursing services to addicted clients. Nurses who qualify and specialize in the care of addicted clients are now recognized as Certified Addictions Registered Nurses (CARN). The National Nurses Society on Addictions, established in 1975, develops publications to help nurses prepare for the CARN exam. In 1995, 1,300 nurses were certified (Landry 1995). In 1992 the American Association of

Dental Schools (AADS) published its "Curriculum Guidelines for Education in Substance Abuse, Alcoholism, and Other Chemical Dependencies." The curriculum includes a brief definition and history of the disease and its psychophysiological characteristics, patient health care considerations, and impaired professional issues. Also included are related concerns such as codependency, adult children of alcoholics, chemically dependent dental professionals, clinical interventions, and the essential elements of chemical dependency programs. Methods of referral and current treatment modalities are also recommended.

7. Law schools have been slow to incorporate substance abuse education into their curricula. The Ohio Bar is reportedly the first to require a certificate from law schools certifying that students have successfully completed instruction in substance abuse, including causes, prevention, detention, and treatment alternatives. However, this 1993 requirement calls for only one hour of instruction during law school. The requirement for continuing legal education is even less—at least 30 minutes of instruction on substance abuse during each two-year reporting period (Christoff 1992).

8. An anonymous, self-reporting pre- and post-test questionnaire was given to 71 students who had completed the program and to 69 students at another dental school who had received no comparable instruction. The survey showed that twice as many participating students (44.8 percent) as the comparison group (21.4 percent) switched from high-risk category at pretest (drinking four or more drinks on occasion) to a low-risk group post-test—never exceeding zero to three drinks on any given day.

5. *Developmental Stages*

1. For a compelling example of a physician's accidental death as a result of overdosing, see the videotape "Wearing Masks," produced by the Association of Anesthesia Program Directors, Rainbow Productions, Chicago, 1993.

6. *Recovery Tools*

1. The pharmacological agents used in detoxification programs vary. Programs that focus on narcotics dependence often use methadone for staged withdrawal over 21 days. A more recent strategy uses Clonidine, a blood-pressure medication, to detoxify opiate addicts by suppressing the autonomic signs and symptoms of withdrawal (Spencer and Gregory 1989). The latter has also been used with some success to detoxify nicotine, benzodiazepine, and alcohol addicts. Clonidine-assisted detoxification makes the transition from opiate abuse to opiate antagonists (e.g., naltrexone treatment) easier and more accessible to patients (*Drug Abuse and Drug Abuse Research* 1991, p. 56). Acupuncture may also be used in the management of opiate withdrawal (see the section "Holistic Care" later in this chapter).

2. Not every addict easily embraces the disease perspective. For a humorous

account by a novelist who found it difficult to compare his alcoholism with his earlier polio and cancer in remission, see Sheed (1995).

3. Some hospitals have implemented random urine screening to ensure safe patient care. In 1990, for example, the Johns Hopkins Hospital announced that all new employees—including nurses and physicians—would undergo random testing for alcohol and other drugs of abuse (Orentlicher 1990). "Issues of personal freedom and tradition," a press release stated, "are clearly secondary to the need to protect our patients and to come to grips with the public's growing wish for reassurance" (Johns Hopkins University 1990; also see Lewy 1988).

4. Other requirements may include (1) spending a specified time in an after-care program, including individual or group therapy, (2) submitting to random urine analysis for three years, (3) attending 90 meetings of Alcoholics Anonymous or Narcotics Anonymous during the first three months after signing the contract; (4) accepting an AA-specified sponsor in these programs, (5) attending additional private and/or group therapy sessions as decided by the after-care counselor, (6) encouraging spouses and other significant persons to attend support groups, (7) sending monthly progress reports to the committee representatives, (8) calling the committee representative at least once a month to report progress, (9) complying with regulations of the state licensing board, (10) assuming financial responsibility for urinalysis and other contract stipulations, (11) notifying the committee of any changes in the address or telephone number of the testing laboratory within 14 days, (12) not withdrawing from the contract without the written consent of the committee, and (13) disclosing the names of all states in which a clinical license is utilized (Smith and Starnes 1988; Kendall 1991).

5. For a review of the literature see Institute of Medicine (1989, pp. 61–63) and *Seventh Special Report to the U.S. Congress on Alcohol and Health* (1990).

7. Self-Help Recovery

1. Other Twelve-Step derivatives include Adult Children Anonymous, Al-Atot, Bulimics/Anorexics Anonymous, Child Abusers Anonymous, Co-dependents of Sex Addicts, Debtors Anonymous, Emotions Anonymous, Fundamentalists Anonymous, Gamblers Anonymous, Parents Anonymous, Sex Addicts Anonymous, Sexaholics Anonymous, Sex and Love Addicts Anonymous, Shoplifters Anonymous, Smokers Anonymous, Spenders Anonymous, and Workaholics Anonymous (Friel and Friel 1988).

2. To locate a group in most cities throughout the world, look in the telephone directory or write to AA World Services, Box 459 Central Station, New York, NY 10163.

3. "Working the 12 steps" requires participants to struggle laboriously and often painfully with each step, such as itemizing and publicly discussing their painful memories of hurting self and others when under the influence. Chappel (1991) explains that steps 1, 2, and 3, the surrender steps, help the addict overcome denial, pride, and an inflated ego. Steps 4 and 5, the in-

ventory steps, help overcome the guilt, shame, and grief that lead to depression. Steps 6 and 7, the character-change steps, promote awareness of such defects as selfishness, self-centeredness, and antisocial traits and a willingness to let them go. Steps 8 and 9, the relational steps, help the addict repair damaged relationships and make amends. Steps 8 and 9 also promote skills important for long-term social bonds by helping the addict overcome interpersonal resentments, blaming, and attempts to control others. Steps 10 and 11, the maintenance steps, encourage regular attention to personal, relational, and spiritual health. Step 10 reviews steps 4–9, and step 11 reviews steps 1–3. Step 12, the service step, overcomes the barriers of narcissism, shyness, and constraints on time and energy by involving members in serving as sponsors and visiting the chemically dependent in their homes, hospital rooms, prisons, and treatment facilities.

4. For information call (310) 478-0776 or write to Life Management Skills, Inc., 1990 S. Bundy, West Los Angeles, CA 90025.

5. The following MM Ground Rules are read at the beginning of each meeting: "(1) MM members accept responsibility for their own actions and have a sincere desire to moderate their drinking behavior; (2) MM meetings are anonymous; (3) members should never come to MM meetings intoxicated; (4) MM has a 'zero tolerance' policy toward drinking and driving. The only safe blood-alcohol level prior to driving is zero; (5) MM does not condone underage drinking; (6) problems related to the abuse of illegal drugs are outside the scope of MM meetings; (7) MM meetings are for problem drinkers. This program is not intended for chronic drinkers or others who should not drink; (8) MM discourages members from socializing together in drinking situations; (9) MM never permits alcohol at meetings or other MM-related activities; (10) MM suggests that members make their MM meeting days non-drinking days" (Kishline 1994, p. 79).

   MM offers nine steps to help members attain their self-management goals: "(1) attend meetings and learn about the program of Moderation Management; (2) abstain from alcoholic beverages for 30 days and complete steps 3 through 6 during this time; (3) examine how drinking has affected your life; (4) write down your priorities; (5) take a look at how much, how often, and under what circumstances you used to drink; (6) learn the MM guidelines and limits for moderate drinking; (7) set moderate drinking limits and start weekly 'small steps' toward positive lifestyle changes; (8) review your progress at meetings and update your goals; (9) after achieving your goal of moderation, attend MM meetings any time you feel the need for support, or would like to help newcomers" (Kishline 1994, pp. 85–86).

6. See Carey (1995) for a description of Drinkwise, another moderation program begun in Ontario in 1991 by psychologist Martha Sanchez-Craig. It teaches people to keep their drinking within specific boundaries: a maximum of 12 a week for women (never more than 3 daily) and 14 for men (never more than 4 daily).

7. In 1979 the American Dental Association House of Delegates passed a resolution calling for the establishment of a national clearinghouse of infor-

mation about alcohol and chemical-dependency programs in the dental profession (Crosby 1995).

8. Formal Recovery Programs

1. See Hubbard (1992) for a review of outcome studies.
2. The earliest residential treatment program for chemically impaired professionals, the Georgia Medical Society's Impaired Physician Program (IPP), began in 1974 sponsored by the Medical Association of Georgia (see Talbott 1982; Talbott and Martin 1984; Talbott et al. 1987).
3. Methadone maintenance, a form of drug-replacement therapy, frees opiate addicts from the withdrawal that impels them to use illicit opiates. It is not a treatment for alcoholism or cocaine dependence. Participants' daily lives are oriented around a treatment center and recovery program rather than people and places that involve drug use and crime, and they can begin to deal with their problems and establish new lifestyles.

   Taken orally, methadone is distributed under close supervision. State and federal regulations require the participant to have (1) a documented history of opiate addiction—legal records of arrest records, etc., of at least two years; (2) a confirmed history of two or more unsuccessful attempts at detoxifying from illicit opiates; (3) a physician's certification of at least one year of addiction; and (4) evidence of current narcotic dependence, including early signs of withdrawal (State of California Department of Alcohol and Drug Program 1992, p. 32). Urine specimens, randomly given, must be provided at least monthly, and arms are checked periodically for needle marks and bruises. When an addict is stabilized on a daily methadone dose so that she no longer has withdrawal complaints or sedative effects, a treatment plan is negotiated, including long-term goals (e.g., finding a job) and short-term goals (e.g., completing job application forms). Counseling with contracts rewards participants for achievements and teaches problem solving, decision making, stress management, relaxation skills, nutrition, and physical exercise. Although methadone treatment substantially reduces illicit narcotic use, it does not eliminate use of alcohol or other drugs. But studies have shown that the majority of methadone patients substantially reduce overall use of these other substances (Zweben and Payte 1990; Ball and Ross 1991).
4. In one program (O'Connor n.d.), for example, new participants may attend two group-therapy sessions from 6:30 to 10:00 four nights a week for six to eight weeks. Biweekly, random, supervised urine drug screens are obtained during the initial phases, and participants are encouraged to attend self-help meetings during the week. Clients advance through structured stages.
5. The Matrix/UCLA Alcoholism and Addiction Medical Service, for example, offers comprehensive behavioral treatment at several locations in southern California, but it also includes 12-step participation and pharmacologic support when appropriate. For a review see Matrix Center (1991); Rawson et al. (1990).

6. In 1984 California created the Impaired Pharmacist Program (IPP) and required the Board of Pharmacy to identify and rehabilitate pharmacists whose competency is affected by alcohol, other drugs, or mental illness. The board now contracts with an independent organization that offers confidential assessments, referral, and monitoring services for the IPP (Whitmore n.d.). The California Pharmacists Association and the California Society of Hospital Pharmacists recruit licensed pharmacists as IPP volunteers, who provide information and support for impaired pharmacists. A toll-free telephone line is staffed 24 hours a day, seven days a week.

7. In 1982 the American Nurses' Association passed a resolution urging treatment for addicted nurses. However, the change from punishment to diversion has been difficult, and most programs are now run by state nurses' associations with small budgets and volunteer staff. "Addicted physicians are rehabilitated, addicted nurses are punished," Lippman (1992, p. 36) observes.

   Florida enacted the first diversion law for nurses in 1983, followed by 12 other states, with another 18 reportedly considering similar action. The Diversion Program for the California board of Registered Nursing during its first six years (1985–1990) saw more than 1,000 nurses referred; more than 300 completed the two-to-five-year program and returned to practice drug-free; about 400 other nurses are currently in the program. Before 1985 these nurses were typically fired or faced criminal charges for drug theft. To protect the public, the board removed impaired nurses from practice by revoking their professional licenses. This costly disciplinary process required several years, became part of the nurse's record, and consumed nearly half of the board's budget. The diversion program expedites initial treatment in almost the same time it takes to investigate and prosecute a disciplinary action, and the average of three years' participation costs about one-third of the money it takes to pursue traditional discipline on a single violation (State of California Department of Consumer Affairs 1992).

8. Lawyers only recently adopted the diversion approach. A Supreme Court ruling in 1991 created a method whereby an attorney in trouble can be diverted from the disciplinary system into diversion programs. Using a demanding diversion contract, attorneys are carefully monitored over an extended period.

9. In the early 1970s, when rehabilitation was dimly understood, alcoholics were prone to relapse, and FAA policies were punitive. Since it would jeopardize their livelihood, airline pilots were reluctant to seek help, and fellow pilots were resistant to reporting colleagues. Grass-roots efforts by pilots changed this. Through the Air Line Pilots Association (ALPA), they developed their own alcoholic rehabilitation programs and challenged the Office of Aviation Medicine to provide a way for rehabilitated alcoholic airline pilots to return to work. Now a commercial airline pilot, sponsored by an appropriate medical department or ALPA medical representative, can return to duty three months after completing an initial intensive re-

habilitation program, which usually includes one month at an inpatient drug-rehabilitation facility. The pilot also reports regularly to the medical sponsor and attends AA (Reighard 1980).

10. The FAA's Aviation Medical Program routinely assesses the medical fitness of more than 800,000 U.S. pilots. Alcoholism brings a mandatory denial of medical certification (Reighard 1980, p. 24). When an alcoholic pilot becomes sufficiently rehabilitated that he no longer threatens aviation safety, an "exemption" is granted. The longer the abstinence, the greater the probability an exemption will be granted. It is unusual for an exemption to be granted for less than two years' abstinence without stringent medical surveillance. Most pilots with a history of more than five years of abstinence receive an exemption. Once medical certification is restored, continued licensing is conditional upon total abstinence. The FAA currently identifies substance-abusing pilots by examining their automobile driving records. Pilots applying for a medical certificate from the FAA must consent to the release of information from the National Driver Register to allow the FAA to review records of motor-vehicle offenses (Wood 1995). Pilots must also provide written notification to the FAA within 60 days after the occurrence of any alcohol/drug-related driving conviction. Pilots who violate drunken-driving laws or are convicted of traffic offenses involving drugs are grounded.

11. In 1986 Congress passed the Health Care Quality Improvement Act to establish a National Practitioner Data Bank as a repository for adverse information on physicians and dentists (Cullan and Cullan 1991). Administered by the U.S. Public Health Service, the bank's purpose is to identify impaired or incompetent physicians and dentists who stay one step ahead of the law by moving from state to state without disclosing previous damaging or incompetent practices. The statute requires state professional licensing boards to report license revocations, suspensions, or restrictions to the data bank. Also reported are censures, reprimands, or probations that relate to professional competence or conduct. Significantly, the surrender of a license as a result of admission to a drug, alcohol, or psychiatric rehabilitation program for 30 days or more is not reportable (see also Chen 1989).

Located in a high-security facility in Camarillo, California, the $15.9-million data bank tracks malpractice actions and disciplinary proceedings against all of the nation's 600,000 physicians and 147,000 dentists. Actions against all physicians and dentists must be reported, but it is left up to individual hospitals to decide whether to report nurse anesthetists, pharmacists, and other health practitioners. The law requires all insurance companies to report both to the data bank and to the appropriate state licensing board any malpractice payments on behalf of a licensed health practitioner. Professional organizations must report any formal actions taken as a result of a peer-review process. State licensing boards and more than 7,000 hospitals are urged to waste no time in consulting the registry. Hospitals are required to query the data bank regarding any practitioner they hire, and to check every two years on professionals who currently have clinical privileges. The public and the press are denied access to this information.

12. The DEA estimates that several hundred million doses of prescription drugs are each year diverted to illicit use from the more than 1.5 billion prescriptions dispensed annually. As of May 1992, 11 states (California, Hawaii, Indiana, Illinois, Indiana, Massachusetts, Michigan, New York, Oklahoma, Rhode Island, and Texas) had monitoring programs to deter and detect such diversion. Using prescription records for selected drugs, they evaluate physicians' prescribing patterns, pharmacists' dispensing patterns, and patients' purchasing habits.

The DEA claims that this strategy significantly reduces drug crimes, but the American Medical Association, the American Civil Liberties Union, and some health experts argue that it jeopardizes the right of privacy between doctor and patient and that legitimate prescribing will be curtailed. Law-enforcement officials respond that the new system is simply a faster and more cost-effective way of gathering data that are already available. A review of 10 state programs by the U.S. General Accounting Office found only one instance in which the monitoring program had adversely affected patient care *(Prescription Drug Monitoring* 1992). There is no evidence that prescription monitoring affects patient care. All state monitoring programs have controls to protect patient privacy (Celis 1992).

13. EAPs initially focused primarily on alcoholism and substance abuse in the workplace (Roman and Blum 1994). Over time the emphasis broadened to include psychiatric disorders, stress-related disorders, adjustment or "transient situational disorders" (for example, marriage breakdown, parenting problems, interpersonal conflicts), financial and legal concerns, and lifestyle issues (Solursh 1989). By 1988 more than 60 percent of Fortune 500 companies and a growing number of smaller companies provided counseling services to employees (Dixon 1988).

14. In 1983 United Airlines reported a 93 percent success rate for more than 120 pilots; only 7 percent relapsed within a three-year period (Harper 1983). Palmer (1983, p. 953) notes that "mandatory license proficiency checks performed at least five times a year also assist in early detection. Four checks are completed in the sophisticated computerized flight simulators, which are exact replicas of aircraft cockpits and are capable of creating, with extreme fidelity, every conceivable emergency as well as depicting a realistic external visual environment . . . If a pilot fails his test, he is required to undergo a thorough re-training program before being allowed to attempt another relicensing assessment. Prior to the re-training, or even in cases of marginal performance, an in-depth interview and counseling take place with the chief pilot and the flight operations director. In this way, many cases of alcoholism have been thwarted."

15. A successful EAP at the Medical College of Georgia, cosponsored by the Georgia State Committee for Impaired Professionals, serves more than 6,000 employees and their families free of charge (Solursh 1989). Located

in a renovated house on a residential street near the campus, the EAP sponsors a drug-abuse awareness program, crisis intervention and psychotherapy for "at-risk impaired employees/faculty," educational sessions on wellness, stress reduction, and time management, and problem-solving consultation with management. It also conducts evaluation research to improve its services. During its first nine months this EAP received 108 consultation phone calls, 92 percent of which were self-referrals. Alcohol was the drug of abuse most frequently cited by physicians and other health-care professionals—about 20 percent of participants.

16. The committee chair at an exclusive urban hospital explained: "All California hospitals are required under federal law [Title 22] to provide a committee to examine reports or suspicions of any staff members who may constitute a potential or real threat to patients, staff, or hospital reputation. Educating medical staff is an auxiliary function. All reports are funneled to the department chairman, who appoints a subcommittee to meet with the suspect physician and examine the charges. When confronted, the physician may either comply or decline further examination. If he complies with the recommendations of the well-being committee, it is not essential for the chair to report him to the chief of staff. If he declines, he is reported to the chief of staff for action. If there is evidence of impairment, his hospital privileges are suspended, and he has 23 days to reply. If he fails to do so, the problem is automatically reported to the California Medical Board" (MD, age 43).

17. During its first ten years, the AIMS program at the University of Tennessee Medical School worked with 18 chemical-abuse or -dependency cases. Four impaired students voluntarily requested evaluation and treatment, and 14 were identified by fellow medical students, residents, or faculty. In most case, initial contact with the AIMS program was made through a student representative. Ten students successfully completed initial treatment. Nine maintained remission without relapse. Eight of the 10 subsequently graduated, while 2 remained enrolled, making satisfactory academic progress. One student relapsed during residency and withdrew from training. He later refused assistance from his state impaired-physicians' program and subsequently committed suicide (Ackerman and Wall 1994).

18. "In order to comply with the Drug-Free Schools and Communities Act, institutions must now annually distribute a statement in writing to each employee and student containing the following: (1) standards of conduct clearly prohibiting the unlawful possession, use, or distribution of illegal drugs and alcohol by students or employees on the institution's property or on any part of the institution's activities; (2) a description of the applicable legal sanctions under local, state, or federal law for the unlawful possession or distribution of illicit drugs and alcohol; (3) a description of the health risks associated with the use of illicit drugs and the abuse of alcohol; (4) a description of any drug or alcohol counseling, treatment, rehabilitation, or re-entry programs that are available to students or employees; and (5) a clear statement that the institution will impose sanctions on

students and employees for violating the institution's standards concerning drugs and alcohol, together with the description of those sanctions (which, under the act, may include completion of an appropriate rehabilitation program and may also include expulsion, termination of employment, and referral for prosecution" (American Association of Law Schools 1993, p. 28).

Epilogue

1. According to calculations by William F. Buckley Jr., the annual cost to the nation as a result of the criminalization of drug use is as follows: "Incarceration: 700,000 times $30,000 per prisoner, or $21 billion. New prison construction: 52 weeks times 1,200 beds times $70,000 per bed times 50 percent (one-half of prisoners are there for drug violations), or $2.2 billion. Justice system and trial costs: 1,200,000 cases times $5,000 per case, or $6 billion. Law enforcement: 220,000 officers times $35,000 per officer, or $7.7 billion. Custom Service and Coast Guard and other armed forces involvement in the drug war: $2 billion. Wasted consumer spending on marijuana, estimated 15 million users (the difference between what consumers pay for illegal drugs and what they cost to produce): 4 ounces per consumer times 15,000,000 times overpayment per ounce: $12.9 billion. Wasted on cocaine: 2,500,000 users times three-quarters of a gram per day times $250 per eight ball times eight balls per ounce, divided by 28 grams per ounce, or $48.9 billion. All other drugs combined, or $5 billion. If 15 percent of addicts resort to crime to support their habit, we have 150,000 addicts committing crime. Assume the average cocaine addict uses 2 grams of cocaine per day: 150,000 addicts times 2 grams per day times 265 days per year times $300 per eight ball times eight balls per ounce divided by 28 grams per ounce, or $9.4 billion. Stolen goods sell for much less than their value. So at one-fifth of value, to realize $9.4 billion requires stealing $47 billion worth of goods. Health costs attributed to dirty needles: $3 billion. Lost revenue (untaxed illegal drugs): $6 billion. Environmental and industrial impact (the uses of marijuana for commerce and medicine): $5 billion. Collateral costs in extra firearms, court congestion, banking use, insurance against burglary, health costs, emergency care—my correspondent cannot estimate these costs, and therefore adds up the costs independent of these: The bottom line: $205,000,000,000" (Buckley quoted in *Alcohol and Drugs* 1995, pp. 4–5).

References

Ackerman, Terrence F., and Hershel P. Wall. 1994. "A Programme for Treating Chemically Dependent Medical Students." *Medical Education* (U.K.), 28: 40–46.

Adams, John D. 1988. "A Healthy Cut in Costs." *Personnel Administrator,* August: 42–47.

AIMS: Aid for the Impaired Medical Student. N.d. Brochure. University of Tennessee–Memphis, Health Science Center, College of Medicine.

Alcohol and Health: Seventh Special Report to the U.S. Congress from the Secretary of Health and Human Services. 1990. (ADM)90-1656. Rockville, Md.: U.S. Department of Health and Human Services, Public Health Service.

"Alcohol and Nutrition." 1993. *Alcohol Alert* (National Institute of Alcohol Abuse and Alcoholism, U.S. Public Health Service), 346(22): 1–4.

Alcoholics Anonymous General Service Office. 1995. Personal communication from staff member, New York City, July 11.

—— 1996. Personal communication from staff member, New York City, October 15.

Alcoholics Anonymous World Services. 1976. *Alcoholics Anonymous: The Story of How Many Thousands of Men and Women Have Recovered from Alcoholism.* New York.

—— 1982. *AA as a Resource for the Medical Profession.* Brochure. New York.

Alexander, D., and J. O'Quinn-Larson. 1990. "When Nurses Are Addicted to Drugs: Confronting an Impaired Co-Worker." *Nursing90,* August: 55–58.

"Alternative Medicine: The Facts. Acupuncture." 1994. *Consumer Reports,* January: 51–59.

American Association of Dental Schools. 1992. "Curriculum Guidelines for Education in Substance Abuse, Alcoholism, and Other Chemical Dependencies." *Journal of Dental Education,* 56: 405–408.

American Council on Alcoholism News. 1993. Quoted in American Pharmaceutical Association, Pharmacists Recovery Network, *PRN Memo,* no. 35 (April): 8–9.

American Pharmaceutical Association, Pharmacists Recovery Network. 1992. "Texas Health Care Professionals Fear Diversion of Drug Samples." *PRN Memo*, no. 33 (October): 13–14.

——— 1994. *PRN Memo*, no. 40 (July–September).

American Society of Addiction Medicine. 1992. *Advancing the Field of Addiction Medicine*. Washington, D.C.

American Society of Anesthesiologists and Janssen Pharmaceutica. 1994. *Unmasking Addiction: Chemical Dependency in Anesthesiology*. With William J. Farley, M.D., and William P. Arnold III, M.D. Videotape. Park Ridge, Ill.

American Sociological Association. 1994. Comments at annual meeting in Los Angeles, August.

Anderson, David S., and Angelo F. Gadaleto. 1991. "Results of the 1991 College Alcohol Survey: Comparison with 1988 Results and Baseline Year." Copies available from David S. Anderson, Center for Health Promotion, George Mason University, Fairfax, VA 22030.

Anglin, M. Douglas, M. L. Brecht, and E. Maddahian. 1989. "Pre-Treatment Characteristics and Treatment Performance of Legally Coerced versus Voluntary Methadone Maintenance Admission." *Criminology*, 27: 537–557.

Anglin, M. Douglas, E. P. Deschens, and G. Speckart. 1987. "The Effect of Legal Supervision on Narcotic Addiction and Criminal Behavior." Paper presented at the annual meeting of the American Society of Criminology, Montreal, November.

Anglin, M. Douglas, and Yih-Ing Hser. 1991. "Criminal Justice and the Drug-Abusing Offender: Policy Issues of Coerced Treatment." *Behavioral Sciences and the Law*, 9: 243–267.

Annis, H. M, and C. S. Davis. 1988. "Self-Efficacy and the Prevention of Alcoholic Relapse: Initial Findings from a Treatment Trial." In *Assessment and Treatment of Addictive Disorders*, ed. T. B. Baker and D. Cannon. New York: Praeger. Pp. 88–112.

Anonymous. N.d. "The Mind and Body Seek Fulfillment for Issues That Only the Soul Can Satisfy." Shared with author by H. Khouzam, personal correspondence.

——— 1988. Letter to the editor. *Journal of Nursing Scholarship*, 20 (Fall): 175.

Anonymous. 1993. Personal communication.

Apostolides, Marianne. 1996. "How to Quit the Holistic Way." *Psychology Today*, September/October: 35–43.

"The Appearance of Propriety." 1989. *Texas Bar Journal*, March: 310–311.

Arnold, Kathryn, and Kathleen Finn. 1994. "The Body & Soul of Healing." *Delicious!* October: 14–16.

Arron, Deborah L. 1991. *Running from the Law: Why Good Lawyers Are Getting Out of the Legal Profession*. Berkeley, Calif.: Ten Speed Press.

Arthur, Mark S. 1982. "Drug and Alcohol Abuse: Dentists' Call for Help." *Dental Management*, July: 45–48.

Association of American Law Schools. 1993. "Report of the AALS Special Committee on Problems of Substance Abuse in the Law Schools." Submitted to the Executive Committee, Washington, D.C., May.

Association of American Medical Colleges, Section for Educational Research. 1991. *1991 Graduating Student Survey Results.* Washington, D.C.

—— 1992a. *1992 Graduating Student Survey Results.* Washington, D.C.

—— 1992b. "Reaffirming Institutional Standards of Behavior in the Learning Environment." Memorandum no. 92-38. Washington, D.C., July 28.

Association of Anesthesia Program Directors. 1993. *Wearing Masks.* Videotape. Chicago: Rainbow Productions.

Aston, Roy. 1984. "Drug Abuse: Its Relationship to Dental Practice." *Dental Clinics of North America,* 28: 595–609.

Bagelos, Roy P. 1991. "Are Prescription Drug Prices High?" *Science,* 252 (May): 1043–84.

Baldwin, DeWitt C., et al. 1991. "Substance Use among Senior Medical Students: A Survey of 23 Medical Schools." *Journal of the American Medical Association,* 265: 2074–78.

Baldwin, W. A., et al. 1993. "Substance Abuse-Related Admissions to Adult Intensive Care." *Chest,* 103(1): 21–25.

Ball, John C., and Alan Ross. 1991. *The Effectiveness of Methadone Maintenance Treatment: Patients, Programs, Services, and Outcomes.* New York: Springer-Verlag.

Barber, James G. 1992. "Relapse Prevention and the Need for Brief Social Intervention." *Journal of Substance Abuse Treatment,* 9: 157–158.

Barde, Barbara, and Anne Pick. 1993. *Nurses: The Web of Denial.* Videotape. Boston: Fanlights Productions.

Beck, Melinda, and Jerry Buckley. 1983. "Nurses with Bad Habits." *Newsweek,* August 22: 54.

Beckley-Barrett, Lisa M., and Patricia B. Mutch. 1990. "Position of the American Dietetic Association: Nutrition Intervention in Treatment and Recovery from Chemical Dependency." *Journal of the American Dietetic Association, ADA Reports,* 90(9): 1274–77.

Beckman, L. J. 1993. "Alcoholics Anonymous and Gender Issues." In *Research on Alcoholics Anonymous: Opportunities and Alternatives,* ed. B. S. McCrady and W. R. Miller. New Brunswick, N.J.: Rutgers Center on Alcohol Studies. Pp. 233–248.

Benjamin, G. Andrew H. 1985. "Psychological Distress in Law Students and New Lawyers." *Washington State Bar News,* December: 13–15.

Benjamin, G. Andrew H., Elaine J. Darling, and Bruce D. Sales. 1990. "The Prevalence of Depression, Alcohol Abuse, and Cocaine Abuse among United States Lawyers." *International Journal of Law and Psychiatry,* 13: 233–246.

Benjamin, G. Andrew H., Bruce D. Sales, and Elaine J. Darling. 1992. "Comprehensive Lawyers Assistance Programs: Justification and Model." *Law and Psychology Review,* 16: 113–136.

Benjamin, G. Andrew H., et al. 1986. "The Role of Legal Education in Producing Psychological Distress among Law Students and Lawyers." *American Bar Foundation Research Journal,* 225: 225–252.

Benson, Herbert. 1975. *The Relaxation Response.* New York: Avon.

Benson, Herbert, and Mary Stark. 1996. *Timeless Healing: The Power and Biology of Belief*. New York: Scribner.

Bernard, Mike. 1988. "Intervention: A Lifeline in the Tunnel of Despair." *Ohio Dental Journal*, 62(10): 36–38.

Bernstein, Arnold, and Henry L. Lennard. 1973. "Drugs, Doctors and Junkies." *Society*, 10 (May/June): 14–25.

Berridge, Kent C., and Terry E. Robinson. 1995. "The Mind of an Addicted Brain: Neural Sensitization of Wanting versus Liking." *Current Directions in Psychological Science*, 4(3): 71–76.

Bertram, Eva, et al. 1996. *Drug War Politics: The Price of Denial*. Berkeley: University of California Press.

Biernacki, Patrick. 1986. *Pathways from Heroin Addiction: Recovery without Treatment*. Philadelphia: Temple University Press.

Biery, Janet Reid, J. H. Williford, and Elsa A. McMullen. 1991. "Alcohol Craving in Rehabilitation: Assessment of Nutrition Therapy." *Journal of the American Dietetic Association, ADA Reports*, 91(4): 463–466.

Bird Word. 1992. Spring newspaper of Birds of A Feather International.

Bishop, Katherine. 1990. "Band's Marching Orders Are No More Encores." *New York Times*, November 17: L9, N10.

Bissell, LeClair. 1989. "An Historical Review: Alcohol and Drugs in the Professions." In *Professionals and Their Addictions*, ed. Thomas W. Hester. Macon, Ga.: Charter Medical. Pp. 3–23.

——— 1992. "Is Alcoholics Anonymous (AA) for the Dental Professional?" In *Dentistry Faces Addiction: How to Be Part of the Solution*, ed. Arthur G. Williams. New York: Mosby Year Book. Pp. 73–76.

Bissell, LeClair, P. W. Haberman, and R. L. Williams. 1989. "Pharmacists Recovering from Alcohol and Other Drug Addictions: An Interview Study." *American Pharmacy*, n.s., 29(6): 19–30.

Bissell, LeClair, and R. W. Jones. 1981. "The Alcoholic Nurse." *Nursing Outlook*, February: 96–101.

Bissell, LeClair, and Jane K. Skorina. 1987. "One Hundred Alcoholic Women in Medicine." *Journal of the American Medical Association*, 257: 2939–44.

"Bladder Buster." 1992. *Prevention Pipeline* (Center for Substance Abuse Prevention), January/February: 42.

Bliss, Shepherd, et al., eds. 1985. *The New Holistic Health Handbook: Living Well in a New Age*. Lexingon, Mass: Stephen Greene Press.

Blum, Kenneth, Michael C. Trachtenberg, and Gerald P. Kozlowski. 1989. "Cocaine Therapy: The 'Reward Cascade' Link." *Professional Counselor*, January/February: 27–35.

Blum, Kenneth, et al. 1996. "Reward Deficiency Syndrome." *American Scientist*, 84: 132–144.

Bohlmann, Brian J. 1995. "Binge Drinking in College." Letter to the editor. *Journal of the American Medical Association*, 273: 1903.

Borenstein, Daniel B. 1985. "Availability of Mental Health Resources for Residents in Academic Medical Centers." *Journal of Medical Education*, 60: 517–523.

Borenstein, Daniel B., and Karen Cook. 1982. "Impairment Prevention in the Training Years." *Journal of the American Medical Association*, 247: 2700–03.

Bowermaster, Don P. 1988. "Chemical Dependency and the Dental Student." *Dentistry*, December: 16–19.

——— 1989. "Chemical Dependency: Are Dental Students at Risk?" *Ohio Dental Journal*, 63(2): 26–30.

Brandon, Thomas H. 1994. "Negative Affect as Motivation to Smoke." *Current Directions in Psychological Science*, 3(2): 33–37.

Brandsma, J. M., M. C. Maultsby, Jr., and R. J. Welsh. 1980. *Outpatient Treatment of Alcoholism: A Review and Comparative Study.* Baltimore: University Park Press.

Brenner, Lawurence H. 1988. "Corporate Responsibility for Physician Impairment." *Quality Review Bulletin*, 14 (April): 123–128.

Brewster, J. M. 1986. "Prevalence of Alcohol and Other Drug Problems among Physicians." *Journal of the American Medical Association*, 255: 1913–20.

Brooke, Deborah, Griffith Edwards, and Colin Taylor. 1991. "Addiction as an Occupational Hazard: 144 Doctors with Drug and Alcohol Problems." *British Journal of Addictions*, 86: 1011–16.

Brumbaugh, A. G. 1993. "Acupuncture: New Perspectives in Chemical Dependency Treatment." *Journal of Substance Abuse Treatment*, 10: 35–43.

Buckley, William F., Jr. 1995. Weekly newspaper column, reprinted in American Sociological Association's Alcohol and Drugs Section newsletter, *Alcohol and Drugs*, 4 (Spring): 4–5.

"Bucky's Backyard, Quarter Beer Machines, and Other Forms of Perdition." 1989. *Texas Bar Journal*, March: 292–293.

Burke, Christopher. 1991. "Two Lives." *Rhode Island Bar Journal*, November: 6.

Busch, Linda. 1982. "Rehabilitating the Impaired Dentist: A Look at What the Profession Is Doing to Help." *Journal of the American Dental Association*, 105 (November): 781–787.

Bushman, Brad J. 1993. "Human Aggression While under the Influence of Alcohol and Other Drugs: An Integrative Research Review." *Current Directions in Psychological Science*, 2(5): 148–152.

Byrd, Randolph C. 1988. "Positive Therapeutic Effects of Intercessory Prayer in a Coronary Care Unit Population." *Southern Medical Journal*, 81: 826–829.

Canavan, David I. 1983. "The Impaired Physicians Program: Education." *Journal of the Medical Society of New Jersey*, 80: 205–206.

——— 1984. "Monitoring." *Journal of the Medical Society of New Jersey*, 81: 65–66.

Carey, Benedict. 1995. "The Drinking Cure." *Health*, July/August: 79–84.

Carey, Gale Beliveau. 1989. "Nutrition and Alcholism: Problems and Therapies." *Occupational Medicine: State of the Art Reviews*, 4(2): 311–323.

Carey, Kate B., and Michael P. Carey. 1993. "Changes in Self-Efficacy Resulting from Unaided Attempts to Quit Smoking." *Psychology of Addictive Behaviors*, 7: 219–224.

Carol. 1986. "Addicted Nurses." *NursingLife*, May/June: 41–43.

Cassell, Dana K. 1979. "Understanding the Alcoholic Dentist." *Dental Economics,* February: 52–57.

Cekola, Anna, and Susan Marquez Owen. 1994. "Doctor Convicted of 2nd-Degree Murder in 2 Traffic Deaths." *Los Angeles Times,* December 29: A3, A13.

Celis, William III. 1992. "As Computers Begin to Track Drugs, Fears of Snooping and Abuse Arise." *New York Times,* January 17: A7, A12.

Center for Substance Abuse Prevention. 1991. *What You Can Do about Drug Use in America.* (ADM)91-1572. Rockville, Md.: U.S. Department of Health and Human Services, National Clearinghouse for Alcohol and Drug Information.

———— 1994. *Directory of Projects, Faculty Development Program in Alcohol and Other Drug Abuse.* Rockville, Md.: U.S. Department of Health and Human Services, Substance Abuse and Mental Health Services Administration, Public Health Service.

Centers for Disease Control and Prevention. 1993. "Smoking Cessation during Previous Year among Adults—United States, 1990 and 1991." *Morbidity and Mortality Weekly Report,* 42 (July): 504–507.

Chappel, John N. 1991. "The Use of Alcoholics Anonymous and Narcotics Anonymous by the Physician in Treating Drug and Alcohol Addiction." In *Comprehensive Handbook of Drug and Alcohol Addiction,* ed. Norman S. Miller. New York: Marcel Dekker. Pp. 1079–88.

Chen, Edwin. 1989. "Data Bank on Physicians, Dentists to Start in April." *Los Angeles Times,* November 28: A4.

Christenson, Andrew, and Neil S. Jacobson. 1994. "Who (or What) Can Do Psychotherapy: The Status and Challenge of Non- Professional Therapies." *Psychological Science,* 5(1) (January): 8–14.

Christoff, Susan B. (Counsel-Clerk's Office, Supreme Court of Ohio). 1992. Personal communication, October 29.

Chopra, Deepak. 1991. *Perfect Health: The Complete Mind/Body Guide.* New York: Harmony Books.

Ciotti, Paul. 1988. "Unhappy Lawyers: They're Highly Trained and Highly Paid, So Why Do Many Feel So Low about Their Jobs?" *Los Angeles Times,* August 25: sec. V, pp. 1, 8–9.

Clark, David C. 1988. "Alcohol and Drug Use and Mood Disorders among Medical Students: Implications for Physician Impairment." *Quality Review Bulletin,* 14 (February): 50–54.

Clark, David C., and S. R. Daugherty. 1990. "A Norm-Referenced Longitudinal Study of Medical Student Drinking Patterns." *Journal of Substance Abuse,* 2: 15–37.

Clark, David C., and Peter B. Zeldow. 1988. "Vicissitudes of Depressed Mood during Four Years of Medical School." *Journal of the American Medical Association,* 260: 2521–28.

Clark, David C., et al. 1987. "Alcohol-Drug Use Patterns through Medical School: A Longitudinal Study of One Class." *Journal of the American Medical Association,* 257: 2921–26.

Clark, J. H., G. T. Chiodo, and F. F. Cowan. 1988. "Chemical Dependency among Dentists: Prevalence and Current Treatment." *General Dentistry*, 36: 227–229.

Clarno, J. C. 1986. "The Impaired Dentist: Recognition and Treatment of the Alcoholic and Drug-Dependent Professional." *Dental Clinics of North America*, 30(4): S45–53.

Cocores, James. 1991. "Outpatient Treatment of Drug and Alcohol Addiction." In *Comprehensive Handbook of Drug and Alcohol Addiction*, ed. Norman S. Miller. New York: Marcel Dekker. Pp. 1213–22.

Commission on Substance Abuse at Colleges and Universities. 1994. *Rethinking Rites of Passage: Substance Abuse on America's Campuses*. New York: Center on Addiction and Substance Abuse, Columbia University.

Conard, Scott, et al. 1988. "Substance Use by Fourth-Year Students at 13 U.S. Medical Schools." *Journal of Medical Education*, 63: 747–757.

Coombs, Robert H. 1978. *Mastering Medicine: Professional Socialization in Medical School*. New York: Free Press.

——— 1981a. "Back on the Streets: Therapeutic Communities' Impact upon Drug Users." *American Journal of Drug and Alcohol Abuse*, 8(2): 185–201.

——— 1981b. "Drug Abuse as Career." *Journal of Drug Issues*, 11(4): 369–387.

——— 1986. "The Impaired Physician Syndrome: A Developmental Perspective." In *Heal Thyself: The Health of Health Professionals*, ed. Cynthia Scott and Joanne Hawk. New York: Brunner/Mazel. Pp. 44–55.

——— 1991. "Marital Status and Personal Well-Being: A Literature Review." *Family Relations: Journal of Applied Family and Child Studies*, 40: 97–102.

———, ed. 1975. *Junkies and Straights: The Camarillo Experience*. Lexington, Mass: Lexington Books.

——— 1988. *The Family Context of Adolescent Drug Use*. New York: Haworth Press.

Coombs, Robert H., and Kate Coombs. 1988. "Developmental Stages in Drug Use: Changing Family Involvements." *Journal of Chemical Dependency Treatment*, 1(2): 73–98.

Coombs, Robert H., and Hori Hovanessian. 1988. "Stress in the Role Constellation of Female Resident Physicians." *Journal of the American Medical Women's Association*, 43 (January/February): 21–27.

Coombs, Robert H., and Morris J. Paulson. 1990. "Is Premedical Education Dehumanizing?" *Journal of Medical Humanities*, 11(1) (Spring): 13–22.

Coombs, Robert H., Karen Perell, and J. Ruckh. 1990. "Primary Prevention of Emotional Impairment among Medical Trainees." *Academic Medicine: Journal of the Association of American Medical Colleges*, 65: 567–581.

Coombs, Robert H., and Jill St. John. 1979. *Making It in Medical School*. Jamaica, N.Y.: Spectrum Publications Medical and Scientific Books. Reprint, Los Angeles: Medicine and Society Press, 1981.

Coombs, Robert H., and Bernard Virshup. 1994. "Enhancing the Psychological Health of Medical Students: The Student Well-Being Committee." Special issue, *Medical Education* (U.K.), 28: 47–54.

——— 1995. "The Helping Professionals." In *Handbook of Drug Abuse Preven-*

tion: A Comprehensive Strategy to Prevent the Abuse of Alcohol and Other Drugs, ed. Robert H. Coombs and Douglas Ziedonis. Boston: Allyn and Bacon.

Coombs, Robert H., et al. 1993. "Medical Slang and Its Functions." *Social Science and Medicine: An International Journal,* 36(8): 987–998.

Coombs, Robert H., Lincoln J. Fry, and Patricia Lewis, eds. 1976. *Socialization in Drug Abuse.* Cambridge, Mass: Schenkman Publishing/Transaction Books.

Coombs, Robert H., D. Scott May, and Gary W. Small, eds. 1986. *Inside Doctoring: Stages and Outcomes in the Professional Development of Physicians.* New York: Praeger.

Coombs, Robert H., and Louis J. West, eds. 1991. *Drug Testing: Issues and Options.* New York: Oxford University Press.

Coombs, Robert H., and Douglas Ziedonis, eds. 1995. *Handbook of Drug Abuse Prevention: A Comprehensive Strategy to Prevent the Abuse of Alcohol and Other Drugs.* Boston: Allyn and Bacon.

Cosper, R., and Florence Hughes. 1982. "So-Called Heavy Drinking Occupations: Two Empirical Tests." *Journal of Studies on Alcohol,* 43: 110–118.

Crawshaw, Ralph, et al. 1980. "An Epidemic of Suicide among Physicians on Probation." *Journal of the American Medical Association,* 243: 1915–17.

Crosby, Linda R. 1995. Personal communication.

——— 1996. "Taking Steps to Heal Mind, Body, and Spirit." *Georgia Dental Association Action,* May: 20.

Crosby, Linda R., and LeClair Bissell. 1989. *To Care Enough: Intervention with Chemically Dependent Colleagues. A Guide for Healthcare and Other Professionals.* Minneapolis: Johnson Institute.

Cross, Gerald M., et al. 1990. "Alcoholism Treatment: A Ten-Year Follow-up Study." *Alcoholism: Clinical and Experimental Research,* 14(2): 169–173.

Cruse, J. 1981. "Confronting Impaired Colleagues with Compassion." *Consultant,* November: 297–302.

Cullan, Daniel B., and Samuel K. Cullan. 1991. "Black Marks on Your Soul . . . : The National Practitioner Data Bank." *Missouri Medicine,* 88(5) (May): 285–288.

Cummings, Nicholas A. 1991. "Inpatient versus Outpatient Treatment of Substance Abuse: Recent Developments in the Controversy." *Contemporary Family Therapy,* 13 (October): 507–520.

Davies, John Booth. 1992. *The Myth of Addiction: An Application of the Psychological Theory of Attribution to Illicit Drug Use.* New York: Harwood Academic.

Davis, Thomas N. 1992. "Can Prayer Facilitate Healing and Growth?" Paper presented at the California Society of Addiction Medicine, preconference review course and workshops, November 5–7, Long Beach.

Dean's Office, UCLA School of Nursing. 1995. Personal communication, July.

Delbanco, Andrew, and Thomas Delbanco. 1995. "AA at the Crossroads." *New Yorker,* March 20: 50–53, 59–63.

Dickinson, Kenneth M. 1988. "The Recovering Impaired Pharmacist: Re-entry into Practice." *Pennsylvania Pharmacist,* June: 216–217.

Dixon, K. 1988. "Employee Assistance Programs: A Primer for Buyer and Seller." *Hospital and Community Psychiatry,* 39: 623–627.

Dizon, Lily, and Leslie Berkman. 1993. "Doctor Arrested in Head-on Collision That Killed Two and Injured Three." *Los Angeles Times,* July 13: D3.

Dossey, Larry. 1993. *The Power of Prayer and the Practice of Medicine.* New York: HarperCollins.

Dowell, Laurie Bilz. 1988. "Attorneys and Alcoholism." *North Kentucky Law Review,* 16: 169–189.

Dr. Jon. 1992. "The Nitrous Nightmare." In *Dentistry Faces Addiction: How to Be Part of the Solution,* ed. Arthur G. Williams. New York: Mosby Year Book. Pp. 39–40.

Drug Abuse and Drug Abuse Resarch. 1991. The Third Triennial Report to Congress from the Secretary. (ADM)91-1704. Washington, D.C.: U.S. Department of Health and Human Services.

Drugs, Crime & Campaign '94. 1994. Forum at the National Press Club, Washington, D.C., cosponsored by Drug Strategies and the Washington Center for Politics and Journalism, April 5.

"Drug Testing for Highflyers." 1991. *Time.* March 4: 65.

Eaton, William J. 1994. "College Binge Drinking Soars, Study Finds." *Los Angeles Times,* June 8: A21.

Eigen, Lewis D. 1992. "New Problems, New Challenges on Campus." *Prevention Pipeline* (Center for Substance Abuse Prevention), September/October: 85.

——— 1995. "College Students." In *Handbook of Drug Abuse Prevention: A Comprehensive Strategy to Prevent the Abuse of Alcohol and Other Drugs,* ed. Robert H. Coombs and Douglas Ziedonis. Boston: Allyn & Bacon. Pp. 267–298.

"Elected Officials Endorse Treatment." 1992. *SOAR Foundation Special Report* (Des Moines), June: 1–8.

Elliot, Robert W. N.d. "Substance Abuse: Myths and Facts." Manuscript. Available from Robert W. Elliot, 629 27th St., Manhattan Beach, CA 90266.

Ellis, Albert. 1962. *Reason and Emotion in Psychotherapy.* North Vale, N.J.: Lyle Stuart.

Ellis, Albert, and Eugene Schoenfeld. 1990. "Divine Intervention and the Treatment of Chemical Dependency." Editorial. *Journal of Substance Abuse,* 2: 459–468.

Elzea, Debby. 1989. "Employee Assistance Programs." *Georgia State Bar Journal,* 25: 118.

"Employed Pharmacists Share Job Concerns, Recommend Ways to Increase Job Satisfaction." 1990. *American Pharmacy,* n.s., 30: 32–33.

Emrick, C. D. 1989. "Alcoholics Anonymous: Membership Characteristics and Effectiveness as Treatment." In *Recent Developments in Alcoholism,* ed. Marc Galanter. New York: Plenum. Pp. 37–53.

Erickson, Carlton. 1995. "The Neurochemistry of Craving." *Treatment Today,* 7(2) (Summer): 8–9.

Fawzy, Fawzy I., Robert H. Coombs, and Barry Gerber. 1983. "Generational

Continuity in the Use of Substances: The Impact of Parental Substance Use on Adolescent Substance Use." *Addictive Behaviors,* 8: 109–114.

Finkelstein, Peter. 1986. "Studies in the Anatomy Laboratory: A Portrait of Individual and Collective Defense." In *Inside Doctoring: Stages and Outcomes in the Professional Development of Physicians,* ed. Robert H. Coombs, D. Scott May, and Gary W. Small. New York: Praeger. Pp. 22–43.

Finn, Peter, and Andrea Kay Newlyn. 1993. "Miami's Drug Court: A Different Approach." National Institute of Justice, Program Focus, U.S. Department of Justice, Washington, D.C., June.

Finnegan, John, and Daphe Gray. 1990. *Recovery from Addiction: A Comprehensive Understanding of Substance Abuse with Nutritional Therapies for Recovering Addicts and Co-Dependents.* Berkeley, Calif.: Celestial Arts.

Fisher, J., R. Mason, and K. Keeley. 1975. "Physicians and Alcoholics: The Effect of Medical Training on Attitudes towards Alcoholics." *Journal of Studies on Alcohol,* 36: 949–955.

Fisher, Karen, and Ellen Weisman. 1988. "Special Issue on Impaired Health Care Professionals." *Quality Review Bulletin,* 14 (April): 98–99.

Flynn, C. F., et al. 1993. "Alcoholism and Treatment in Airline Aviators—One Company's Results." *Aviation, Space, and Environmental Medicine,* April: 314–318.

"A Foolish Capacity: I'm a Chemically Dependent Dentist/Case II." 1990. *Journal of the California Dental Association,* 18 (February): 49.

Ford, C. V. 1983. "Emotional Distress in Internship and Residency: A Questionnaire Study." *Psychiatric Medicine,* 1: 143–150.

Fotos, Christopher P. 1989. "NTSB Asserts Captain's Cocaine Use Contributed to Crash of Continental Express Metro 3." *Aviation Week and Space Technology,* February 6: 59.

Friel, John, and Linda Friel. 1988. *Adult Children: The Secrets of Dysfunctional Families.* Deerfield Beach, Fla.: Health Communications.

Friesendorf, Sarah. 1994. " 'Lucky' Attorney Drank Her Way through Life." *California Bar Journal,* June: 6.

"From Joker to Justice." 1992. *Texas Bar Journal,* March: 252–253.

Fulco, Carolyn E., Catharyn T. Liverman, and Laurence E. Farley, eds. 1995. *Development of Medications for the Treatment of Opiate and Cocaine Addictions: Issues for the Government and Private Sector.* Washington, D.C.: National Academy Press.

Furtado, Teo. 1992. "Drugs: The Over-the-Counter Culture." *People,* July 6: 28, 30.

Gabbard, Glen O. 1985. "The Role of Compulsiveness in the Normal Physician." *Journal of the American Medical Association,* 254: 2926–29.

Galanter, Marc. 1991. "Office Practice in Drug and Alcohol Addiction." In *Comprehensive Handbook of Drug and Alcohol Addiction,* ed. Norman S. Miller. New York: Marcel Dekker. Pp. 1223–30.

——— 1993. "Network Therapy for Substance Abuse: A Clinical Trial." *Psychotherapy,* 30(2): 251–258.

——— 1994. "Network Therapy for the Office Practitioner." In *The American*

Psychiatric Press Textbook of Substance Abuse Treatment, ed. Marc Galanter and Herbert D. Kleber. Washington, D.C. Pp. 253–262.

Galanter, Marc, Susan Egelko, and Helen Edwards. 1993. "Rational Recovery: Alternative to AA for Addiction?" *American Journal of Drug and Alcohol Addiction,* 19(4): 499–510.

Galanter, Marc, et al. 1990. "Combined Alcoholics Anonymous and Professional Care for Addicted Physicians." *American Journal of Psychiatry,* 147: 64–68.

Galbraith, John Kenneth. 1971. *The New Industrial State.* Boston: Houghton Mifflin.

Galbraith, Susan, and Christine Lubinski. 1992. "Alcohol and Drug Problems among Women." In *Dentistry Faces Addiction: How to Be Part of the Solution,* ed. Arthur G. Williams. New York: Mosby Year Book.

Gallagher, Winifred. 1986. "The Looming Menace of Designer Drugs." *Discover,* August: 24–35.

Gallegos, Karl V., and Merrill Norton. 1984. "Characterization of Georgia's Impaired Physicians Program Treatment Population: Data and Statistics." *Journal of the Medical Association of Georgia,* 73 (November): 755–758.

Gallegos, Karl V., et al. 1988. "Addiction in Anesthesiologists: Drug Access and Patterns of Substance Abuse." *Quarterly Review Board,* 14 (April): 116–122.

Gelderloos, Paul, et al. 1991. "Effectiveness of the Transcendental Meditation Program in Preventing and Treating Substance Misuse: A Review." *International Journal of the Addictions,* 26(3): 293–325.

Gelernter, Joel, David Goldman, and Neil Risch. 1993. "The A-1 Allele at the D2 Dopamine Receptor Gene and Alcoholism: A Reappraisal." *Journal of the American Medical Association,* 269: 1673–77.

Gellene, Denise. 1995. "New 'Draft' Soft Drink Stirs a Brouhaha." *Los Angeles Times,* July 21: D1, D3.

"The Genetics of Alcoholism." 1992. *Alcohol Alert* (National Institute of Alcohol Abuse and Alcoholism, U.S. Public Health Service), 328(18): 1–4.

Gentilello, Larry M., et al. 1995. "Alcohol Interventions in Trauma Care." *Journal of the American Medical Association,* 274: 1043–47.

Gerstein, Dean R., and Henrick J. Harwood, eds. 1990. *Treating Drug Problems.* Washington, D.C.: National Academy Press.

Gillespie, E. 1987. "Don't Drop Your Zipper for the Gipper." *New Statesman,* December: xix.

Girard, D. E., et al. 1980. "Survival of the Medical Internship." *Forum Medicine,* 3: 460–463.

Gladden, Joan (California Physician's Diversion Program). 1994. Personal communication.

Glasser, William. 1976. *Positive Addictions.* New York: Harper and Row.

Goff, Michelle. 1987. "The Oregon State Bar Professional Liability Fund Attorney Assistance Program." In *Drug Free Workplace: A Guide for Supervisors,* ed. Dale A. Msai. Washington, D.C.: Buraff. Pp. 145–151.

Golden, Sarah J., Edward J. Khantzian, and William E. McAuliffe. 1994. "Group

Therapy." In *The American Psychiatric Press Textbook of Substance Abuse Treatment,* ed. Marc Galanter and Herbert D. Kleber. Washington, D.C. Pp. 303–315.

Goldman, Brian. 1991. "How to Thwart a Drug Seeker." *Emergency Medicine,* March 30.

Goodwin, D. W. 1985. "Alcoholism and Genetics." *Archives of General Psychiatry,* 42: 171–174.

Gordis, Enoch. 1995. Open letter from Director, National Institute on Alcohol Abuse and Alcoholism, U.S. Department of Health and Human Services, Public Health Service, February 6.

Gordon, Gregory. 1991. "FAA Figures Show 400 Pilots Convicted of Alcohol Offenses." *Des Moines Register,* September 23: 3A.

Gorelick, David A. 1993. "Overview of Pharmacologic Treatment Approaches for Alcohol and Other Drug Addiction: Intoxication, Withdrawal, and Relapse Prevention." *Psychiatric Clinics of North America,* 16(1) (March): 141–156.

Granfield, Robert, and William Cloud. 1994. "Terminating Addiction Naturally: Post Addict Identity and the Avoidance of Treatment." Paper presented at the annual meeting of the American Sociological Association, Los Angeles, August.

Graves, Tucker. 1992. "Party Time Means Problem Time." *Texas Bar Journal,* March: 261.

Green, Pat. 1989. "The Chemically Dependent Nurse." *Nursing Clinics of North America,* 24 (March): 81–94.

Greenstein, Robert A., Paul J. Fudala, and Charles P. O'Brien. 1992. "Alternative Pharmacotherapies for Opiate Addiction." In *Substance Abuse: A Comprehensive Textbook,* ed. Joyce H. Lowinson, Pedro Ruiz, and Robert B. Millman. Baltimore: Williams and Wilkins. Pp. 562–573.

Grisham, John. 1992. *A Time to Kill.* New York: Dell.

Gropper, Bernard A., and Judy A. Reardon. 1993. "Developing Drug Testing by Hair Analysis." National Institute of Justice, Research in Brief, U.S. Department of Justice, Washington, D.C., October.

Groves, James E. 1978. "Taking Care of the Hateful Patient." *New England Journal of Medicine,* 298: 883–887.

Gualtieri, Antony C., Joseph P. Cosentino, and Jerome S. Becker. 1983. "The California Experience with a Diversion Program for Impaired Physicians." *Journal of the American Medical Association,* 249: 226–229.

Haack, Mary R. 1988. "Stress and Impairment among Nursing Students." *Research in Nursing and Health,* 11: 125–143.

Haack, Mary R., and Thomas C. Harford. 1984. "Drinking Patterns among Student Nurses." *International Journal of the Addictions,* 19(5): 577–583.

Haaga, John G., and Elizabeth A. McGlynn. 1993. *The Drug Abuse Treatment System: Prospects for Reform.* Santa Monica, Calif.: Drug Policy Research Center, Rand Corporation.

Hackett, P., Mary Henry, and Mary P. Manke. 1991. "Courses in Substance Use and Abuse: A Survey of Colleges and Universities." *Journal of Alcohol and Drug Education,* 37(1): 58–64.

Haislip, Gene R. 1993. "Drug Diversion Control Systems, Medical Practice, and Patient Care." In *Impact of Prescription Drug Control Systems on Medical Practice and Patient Care,* ed. James R. Cooper et al. NIH 93-3507. Rockville, Md.: U.S. Department of Health and Human Services, Public Health Service. Pp. 120–131.

Haldane, David. 1990. "Legal Remedies." *Los Angeles Times,* June 7: E1–2.

Hallgren, Jeanette, and Bill Beach. 1989. "Addiction among Nurses: Facing the Issue." *AARN,* January: 25–26.

Halzer, John E., Audrey Burnham, and Lawerence McEvoy. 1991. "Alcohol Use and Dependence." In *Psychiatric Disorders in America: The Epidemiologic Catchment Area Study,* ed. Lee N. Robins and Darrel A. Regier. New York: Free Press. Pp. 81–115.

Hanson, Judith. 1992. "Attorneys and Judges Assistance Programs." *Hawaii Bar News,* March: 26.

"A Hard Charging, Hard Drinking Trial Lawyer." 1989. *Texas Bar Journal,* March: 294–295.

Harper, Charles R. 1983. "Airline Pilot Alcoholism: One Airline's Experience." *Aviation, Space, and Environmental Medicine,* July: 590–591.

Harrison, Patricia Ann, Norman G. Hoffman, and Susan G. Streed. 1991. "Drug and Alcohol Treatment Outcome." In *Comprehensive Handbook of Drug and Alcohol Addiction,* ed. Norman S. Miller. New York: Marcel Dekker. Pp. 1163–97.

Hazelden Physician Survey. 1996. Center City, Minn.: Hazelden Educational Services.

Hernandez, Tom. 1993. "Members of SOS Abandon the AA Ship and Save Themselves." *Sober Times,* February: 39.

Hester, Reid K. 1994. "Outcome Research: Alcoholism." In *The American Psychiatric Press Textbook of Substance Abuse Treatment,* ed. Marc Galanter and Herbert D. Kleber. Washington, D.C. Pp. 35–44.

Hester, Thomas W., ed. 1989. *Professionals and Their Addictions.* Macon, Ga.: Charter Medical.

Hiatt, John F. 1986. "Spirituality, Medicine, and Healing." *Southern Medical Journal,* 79: 736–743.

Hickey, Mary C. 1990. "Attorney Alcoholism." *Washington Lawyer,* March/April: 32–42.

"The High and the Mighty." 1990. Editorial. *Los Angeles Times,* August 22: B6.

Hilfiker, David. 1986. *Healing the Wounds: A Physician Looks at His Work.* New York: Pantheon.

Hirning, Fred. 1991. "Pharmacists Are Not Immune." *California Journal of Hospital Pharmacy,* March: 12–15, 18.

Hochschild, Arlie. 1989. *The Second Shift.* New York: Avon.

Hodge, Judy. 1988. "A Special Report. Nurses and Drugs: A Hidden Problem?" *Good Housekeeping,* February: 87–90.

Hoffman, Norman G. 1993. "Continuing Care Is a Good Investment." *Professional Update* (Betty Ford Center), 2 (Spring): A–C.

Holloway, Marguerite. 1991. "Trends in Pharmacology—Rx for Addiction." *Scientific American,* 264: 94–103.

Hubbard, Robert L. 1992. "Evaluation and Treatment Outcome." In *Substance Abuse: A Comprehensive Textbook,* ed. Joyce H. Lowinson, Pedro Ruiz, and Robert B. Millman. Baltimore: Williams and Wilkins. Pp. 596–611.

Hubbard, Robert L., et al. 1984. "Treatment Outcome Prospective Study (TOPS): Client Characteristics and Behaviors before, during, and after Treatment." In *Drug Abuse Treatment Evaluation: Strategies, Progress, and Prospects.* Rockville, Md.: U.S. Department of Health and Human Services, National Institute on Drug Abuse.

Hubbard, Robert L., et al., eds. 1989. *Drug Abuse Treatment: A National Study of Effectiveness.* Chapel Hill: University of North Carolina Press.

Hudson, Mary Ann. 1994. "Delino DeShields Is Taking a New Tack." *Los Angeles Times,* March 2: C1, C10.

Hughes, Patrick H., et al. 1991. "Resident Physician Substance Use in the U.S." *Journal of the American Medical Association,* 265: 2069–73.

——— 1992. "Prevalence of Substance Use among U.S. Physicians." *Journal of the American Medical Association,* 267: 2333–39.

Huie, H. Stel, and Donna L. Spilis. 1991. "Preparing for the Unexpected: Leave for Treatment of Chemical Dependency—One Firm's Experience." *Oregon State Bar Bulletin,* August/September: 35–37.

Hurwitz, T. A., et al. 1987. "Impaired Interns and Residents." *Canadian Journal of Psychiatry,* 32 (April): 165–169.

Hutchinson, Sally A. 1987. "Chemically Dependent Nurses: Implications for Nurse Exectuvies." *Journal of Nursing Administration,* 17: 23–29.

Ikeda, Richard, and Chet Pelton. 1990. "Diversion Programs for Impaired Physicians." *Western Journal of Medicine,* 152(5): 617–621.

"I'm a Chemically Dependent Dentist." 1990. *Journal of the California Dental Association,* 18 (February): 17, 25.

"I'm a Dentist and a Drug Addict." 1990. *Missouri Dental,* 70(4) (July/August): 16–20.

"I'm a Doctor and a Drug Addict." 1980. *Medical Economics,* 18 (February): 90.

"An Inherited Problem/Case III." 1990. *Journal of the California Dental Association,* 18 (February): 55.

Institute of Medicine. 1989. *Prevention and Treatment of Alcohol Problems: Research Opportunities.* Report of a Study by a Committee of the Institute of Medicine, Division of Mental Health and Behavioral Medicine. Washington, D.C.: National Academy Press.

——— 1994. *Development of Anti-Addiction Medications: Issues for the Government and Private Sector.* Washington, D.C.: Institute of Medicine, Division of Biobehavioral Sciences and Mental Disorders.

International Doctors of Alcoholics Anonymous. N.d. "History and Objectives." Membership form.

"It's O.K. to Feel Bad." 1994. *Prevention Pipeline* (Center for Substance Abuse Prevention), March/April: 123.

Jacobsen, Gary A. 1991. "Puzzled by Addiction?" *Oregon State Bar Bulletin*, August/September: 21–23.

Jaffe, Dennis T. 1980. *Healing from Within*. New York: Alfred A. Knopf.

Jalon, Allan. 1986. "Inside the Pill Trade." *Los Angeles Times Magazine*, June 8: 10–15, 23–24, 26.

Jarvis, Janice. 1984. "The Nurse, the Addict." *Fort Worth Star Telegram*, April 8: C1.

Jennings, P. S. 1991. "To Surrender to Drugs: Grief Process in Its Own Rite." *Journal of Substance Abuse Treatment*, 8: 221–226.

Jim. 1992. "Learning the Truth Too Late." Conference syllabus, American Bar Association, International Workshop on Lawyer Substance Abuse, sponsored by the Commission on Impaired Attorneys, San Diego, September 15–18.

Johns Hopkins University. 1990. Press release, December 6.

Johnson, N. Peter (University of South Carolina Department of Neuropsychiatry and Biobehavioral Science, Columbia, S.C.). 1990. Personal communication.

Johnson, Richard P., and John C. Connelly. 1981. "Addicted Physicians: A Closer Look," *Journal of the American Medical Association*, 245: 253–257.

Johnson, Vernon. 1973. *I'll Quit Tomorrow*. New York: Harper and Row.

Johnston, Lloyd D., Patrick M. O'Malley, and J. G. Bachman. 1994. *National Survey Results on Drug Use from the Monitoring the Future Study, 1975–1993*. Vol. 2 of *College Students and Young Adults*. Rockville, Md.: University of Michigan Institute for Social Research and National Institute on Drug Abuse, U.S. Department of Health and Human Services, Public Health Service.

Kabb, Greer M. 1984. "Chemical Dependency: Helping Your Staff." *Journal of Nursing Administration*, 14: 18–23.

Kahler, Joseph K. 1989. "Special Issues and Character of the Alcoholic Professional." *Texas Bar Journal*, March: 288–289.

Kaminer, Wendy. 1992. *I'm Dysfunctional, You're Dysfunctional: The Recovery Movement and Other Self-Help Fashions*. Reading, Mass: Addison-Wesley.

Kandel, D. B., R. C. Kessler, and R. Z. Margulies. 1978. "Antecedents of Adolescent Initiation into Stages of Drug Use: A Developmental Analysis." *Journal of Youth and Adolescence*, 7(1): 13–40.

Kaskutas, Lee. 1989. "Women for Sobriety: A Qualitative Analysis." *Contemporary Drug Problems*, 16 (Summer): 177–200.

——— 1994. "What Do Women Get out of Self-Help? Reasons for Attending Women in Sobriety and AA." *Journal of Substance Abuse Treatment*, 11: 185–194.

Kathleen. 1992. "A Woman's Fight with Alcohol." Conference syllabus, American Bar Association, International Workshop on Lawyer Substance Abuse, sponsored by the Commission on Impaired Attorneys, San Diego, September 15–18.

Kaufman, Edward. 1994. "Family Therapy: Other Drugs." In *The American Psychiatric Press Textbook of Substance Abuse Treatment,* ed. Marc Galanter and Herbert D. Kleber. Washington, D.C. Pp. 331–350.

Kaufman, Edward, and Linda Borders. 1988. "Ethnic Family Differences in Adolescent Substance Use." In *The Family Context of Adolescent Drug Use,* ed. Robert H. Coombs. New York: Haworth Press. Pp. 99–121.

Kaufman, Edward, and J. P. McNaul. 1992. "Recent Developments in Understanding and Treating Drug Abuse and Dependency." *Hospital and Community Psychiatry,* 43: 223–236.

KCET Video Lifeguides. 1991. *The Journey Back: Professionals Recovering from Addiction.* Videotape. Hosted by Michael Meyers, M.D. Los Angeles.

Keegan, John W. 1995. Open letter to members of the American Bar Association, reporting on Model Lawyer Assistance Program, June 7.

Kempster, Norman. 1993. "What Really Happened at Tailhook Convention." *Los Angeles Times,* April 24: A1, A18.

Kendall, James D. 1987. "The Chemically Impaired Pharmacist: The Right Approach." *Topics in Hospital Pharmacy Management,* 7(3) (November): 84–92.

——— 1991. "Considerations in Employing a Pharmacist Recovering from Chemical Dependence." *American Journal of Hospital Pharmacy,* 48: 326–329.

Kern, Marc. n.d. "Unhooking Your Habits: A Lifetime Mastery Training Course with Your Own Personal Addiction Therapist." Mimeograph. Life Management Skills, West Los Angeles.

——— 1993. "Overcoming Your Bad Habits." Workshop presented in Woodland Hills, Calif., November.

——— 1994. *Take Control Now.* West Los Angeles: Life Management Skills.

——— 1995. Personal communication.

Khantzian, Edward J. 1985. "The Self-Medication Hypothesis of Addictive Disorders: Focus on Heroin and Cocaine Dependence." *American Journal of Psychiatry,* 142: 1259–64.

Khouzam, Hani R. 1993. "Spirituality and Recovery from Opiate Dependence." Letter to the editor. *Substance Abuse,* 14: 166–167.

Kilburg, Richard R., Peter E. Nathan, and Richard W. Thoreson. 1986. "Alcoholism Treatment for Professionals." In *Professionals in Distress: Issues, Syndromes, and Solutions in Psychology,* ed. Kilburg, Nathan, and Thoreson. Washington, D.C.: American Psychiatric Press. Pp. 92–117.

Kirkpatrick, Jean. 1977. *Turnabout: New Help for Women Alcoholics.* New York: Bantam Books.

Kishline, Audrey. 1994. *Moderate Drinking: The New Option for Problem Drinkers.* Tucson: See Sharp Press.

Kleber, Herbert D. 1994. "Opioids: Detoxification." In *The American Psychiatric Press Textbook of Substance Abuse Treatment,* ed. Marc Galanter and Herbert D. Kleber. Washington, D.C. Pp. 191–208.

Kleiman, Mark A. R. 1992. *Against Excess: Drug Policy for Results.* New York: Basic Books.

Kliner, Dale J., Jerry Spicer, and Peggy Barnett. 1980. "Treatment Outcomes of Alcoholic Physicians." *Journal of Studies on Alcohol,* 41: 1217–20.

Kloeffler, Gale D. 1986. "Dentistry's Conspiracy of Silence: Chemical Dependency and Rehabilitation in Dentistry." *California Dental Association Journal,* 14 (February): 28–31.

Koenenn, Connie. 1995. "Just How Dangerous Is Your Job, Anyway?" *Los Angeles Times,* July 20: E1, E9.

Kotzsch, R. E. 1993. "Brain Fitness—Develop Your Powers of Mind." *Natural Health,* May–June: 159–160.

Kramer, Peter D. 1993. *Listening to Prozac: A Psychiatrist Explores Antidepressant Drugs and the Remaking of the Self.* New York: Viking.

"Kudzu Extract May Cut Alcohol Craving (Harvard Medical School Research)." 1993. *Los Angeles Times,* November 1: A20.

Kuhn, Clifford C. 1988. "A Spiritual Inventory of the Medically Ill Patient." *Psychiatric Medicine,* 6: 87–99.

LaGodna, Gretchen E., and Melva Jo Hendrix. 1989. "Impaired Nurses: A Cost Analysis." *Journal of Nursing Administration,* 19: 13–17.

Lahoz, Monina, and Holly L. Mason. 1990. "Burnout among Pharmacists." *American Pharmacy,* n.s., 30: 28–33.

Landry, Paige (National Nurses' Society on Addictions, Raleigh, N.C.). 1995. Personal communication, July 18.

Langenburcher, James W. 1994. "Rx for Health Care Costs: Result in Addictions in the General Medical Setting." *Alcoholism: Clinical and Experimental Research,* 18(5): 1033–36.

——— 1995. Personal communication, July.

Langenburcher, James W., et al. 1993. *Socioeconomic Evaluation of Addictions Treatment.* Washington, D.C.: U.S. Government Printing Office.

"Lawyer's Assistance Programme—Codependency—Part II." 1992. *The Advocate,* 50: 623–625.

Lawyers Concerned for Lawyers. N.d. *Where There Is a Problem . . . There Is Hope.* Brochure. Copies available from P.O. Box 11901, Harrisburg, PA 17108-1901.

Leahy, Vincent F. 1991. "I Am an Alcoholic. I Am Also a Judge." *Family Advocate,* Summer: 52–53.

LeDoux, Joseph E. 1994. "Emotion, Memory, and the Brain." *Scientific American,* 270: 50–57.

Lee, Cynthia. 1993. "Clinic Helps Patients Cope with Fear of Dentists." *UCLA Today,* 14 (January): 6–7.

Lewis, David C. 1986. "Doctors and Drugs." *New England Journal of Medicine,* 315: 826–828.

——— 1991. "Comparison of Alcoholism and Other Medical Diseases: An Internist's View." *Psychiatric Annals,* 215: 256–264.

——— 1995. "Fighting the War on Drugs." *Prevention Pipeline* (Center for Substance Abuse Prevention), March/April: 52–59.

Lewis, David C., et al. 1987. "A Review of Medical Education in Alcohol and

Other Drug Abuse." *Journal of the American Medical Association,* 257: 2945–48.

Lewy, Robert. 1988. "Pre-Employment Drug-Testing of Housestaff Physicians." *New York State Journal of Medicine,* October: 553–554.

Lippman, Helen. 1992. "Addicted Nurses: Tolerated, Tormented, or Treated?" *RN,* April: 36–41.

Litman, G. K. 1986. "Alcoholism Survival: The Prevention of Relapse." In *Treating Addictive Behaviors: Processes of Change,* ed. W. R. Miller and N. Heather. New York: Plenum. Pp. 391–405.

Little, L. F. 1988. Presentation at the Third Annual Conference on Work and Mental Health. *Journal of the American Medical Association,* 259: 3097–98.

Lutsky, Irving, et al. 1991. "Substance Abuse by Anesthesiology Residents." *Academic Medicine,* 66: 164–166.

Madera, Edward, ed. N.d. *Self-Help Source Book.* Denville, N.J.: Self-Help Clearing House, St. Clare's Riverside Hospital.

Mäkelä, Klaus. 1996. *Alcoholics Anonymous as a Mutual-Help Movement.* Madison: University of Wisconsin Press.

Malaman, Geoff. 1993. "Softball Used to Help Alcoholics Recover." *Culver City Star/Westchester Star,* August 25: 3.

Mammo, Abate, and Donald F. Weinbaum. 1993. "Some Factors That Influence Dropping Out from Outpatient Alcoholism Treatment Facilities." *Journal of Studies on Alcohol,* 54(1): 92–101.

Mann, George A. 1991. "History and Theory of a Treatment for Drug and Alcohol Addiction." In *Comprehensive Handbook of Drug and Alcohol Addiction,* ed. Norman S. Miller. New York: Marcel Dekker. Pp. 1201–12.

Mark. 1992. Quoted in Donald Muccigrosso and Donna L. Spilis, "Salvation for Solos: Help for Recovery from Addiction." Conference syllabus, American Bar Association, International Workshop on Lawyer Substance Abuse, sponsored by the Commission on Impaired Attorneys, San Diego, September 15–18.

Markham, Margaret. 1981. "Alcoholism among Pilots May Be on Increase." *Psychiatric News,* July 3: 9.

Marlatt, G. Alan. 1985a. "Relapse Prevention: Theoretical Rationale and Overview of the Model." In *Relapse Prevention: Maintenance Strategies in the Treatment of Addictive Behaviors,* ed. G. Alan Marlatt and Judith R. Gordon. New York: Guilford Press. Pp. 3–70.

——— 1985b. "Situational Determinants of Relapse and Skill-Training Interventions." In ibid., pp. 71–127.

——— 1985c. "Cognitive Assessment and Intervention Procedures for Relapse Prevention." In ibid., pp. 201–275.

Marlatt, G. Alan, and Kimberly Barrett. 1994. "Relapse Prevention." In *The American Psychiatric Press Textbook of Substance Abuse Treatment,* ed. Marc Galanter and Herbert D. Kleber. Washington, D.C. Pp. 285–302.

Marlatt, G. Alan, and Judith R. Gordon, eds. 1985. *Relapse Prevention: Maintenance Strategies in the Treatment of Addictive Behaviors.* New York: Guilford Press.

Martin, Albert R. 1986. "Stress in Residency: A Challenge to Personal Growth." *Journal of General Internal Medicine*, 1 (July/August): 252–257.

Martinez, Esperison. 1987. "FAA Gives Pilots Amnesty." *Airline Pilot*, December: 6.

Massing, Michael. 1992. "Under the Influence." *Modern Maturity*, February/March: 38–41, 93.

Matrix Center. 1991. *The Matrix Model for the Outpatient Treatment of Alcohol Related Problems: A Therapist Manual.* Beverly Hills.

Maugh, Thomas H., II. 1995. "U.S. Approves First New Drug to Treat Alcoholism in 47 Years." *Los Angeles Times*, January 17: A14.

McAuliffe, William E. 1984. "Nontherapeutic Opiate Addiction in Health Professionals: A New Form of Impairment." *American Journal of Drug and Alcohol Abuse*, 10(1): 1–22.

McAuliffe, William E., et al. 1985. "The Role of Euphoric Effects in the Opiate Addictions of Heroin Addicts, Medical Patients and Impaired Health Professions." *Journal of Drug Issues*, 15(2): 203–224.

——— 1987a. "Risk Factors of Drug Impairment in Random Samples of Physicians and Medical Students." *International Journal of the Addictions*, 22(9): 825–841.

——— 1987b. "Use and Abuse of Controlled Substances by Pharmacists and Pharmacy Students." *American Journal of Hospital Pharmacy*, 44: 311–317.

——— 1991. "Alcohol Use and Abuse in Random Samples of Physicians and Medical Students." *American Journal of Public Health*, 81: 177–182.

McCarthy, Nancy. 1994. "Drunk, Drugged, and Stressed: Problems Pervade Lawyers' Lives." *California Bar Journal*, June: 1, 6–7.

McCormick, Lawrence, and Robert M. Schmidt. 1989. Abstract in special issue, Program of the 42nd Annual Scientific Meeting: "Aging Differently." *The Gerontologist*, 29 (October): 93A–94A.

——— 1991. Abstract in special issue, Program of the 44th Annual Scientific Meeting: "New Knowledge: The Key to Meeting the Challenge of Aging." *The Gerontologist*, 31 (October): 116.

McGann, K. Patricia. 1990. "AIMS Council Report for 1989–90." Wake Forest University, Bowman Gray School of Medicine, Winston-Salem, N.C.

McGlone, Karen. 1991. "Alone in the Hallway." Interview with Larry O. *Oregon State Bar Bulletin*, August/September: 33.

McKee, Denise D., and John N. Chappel. 1992. "Spirituality and Medical Practice." *Journal of Family Practice*, 35: 201–208.

McLellan, A. Thomas, et al. 1993. "Acupuncture Treatment for Drug Abuse: A Technical Review." *Journal of Substance Abuse Treatment*, 10: 569–576.

McPeake, J. D., B. P. Kennedy, and S. M. Gordon. 1991. "Altered States of Consciousness Therapy: A Missing Component in Alcohol and Drug Rehabilitation Treatment." *Journal of Substance Abuse Treatment*, 8: 75–82.

"Me? An Addict?" 1992. *Texas Bar Journal*, March: 254–255.

Mecca, Andrew. 1994. "Evaluating Recovery Services: The California Drug and Alcohol Treatment Assessment, Executive Summary Fact Sheet." Press release, State of California Department of Alcohol and Drug Programs, Sacramento, August 29.

Medical Board of California. 1995. *The Medical Board's Diversion Program.* Mission statement. Sacramento.

Meehan, Bob. 1984. *Beyond the Yellow Brick Road.* Chicago: Contemporary Books.

Mehren, Elizabeth. 1992. "A Sobering Alternative: Alternative to Alcoholics Anonymous, Jack Trimpey, Founder of Rational Recovery Systems." *Los Angeles Times,* April 13: E1.

——— 1993. "Making Peace with Prozac," *Los Angeles Times,* December 1: E1–2.

Mieczkowski, Tom, et al. 1993. "Testing Hair for Illicit Drug Abuse." National Institute of Justice, Research in Brief, U.S. Department of Justice, Washington, D.C.

Milam, James R. 1992. "The Alcoholism Revolution." *Professional Counselor,* August: 1–8.

Milam, James R., and K. Ketcham. 1983. *Under the Influence: A Guide to the Myths and Realities of Alcoholism.* New York: Bantam Books.

Miles, Richard B. 1985. "Humanistic Medicine and Holistic Health Care." In *The New Holisitic Health Handbook: Living Well in a New Age,* ed. Shepherd Bliss et al. Lexington, Mass.: Stephen Greene Press. Pp. 8–13.

Miller, Norman S. 1991. "Drug and Alcohol Addiction as a Disease." In *Comprehensive Handbook of Drug and Alcohol Addiction,* ed. Norman S. Miller. New York: Marcel Dekker. Pp. 295–309.

Miller, Norman S., and Mark S. Gold. 1988a. "Alcoholism and Drug Addiction among Physicians: Humanitarian Approach." *Psychiatry Letter,* 6: 43–46.

——— 1988b. "Alcohol Use in Cocaine Addicts." *Substance Abuse,* 9: 216–221.

——— 1990. "The Diagnosis of Cannabis Dependence in Cocaine Addicts." *Journal of Substance Abuse,* 2: 107–111.

Miller, William R. 1992. "The Effectiveness of Treatment for Substance Abuse: Reasons for Optimism." *Journal of Substance Abuse Treatment,* 9: 93–102.

——— 1993. "Alcoholism: Toward a Better Disease Model." *Psychiatry of Addictive Behavior,* 7(2): 129–136.

Miller, William R., and R. K. Hester. 1986. "Inpatient Alcohol Treatment: Who Benefits?" *American Psychologist,* 41: 794–805.

Modlin, Herbert C., and Alberto Montes. 1964. "Narcotic Addiction in Physicians." *American Journal of Psychiatry,* 121: 358–363.

Moffit, Mary. 1986. "The Impaired Dentist." *Contact Point* (University of the Pacific School of Dentistry), 64(1): 24–29.

Moore, Andrew G. T. 1991. "Ending the Code of Silence." *Delaware Lawyer,* Spring: 6–8.

Moore, Thomas. 1992. *Care of the Soul: A Guide for Cultivating Depth and Sacredness in Everyday Life.* New York: HarperCollins.

——— 1993. "Care of the Soul: The Benefits and Costs of a More Spiritual Life." *Psychology Today,* May/June: 28, 30, 76–77.

Morrison, Martha. 1987. "My 17 Years as a Drug Addict." *Reader's Digest,* May: 126.

Morse, Robert M., and Daniel K. Flavin. 1992. "The Definition of Alcoholism." *Journal of the American Medical Association,* 268: 1012–14.

Muccigrosso, Donald, and Donna L. Spilis. 1992a. "Report of the American Bar Association International Workshop on Lawyer Substance Abuse." Handout at American Bar Association, International Workshop on Lawyer Substance Abuse, sponsored by the Commission on Impaired Attorneys, San Diego, September 15–18.

———— 1992b. "Salvation for Solos: Help for Recovery from Addiction." Paper presented at American Bar Association, International Workshop on Lawyer Substance Abuse, sponsored by the Commission on Impaired Attorneys, San Diego, September 15–18.

Musto, David F. 1987. *The American Disease.* New York: Oxford University Press.

Myers, David G. 1992. *The Pursuit of Happiness: Discovering the Pathway to Fulfillment, Well-Being, and Enduring Personal Joy.* New York: Avon.

Myers, T., and E. Weiss. 1987. "Substance Use by Internes and Residents: An Analysis of Personal, Social, and Professional Differences." *British Journal of Addiction,* 82(10): 1091–99.

Naegle, Madeline A. 1988. "Drug and Alcohol Abuse in Nursing: An Occupational Hazard?" *Nursing Life,* January/February: 42–54.

Nagel, Sigrid. 1992. "Recovering the Hard Way" *RN,* April: 40.

Nather, David. 1989. "Have One for the Runway." *Washington Monthly,* April: 12–16.

National Council against Health Fraud. 1991. "Acupuncture: The Position Paper of the National Council against Health Fraud." *American Journal of Acupuncture,* 19(3): 273–279.

National Household Survey on Drug Abuse: Population Estimates, 1991. 1991. (ADM)92-1887. Rockville, Md.: U.S. Department of Health and Human Services, Public Health Service.

National Institute on Drug Abuse. 1993. *Drug Abuse and the Brain.* NCADI Videotape Resource no. 57. Rockville, Md.: National Clearinghouse for Alcohol and Drug Information.

National Transportation Safety Board. 1984. *Statistical Review of Alcohol-Involved Aviation Accidents.* Washington, D.C.

"A Near Fatal Combination." 1990. *Journal of the California Dental Association,* 18 (February): 25.

"New Insights into Alcoholism." 1983. *Time,* 25: 64, 69.

"New Law Attempts to Stop Spread of Cat." 1994. *Prevention Pipeline* (Center for Substance Abuse Prevention), March/April: 26.

"NIAAA's Genetic Research." 1992. *Alcohol Alert Supplement* (National Institute on Alcohol Abuse and Alcoholism, U.S. Public Health Service), 328S(18): 1–2.

Noble, Ernest P., et al. 1993. "Allelic Association of the D2 Dopamine Receptor Gene with Cocaine Dependence." *Drug and Alcohol Dependence,* 33: 271–285.

———— 1994. "D2 Dopamine Receptor TaqI A Alleles in Medically Ill Alcoholic and Nonalcoholic Patients." *Alcohol and Alcoholism,* 29 (November): 729–744.

Noel, Nora E., et al. 1987. "Predictors of Attrition from an Outpatient Alcoholism Treatment Program for Couples." *Journal of Studies on Alcohol,* 48: 229–235.

Normark, James W., et al. 1985. "Impairment Risk in North Carolina Pharmacists." *American Pharmacy,* n.s., 25: 373–376.

North Carolina Bar Association. 1991. *Report of the Quality of Life Task Force and Recommendations.* Raleigh.

Norton, Merrill A. 1989. "Current Issues Pertaining to Pharmacists." Paper presented at The Professionals and Their Addictions Conference, Atlanta, April 5.

Nyman, David J., and James Cocores. 1991. "Coaddiction: Treatment of the Family Member." In *Comprehensive Handbook of Drug and Alcohol Addiction,* ed. Norman S. Miller. New York: Marcel Dekker. Pp. 877–888.

Oberg, S. William. 1989. "There Are 18,000 Dentists Who Need Our Special Attention (Part I)." *Journal of the American College of Dentists,* 56: 4–8.

——— 1990. "The 2,106 Most Wanted List." *Journal of the California Dental Association,* 18: 51–53.

——— 1994. Open letter to the Constituent and Component Dental Society Well-Being Committee, University of Utah School on Alcoholism and Other Drug Dependencies, March 15.

O'Brien, Charles P. 1994. "Opioids: Antagonists and Partial Agonists." In *The American Psychiatric Press Textbook of Substance Abuse Treatment,* ed. Marc Galanter and Herbert D. Kleber. Washington, D.C. Pp. 223–238.

O'Connell, William L. 1989. "The Committee on Chemical Dependency: A Report." *New York State Dental Journal,* August/September: 20–21.

O'Connor, Garrett. N.d. *REPAIR.* Manual. Available from Garrett O'Connor, 9100 S. Sepulveda Blvd., Suite 123, Los Angeles, CA 90045.

——— 1992. Presentation at meeting of the California Society for Addiction Medicine, Long Beach, November.

O'Doherty, Fiona O. 1991. "Is Drug Use a Response to Stress?" *Drug and Alcohol Dependence,* 29: 97–106.

Oregon State Bar Bulletin. 1991. *Drugs, Alcohol, and Lawyers: Special Issue. Lawyer.* August/September.

——— 1993. *Stress, Burnout, and the Oregon Lawyer: Special Issue.* February/March.

O'Reilly, Brian. 1991. "Drugmakers." *Fortune,* July 29: 48, 50, 54–55, 60, 63.

Orentlicher, David. 1990. "Drug Testing of Physicians." *Journal of the American Medical Association,* 264: 1039–40.

Ortmeier, Brian G., and Alan P. Wolfgang. 1991. "Job Related Stress: Perceptions of Employee Pharmacists." *American Pharmacy,* n.s., 31: 27–30.

"Out of the Abyss." 1991. *Oregon State Bar Bulletin,* August/September: 12–19.

Oyler, J. 1986. "Drugs and Alcohol: A Dentist's Story of Addiction." *Florida Dental Journal,* Winter: 4–9.

Pakull, Barton. 1990. *Position Paper on Aftercare: Continuing Care.* Washington, D.C.: U.S. Department of Transportation, FAA Office of Aviation Medicine.
———— 1996. Personal communication, October 3.

Palmer, P. V. 1983. "The Air Canada Programme for Rehabilitation of the Alcoholic Employee/Pilot." *Aviation, Space, and Environmental Medicine,* July: 592–594.

Pasnau, Robert O., and Paula Stoessel. 1994. "Mental Health Service for Medical Students." *Medical Education,* 28: 33–40.

Pauwels, Judith A., and David G. Benzer. 1989. "The Impaired Health Care Professional." *Journal of Family Practice,* 29(5): 477–484.

Peck, M. Scott 1991. *Further Along the Road Less Traveled.* New York: Simon and Schuster.

Peele, Stanton. 1989. *Diseasing of America: Addiction Treatment Out of Control.* Lexington, Mass.: Lexington Books.
———— 1992. "Alcoholism, Politics, and Bureaucracy: The Consensus against Controlled-Drinking Therapy in America." *Addictive Behaviors,* 17: 49–62.
———— 1996. "Recovering from an All-or-Nothing Approach to Alcohol." *Psychology Today,* September/October: 35.

Peele, Stanton, and Archie Brodsky. 1991. *The Truth about Addiction and Recovery.* New York: Simon and Schuster.

Pekkanen, John. 1988. *M.D.: Doctors Talk about Themselves.* New York: Delacorte Press.

Pelton, Chet, and Richard M. Ikeda. 1991. "The California Physicians Diversion Program's Experience with Recovering Anesthesiologists." *Journal of Psychoactive Drugs,* 23(4): 427–431.

Perry, Tony. 1995. "AA Quietly Marks 60 Years of Deep Impact on Society." *Los Angeles Times,* July 1: A1, A34–35.

"Personal Stories of Recovery." 1991. *Michigan Bar Journal,* February: 162–165.

Peters, Alfred C. 1987. "Chemical Dependency and Dental Practice." *Journal of the American Dental Association,* 114 (April): 509–515.
———— 1990a. "ADA Policy Statement on Chemical Dependency." *Journal of the California Dental Association,* 18 (February): 27–30.
———— 1990b. "Chemical Dependency: An Overview." *Journal of the California Dental Association,* 18 (February): 19–23.

Peterson, Ruth Lang. 1988. "Reaching the Impaired Practitioner: The Peer Assistance Network." *Journal of the Michigan Dental Association,* 70 (June): 265–269.

Peterson, Ruth Lang, and J. K. Avery. 1988. "The Alcohol-Impaired Dentist: An Educational Challenge." *Journal of the American Dental Association,* 117 (November): 743–748.

Pfifferling, John-Henry, and Richard W. Corbin. 1988. "The Stress of Dental Life." *Bulletin of the Society for Professional Well-Being,* 1 (December): 1–2.

Phillips, Don. 1991. "Rarer than Disaster: Praise from Safety Board." *Washington Post,* July 10: A19.

Pitulla, Joanne. 1992. "Abusers Anonymous: Model Rule Amendment Permits Confidential Assistance." *American Bar Association Journal*, June: 108.

Platman, Stanley R., and Michael C. Llufrio. 1990. "The Physician Rehabilitation Program of Maryland." *Maryland Medical Journal*, 39 (November): 1029–32.

Pokorny, Alex D., and Joel Solomon. 1983. "A Follow-up Survey of Drug Abuse and Alcoholism Teaching in Medical Schools." *Journal of Medical Education*, 58: 316–321.

Poplar, Jimme F. 1969. "Characteristics of Nurse Addicts." *American Journal of Nursing*, 69: 117–119.

Powell, Burnele V. 1991. "Retribution or Rehabilitation." *Family Advocate*, Summer: 51.

"The Power of Understanding." 1990. *Journal of the California Dental Association*, 18 (February): 61.

Preliminary Estimates from the 1995 National Household Survey on Drug Abuse. 1996. (SMA)96-3107. Rockville, Md.: U.S. Department of Health and Human Services, Public Health Service.

Prescription Drug Monitoring: States Can Readily Identify Illegal Sales and Use of Controlled Substances. 1992. Gaithersburg, Md.: U.S. General Accounting Office.

"A Progressive Disease." 1992. *Texas Bar Journal*, March: 250–251.

"Projecting Future Cocaine Use and Evaluation Control Strategies." 1995. Research brief. Santa Monica, Calif.: Rand Drug Policy Research Center.

Public Citizen Health Research Group. 1994a. "Narcotic Lollipops." *Health Letter*, 10 (March): 6, 12.

——— 1994b. "Outrage of the Month: 4,000 More Physicians Should Be Disciplined Each Year." *Health Letter*, 10 (June): 10, 12.

"Questionable Call." 1992. *Los Angeles Times*, January 2: C3.

Rankin, Jane A., and Mary B. Harris. 1990. "Stress and Health Problems in Dentists." *Journal of Dental Practice Administration*, January/March: 2–8.

Rawson, Richard A., et al. 1990. "Neurobehavioral Treatment for Cocaine Dependency." *Journal of Psychoactive Drugs*, 22: 159–171.

——— 1993. "Relapse Prevention Strategies in Outpatient Substance Abuse Treatment." *Psychology of Addictive Behaviors*, 7: 85–95.

Redmond, Pat. 1979. "Doctor, You Are Not Alone." *Dental Economics*, February: 50–51.

Reed, Leonard. 1992. "Life and Death Resolutions." *Los Angeles Times*, December 31: 58–59.

"Reflections of the Drug Czars." 1995. *Prevention Pipeline* (Center for Substance Abuse Prevention), March/April: 117–120.

Regier, Darrel A., et al. 1988. "One-Month Prevalence of Mental Disorders in the United States, Based on Five Epidemiologic Catchment Area Sites." *Archives of General Psychiatry*, 45: 977–986.

——— 1990. "Co-Morbidity of Mental Disorders with Alcohol and Other Drug Abuse. Results from the Epidemiologic Catchment Area (ECA) Study." *Journal of the American Medical Association*, 264: 2511–18.

Reid, Fred, and Dr. L. 1990. "The 'Dream Profession' Was Nightmare for an Alcoholic Dentist." *Arizona Dentistry*, 3(11) (April): 10–14.

Reighard, Homer L. 1980. "FAA Addresses Alcohol's Impact." *U.S Medicine*, 15 (January): 23–24.

Reimenschneider, Jerry. 1990. "One More Day, One More Miracle." *Pharmacy Update*, 1(20): 1, 4–5, 8–9.

Remen, Rachel Naomi. 1991. "Spirit: Resource for Healing." In *Noetic Sciences Collection, 1980–90.* Sausalito, Calif.: Institute for Noetic Sciences. Pp. 61–65.

Resnick, Rosalind. 1990. "There Is Hope for Addicted Lawyers." *National Law Journal*, 13 (December 10): 27.

Rhode Island Bar Journal. 1991. *An Overview of Rhode Island Employees Assistance Programs: Special Issue on Attorney Impairment*, 40: 21–22, 34.

Richardson, Elizabeth. 1990. "Systems Form to Help Impaired Pharmacists." *Drug Store News*, November 19: 1, 16.

Ricker, Darlene. 1990. "Under the Influence." *Student Lawyers*, 19 (October): 21–26.

Robb, Nigel D. 1990. "Alcoholism and the Dentist." Editorial. *British Journal of Addiction*, 85(4): 437–439.

Robbins, J. H., and Tim F. Branaman. 1992. "The Personality of Addiction." *Texas Bar Journal*, March: 266–267.

Robins, Lee N. 1993. "Vietnam Veterans' Rapid Recovery from Heroin Addiction: A Fluke or Normal Expectation?" *Addiction*, 88(8): 1041–54.

Robins, Lee N., et al. 1984. "Lifetime Prevalence of Specific Psychiatric Disorders in Three Sites." *Archives of General Psychiatry*, 41: 949–958.

Rogers, Peter D. 1995. "Physician Learns to Heal Himself." *Los Angeles Times*, July 28: E1, E8.

Rohrlich, Ted. 1990. "Attorneys Report Big Jump in Drinking in ABA Survey." *Los Angeles Times*, December 5: A5.

Roman, Paul M., and Terry C. Blum. 1994. "Employee Assistance Programs." In *The American Psychiatric Press Textbook of Substance Abuse Treatment*, ed. Marc Galanter and Herbert D. Kleber. Washington, D.C. Pp. 369–384.

Rosecan J. S., H. I. Spitz, and B. Gross. 1987. "Contemporary Issues in the Treatment of Cocaine Abuse." In *Cocaine Abuse: New Directions in Treatment and Research*, ed. H. I. Spitz and J. S. Rosecan. New York: Brunner/Mazel. Pp. 315–323.

Rosenberg, Harold. 1993. "Prediction of Controlled Drinking by Alcoholics and Problem Drinkers." *Psychological Bulletin*, 113: 129–139.

Rosenblatt, Leon. 1989. "It's All Right, I'm a Doctor." *Miami Herald, Tropic,* July 9: 9–15.

Ross, Leonard E., and Susan M. Ross. 1988. "Pilots' Attitudes toward Alcohol and Flying." *Aviation, Space, and Environmental Medicine*, October: 913–919.

Ross, Susan M., and Leonard E. Ross. 1990. "Pilots' Knowledge of Blood Alcohol Levels and the 0.04% Blood Alcohol Concentration Rule." *Aviation, Space, and Environmental Medicine*, May: 412–417.

Rounsaville, Bruce J., and Kathleen M. Carroll 1992. "Individual Psychotherapy for Drug Abusers." In *Substance Abuse: A Comprehensive Textbook,* ed. Joyce H. Lowinson, Pedro Ruiz, and Robert B. Millman. Baltimore: Williams and Wilkins. Pp. 496–507.

Russell, Julia C., and Audie W. Davis. 1985. *Alcohol Rehabilitation of Airline Pilots.* Oklahoma City: Civil Aeromedical Institute, Federal Aviation Administration.

Samborn, Randall. 1990. "Firms Slowly Come to Grips with Addiction." *National Law Journal,* 13 (December 10): 25–26.

Sammon, Patrick J., et al. 1991. "Teaching an Alcohol Prevention Course in the Dental School Chemical Dependency Curriculum: A Preliminary Report." *Journal of Dental Education,* 55(1): 30–31.

Samuel, Steven E., et al. 1991. "Investigating Stress Levels of Residents: A Pilot Study." *Medical Teacher,* 13(1): 89—92.

Sandor, Richard S. 1994. "Why Spirituality?" *California Society of Addiction Medicine,* Winter: 4–6.

Sandoval, Victor A., William D. Hendrickson, and Robert A. Dale. 1988. "A Survey of Substance Abuse Education in North American Dental Schools." *Journal of Dental Education,* 52(3): 167–169.

Sandoval, Victor A., et al. 1990. "Substance Use Trends in a Dental School Population: Preliminary Report." *Journal of Dental Education,* 54(1): 36.

Schafer, Walter. 1992. *Stress Management for Wellness.* New York: Holt, Rinehart and Winston.

Schatzberg, Alan F., and Charles B. Nemeroff, eds. 1995. *The American Psychiatric Press Textbook of Psychopharmacology.* Washington, D.C.: American Psychiatric Press.

Schoenborn, Charlotte A. 1991. *Exposure to Alcoholism in the Family: United States, 1988.* (PHS)91-1250. Rockville, Md.: U.S. Department of Health and Human Services, Public Health Service.

Schuckit, Marc A. 1994. "MDMA (Ecstasy): An Old Drug with New Tricks." *Drug Abuse & Alcoholism Newsletter,* 23 (April).

——— 1995a. "Abuse and Dependence on Nitrous Oxide." *Drug Abuse & Alcoholism Newsletter,* 24 (August).

——— 1995b. "Alcohol Dependence in Women: Is It Really Unique?" *Drug Abuse & Alcoholism Newsletter,* 24 (February).

——— 1995c. *Drug and Alcohol Abuse: A Clinical Guide to Diagnosis and Treatment.* 4th ed. New York: Plenum Medical Books.

——— 1995d. "Is There a Clinically Significant Marijuana Withdrawal Syndrome?" *Drug Abuse & Alcoholism Newsletter,* 24 (April).

Schulz, Jerome E. 1991. "12-Step Programs in Recovery from Drugs and Alcohol Addiction." In *Comprehensive Handbook of Drug and Alcohol Addiction,* ed. Norman S. Miller. New York: Marcel Dekker. Pp. 1255–65.

Schwartz-Barcott, Donna, and T. P Schwartz. 1990. "Are Nurses Healthier and Happier than the General Public?" *Nursing Forum,* 25: 19–34.

Scriven, Paul. 1994. "The Culture Club of the Twelve Step Meeting: A Counter to Critics of the Recovery Movement." Paper presented at the annual meeting of the American Sociological Association, Los Angeles, August.

Secretary-Treasurer of International Nurses Anonymous. 1995. Personal communication, July 10 and 17.

Secular Organizations for Sobriety. 1993a. Weekly meeting flier, Summer–Fall.

———— 1993b. International newsletter.

"The Seduction of Substance Abuse: Two Personal Accounts." 1988. *New York Journal of Dentistry*, 58(5): 176–180.

Seidenberg, Robert. 1971. "Drug Advertising and Perception of Mental Illness." *Mental Hygiene*, 55 (January): 21–51.

Senay, Edward C. 1994. "Opioids: Methadone Maintenance." In *The American Psychiatric Press Textbook of Substance Abuse Treatment*, ed. Marc Galanter and Herbert D. Kleber. Washington, D.C. Pp. 209–222.

Shaffer, Howard J., and Stephanie B. Jones. 1989. *Quitting Cocaine: The Struggle against Impulse*. Lexington, Mass.: Lexington Books.

Sharfstein, Joshua. 1993. "Buying Gratitude on the Cheap: Drug Industry Woos Medical Students." *Public Citizen Health Research Group Health Letter*, ed. Sidney M. Wolf, 9(7): 7.

Shedler, Jonathan, and Jack Block. 1990. "Adolescent Drug Use and Psychological Health: A Longitudinal Inquiry." *American Psychologist*, 45: 612–630.

Sheed, Wilfrid. 1995. "Down in the Valley." *Psychology Today*, November/December: 26–28.

Sheehan, K. H., et al. 1990. "A Pilot Study of Medical Student Abuse: Student Perceptions of Mistreatment and Misconduct in Medical School." *Journal of the American Medical Association*, 263: 533–537.

Sheets, Vicki (Director for Nursing Practice and Education, National Council of State Boards of Nursing). 1995. Personal communication, July 17.

Sheffield, Jean W. 1992. "The Special Needs of Women Pharmacists in Recovery." *American Pharmacy*, n.s., 32: 581–583.

Sheridan, Edward P., and Kathleen Sheridan. 1980. "The Troubled Attorney." *Barrister*, 7(3): 42–45.

Shneidman, Edwin S. 1993. "Suicide as Psychache." *Journal of Nervous and Mental Disease*, 181(3): 145–147.

Shore, James H. 1987. "The Oregon Experience with Impaired Physicians on Probation: An 8-Year Follow-up." *Journal of the American Medical Association*, 257: 2931–34.

Sikora, Ann. 1988. "TRAPIN Rescues Impaired Nurses." *Texas Hospitals*, September: 24–26.

Silas, Faye A. 1987. "A Profession's Scourge: Lawyers on Drugs." *Bar Leader*, 13(3) (November/December): 12–16.

Silver H. K., and A. D. Glicken. 1990. "Medical Student Abuse: Incidence, Severity, and Significance." *Journal of the American Medical Association*, 263: 527–532.

Simpson, D. Dwayne. 1993. "Drug Treatment Evaluation Research in the United States." *Psychology of Addictive Behaviors*, 7: 120–128.

Singleton, James A. 1989. *California Occupational Mortality, 1979–1981, Adjusted for Smoking, Alcohol, and Socioeconomic Status*. Sacramento: California Department of Health Services.

Sipe, Fred. 1993. "Drug and Alcohol Treatment." *Professional in Residence Journal* (Betty Ford Center): 2.

Skinner, B. F. 1977. "A Humanist Alternative to AA's Twelve-Steps." *The Humanist,* July–August: 5.

Skuter, Claudia. 1990. "Physicians Recovery Network Targets Attitudes about Impairment." *Michigan Medicine,* December: 30–32.

Sloan, S. J., and C. L. 1984. "Health-Related Lifestyle Habits in Commerical Airline Pilots." *British Journal of Aviation,* 2: 32–41.

Smith, Chris. 1992. "Under the Influence." *AGD Impact,* February: 7–9.

Smith, Harold E., G. Douglas Talbott, and Martha A. Morrison. 1985. "Chemical Abuse and Dependence: An Occupational Hazard for Healthy Professionals." *Topics in Emergency Medicine,* 7(3): 69–78.

Smith, Howard L., et al. 1989. "Substance Abuse among Nurses: Types of Drugs." *Dimensions of Critical Care Nursing,* 8: 159–168.

Smith, Jay W., William F. Denny, and Donald B. Witzke. 1986. "Emotional Impairment in Internal Medicine House Staff." *Journal of the American Medical Association,* 255: 1155–78.

Smith, Lynn. 1994. "Testament to the Downward Spiral of Drugs and Teen Angst." *Los Angeles Times,* February 16: E1, E3.

Smith, Rickey, and Howard W. Starnes. 1988. "Hospital Pharmacy Employment Considerations for the Chemically Dependent Health Care Professional." *American Journal of Hospital Pharmacy,* 45 : 2102–07.

Smith, Stephen R. 1992. "Medical Training: A Matter of Survival." Introductory remarks at the American Medical Student Association's preconvention Conference on Medical Education Student Well-Being, Arlington, Va.

Solari-Twadell, Ann. 1988. "Nurse Impairment: The Significance of Professional Culture." *Quality Review Bulletin,* April: 103–104.

Solursh, Diane S. 1989. "An EAP Program for the Health Profession." In *Professionals and Their Addictions,* ed. Thomas W. Hester. Macon, Ga.: Charter Medical. Pp. 105–117.

Spencer, Laurene, and Margaret Gregory. 1989. "Clonidine Transdermal Patches for Use in Outpatient Opiate Withdrawal." *Journal of Substance Abuse Treatment,* 6: 113–117.

Spencer-Strachan, F. Louise. 1990. "Attitudes of Registered Nurses toward Perceived Substance Abusing Peers: An Education Specific to Substance Abuse." *ABNF Journal,* Fall: 27–32.

Spicer, Jerry, Peggy Barnett, and Dale Kliner. 1978. *Characteristics and Outcomes of Professionals Admitted to the Hazelden Rehabilitation Center, 1973–1976.* Center City, Minn.: Hazelden Educational Services.

Spierer, Diane. 1986. Testimony at San Diego hearing, Attorney General's Commission on the Prevention of Drug and Alcohol Abuse, January 9.

Spilis, Donna L. 1992. *Report of the ABA International Workshop on Lawyer Substance Abuse.* San Diego: American Bar Association, Commission on Impaired Attorneys.

——— (American Bar Association, Commission on Impaired Attorneys). 1995. Personal communication.

Stammer, M. Ellen. 1991. *Women and Alcohol: The Journey Back.* New York: Gardner Press.

Starr, Cynthia. 1989. "Breaking Out, Part I: Pharmacists in Recovery." *Drug Topics,* June 5: 30–34.

State of California Department of Alcohol and Drug Programs. 1992. *The Treatment of Addiction Using Methadone: A Counselor's Manual.* Sacramento.

State of California Department of Consumer Affairs. 1992. *The California Board of Registered Nursing's Diversion Program.* Sacramento.

Steindler, Emanuel M. 1987. "Alcoholic Women in Medicine: Still Homeless." *Journal of the American Medical Association,* 257: 2954–55.

Steinglass, Peter. 1994. "Family Therapy: Alcohol." In *The American Psychiatric Press Textbook of Substance Abuse Treatment,* ed. Marc Galanter and Herbert D. Kleber. Washington, D.C. Pp. 315–331.

Stone, Hal, and Sidra Winkelman. 1989. *Embracing Ourselves: A Voice Dialogue Manual.* San Rafael, Calif.: New World Library.

Storti, Ed. 1990. Untitled brochure. Copies available from Intervention Specialist, Inc., P.O. Box 2635, San Pedro, CA 90731.

——— 1992. Personal communication.

Substance Abuse Workshop. 1988. Annual meeting of the American Bar Association, Toronto, August.

Sullivan, Eleanor, LeClair Bissell, and Doris Leffler. 1990. "Drug Use and Disciplinary Actions among 300 Nurses." *International Journal of the Addictions,* 25(4): 375–391.

Sullivan, Eleanor, LeClair Bissell, and Etta Williams. 1988. *Chemical Dependency in Nursing: The Deadly Diversion.* Reading, Mass.: Addison-Wesley.

Swann, William B., T. Gregory Hixon, and Chris de la Ronde. 1992. "Embracing the Bitter Truth: Negative Self-Concepts and Marital Commitment." *Psychological Science,* 3(2) (March): 118—121.

Swift, Herald A., and T. Williams. 1975. *Recovery for the Whole Family.* Center City, Minn.: Hazelden Educational Services.

Talbott, G. Douglas. 1982. "The Impaired Physician and Intervention: A Key to Recovery." *Journal of the Florida Medical Association,* 69: 793–797.

——— 1987. "The Impaired Physician: The Role of the Spouse in Recovery." *Journal of the Medical Association of Georgia,* 76 (March): 190–192.

——— 1996. Personal communication, October 15.

Talbott, G. Douglas, and Karl V. Gallegos. 1990. "Intervention with Health Professionals." *Addiction and Recovery,* September: 13–16.

Talbott, G. Douglas, and Carolyn A. Martin. 1984. "Relapse and Recovery: Special Issues for Chemically Dependent Physicians." *Journal of the Medical Association of Georgia,* 73 (November): 763–769.

——— 1986. "Treating Impaired Physicians: Fourteen Keys to Success." *Virginia Medical,* 113 (February): 95–99.

Talbott, G. Douglas, et al. 1987. "The Medical Association of Georgia's Impaired

Physicians Program: Review of the First 1000 Physicians, Analysis of Specialty." *Journal of the American Medical Association*, 257: 2927–30.

Talley, C. Richard. 1988. "Chemical Impairment." *American Journal of Hospital Pharmacy*, 54: 2077.

TenBroeck, Arlyce (California Board of Dental Examiners). 1995. Personal communication.

Texas Young Lawyers Association. 1990. *A Secret Sickness: Just How Secret Is It?* Videotape. Austin.

"This Is Your Captain Snoring." 1991. *Time*, October 7: 15.

Thomas, A., et al. 1986. "Family Treatment in Short-Term Detoxification." Paper presented at the National Council on Alcoholism Forum, San Francisco.

Trans World Airlines. N.d. *Special Health Services Orientation for the TWA Pilot: The Medical Disorder Alcoholism*. New York.

Trimpey, Jack. 1992. *The Small Book: A Revolutionary Alternative for Overcoming Alcohol and Drug Dependence*. New York: Delacorte Press.

Trinkoff, Alison M., William W. Eaton, and James C. Anthony. 1991. "The Prevalence of Substance Abuse among Registered Nurses." *Nursing Research*, 40(3): 172–175.

Trinkoff, Alison M., and C. L. Storr. 1994. "Relationship of Specialty and Access to Substance Abuse among Registered Nurses: An Exploratory Analysis." *Drug and Alcohol Dependence*, 36: 215–219.

Tuchfeld, Barry S. 1981. "Spontaneous Remission in Alcoholics: Empirical Observations and Theoretical Implications." *Journal of Studies on Alcohol*, 42: 626–641.

Tucker, Deborah R., Mary C. Gurnee, and Mario F. Sylvestri. 1988. "Psychoactive Drug Use and Impairment Markers in Pharmacy Students." *American Journal of Pharmaceutical Education*, 52 (Spring): 42–46.

"Two Psychiatrists View AA—50 Years Apart." 1995. *Newsletter for Professionals: About AA* (Alcoholics Anonymous World Services), Spring.

"Two Sides to Every Story." 1992. *Texas Bar Journal*, March: 260–261.

Uboise, Jeff. 1992. "The Electronic Sweatshop: Law and Technology." *Midrange Systems*, 5 (July 21): 45–45.

U.S. Department of Health and Human Services. 1985. *Alcoholism: An Inherited Disease*. Washington, D.C.: U.S. Government Printing Office.

Vaillant, George E. 1982. "Adaptation of a Lecture: When Doctors Fail to Care for Themselves." *Harvard Medical Alumni Bulletin*, 56: 18–21.

——— 1983. *The Natural History of Alcoholism: Causes, Patterns, and Paths to Recovery*. Cambridge, Mass.: Harvard University Press.

Vaillant, George E., Jane R. Brighton, and Charles McArthur. 1970. "Physicians' Use of Mood-Altering Drugs: A Twenty-Year Follow-up Report." *New England Journal of Medicine*, 282: 365–370.

Vaillant, George E., N. C. Sobowale, and C. McArthur. 1972. "Some Psychologic Vulnerabilities of Physicians." *New England Journal of Medicine*, 287: 372–375.

Visocan, Barbara J. 1983. "Nutritional Management of Alcoholism." *Journal of the American Dietetic Association, ADA Reports*, 83(6): 693–696.

Wachter, Nicholas J. 1989. "Cocaine Blocks Out Everything, but You Don't Care." *Los Angeles Times,* June 4: sec. V, p. 5.

Waldorf, Dan. 1983. "Natural Recovery from Opiate Addiction: Some Social-Psychological Processes of Untreated Recovery." *Journal of Drug Issues,* 13(2): 237–280.

Waldorf, Dan, Craig Reinarnan, and Sheigla Murphy. 1991. *Cocaine Changes: The Experience of Using and Quitting.* Philadelphia: Temple University Press.

Wall, Keith. 1991. "Doctors on Drugs." *Physician,* January/February: 2–5.

Wallace, John. 1990. "The New Disease Model of Alcoholism." *Western Journal of Medicine,* 152(5): 502–505.

Walsh, D. C., et al. 1991. "A Randomized Trial of Treatment Options for Alcohol-Abusing Workers." *New England Journal of Medicine,* 325: 775–782.

Wamsley, Francis. 1978. "Dentistry through a Bottle, Darkly." *Dental Management,* November: 27–34.

Ward, C. F., Gretchen C. Ward, and Lawrence J. Saidman. 1983. "Drug Abuse in Anesthesia Training Programs." *Journal of the American Medical Association,* 250: 922–925.

Ward, Jeff, Richard P. Mattick, and Wayne Hall. 1994. "Effectiveness of Methadone Maintenance Treatment: An Overview." *Drug and Alcohol Review,* 13(3): 327–336.

Washburn, A. M., et al. 1993. "Acupuncture Heroin Detoxification: A Single-Blind Clinical Trial." *Journal of Substance Abuse Treatment,* 10: 345–351.

Washton, Arnold M. 1992. "Structured Outpatient Group Therapy with Alcohol and Substance Abusers." In *Substance Abuse: A Comprehensive Textbook,* ed. Joyce H. Lowinson, Pedro Ruiz, and Robert B. Millman. Baltimore: Williams and Wilkins. Pp. 508–519.

Wechsler, Henry, et al. 1994. "Health and Behavioral Consequences of Binge Drinking in College." *Journal of the American Medical Association,* 272: 1672–77.

Weikel, Dan. 1996. "Drug Firms Battle Rule on Prescription Forms." *Los Angeles Times,* August 19: A1, A10–11.

Weiss, Roger D. 1994. "Inpatient Treatment." In *The American Psychiatric Press Textbook of Substance Abuse Treatment,* ed. Marc Galanter and Herbert D. Kleber. Washington, D.C. Pp. 359–368.

"Wellness Project on '95 Agenda." 1995. *Highlights: A Questionnaire Newsletter from the American Bar Association Commission on Impaired Attorneys,* 1 (Spring): 5.

Wen, H. L., and S. Y. C. Cheung. 1973. "How Acupuncture Can Help Addicts." *Drugs and Society,* 2: 8–18.

Wertsch, Mary Edwards. 1992. "The Pathology Is Alcohol: Acceptance of Drunkenness in the Military Has Led to Institutionalized Sexual Harassment Culminating in the Tailhook Scandal." *Los Angeles Times,* August 16: M5.

Wharton, Lawrence H. 1989. "The Disease of Addiction." *Texas Bar Journal,* March: 286–287.

"What's So Great about a Drug-free Lifestyle?" 1991. *Prevention Pipeline* (Center for Substance Abuse Prevention), November/December: 36.

Whitaker, Eric E. 1991. "Ethics of a Doughnut." *New Physician,* September: 48.

Whitmore, Maureen. N.d. "The Impaired Pharmacist Program: An Alternative Choice." *California Journal of Hospital Pharmacy,* 22–23.

Williams, Arthur G., ed. 1992. *Dentistry Faces Addiction: How to Be Part of the Solution.* St. Louis: Mosby Year Book.

Williams, Etta, LeClair Bissell, and Eleanor Sullivan. 1991. "The Effects of Co-Dependence on Physicians and Nurses." *British Journal of Addictions,* 86: 37–42.

Williams, Ronald L., ed. 1994. American Pharmaceutical Association, *PRN Memo,* no. 39 (April–June): 1–16.

Willis, Eugene F. (Director, Impaired Dentists Program of the Georgia Dental Association). 1990. Personal communication, June 20.

――― 1992. "Nitrous Oxide: Dentistry's Own Spread Addiction." In *Dentistry Faces Addiction: How to Be Part of the Solution,* ed. Arthur G. Williams. New York: Mosby Year Book. Pp. 33–38.

Willis, Susi. 1992. "What We Won't See: Women and Addiction." *Texas Bar Journal,* March: 271–272.

Wilsnack, Sharon C., Richard W. Wilsnack, and Susanne Hiller-Sturmhold. 1994. "How Women Drink: Epidemiology of Women's Drinking and Problem Drinking." *Alcohol, Health & Research World,* 18: 173–182.

Wolf, Thomas M. 1994. "Stress, Coping and Health: Enhancing Well-Being during Medical School." *Medical Education,* 28: 8–17.

Wolf, Thomas M., and G. E. Kissling. 1984. "Changes in Lifestyle Characteristics, Health, and Mood of Freshman Medical Students." *Journal of Medical Education,* 59: 806–814.

Wolfgang, Alan P. 1988. "Job Stress in the Health Professions: A Study of Physicians, Nurses, and Pharmacists." *Behavioral Medicine,* 14(1) (Spring): 43–47.

"A Woman's Story." 1989. *Texas Bar Journal,* March: 296–297.

Wood, Don (Federal Aviation Administration Department of Medical Services, Oklahoma City). 1995. Personal communication, July.

Woodruff, Ruth. 1992. "Cocaine Addiction and the Lawyer Next Door." *Professional Lawyer,* 3 (August): 7, 9.

Woody, George E., Delinda Mercer, and Lester Luborsky. 1994. "Individual Psychotherapy: Other Drugs." In *The American Psychiatric Press Textbook of Substance Abuse Treatment,* ed. Marc Galanter and Herbert D. Kleber. Washington, D.C. Pp. 275–284.

Wright, Curtis. 1990. "Physician Addiction to Pharmaceuticals: Personal History, Practice Setting, Access to Drugs, and Recovery." *Maryland Medical Journal,* 39 (November): 1021–25.

Yalisove, Daniel. 1993. "The Role of Acupuncture in an Outpatient Alcohol Treatment Program." *American Psychiatric Association Division of Addictions,* 1 (Summer).

Yates, Nona. 1992. "Wishing You the Very (Sober) Best." *Los Angeles Times,* July 13: 1.

Yesavage, Jerome A., and Von Otto Leirer. 1986. "Hangover Effects on Aircraft Pilots 14 Hours after Alcohol Ingestion: A Preliminary Report." *American Journal of Psychiatry,* 143: 1546–50.

Young, Bernadette F. 1986. "Drug Abuse: What Dental Professionals Should Know." *Dental Hygiene,* 60(12) (December): 546–550.

Zackon, Fred, William E. McAuliffe, and James M. N. Ch'ien. 1993. *Recovery Training and Self-Help: Relapse Prevention and Aftercare for Drug Addicts.* (NIH) 93-3521. Washington, D.C.: U.S. Department of Health and Human Services, Public Health Service.

Zweben, Joan Ellen, and Thomas Payte. 1990. "Methadone Maintenance in the Treatment of Opiate Dependence: A Current Perspective." *Addiction Medicine.* Special issue, *Western Journal of Medicine,* 152(5): 588–599.

Acknowledgments

Writing this book has been a rewarding adventure. I presumed it would be difficult to persuade addicted professionals to reveal the intimate circumstances of their personal and professional lives for publication. Although I had successfully arranged for a few to tell their experiences to UCLA students in a classroom setting, I did not anticipate that so many would be willing to share their stories of pain and recovery. Each interview is an invaluable gift, offered freely to help others who may be at risk for addiction.

Skilled and generous volunteers came to my assistance at each stage. Three colleagues—Ruthie McCrary, Carol Jean Coombs, and another associate who requested anonymity—played a crucial role in locating and interviewing subjects.

I thank executives and staff of the Betty Ford Center (BFC), in Rancho Mirage, California, for allowing me to spend 10 highly stimulating and informative 12- to-14-hour days participating with their clients and families. Their award of two BFC Professional-in-Residence scholarships allowed me to spend one week in their inpatient program and another in their family and outpatient programs. I also thank Garrett O'Connor, M.D., who let me participate briefly in REPAIR, his outpatient treatment program, and provided program descriptions; and Karen Miotto, M.D., who made available the UCLA Matrix Center Treatment manual.

The people who direct and staff the professional organizations' well-being programs responded to my inquiries with personalized care; they invited me to their conferences, arranged interviews with recovering addicts, and gave me pertinent publications and videos. I am especially grateful to Linda R. Crosby, former manager of the American Dental Association's Well-Being Program; Donna L. Spilis and Donald Muccigrosso of the American Bar Association Commission on Impaired Attorneys; Barton Pakull of the Federal Aviation Administration; and S. William Oberg, former manager of the American Dental Association's Well-Being Program. Jean Sheffield of the Texas Pharmaceutical Association Pharmacist Recovery Network sent printed information and arranged interviews with pharmacists from several states. Ronald Williams, director of the Pharmacy Recovery Program in Washington, D.C., provided valuable information and support. The secretary of International Nurses Anonymous and Vickie Sheets of the National Council of State Boards of Nursing provided helpful information regarding nurses. The National Clearinghouse for Alcohol and Drug Information responded to many queries promptly, pleasantly, and informatively.

I thank the following addictionologists and treatment experts who allowed us to interview them about their experiences with addicted professionals: Robert Ashburn, Jamie Caraway, Bill Chamberlain, M.D., Kathy D'Mato-Smith, Robert W. Elliot, Ph.D., Roger Goetz, M.D., Marc Greenberg, Paul Hoover, Marc Kern, Ph.D., Tom Mangold, Nancy Porter, Johanna O'Flaherty, Johanne Rose, Lic. Ac., Howard Shapiro, M.D., and Max Weisman, M.D. Others permitted us to tape-record their presentations at professional conferences: David Canavan, M.D., Anne Geller, M.D., John W. Kegan, J.D., and Penny Ziegler, M.D., at the 1993 Princeton House Conference; and Richard Sandor, M.D., who lectured at UCLA. LeClair Bissell, renowned author of numerous books and articles about chemical dependency, generously offered insights and technical information. Ed Storti and Dean Lang, D.D.S., also provided helpful information.

The following organizations and colleagues provided information, manuscripts, or videos: Association of Anesthesia Program Directors; American Medical Association; DeWitt Baldwin, M.D.; Nan H. Davis, R.Ph., pharmacy counselor; Vicky Eckland, R.N., Virginia Nursing Association; Famlight Productions, Boston ("Nurses Web of Denial," 617/524–0980); Adrian Hill, J.D.; Fred Hirning, PharmD., Southwest Pharmacy Recovery Network; Don P. Jones and Leland A. Reinhard, P.C., Texas Lawyers Assistance Program; Hani R. Khouzam, M.D., New Hampshire Department of Veterans Affairs; James Langenbucher, Ph.D., Rutgers Center for Alcohol Studies; Chet Pelton and Joan Gladden, California Physicians Diversion Program; Patrick J. Sammon, Ph.D., University of Kentucky College of Dentistry; and Robert A. Stein, Dean, University of Minnesota Law School.

Data processing was coordinated at UCLA by Carla Cronkhite Vera and Carol Jean Coombs. Noël O'Connor, director of Volunteer Services at the UCLA Neuropsychiatric Institute and Hospital, arranged for volunteer research assistants to help with many tasks. Jean Albert, Sam Kaiser, Jennifer Lebe, Muriel Marks, Seymour Stuart, and Ray Terrazas assisted with library retrieval and data processing. Special thanks are due to David Libby for retrieving hundreds of reference materials and to Hilda Zech for identifying pertinent literature and retrieving interlibrary loan documents.

Virginia Hansen devoted months to checking the accuracy of cited publications, and Tracy Lam, a UCLA undergraduate, compiled numerical information cited in Chapter 5 about developmental stages. I thank Bernard Virshup, M.D., my colleague and friend, who with Wendy Kohatsu, at that time a UCLA medical student, spent an entire summer networking with training institutions and other organizations to obtain the latest information about primary, secondary, and tertiary drug-prevention programs.

Ruth Fontaine, an anesthesiologist, verified technical information about drugs and their effects. I also thank Lewis Baxter, M.D.; Linda Crosby, American Dental Association; Don Hudson, M.D., ALPA Aeromedical adviser; Marc Kern, Ph.D.; Paul Scriven, Ph.D.; and Hershel P. Wall, M.D., for offering valuable suggestions on the manuscript.

Kathryn Coombs, my daughter, improved the manuscript significantly by closely editing and critiquing each section. Ann Hawthorne, senior editor at Harvard University Press, improved the manuscript with critical suggestions and thorough editing.

I owe a profound debt of gratitude to Carla Cronkhite Vera, who assisted in every aspect of this project. Her "fingerprints" are on every paragraph. I can't imagine a more productive or harder-working associate. She typed and retyped numerous drafts, located and checked references, and supervised others in a wide variety of tasks. She moved the project along energetically, cheerfully, and efficiently.

Finally, I thank Carol Jean Coombs, my life's companion, for her unstinting help, support, and encouragement. She participated in every major decision and time and again pointed me in the right direction. She traveled with me to professional conferences, arranged and conducted interviews, networked with numerous individuals, assisted with library research, tracked down references, and edited several drafts of the manuscript.

Index